Keeping Mozart in Mind

Keeping Mozart in Mind

Gordon L. Shaw, Ph.D.

M.I.N.D. Institute/University of California
Irvine, California

ACADEMIC PRESS

A Harcourt Science and Technology Company

San Diego   San Francisco   New York   Boston   London   Sydney   Tokyo

Academic Press
A Harcourt Science and Technology Company
525 B Street, Suite 1900, San Diego, California 92101-4495, USA
http://www.apnet.com

Academic Press
24-28 Oval Road, London NW1 7DX, UK
http://www.hbuk.co.uk/ap/

Library of Congress Catalog Card Number: 99-65095

International Standard Book Number: 0-12-639290-0
International Standard Book Number: 0-12-639291-9 (CD-ROM)

This book is printed on acid-free paper. ∞

PRINTED IN THE UNITED STATES OF AMERICA
99   00   01   02   03   04   EB   9   8   7   6   5   4   3   2   1

CONTENTS

Preface   ix

Acknowledgments   xi

Prologue   xiii

PART **I**

Higher Brain Function: Music, Mathematics, Chess

Chapter 1 History, Anecdotes, Correlations, and Interviews   3

Chapter 2 Spatial-Temporal and Language-Analytic
Reasoning in Learning Math and Science   17

Chapter 3 Music Enhances Spatial-Temporal Reasoning   29

Chapter 4 Implications: Scientific, Educational, Clinical   35

PART **II**

Structured Brain and Symmetry

Chapter 5 Symmetry as a Common Theme   43

v

Chapter 6 Introduction to the Brain: Basic Brain Features
and Brain Imaging   53

Chapter 7 Mountcastle Theory of Mammalian Cortex:
Internal Neural Language of Higher Brain
Function   73

Chapter 8 Trion Model and Symmetries   87

Chapter 9 Trion Music: Reasoning and Creativity   121

Chapter 10 Trion Model of Higher Brain Function:
Prediction that Music Enhances Spatial-Temporal
Reasoning   141

PART **III**

Tests of Predictions in Human Behavior

Chapter 11 Highly Accurate Mental Rehearsals: Correlation
with Top Performance in Sports   147

Chapter 12 Listening to Mozart Sonata (K.448) Enhances
Spatial-Temporal Reasoning: The "Mozart Effect"   159

Chapter 13 Music Training Enhances Spatial-Temporal
Reasoning in Preschool Children   169

Chapter 14 Music Training Plus Spatial-Temporal Training
Equals Improved Math   185

PART **IV**

Tests from Brain Imaging and Animal Studies

Chapter 15 EEG and fMRI Studies of Mozart Effect   205

Chapter 16 Symmetry in Primate Higher Brain Function   211

Chapter 17 Musical Structure of the Internal Neural
            Language of the Brain: Using Music as the
            Rosetta Stone to Help Decode this Internal
            Language   229

Chapter 18 Animal Behavior While Listening to Music and
            Doing Higher Brain Functions   239

PART **V**

*The Future of Music as a Window into Higher
Brain Function*

Chapter 19 Child Brain Development and Adult Brain
            Reorganization   255

Chapter 20 Education: Music Training Plus Spatial-Temporal
            Training Improves Math   269

Chapter 21 Clinical Implications   281

Chapter 22 The Spatial-Temporal Thinking Machine   295

Chapter 23 Final Thoughts   301

            Glossary   323
            Notes   335
            References   351
            Index   365

PREFACE

On October 14, 1993, our publication in the British scientific journal *Nature* announced that listening to 10 minutes of the Mozart Sonata for Two Pianos in D Major (K.448) would cause a subsequent enhancement in reasoning lasting from some 10–15 minutes. This "Mozart effect," as coined by the media, created a worldwide interest far beyond what I as a physicist could have imagined. It quickly became part of a popular folk lore and was referred to in comic strips, ads for German cars and CDs to make you smarter. The "Mozart Effect" has even been trademarked by someone. Note that neither my colleague Frances Rauscher nor I have been associated with them or endorsed them in any manner.

In February 1997, our article in the journal *Neurological Research* announced that 6 months of piano keyboard training causes enhancement of spatial-temporal reasoning in preschool children. This effect, which lasts at least several days, has potentially enormous educational implications.

Although these two publications created huge public interest, they raised many questions and misconceptions in people who learned of the results from the popular media. Almost none had seen or would have the scientific background to read the original articles and the perhaps dozen crucially relevant preceding and subsequent papers. I have written this book to make all of this material, as well as our recent research results and research in progress, accessible to everyone. A glossary of scientific and technical terms helps make this possible. The first time each such term is used, it appears in **bold** type. At the beginning of each chapter a brief guide will outline the key points and suggest how the nonexpert might approach the more technical sections, for example, whether to skim or skip them, without losing the thread of the main features of the book.

SYLVIA   by Nicole Hollander

FIGURE 0.1   Nicole Hollander's "Sylvia" comic strip (released December 13, 1993) motivated by our Mozart effect results. Courtesy of N. Hollander.

This book is our story of higher brain function: how humans think, reason, and create. It is based on a structured model of the brain that Xiaodan Leng and I proposed in 1991; it demonstrates how music is a window into higher brain function. This book is not about music, but about how music can help us understand how the brain works and how music can enhance how we think, reason, and create. We are at the very beginning of this quest: much additional research remains to be done. However, I believe that we have made considerable progress and that all the pieces of the story presented here fit into a coherent and compelling picture. I hope this interdisciplinary book will be of strong interest and use to parents, educators, scientists, and clinicians.

Before you read further, I suggest that you slip the CD out of the book, make yourself comfortable, and listen to the magic genius of Wolfgang Amadeus Mozart in his Sonata for Two Pianos in D Major (K.448).

ACKNOWLEDGMENTS

This book represents over 25 years of my research on the brain. Throughout the text, I have explicitly mentioned my collaborators, who included a wide range of highly talented individuals from beginning undergraduates to world-renown scientists. Working with them was a great pleasure, and *this work could not have been done without them*. Further, to me the greatest pleasure in scientific research is the collaborative effort in the quest for new and exciting insights into nature: Understanding how we think, reason, and create was and is my goal. So, I thank them for all the fun I had and am still having exploring the brain with them; these are golden years.

In addition to the collaborations, I have explicitly mentioned in the Prologue the support for the main ideas in this work that has come from many top scientists. This support has been extremely helpful to me and has carried me through some tough periods: Imagine going against the "standard accepted wisdom" in one area of science, and then consider that our studies have crossed many diverse boundaries in science.

Special thanks go to Ted Bullock, Peter Fuerbringer, Ted Jones, Bill Little, Bill Lucas, George Patera, Martin Perl, Jan Plastino, and Ed Thorp for helping give direction to the M.I.N.D. Institute. The proceeds from this book will go to support research done at the M.I.N.D. Institute. For new results from this research, and the status of S.T.A.R., check the Web site at www.MINDinst.org.

The preschool study and the 2nd grade study could not have been done without the support, encouragement, and complete cooperation of the heads of the participating schools, Marti Baker, Bruce Barron, Helen Clemmons, Patty DeBaun, Jim Kolinski, Gwen Morgan-Beazell, and Marge Rice, and their teachers. I thank Bruce Johnson and Al Landau for technical assistance.

I want to acknowledge the necessary financial support of this research during the past 10 years, all from the private sector: The Ralph and Leona Gerard

Family Trust, Herbert Lucas, Mary Lyons, National Association of Music Merchants, Philharmonic Society of Orange County, Marjorie Rawlins, The Seaver Institute, Texaco Foundation, Edward and Vivian Thorp, and the Yamaha Corporation of America. Dean Corey (PSOC), Anne Dowling (Texaco), Joanne Fuerbringer (PSOC), Pat Foster (Gerard Trust), and Pat and Sonia Seaver (Seaver Institute) must be singled out for their special help. Karl Bruhn has been my biggest source of encouragement for many years.

Thanks go to those who specifically helped make this book a reality. Kate Hendricks, a Seattle lawyer, has given me excellent advice concerning the M.I.N.D. Institute and S.T.A.R. Kate convinced me in November 1997 that writing this book at this time was important. Thanks goes to Reidun Torp, a dynamic neuroanatomist from Norway, who has given me help at many levels.

I thank Graham Lees, Vice President, Academic Press for all his interest, help, ideas, and encouragement. Graham reviewed my proposal and granted a contract to me for the book and to Matthew Peterson for the S.T.A.R. software demo version included with this volume. Matthew not only created this extremely valuable scientific and educational tool, but designed the M.I.N.D. Institute logo on the cover of the book. Reidun Torp gave me continued and important encouragement for writing the book as well as detailed and invaluable comments on the manuscript. Mark Bodner and Jill Hansen also gave very detailed and invaluable suggestions on the manuscript, as did Matthew Peterson and Bruce Shaw. Jill Hansen, Meredith Crosby, and Piper Pack worked hard on the many figures in this book. Although she's still an undergraduate, Jill runs my research lab and her contributions to this book have been absolutely crucial to so many aspects.

Graham Lees introduced me to the top people at Academic Press to work on the book. Many thanks to Lori Asbury, Senior Developmental Editor; Debby Bicher, Senior Art Consultant; and Cindy MacDonald, Editorial Manager. I also thank my copy editor, John Thomas, for an outstanding job. He not only greatly improved my English, but also greatly improved how I presented the material.

I thank three longtime, special friends for regularly being there to listen to how things were going with my research and the book and for giving excellent advice: Jim Mercereau, Ed Thorp, and Rita Viner.

Certainly not least has been the necessary, unconditional support and love of my son Bruce (and wife, Jackie), my daughter Karen (and husband John), my daughter Robin (and husband, Pat), and my wife, Lorna, who has always been ready to help with anything and everything.

PROLOGUE

This is the personal story of my 25-year adventure in the scientific study of the brain with the essential collaboration and inspiration of a number of wonderful colleagues. Because the main theme of this book is "music as a window into higher brain function," I will start here with how this thread of inquiry came about. I will also acknowledge the tremendous debt I owe to the many outstanding scientists that I have worked with and learned from in my journey.

I did my graduate studies in physics at Cornell University under the direction of Hans Bethe, a superb theorist now for seven decades and a Nobel laureate. He taught me how to do independent, goal-directed research. I was greatly influenced at Cornell by the brilliance and courage of Jon Sakurai, a fellow graduate student. Even as a student, Jon stood up to the entire physics community, which was criticizing his bold new (and subsequently proven correct) concepts. My first postdoctoral position was at Indiana University, where I worked in **elementary particle** theory with Marc Ross, who helped me increase my creativity. This was followed by a research position in theoretical physics at the University of California (UC) at San Diego, where I continued to learn how to do good science from David Wong and Keith Brueckner. Next, during an assistant professorship at Stanford University, I had the wonderful opportunity to teach graduate and undergraduate courses to the outstanding students there and to direct my first two graduate students in their Ph.D. research in elementary particle theory. There I met William Little and Martin Perl, two brilliant physicists who were to play major roles in my later research. The 1960s were golden years in physics: plenty of faculty positions, grants, and fantastic discoveries in elementary particle physics. I joined the brand new UC campus at Irvine in 1965 and have been there ever since, becoming full professor in 1968 and professor emeritus in 1994.

My detour from elementary particle physics to brain theory began in 1973, when I received a preprint from Bill Little that proved to be the seminal paper in bringing the powerful techniques of **statistical physics** to brain theory. I had recently heard a lecture by J. G. Taylor about the **fluctuations** in the release of **neurochemicals** at the junction between input and target **neuron** as demonstrated by Bernard Katz and collaborators. R. Vasudevan and I were then able to show that the **physiological** basis for some aspects of the equations in Little's model followed from these fluctuations in neurochemical transmission. I soon had the rewarding opportunity to collaborate with Bill on two papers. Thus began my gradual shift in research interest from elementary particle theory to brain theory. Over the past 20 years, Bill has provided continued insight, inspiration, and encouragement to me in my quest to understand how we think and reason.

In 1978, Bill and I published some important mathematical results from studies of the huge **memory storage capacity** of a system of neurons. Then, in trying to elaborate a physiological interpretation of our expressions, I was led to the insight that the basic unit in the brain was a small group of neurons rather than the individual neurons. At this time, Vernon Mountcastle presented his dramatic **columnar organizational principle** of mammalian **cortex** as a way to understand higher brain function, in which the internal **neural language** is manifested by the **spatial-temporal firing patterns** of groups of neurons. Vernon is one of the top neuroscientists of the past 50 years, and his columnar principle struck me as the way to proceed. Then in 1980, the amazing theoretical results of Michael Fisher and Walter Selke appeared on how **structured** physical systems yield an enormous variety of physical behavior compared to nonstructured models. It became clear to me that a combination of Bill Little's model and the insights from Mountcastle, Fisher, and Selke would lead me to a useful mathematical model of higher brain function. There were a number of intermediate steps, but the knowledge and importance of **symmetry** that I learned from George Patera and Dick Slansky proved to be the final ingredients in our **trion model** of higher brain function, which we published in 1985. George is perhaps the leading expert on bringing the mathematics of symmetry to physical sciences. I came up with the name trion because it represented a group of neurons and had three levels of **firing activity**.

My colleagues and I were finding some quite interesting properties of the trion model that were relevant to higher brain function. In 1988 it occurred to my graduate student Xiaodan Leng and me that it would be interesting to **map** the computer-generated spatial-temporal sequences of **memory patterns** in the trion model onto music in order to have another means of understanding these patterns and all their symmetry relations. Xiao's results were totally unexpected to us: Different mappings gave different recognizable styles of music! Xiao and I realized that in our quest to understand how we think, reason, and create, we could use "music as a window into higher brain function." This has been the dominant focus of our lab ever since.

Xiao and I recognized the significance of the trion model to music and higher brain functions such as chess and math. We saw the brain's innate ability to relate (through symmetry operations) patterns developing in space and time as the unifying physiological mechanism, and we predicted in our 1991 paper that music training for young children (when their brains are developing the most) would enhance their ability to do **spatial-temporal reasoning**, which is important in doing math and science.

The next big step was to test this bold idea with very little research funding. After a nationwide search, I was lucky to hire Frances Rauscher as a postdoctoral researcher. When my "child development advisor" Linda Levine and I interviewed Franny, it took no time at all to agree that she would be perfect, as indeed it turned out. Her parents were both professors of music at Manhattan School of Music and started her off on the cello at the age of 3. Franny became a concert cellist, but "burned out" at the age of 24. Apparently, being a concert musician is not as romantic as it seems to the outside observer such as myself, requiring perhaps 10 hours of practice a day to maintain one's peak skills. She quit music totally and went back to school at Columbia University, where she obtained her Ph.D. in psychology.

Franny immediately set up a pilot study with two groups of 3-year-old children. It soon became clear to us that these experiments with preschool children would take us years at considerable financial cost. Thus we came up with the idea for the **Mozart effect** experiments, which could be done relatively quickly. In these experiments, college students scored significantly higher on spatial-temporal reasoning after listening to the first 10 minutes of the Mozart Sonata for Two Pianos in D Major (K.448) compared to other students under control conditions. These results, published in 1993, were the first to demonstrate a causal link that music enhanced spatial-temporal reasoning. (Understanding how it does so and determining which among different types of music will also produce the Mozart effect are of great general and scientific interest in helping us understand the brain.)

The preschool study, published in 1997, showed that the children receiving 6 months of piano keyboard training improved on spatial-temporal reasoning by 30% more than children in **control groups** (including those receiving language training on a computer). This enhancement lasted at least several days (unlike the 10–15 minutes' duration of the Mozart effect), which meant that it should be of strong educational interest. The next steps in bringing the educational implications of these preschool results to reality are now in progress.

Thus we had shown that spatial-temporal reasoning could be used in a complementary manner to learn math and science concepts known to be difficult to teach with the usual **language-analytic** methods used in schools. These ideas are based again on studies (with John McGrann and Krishna Shenoy) of our structured trion model, in which the symmetry operations that, we are born with and that are enhanced through experience form the basis of higher brain function.

The realization of this new approach to teaching math has led to the development of **S.T.A.R.**—Spatial-Temporal Animation Reasoning—computer software for math reasoning, with Matthew Peterson as its architect and developer. The first exciting results, as found by Amy Graziano and Matthew in two elementary schools in Orange County, California, demonstrate that S.T.A.R. can be used to teach **proportional math**. Even more exciting are the results from the inner-city 95th Street School in Los Angeles, where we demonstrated that *music training along with S.T.A.R. gives a significant additional advantage to 2nd grade children learning proportional math and fractions*. We must now prove that our methods can be readily integrated into a standard curriculum and then shown to yield enhanced math in any classroom setting. For those of you who have a computer, at this time you might want to play with Matthew's great S.T.A.R. Demo that is included with this book.

Crucial parts of our research program involve investigations of the **neurophysiological** bases of these theoretical and behavioral results and ideas. These experiments not only are necessary from a scientific standpoint to truly establish the results, but are equally important in guiding the theory and behavioral studies to further breakthroughs. Our first brain mapping studies, published in 1997 in collaboration with scientists at the University of Vienna using **EEG** (**electroencephalogram**) methods pioneered there by Hellmuth Petsche, showed qualitative neurophysiological support for the Mozart effect. **Functional MRI** (**magnetic resonance imaging**) studies now in progress in Orhan Nalciolgu's lab here at UC Irvine show further and dramatic neurophysiological support from its first four subjects. New methods of analyzing neurophysiological data based on symmetry methods from the trion model have been developed by Mark Bodner and applied by him to single-neuron data from primate brains. This study, published in 1997, found **families of firing patterns** related by symmetries (as predicted by our model) and opened up exciting new possibilities for studying the neurophysiology of higher brain function.

A fascinating recent experiment by Fran Rauscher, now at the University of Wisconsin, Oshkosh, showed that long-term listening (12 hours per day for over 2 months) to the Mozart Sonata (K.448) by rats led to improved learning performance (versus rats in control groups) in a standard (complicated) **spatial maze**. These results, as we shall see, have several major consequences and implications for the Mozart effect: (i) it lasts at least 4 hours; (ii) an **animal model** is established; (iii) the effect is not due to cultural bias; and (iv) the results should generate philosophical discussions.

If these results are accurate, then they should have major **clinical** importance. Controlled studies now under way are investigating the Mozart effect in spatial-temporal reasoning in **Alzheimer disease** patients, recovery of spatial-temporal motor function following **stroke**, and reduction of **neurologically** measured electrical brain pathology in patients with **epilepsy**, as well as the effects of piano keyboard training on the spatial-temporal reasoning of children with the rare **Williams syndrome**. Encouraging first results with Alzheimer subjects were found by Julene Johnson and Carl Cotman here at UC Irvine. Extremely exciting results on the temporary reduction of abnormal cortical firing during listening to the Mozart Sonata (K.448), and not during control music, in 29 of 36 epileptic patients (many even in a coma) have been found by John Hughes at the University of Illinois at Chicago! These results for subjects in a coma dramatically demonstrated that the effect of the Mozart Sonata could not be attributed to relaxation or to whether the subject was attending to the music.

It is very important to note that much of what we present in this book is not without controversy. On the other hand, many renowned scientists have over the years been very supportive, among them Ted Bullock, Carl Cotman, Michael Fisher, Joaquin Fuster, Ted Jones, Bill Little, Gary Lynch, Jim McGaugh, Vernon Mountcastle, (the late) Ken Norris, George Patera, Martin Perl, Hellmuth Petsche, (the late) Fred Reines, (the late) Abdus Salam, (the late) Dick Slansky, and John Ward. In the early stages when I was developing the trion model, Salam said that the ideas "smelled right." I use this opportunity to thank these gifted scientists for encouraging me to pursue the ideas presented in this book. Of course, these ideas must be tested again and again in more detail and in further directions and modified to take into account the new results. Science is a dynamic process.

Two giants in experimental elementary particle physics, Martin Perl and Fred Reines, shared the 1995 Nobel Prize in Physics, each having made separate monumental contributions in going against the conventional wisdom. Each has played a major role in my career. As the first Dean of Physical Science at UC Irvine, Fred gave me the encouragement to pursue my interests in brain theory. His office, down the hall from mine, was always open to me to discuss my latest ideas, especially those on music enhancing spatial-temporal reasoning. Many people ask me if I still do some elementary particle physics, and the answer is yes, I still pursue, in a very limited way, searches for free **quarks**. Quarks have **fractional electric charge** and are the fundamental building blocks of **protons and neutrons**, and are generally thought to be "**confined**." Perhaps the best experiment yet devised to search for free quarks is being done by Martin Perl in his lab at Stanford University. (Positive results would be of *enormous* interest.) I take great satisfaction in having been part of this effort, along with my friends Chuck Hendricks and Klaus Lackner. Martin has always kept up on my research on the brain.

The ideas presented in this book cross many boundaries, including brain theory, neurophysiology, child development, music **cognition**, education,

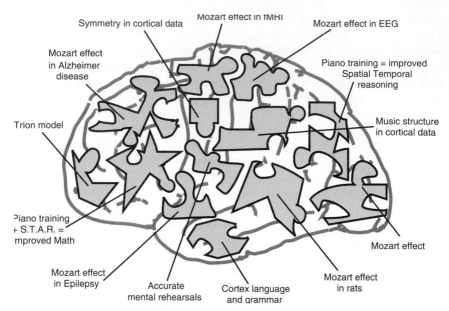

Symmetry in cortical data

Mozart effect in fMRI

Mozart effect in EEG

Mozart effect in Alzheimer disease

Piano training = improved Spatial Temporal reasoning

Trion model

Music structure in cortical data

Piano training + S.T.A.R. = Improved Math

Mozart effect

Mozart effect in Epilepsy

Accurate mental rehearsals

Cortex language and grammar

Mozart effect in rats

FIGURE 0.2 Pieces of the puzzle in our ongoing study of "Music as a window into higher brain function." I will discuss them all in this book and show how they all fit together.

teaching of music, teaching of math and science, neuropathology, psychology, and the **evolution of the brain**. But why should I write this book now when we are at the very early and controversial stages of this quest to understand how we think and reason by using music as a window into higher brain function? The reason is that I believe this book brings together the diverse experimental data and theory that support this model. Let me present it as a substantial number of pieces in a puzzle: Looking at each piece of the puzzle, a careful thinker would have many questions and doubts about the results from any individual piece. Furthermore, the pieces are not big enough to make the final result obvious. However, by carefully examining each piece and the relationships among the pieces, I believe it becomes *extremely* likely that we are on the right track. In fact, I hope that this book will serve as the necessary guide in completing the puzzle of higher brain function. This leads to what my colleagues and I have done to ensure that the completion of the puzzle is not left to chance.

In 1998, the Music Intelligence Neural Development Institute—**M.I.N.D. Institute**—was formed. The M.I.N.D. Institute (MI) is a community-based, nonprofit, interdisciplinary, basic scientific research institute devoted to using music as a window to understanding higher brain function, with the primary goal of enhancing children's reasoning and creativity. The MI consists of the small team of scientists who did the original groundbreaking research at the University of California at Irvine: Mark Bodner (UC Los Angeles), Xiaodan Leng (Pasadena City College), Matthew Peterson (UC Berkeley), Frances Rauscher (University of Wisconsin, Oshkosh), and myself (UC Irvine). The M.I.N.D. Institute will be building on this research of the past 10 years, including the structured trion model of higher brain function, its predictions, and the striking results of behavioral studies with both preschool children and college students, as noted earlier. Recent developments by the MI team prove that enhanced spatial-temporal reasoning can lead to greatly enhanced learning of specific math and science concepts using Matthew's S.T.A.R. software. An evaluation program—**S.T.A.R. E.P.**—which combines an introduction to S.T.A.R. along with a test, is now being used to assess the results of piano keyboard training plus S.T.A.R. training (or any other enrichment method) in the learning of the specific math and science concepts. We note that S.T.A.R. is meant to complement traditional language-analytic math teaching methods, not replace them. Piano keyboard training plus S.T.A.R. training indeed enhances the learning of proportional math and fractions.

We are at the very beginning of our explorations into the relationship between music and human intelligence. The MI will guarantee that this pioneering work proceeds. The MI Scientific Board consists of five world-renowned researchers: Theodore Bullock (UC San Diego), Edward Jones (UC Davis), William Little (Stanford University), Jiri Patera (University of Montreal), and Martin Perl (Stanford University). It is absolutely essential that the basic neurobiological bases of these important behavioral and educational results be investigated at the highest scientific level. It is the charter of the MI to continue to do this through collaborations with world-class laboratories. The organizational structure of the MI enables it to work directly with the community and to implement its research results directly into the school systems and into medicine. The future of the MI is extremely promising, and I expect that new scientific results will continue to have major educational and clinical relevance.

As I state in the Preface, this book is not about music, but about how music can help us understand how the brain works and how music can enhance how we think, reason, and create. This is a 25-year story and it involves many different disciplines. I have written this book to make all of the relevant scientific research available and understandable to everyone. I present the scientific results and all the insight I have gained in these 25 years, as well as my speculations about higher brain function. I am most pleased with our trion model of the brain. I hope it becomes clear how a mathematical model is *necessary* to help guide experiments into one of the most complicated entities in our solar system, the human brain. So far the trion model has provided fruitful guidance to research into brain theory.

There have been a number of interesting and delightful human aspects to this story and I have included many of them for fun and to help maintain your reading interest. Along this line, I have used a much more informal style than I use in my articles for scientific journals. The Glossary and Notes help explain the material and will assist the reader who wishes to consult the original articles and other publications on brain theory. The brief guide at the beginning of each chapter outlines the important points and objectives, as well as my suggestions on how to read it.

Much of the material in this book will be presented several times, with the plan that ideas and results will become clearer with further discussion. I have done it this way since this is how I learn new concepts best, that is, to start off simply and then to see the concept again and again in increasing detail.

Among the reasons that I felt obliged to write this book were the numerous misuses of our research. For example, the Florida legislature has mandated that classical music be played in licensed daycare centers to enhance the reasoning abilities of young children. It was stated that this initiative was based on our work, but I was never contacted by Florida officials (or officials in Georgia, where parents of newborns are now given CDs of classical music). Many reporters have interviewed me about these state programs, and you will see my comments to them. *In brief, while parents should make informed decisions concerning the upbringing of their children, it is wrong to legislate such decisions in the absence of any directly relevant research.* As a grandparent, I have encouraged my daughter Karen to play Mozart to her two young sons even though the relevant research for young children remains to be done. (You will see my reasons, including the quite important one that no bad side effects from listening in moderation to classical music have been reported.) However, our research has shown that *music training* for 3-year-olds enhances their spatial-temporal reasoning. *I propose that although it should not be legislated without further wide-scale controlled studies, educators should put music training back into the schools.* At worst, the children will learn the very valuable ability to play a music instrument. I *strongly* expect that music training will lead to much more; in particular, it will improve their ability to learn difficult math concepts. I hope you will agree when you finish reading this book.

Higher Brain Function: Music, Mathematics, Chess

BRIEF GUIDE

Part I presents the essential ideas of my theme that music can enhance our ability to think and reason. It briefly discusses how this ability derives from the basic structure of the brain we are born with. Part I is meant to be understandable to a broad audience. Many of the concepts, ideas, and results are not familiar and not so simple on first hearing of them. So, as noted in the Preface, I will present them several times in the book, adding more details as we proceed.

Higher-Brain Function: Music, Mathematics, Chess

CHAPTER 1

History, Anecdotes, Correlations, and Interviews

BRIEF GUIDE

This chapter is devoted mainly to stories relating music and other higher brain functions such as mathematics and chess. You will see that my use of higher brain function focuses on music, math, and chess, rather than more language-based thinking. This comes not only from my background as a physicist, but as you will later see, from my brain model of how we think, reason, and create in terms of the common **internal neural language** using **spatial-temporal firing patterns.** One of the themes of my research is that although much has been learned about how the brain works from studying deficits, I strongly believe that we have just as much to learn from people with exceptional abilities. This chapter introduces you to the concept of the **magic genius,** illustrated by Mozart in music and Ramanujan in math. Some scientific results and concepts are presented, and these will be expanded on in later chapters. Again, note that the scientific terms and abbreviations are put in bold type the first time they are used and are defined in the Glossary.

GENERAL REMARKS

On October 15, 1993, the front page of the Tokyo edition of the *International Herald Tribune* reported on our *Nature* findings (Fig. 1.1) [1]: Students who listened to the Mozart Sonata for Two Pianos in D Major (K.448) as performed by Murray Perahia and Radu Lupu did better on reasoning tasks than after listening to a relaxation tape or silence. This result, coined the "Mozart effect"

Mozart's Notes Make Good Brain Food

By Malcolm W. Browne

New York Times Service

NEW YORK - Can it be that the music of Mozart is not only exalting but can also improve intelligence?

An experiment on students at the University of California at Irvine suggests that listening to 10 minutes of Mozart's piano music significantly improves performance in intelligence tests taken immediately afterward.

The finding was reported Thursday in the British scientific journal Nature by researchers from the university.

The researchers found that after students listened to Mozart's Sonata for two Pianos in D Major (K.448) as performed by Murray Perahia and Radu Lupu, their test scores were a mean of eight or nine points higher than the scores the same students achieved after a period of silence, of after listening to a recorded message suggesting that they image themselves relaxing in a peaceful garden.

The effect was only temporary however. ....

FIGURE 1.1   Taken from the *International Herald Tribune*, Oct. 15, 1993.

FIGURE 1.2   Albert Einstein with his violin. Albert Einstein™ licensed by The Hebrew University of Jerusalem. Represented by the Roger Richman Agency, Inc., Beverly Hills, Calif.

by the media, was widely reported around the world, and continues to receive extensive attention. The particular recording we used sold out immediately in Boston (where many universities are located, including Harvard and MIT).

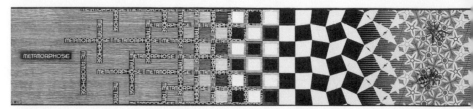

FIGURE 1.3   M.C. Escher's "Metamorphosis III". This amazing picture shows development as viewed from left to right. The complex patterns are full of **symmetry** relations, and transform in space and time (as our eyes follow the development) again and again. © 1998 Cordon Art B.V., Baarn, Holland. All rights reserved.

Why did this huge reaction occur, particularly since a connection between music and math had been discussed for perhaps thousands of years [2]? Somehow the idea that just listening to Mozart made you smarter, even if only for 10–15 minutes, captured the imagination of people around the world. *It was as if you got something for free.* Previously, **anecdotal** [3] and **correlational** [4] connections had been made: persons good or exceptional at math might be good or exceptional at music. Our experiment was the first to present evidence for a cause and effect relationship: music could **causally** enhance reasoning, if even temporarily.

It is of great importance for the nonscientist to understand this distinction between correlation and causation and the distinction between anecdotal studies and controlled studies. For example, important, controlled correlational studies by Marianne Hassler [5] showed higher scholastic performance in students who had years of music training. However, these results might be due to some selection process by parents rather than the music training. Anecdotally, it seems that scientists and mathematicians have an above average interest in classical music. However, I know of no published results on this matter that controlled for possible bias in the sampling. For example, in my gathering of data, I have more everyday contact with scientists than with politicians.

This chapter presents anecdotal and correlational stories relating music and other higher brain functions, since they can be very interesting and enlightening. Also, as elaborated on in Chapter 11, the study of truly exceptional talented individuals can give insights of enormous value if the right questions are addressed.

The relationships and similarities among such higher brain functions as the creativity involved in music, mathematics, and chess have been known for millennia. The ancient Greek **Pythagoreans** [6] considered music as one of the four branches of mathematics; some of the mathematical relations in music were discovered by the Babylonians and introduced into Greece.

FIGURE 1.3   (*Continued*)

For example, take the ratio of two quantities *a* and *b* or *a* divided by *b* (*a/b*) and the ratio of two other quantities *c* and *d* or *c/d*. Proportional math, which the majority of school children have difficulty learning, relates these two ratios *a/b* to *c/d*. (When you are at the supermarket comparing the cost per ounce—price divided by weight—of a big can of corn to a little one, you are doing **proportional math**.)

One of the most important proportions to Pythagoras, the philosopher and mathematician who lived in the sixth century B.C., and the mathematicians under him was called the harmonical proportion since it included those in music concerning harmony and melody. Thus, is it any surprise that learning to play a musical instrument might enhance one's ability to learn ratios and proportions? This is precisely what we were able to prove in our most recent dramatic study with second grade students (see Chapter 2).

Original results have been created before the age of puberty by Mozart and Rossini in music, by Gauss in mathematics, and by Capablanca and Reshevsky in chess [7]. A high percentage of gifted individuals are proficient or highly interested in more than one of these skills. Perhaps one of the most familiar is Albert Einstein, who played the violin (Fig. 1.2). Einstein is undoubtedly the most famous scientist of the twentieth century; his genius as a physicist is universally recognized. He was moved by Mozart's music into an awareness of the mathematical structure of music (the playing of Mozart by his talented pianist mother was one of the few distractions that could draw Albert away from his books) [8].

Einstein explained that music was in some ways an extension of his thinking processes, a method of allowing the subconscious to solve tricky problems. "Whenever he felt that he had come to the end of the road or into a difficult situation in his work," his eldest son has said, "he would take refuge in music, and that would usually resolve all his difficulties." Einstein himself once remarked that "Music has no effect on research work, but both are born of the same source and complement each other through the satisfaction they bestow" [9]. The theme of this book is that this connection goes much deeper—that music and mathematics are causally linked through the built-in, innate ability

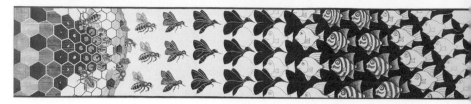

FIGURE 1.3   (*Continued*)

of the brain to recognize symmetries and use them to see how patterns develop in space and time. The transformation and development of spatial patterns is the central theme in the startling masterpieces of the brilliant artist M. C. Escher (Fig. 1.3) [10].

Some research studies in child development have shown correlations between music training (and music ability) and measures of spatial reasoning ability. Our structured trion model of cortex [11] provided a *causative* basis for such relations. The first series of experiments that we performed demonstrated that music enhances spatial-temporal reasoning [12] used in the higher brain functions of math and chess.

It is worthwhile to look for clues to understanding higher brain function from as many points of view as possible, in particular, from glimpses of recognized geniuses. Relevant anecdotes are informative as well as enjoyable to note. It would be remiss not to recount a few:

Mozart: As judged by biographer Davenport (Fig. 1.4) [13]:

> He [God] planted in Wolfgang Mozart what is probably the purest, sheerest genius ever born in man. . . . Until just before his sixth birthday, then, Wolferl [*sic*] led a happy and not too burdened life. . . . He learned his lessons, whatever they were, easily and quickly. His mind was usurped by music until he discovered the rudiments of arithmetic. Suddenly the house erupted with figures scribbled on every bit of space—walls, floors, tables and chairs. This passion for mathematics is plainly in close alliance with his great contrapuntal facility. Music, however, was his only real interest.

Mozart is this magic genius (as defined below) whose music will live forever, and I predict become even more widely listened to. In contrast, the magic genius in math, Srinivasa Ramanujan, is barely known, except to mathematicians (Fig. 1.5). However, I believe it is enormously important to try to understand the origin of Ramanujan's staggering abilities. If a theory of higher brain function is eventually established, it must be able to explain the magic genius of both Mozart and Ramanujan.

Ramanujan: As noted by biographer Kanigel [14], this relatively untaught mathematician is recognized as

FIGURE 1.3   (*Continued*)

"so great that his name transcends jealousies, the one superlatively great mathematician whom India has produced in the last thousand years." His leaps of intuition confound mathematicians even today, seven decades after his death. His papers are still plumbed for their secrets. . . . Ramanujan, in the language of the . . . [renowned] mathematician Mark Kac, was a "magical genius" rather than an "ordinary genius." [According to Kac], "An ordinary genius is a fellow that you and I would be just as good as, if we were only many times better. There is no mystery as to how his mind works. Once we understand what he has done, we feel certain that we, too, could have done it. It is different with the magical genius. They are, to use mathematical jargon, in the orthogonal [no overlap] complement of where we are and the working of their minds is for all intents and purposes incomprehensible. Even after we understand what they have done, the process by which they have done it is completely dark."

The "discovery" of the unknown, not formally trained Ramanujan is a fascinating story. On his own, Ramanujan worked out many problems in mathematics texts, and then after some calculations made simply enormous leaps to write down without proof amazing relationships never before imagined. From his home in Madras, India, he sent several notebooks full of these to the renowned British mathematician G. H. Hardy. The world had the good fortune that Hardy worked through some of these examples and recognized the genius of Ramanujan, and then invited him to come work with him in England. How many more potential math geniuses (with even a *small* fraction of Ramanujan's abilities) are out there waiting to be found and nurtured? Later, I will discuss a potential way of finding such "diamonds in the rough" using Matthew Peterson's **S.T.A.R. E.P.** [15] to measure "raw" spatial-temporal reasoning abilities.

A recently compiled list of India's top mathematicians and scientists indicates that Southern India has produced a remarkably high proportion of them, including Ramanujan. It is noted that [16]

Carnatic music may have been another contributing factor. Being so very precise and mathematical in its structure, it apparently imparted a sense of highly precise, mathematical cadences to the mind . . . thereby somehow "programming" it for scientific thought. . . . Now in the South there has been a strong and very special Carnatic music tradition that has flourished over the centuries. The strength of this tradition

FIGURE 1.3   (*Continued*)

lies in the fact that . . . it has had genuine mass following, drawing people from all
social, economic and age groups.

Thus, perhaps for fun, I might apply Mark Kac's subjective distinction between the ordinary genius and the magic genius and assign Einstein to the
category of "ordinary" genius and Mozart along with Ramanujan to the very
rarefied category of magic genius. Although Einstein's contributions to physics
were monumental, his reasoning process can be understood. Mozart was composing at the age of four, and it was stated that he would sometimes write down
an entire composition without changing a note. When Rauscher and I designed
our listening experiments, it was obvious that we should choose Mozart. I will
share our reasoning with you later.

SPATIAL-TEMPORAL REASONING IN CHESS

There are two complementary ways that we reason: **spatial-temporal** and **language-analytic:** Language-analytic reasoning is more involved when we solve
equations and obtain a quantitative result. Spatial-temporal reasoning is used
in chess when we have to think ahead several moves, developing and evaluating
patterns in space and time totally in our mind.

An important paper by Chase and Simon [17] presents very insightful results
on understanding the bases of chess-playing skill. Their experiments with
groups of chess Masters, class A players, and beginners extend the pioneering
work of de Groot [18] to go beyond the recall of chess positions to analyze the
nature of finding good chess moves.

They show that the amazing recall by the chess Master of a middle game
position takes place through the use of "local clusters of pieces." When the
pieces are randomly arranged at the first trial presentation, the Master's recall
ability is reduced to that of the beginner and class A player and actually falls
below them for subsequent trials! Their conclusions as to the Master's strategy
in choosing a next move in a middle game is fascinating [19]:

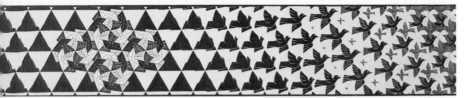

FIGURE 1.3   (*Continued*)

As we have shown, the board is organized into smaller units representing more local clusters of pieces. Since some of these patterns have plausible moves associated with them in long-term memory, the Master will start his search by taking one of these moves and analyzing its consequences. Since some of the recognizable patterns will be relevant, and some irrelevant, to his analysis, we hypothesize that he constructs a more concrete internal representation of the relevant patterns in the mind's eye, and then modifies these patterns to reflect the consequences of making the evoked move. The information processes needed . . . are akin to the mental rotation processes . . . and the mental processes for solving . . . cube-cutting puzzles. . . . When the move is made in the mind's eye—that is, when the internal representation of the position is updated—the result is then passed back through the pattern perception system and new patterns are perceived. These patterns in turn will suggest new moves, and the search continues.

It is clear that the ability of the chess Master to think several moves ahead is a truly amazing feat of spatial-temporal reasoning. It is amusing how structured the chess ratings are: There is no luck or bad referee mistakes that allow chess players to gather the points to improve their ratings. They get their ratings the old-fashioned way, they earn them. A sophisticated formula (you can find it on the official website of the U.S. Chess Federation [20]) determines the number of points a chess player earns when she beats another player depending on the rating of the opponent and the nature of the match or tournament. Rating classifications are Senior Master, above 2399; Master, 2200–2399; Expert, 2000–2199; and Class A, 1800–1999. There are also super levels of Grand Master and International Grand Master, as well as nine levels below Class A.

As a chess player with very modest abilities, I had always been very impressed with the spectacular genius of Bobby Fisher, arguably the most exciting chess genius of all time. It is evident that digital computers work on a totally different principle, and only by linking hundreds of such computers together, each being millions of times faster than the computational time of the human brain, was IBM's "Deep Blue" barely able to defeat the present world champion Garry Kasparov [21]. The number of possibilities when looking ahead 6–8 moves in many situations is just staggering! It becomes impossible for the computer to go through the possibilities that far ahead, whereas a Grand Master like Kasparov is able to see particular sequences of potentially winning possi-

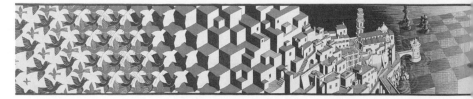

FIGURE 1.3   (*Continued*)

bilities involving that many moves. Deep Blue excels in examining all possibilities when looking ahead "only" perhaps 4–5 moves in complicated situations. Just imagine the technological impact of a computer that could perform spatial-temporal reasoning like a chess Grand Master (see Chapter 22). One day this will surely happen!

We have a lot to learn about higher brain function from studying our best and brightest scientists, musicians, chess players, mathematicians, engineers, artists, and athletes, all of whom use spatial-temporal reasoning at its highest levels. I will show a connection among these abilities and demonstrate that, unlike the influential model of seven separate intelligences proposed by Howard Gardner [22], strong evidence exists that they are not separate: *any higher level brain function must make use of many of the same cortical areas.*

INTERVIEWS WITH RESEARCH MATHEMATICIANS

With the foregoing belief that we can learn much from our best and brightest thinkers, Wendy Boettcher, Sabrina Hahn, and I designed and carried out in-depth interviews with 14 research mathematicians at the University of California at Irvine [23]. In addition to information about each mathematician's research area and math and music background, we were particularly interested in the mixing of the two fields of math and music. One question asked the researcher's opinion about a possible relationship between mathematics and music. Another question asked whether the researcher could listen to music while doing math. We hypothesized that if these activities make use of the same cognitive processes, music should interfere with mathematical operations. The most frequent response to listening to music while doing math was negative, either as a general rule or in particular when doing serious research. Five of the respondents mentioned that Baroque or classical music was particularly distracting.

Maren Longhurst followed up with a more focused interview and a more quantitative measure of the ability of 28 math (including a few physicists)

FIGURE 1.3   (*Continued*)

FIGURE 1.4   Wolfgang Amadeus Mozart, the incomparable magic genius in music, at the age of six. Courtesy of Scala/Art Resource, New York, N.Y.

FIGURE 1.5   A rare photo of S. Ramanujan, the untrained magic genius in math from India. © 1940. Reprinted with the permission of Cambridge University Press.

researchers, at U.C. Irvine and the Mathematical Sciences Research Institute at U.C. Berkeley, to listen to a specific piece of music [the Mozart Sonata (K.448)] while reading an article from a math journal on their desk. These interesting results [24] confirmed that "spatial-temporal reasoning is used extensively by math researchers in their work." Further, "there was no average 'background level' at which the Sonata could be heard that would not interfere with most of the researchers."

Maren had the math researchers listen to a one-minute selection of the Mozart Sonata and recorded the average power (using a gadget built for us by Jim Kelley) going to the headphones. The first trial measured a comfortable listening level, and the second trial used the highest level at which the subject could still maintain concentration while reading a journal article in their specialty (as well as a third trial to determine the threshold hearing level for each researcher). The spread of listening power levels while reading the journal was a surprisingly large factor of roughly 100! This result is quite important, since it would argue *strongly against playing background music to a group of students in order to enhance reasoning during an exam.* The role of listening to music as a setting for creativity is proposed and discussed in Chapter 10. The use of music in this way is thought to be *highly* individual.

A qualitative remark is the often stated one that we know many mathematicians who say that they are respectable musicians, but there are relatively few musicians who say that they are good at math. I suggest that perhaps these musicians are referring to poor performance in language-analytic math reasoning rather than spatial-temporal math reasoning. It is music and spatial-temporal math that are intertwined in our brain.

Wendy Boettcher and I had been discussing the standard methods of teaching math and science concepts to young children. We had suggested that "design and construction of super-friendly computer games to enhance conceptual and reasoning skills" using spatial-temporal reasoning was needed [25]. Matthew Peterson and I have been working on this now for almost five years, leading to Matthew's excitingly successful development and use of the S.T.A.R. (Spatial-Temporal Animation Reasoning) video game for teaching math and its companion evaluation program S.T.A.R. E.P. (You might want to examine Matthew's enclosed S.T.A.R. CD Demo.) The need for this in schools is elaborated on in the next chapter, and the details of S.T.A.R. and S.T.A.R. E.P. are given later.

I anticipate that Matthew's S.T.A.R., included as a demonstration CD to this book, will lead to a major change in how young children learn math and science concepts known to be difficult to teach using the usual language-analytic methods. Amy Graziano, Matthew, and I have shown not only that disadvantaged second graders can rapidly learn ratios and proportional math using S.T.A.R., but that piano training gives an additional significant boost over children in a control group [26]. *This is a big deal!*

CHAPTER 2

Spatial-Temporal and Language-Analytic Reasoning in Learning Math and Science

---

BRIEF GUIDE

I start by discussing how poorly U.S. schoolchildren do in math and science relative to children in other industrialized countries. There are two complementary ways that we reason, specifically in math and science: the spatial-temporal and the language-analytic approaches. The spatial-temporal allows the child to visualize the problem and a solution, which means she understands it conceptually. Understanding the concept allows her to better solve the relevant equations for the quantitative answers in the language-analytic approach. Both approaches are absolutely necessary and complement each other. *Further, as I will later present, spatial-temporal abilities are built into our structured brain.* The big problem is that the spatial-temporal approach is almost entirely neglected in traditional school systems. I present a two-part approach to change this. The first part rests on our results that piano keyboard training in three-year-old children can enhance their ability to do spatial-temporal reasoning. The second part is to design methods using spatial-temporal reasoning to teach math concepts. Computer software has been developed and been shown to work. Like much of the material in this book, these ideas and results will become clearer as they are presented again later on.

It has recently been documented [1] in the Third International Math and Science Study, which involved 45 countries using 500,000 students (who took the test in 30 languages), that the U.S. ranks below average (28th) in math. In particular, U.S. 8th graders are below average in geometry and proportional reasoning, which will of course handicap their science understanding. Further, it was reported that only 14% of American 7th graders and 20% of 8th graders could calculate that raising the price of an item from $0.60 to $0.75 was a 25% increase. It is interesting to note that the top four countries in math were Asian (in order): Singapore, South Korea, Japan, and Hong Kong.

It was shown that these poor showings by U.S. children were not simply due to poor study habits or watching too much TV. The top 20% of U.S. children ranked considerably below the top 20% of the children in the highest-scoring countries. Thus, we cannot simply blame these results on underprivileged children pulling the U.S. scores down. *It would seem obvious that these results deserve immediate and first-hand study.* All parents and educators want their children to do well and be competitive in math and science. It is becoming more and more evident that the competition for jobs is increasingly global, as compared to the more local nature in the times of our grandparents. It is also clear that technology is playing an ever-increasing role in modern society.

It is not our purpose, nor within our ability to analyze the reasons behind these poor math results [2]. Rather, Temple Grandin, Matthew Peterson, and I [3] have proposed a new conceptual strategy to attack this national problem, which we believe could make an enormous difference. But before I tell you of our program, I want to tell you about Temple Grandin, a simply *amazing* person.

Temple Grandin, a Professor of Animal Science at Colorado State University in Fort Collins, is the world's leading expert in the design of livestock-handling facilities. She has designed over half of all such facilities in the U.S. She is also **autistic**, which was clearly evident at the age of three. Some of the symptoms of autism that Temple had were extremely limited language function and very impaired social behavior. Through much effort on the part of others and herself [4], she has been able not only to lead a very productive life, but *she is also the* *best in the world in a very demanding and important technical field. Temple relies entirely on spatial-temporal reasoning.* Although her language skills are now excellent, she cannot do language-analytic math.

Our proposal is based on three important observations:

1. The current educational system concentrates on developing language-analytic reasoning skills, and neglects the complementary form of reasoning that we call spatial-temporal.
2. Some people, like Temple, who are forced to rely almost completely on spatial-temporal reasoning, are able to excel in science and technology.
3. Our recent behavioral experiments have confirmed our predictions that music training can enhance the "cortical hardware" used to solve spatial-temporal tasks.

Our new educational approach combines early music training to enhance spatial-temporal reasoning along with new spatial-temporal methods of teaching math and science. The bottom line is that it works [5]! This approach would complement the usual language-analytic methods, and should be started several years earlier. Integration of spatial-temporal math teaching with language-analytic teaching would follow. We are now implementing such a program in the 95th St. Elementary School in Los Angeles with the crucial support of Dr. Helen Clemmons, Principal, and the work of Linda Rodgers, a 2nd grade teacher. Our next step is to prove that this new program can work in any school. I will now present our program for this.

SPATIAL-TEMPORAL REASONING

Both spatial-temporal and language-analytic reasoning are crucial to how we think, reason, and create, and, in general, in how we go back and forth between the two. Language-analytic reasoning, for example, is more involved when we solve equations and obtain a quantitative result. Spatial-temporal reasoning, on the other hand, is involved in chess when we have to think ahead several moves.

Some key reasoning features that we use in spatial-temporal reasoning are, as suggested by our model of higher brain function:

(a) Mental imaging, by which we transform and relate these mental images in space and time;
(b) Symmetries of the inherent cortical firing patterns used to compare physical and mental images; and
(c) Natural temporal sequences of these inherent cortical firing patterns.

Albert Einstein made many references to his dependence on spatial-temporal reasoning. In a letter to a friend he wrote [6]:

> The words or the language, as they are written and spoken, do not seem to play any role in my mechanism of thought. The psychical entities which seem to serve as elements in thought are certain signs and more or less clear images which can be voluntarily reproduced and combined. . . . Conventional words or other signs have to be sought for laboriously in a secondary stage. . . .

Einstein is an outstanding example of a genius whose strength lay more in his spatial-temporal abilities than in his language-analytic abilities. Two other examples in theoretical physics come to mind. In the 1920s, a revolution in modern physics occurred with the quantum theory of the atom. Until then, there was a patchwork and inconsistent model derived from the work of Einstein and Niels Bohr. In 1925, Werner Heisenberg came up with a brilliant but totally mathematical (matrix) theory. His theory gave no visual picture of the atom. Only six months later, Erwin Schroedinger developed another approach (differential equations). After solving Schroedinger's equations, a pictorial description of the quantum theory atom emerged. The approaches of Heisenberg and Schroedinger were shown to be entirely equivalent.

The second example occurred in 1948, when amazingly accurate experiments on the energy levels of the atom forced the previous quantum theory to be revised. Again, two giants in physics developed seemingly totally different new theories. Julian Schwinger's brilliant theory was again totally mathematical, allowing no visual picture. In contrast, Richard Feynman's theory relied on diagrams that allowed a beautiful visual description. It was later shown that the two theories were exactly equivalent.

The Feynman diagram [7] shown in Fig. 2.1 looks deceptively simple. It conveys an example of the interactions between two electrons. However, accompanying these diagrams are the sophisticated yet straightforward rules laid out by Feynman for doing the full computations that allow one to compare theory with the experimental data. Feynman described the interplay of spatial-temporal and language-analytic approaches as the mysterious process that we all can recognize [8]:

> It's like asking a centipede which leg comes after which—it happens quickly, and I'm not exactly sure what flashes and things go on in the head. I do know it's a crazy mixture of partially solved equations and some kind of visual picture of what the equation is saying is happening, but not as well separated as the words I'm using. . . . Strange! I don't understand how it is that we can write mathematical expressions and calculate what the thing is going to do without being able to picture it.

For the average physicist such as myself, the theories of Schroedinger and of Feynman, which each allowed visual descriptions in addition to mathematical ones, were greatly appreciated and enormously useful. Feynman was perhaps the most important and influential physicist of the second half of this century.

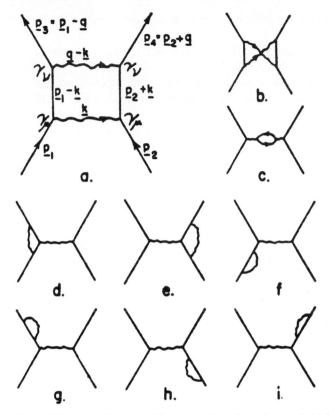

FIGURE 2.1   Richard Feynman's diagrams of the interactions of two electrons (with four vertices, or points where three lines come together). View them as conveying a simple intuitive picture (but with all the underlying, sophisticated, and powerful rules laid out to actually calculate them). From Feynman (1949). Copyright the American Physical Society.

EXTRAORDINARY ACHIEVEMENT IN THINKING IN PICTURES

I first read about Temple Grandin in the book "An Anthropologist on Mars" by the noted neurologist-author Oliver Sacks [9]. She was this "anthropologist" who had a difficult time as an autistic person in understanding the complex and sometimes devious social interactions of humans. What attracted my interest in her was her total reliance on spatial-temporal reasoning. I then read Temple's fascinating autobiography "Thinking in Pictures" [10], which I highly recommend. Every reader will have important insights on the brain, on autism, on courage, and on great accomplishment, and be moved by Temple's beautiful spirit.

I phoned Temple, describing my research interest in spatial-temporal reasoning. We met for dinner during a cattle-handling consulting trip she made to Southern California. It was a delightful dinner spent discussing our common interest in spatial-temporal reasoning and concluded with the outline of a paper that we would coauthor.

To dramatically illustrate the importance of spatial-temporal reasoning, I present here some aspects of Temple Grandin's almost entire reliance on such reasoning. As a very high-functioning person with autism, she describes her exceptional abilities to think in pictures (spatial-temporal reasoning) as an interactive "virtual reality." She is a leading structural designer, and has revolutionized certain areas of structural design that have traditionally been problematic because of the difficulty in visualizing the underlying problems. Her designs for livestock-handling facilities (Fig. 2.2) are revolutionary in that her structures affect animals in such a natural way that livestock are effortlessly directed in a calm and humane manner. In designing these facilities, she is able to visualize herself as the animal going through one of her systems and is thus able to correct for problems that might develop. In her imagination, she walks around and through the structure, and can fly over it in an imaginary helicopter. Remarkably, she moves herself around and through the structure instead of rotating the structure in her imagination.

Temple is able to do practical proportional reasoning at a sophisticated level by relying entirely on spatial-temporal thinking. I believe it is her spatial-temporal reasoning skills that allow her to solve global problems that confound many engineers and architects who rely mainly on language-analytic reasoning. Designing mechanical systems is easy for her because she can test run the equipment in her head. I hope this exceptional example of Temple's spatial-temporal reasoning abilities gets the message across clearly. All of us have this ability to do spatial-temporal reasoning, and it must be nurtured and used.

ROLE OF MUSIC EDUCATION IN LEARNING MATH AND SCIENCE

I have strongly urged that music education be given in our schools, starting preferably in preschool, in order to develop "hardware" in the child's brain for spatial-temporal reasoning. The absolutely crucial (but now neglected) role of

FIGURE 2.2   Example of Temple Grandin's design of a livestock-handling facility. Despite her autism (or perhaps even because of it), she is the world's expert in designing these structures. Courtesy of Temple Grandin.

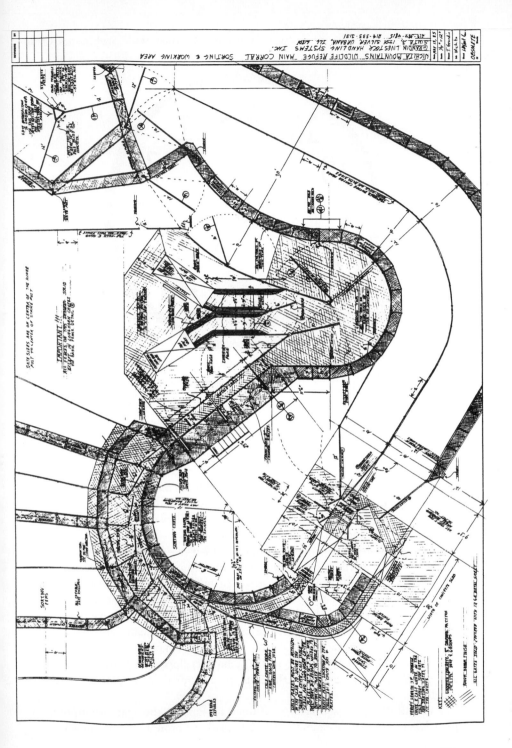

GRANDIN LIVESTOCK HANDLING SYSTEMS INC.
SUITE 3, 1724 SILVER, URBANA, ILL. MAIN
217-384-4815   518-333-5131

FIGURE 2.3   The wall clock at the 95th St. School used by our computer instructor to illustrate the concept of clockwise and counterclockwise rotations and symmetries. (The dotted arrow shows the clockwise rotation of the clock hands about a line or axis out of the paper through the center dot of the clock.) One of the children pointed out that the number 7 is an upside-down 2 on this particular clock. The child had understood symmetry and had incorporated it as part of his thinking.

spatial-temporal reasoning in learning difficult math and science concepts must be explored and exploited. Our success in this with Matthew Peterson's computer software for math reasoning—S.T.A.R.—is a key cornerstone of our present educational program in the **M.I.N.D. Institute.**

Our school program centers around the inner-city 95th St. Grade School in Los Angeles. In April, 1997, I gave a talk at a school in Long Beach to parents and educators about our research. After the talk and the lively discussion was finished, a young woman, Linda Rodgers, introduced herself. She is a 2nd grade teacher in the 95th St. School as well as a violin teacher in the evening. Linda asked if she and her school could be involved in our research aimed at showing that music training could enhance math performance. I saw many advantages to this, and our M.I.N.D. Institute has developed an extremely exciting and productive program with the 95th St. School that we plan to continue indefinitely.

I will illustrate how innate (to human reasoning) the spatial-temporal approach is with a simple example. Matthew had just brought down a new version of S.T.A.R. for the children at the 95th St. School. Our computer instructor Tina Earl was introducing the new concepts and operations: clockwise rotation and counterclockwise rotation using the big clock on the wall. After only three lessons with S.T.A.R., a 3rd grade student pointed out to the class that the number 7 on *this particular clock* was an upside down 2. I along with everyone else saw that he was precisely correct. I had been in this room dozens of times and never noticed this. Matthew immediately said to me that this anecdote should go into the book. Figure 2.3 shows this unusual clock where the 7 is an upside-down 2.

This incident is interesting because it showed how the symmetry concept was immediately understood and became part of the child's thinking, permanently I suspect! This is consistent with our prediction that spatial-temporal reasoning that includes symmetry operations is inherent in our structured brains.

The nature of S.T.A.R. and its companion evaluation program S.T.A.R. E.P. will be presented in Chapter 14, but I want to share with you some of their features (see the enclosed S.T.A.R. CD Demo), and one of its dramatic results, found by Amy Graziano, Matthew and myself [11].

S.T.A.R., as shown in Fig. 2.4, uses the spatial-temporal operations of folding, unfolding, symmetry, development, and evaluation of patterns in space and time within the brain to learn math. Our theory of higher brain function [12] argues that spatial-temporal reasoning is inherent in our structured brain. S.T.A.R. has three additional crucial features, one obvious and two not so obvious:

1. S.T.A.R. is super-friendly, as is most software for young children. However, it uses more of a game format that really captures the children's attention. In fact, we found that even mentally handicapped children were fascinated by it and would play it as a game, whereas they quickly lost interest in similar material presented in a more formal way.

2. S.T.A.R. is essentially a self-teaching program. The children explore the possibilities and learn without much teacher instruction.

3. Just as in a computer game, S.T.A.R. presents an immediate and running score as the children proceed to play this reasoning game. This is an important element. *Children want to know how they are doing and want to compete against themselves and others.* Every time any part of S.T.A.R. is played, the child's score is recorded on a graph that he or she can look at. Every 2nd grade child immediately mastered reading the graphs, a feat that not all college students can do.

An important point is that the children know that the grading in S.T.A.R. is not arbitrary or subjective. S.T.A.R. has no language or cultural bias. In contrast, I well remember a 7th grade science course that I almost flunked: the teacher

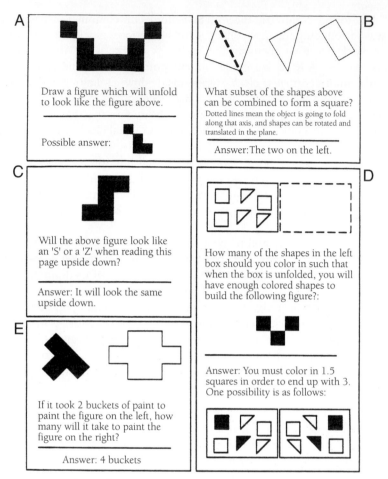

A Draw a figure which will unfold to look like the figure above.
_____
Possible answer:

B What subset of the shapes above can be combined to form a square?
Dotted lines mean the object is going to fold along that axis, and shapes can be rotated and translated in the plane.
_____
Answer: The two on the left.

C Will the above figure look like an 'S' or a 'Z' when reading this page upside down?
_____
Answer: It will look the same upside down.

D How many of the shapes in the left box should you color in such that when the box is unfolded, you will have enough colored shapes to build the following figure?:
_____
Answer: You must color in 1.5 squares in order to end up with 3. One possibility is as follows:

E If it took 2 buckets of paint to paint the figure on the left, how many will it take to paint the figure on the right?
_____
Answer: 4 buckets

FIGURE 2.4 Some (less difficult) examples of concepts presented in the S.T.A.R. software. The software does not include the verbal instructions shown here. Children quickly learned what was expected from each question without instructions. A, B, and C are training problems; D and E apply spatial-temporal reasoning to proportional math and fractions. From Graziano *et al.* (1999a)

gave a zero on any test question in which the answer had a misspelled word (I still cannot spell).

The results shown in Fig. 2.5 show how rapidly the 2nd grade children master the concepts in S.T.A.R. We propose that this is strong support for our trion model predictions that we are tapping into innate higher brain abilities with the spatial-temporal methods used in S.T.A.R. If this were not so, I would

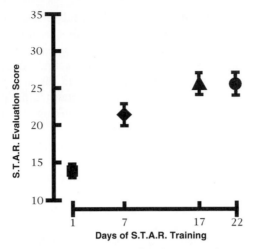

FIGURE 2.5   Results of the S.T.A.R. E.P. testing of math concepts (see Fig. 2.4) as a function of the number of S.T.A.R. training lessons received by 2nd grade children. *This shows how rapidly they master the training.* Each data point represents the average score of a different group on the E.P. It consists of the test plus one day (1-hour lesson) of spatial-temporal training for those children that had no previous training from us. Thus the No Lesson group (square) had one day of training. Group ST-1 (diamond) had 7 days of training, group ST-2 (triangle) had 17 days, and group ST-3 (circle) had 22 days of training. (Chance performance was a score 7.17. Thus the score of the No Lesson group was roughly twice that of chance.) As I discuss later, piano keyboard training further enhances math performance. From Graziano *et al.* (1999a)

predict that the training time required for score improvement would be much longer than we found in Fig. 2.5.

I want to stress that we are clearly not the first to emphasize the important role of spatial-temporal reasoning and how its use in teaching math and science in the school system is totally inadequate. For example, Jean Piaget [13] understood the role of spatial-temporal reasoning. Piaget was perhaps the most influential scholar in child development, publishing extensively from the 1920s to the 1960s, and greatly influenced theories and practice of education. He conceived of four stages of development, and believed that not until the age of six did children reach the more sophisticated operational stages and thus become able to master certain higher brain functions. I think Piaget's ideas must now be reexamined. Our new experiments with very young children (see Chapter 21) clearly show the remarkable higher brain function capabilities of these infants. Our trion model of higher brain function predicts that infants are born with sophisticated spatial-temporal reasoning capabilities that are ready to be influenced by their experiences at a much younger age than that envisioned by Piaget.

Seymour Papert devotes much of his book "Mindstorms: Children, Computers and Powerful Ideas" [14] to the importance of spatial-temporal reasoning. An interesting historical approach is discussed by Eugene Ferguson in an article entitled "The Mind's Eye: Nonverbal Thought in Technology" [15]. He stresses that "thinking with pictures" is an essential part in the intellectual history of technological development. Yet nonverbal (spatial-temporal) thinking has given way to the quantitative language-analytic thinking in schools at all grade levels.

The ideas I present here build on the ideas of others, but there are important differences. In particular, we propose that *there is an inherent neurobiological basis for the early use of spatial-temporal reasoning*. I suggest that the rapid learning shown in Fig. 2.5 supports this. Further, our dramatic contribution is to show how music training can enhance the brain's neural "hardware" for such reasoning. I predict that it is the combination of music training plus spatial-temporal training that will revolutionize how children learn difficult math and science concepts.

CHAPTER 3

Music Enhances
Spatial-Temporal Reasoning

BRIEF GUIDE

In this chapter, I introduce the idea that we are born with a highly structured brain. My mathematical realization of this is the trion model of the cortex. Studies of the trion model led to the prediction that music could enhance spatial-temporal reasoning. I present a first glimpse into the dramatic behavioral experiments that support this prediction: the Mozart effect listening experiment with college students and the preschool experiment involving piano keyboard lessons. All this material will make more sense as details are discussed in later chapters. I felt that it is important in this chapter, and the next one, that I give you a preview of where I am leading you with so many new ideas and results.

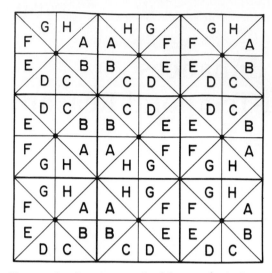

FIGURE 3.1   The Mountcastle columnar principle of the cortex is the basis of our mathematical model of higher brain function. Each square represents a column of neurons, which is assumed to be the fundamental network in mammalian cortex. The triangles represent the minicolumns, which are Mountcastle's irreducible processing units. I will give more details in Chapter 7.

The similarity among higher brain functions such as music, mathematics, and chess has long been discussed [1]. In our model of higher brain function [2], Xiaodan Leng and I proposed, *for the first time,* a causal link between music and spatial-temporal reasoning. In 1988 it occurred to my brilliant graduate student Xiao and me (working with electronic music expert Eric Wright) that it would be interesting to **map** the spatial-temporal sequences of **memory patterns** in our trion model of the brain into music in order to get another means of understanding these patterns with all their symmetry relations.

Xiao's results were totally unexpected to us: Different mappings gave different recognizable styles of music!! Xiao and I recognized that in our quest to understand how we think, reason, and create, we could use "music as a window into higher brain function." This has been the dominant focus of my lab ever since.

Our model of higher brain function was developed from the trion model of the cortex [3]. The trion model (see Chapter 8) is a highly structured mathematical realization of the Mountcastle organization principle with the column as the basic neuronal network in mammalian cortex [4]. Vernon Mountcastle's columnar principle of cortex (Fig. 3.1) is the key to this entire book. We are born with a highly structured brain. Predictions from the trion model yield an inherent **internal neural language** and grammar that we are born with, and that allows us to perform higher brain functions such as music, math, and chess in a manner entirely different from the standard digital computer. In other words, our brains have the innate ability to recognize and manipulate patterns in space and time.

A columnar network of trions has a large repertoire of *inherent* spatial-temporal firing patterns that can be excited and used in memory and higher brain function. According to the model, newborns possess a structured cortex that yields this repertoire of firing patterns at the columnar level. They can be excited and strengthened by small changes in connectivity via a **synaptic learning rule** put forward by the renowned neuroscientist Donald Hebb [5]. These memory firing patterns evolve over time in a **probabilistic** manner from one to another in natural sequences related by specific symmetries, and *form the inherent neural language with a grammar in the cortex.* It was recently shown by Mark Bodner at U.C. Los Angeles that, as predicted, families of symmetric temporal firing patterns are present in primate brain during a short-term memory task [6]. Mark's research is a truly landmark experiment and analysis lending support for the trion model at its most fundamental level.

The results of Xiao were striking when time evolutions of the trion model firing patterns were mapped onto various pitches and instruments, producing recognizable styles of music [7]. This gave us the insight to relate the neuronal processes involved in music and abstract spatial-temporal reasoning.

We proposed that the key component of spatial-temporal reasoning was the "built-in" ability of the columnar networks to recognize the symmetry relations among cortical firing patterns in a sequential manner (see Chapter 8). Spatial-temporal mental processes may last some tens of seconds to minutes, as compared to spatial recognition processes, such as face recognition, which might be accomplished in a fraction of a second.

Music clearly involves spatial-temporal reasoning: the ability to create, maintain, transform, and relate complex mental images even in the absence of external sensory input or feedback.

Although higher brain functions such as music and spatial-temporal reasoning crucially depend on specific, localized regions of the cortex, all higher cognitive abilities draw upon a *wide range of cortical areas.* I will discuss examples of this later, which are clearly demonstrated by the pioneering work by Hellmuth Petsche at the University of Vienna [8].

Recent studies have demonstrated that sophisticated cognitive reasoning abilities are present in children as young as 5 months [9]. Similarly, musical abilities are evident in infants and newborns [10]. One of my favorite experiments was done by Carol Krumhansl [11]. She demonstrated that 4-month-old infants have a remarkable preference for hearing Mozart sonatas as they were written as compared to "unnatural" versions. I will present the details of her experiment along with several other relevant ones in Chapter 19.

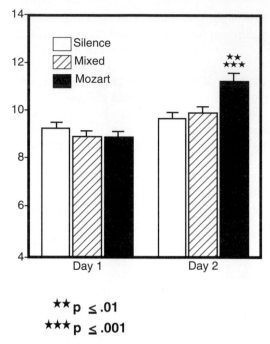

$$\star\star\, p \leq .01$$
$$\star\star\star\, p \leq .001$$

FIGURE 3.2   Results from a Mozart effect follow-up study by Rauscher *et al.* (1995), showing the mean number of correct spatial-temporal test items out of 16 by Silence, Mixed, and Mozart groups. On Day 1, all 79 college students were randomly divided into three groups of equal ability. On Day 2, before doing 16 new items, the Silence group listened first to 10 minutes of silence, the Mixed group listened to 10 minutes of minimalist music by Philip Glass, and the Mozart group listened to (the first) 10 minutes of the Mozart Sonata for Two Pianos in D Major (K.448). (Note a small increase from Day 1 to Day 2 of the Silence and Mixed groups, probably due to a practice effect on the task.) The Mozart group had a large and significant improvement from Day 1 to Day 2 (**probability p** less than 0.001) and scored above the other groups on Day 2 (*p* less than 0.01). This enhancing effect lasts only some 10–15 minutes.

Xiao and I then proposed that music may serve as a "pre-language" (with centers distinct from language centers in the cortex [12]), available at an early age, which can access inherent cortical spatial-temporal firing patterns and enhance the cortex's ability to accomplish spatial-temporal reasoning. You cannot teach your child higher math at the age of three. However, they love music and it plays this very special role in the brain. Thus we predicted in 1991 that music training at an early age might act as exercise for higher brain function [13].

The next step was to test this bold prediction with very little funds. After a nationwide search, I was lucky to hire Frances Rauscher in 1992 as a postdoc-

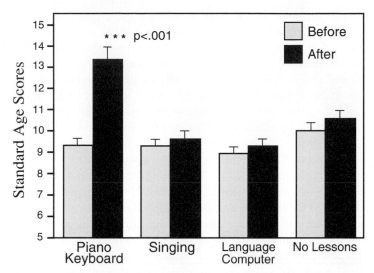

FIGURE 3.3   Spatial-Temporal Task Results Preschool study, showing means for the spatial-temporal age standardized scores before and after training for the (piano) Keyboard, (group) Singing, (English language training on) Computer, and No Lessons groups. The national norms for all ages are 10, showing that these were average children before training. After training, the Keyboard children mean is above the 85% level. The enhancement lasts at least three days, making it potentially significant for education. From Rauscher *et al.* (1997)

toral researcher. Franny set up a pilot study with two groups of three-year-old children. It soon became clear to Franny and me that these experiments with preschool children would take us years at considerable financial cost. Thus we came up with the idea for the "Mozart effect" experiments, which could be done relatively quickly. We found that college students scored significantly higher on spatial-temporal reasoning after listening to the first 10 minutes of the Mozart Sonata for Two Pianos in D Major (K.448), but not for other controls [14]. This experiment, published in 1993, was the first to demonstrate a causal link for certain music-enhancing spatial-temporal reasoning. Further studies have confirmed and explored this astonishing effect with perhaps even more startling results (Fig. 3.2) [15]. These will be presented in later chapters.

I have given many talks on this research to groups ranging from neuroscientists, mathematicians, physicists, educators, parents, music teachers, and the general public. Two of the most frequently asked questions from these audiences are why did we choose Mozart, and will the music of other composers produce the same enhancement. (Clearly, understanding which among different types of music will also produce the Mozart effect is of great general and scientific interest.) In subsequent chapters, I will answer both of these questions, as well as numerous questions posed by these bright and interested audiences and the many sharp media interviewers. I thank all of them for helping me present the diverse and nontrivial concepts in this book in a clearer manner.

The successful Preschool study [16], published in 1997, showed that the three-year-old children receiving 6 months of piano keyboard training improved on spatial-temporal reasoning 30% more than did children in control groups (including those receiving language training on a computer), as shown in Fig. 3.3. This enhancement lasted for at least several days (unlike the 10–15 minutes for the Mozart effect listening), which means that it could be of strong educational interest. These results represent the start, rather than the end, of the story of how music can enhance how we think, reason, and create.

Because the improved spatial-temporal reasoning from the piano keyboard training lasted for a number of days, we suggested that this must involve "long-term" modifications in the brain's neural connections. I expect that the piano training must be continued for some years to truly maintain this improved cortical hardware for spatial-temporal reasoning. This must be further investigated. We also suggested that this improved spatial-temporal reasoning could lead to improved learning of math concepts known to be difficult to teach using standard language-analytic methods alone. Indeed, we now have the first proof (see Chapter 14) that piano training plus spatial-temporal training (using S.T.A.R.) does give greatly improved performance in proportional math and fractions for 2nd grade children [17].

CHAPTER 4

Implications: Scientific, Educational, Clinical

BRIEF GUIDE

This chapter outlines a number of key points so you can clearly see where I am going with them. In particular, three quite startling new results are briefly introduced: Fran Rauscher's Mozart effect studies with rats, Mark Bodner's analysis of primate cortical higher brain function data, and John Hughes' Mozart effect studies with epileptic patients. *All three of these studies have major implications.* The material in this chapter will be gone over in more detail later.

Although a chapter entitled Implications might rightly be expected to appear at the end of the book, I wanted to use this chapter to help readers keep in mind the range of roles and effects of music in higher brain function. We are still at the beginning of this adventure into understanding how we think, reason, and create using music as a scientific tool. Yet it is just as important to apply the results of these scientific studies to the benefit of society through education and medicine.

EDUCATION

We have shown that piano keyboard training enhances spatial-temporal reasoning in preschool children [1], with this effect lasting for days and thus having enormous potential educational implications. (I expect that similar cortical mechanisms are involved in the Mozart effect, so its better understanding should shed considerable light on these preschool results.) We have proposed that spatial-temporal reasoning is crucial in math and science, and in particular in learning proportional math reasoning [2], which has been shown to be difficult to teach using traditional language-analytic methods. We have now shown that this works. and that the music training adds a large additional improvement in math performance [3]. This clearly demonstrates the importance of having young children improve their spatial-temporal reasoning through music training. I am optimistic that the M.I.N.D. Institute will attain its goal of fully integrating music training along with spatial-temporal training into the math and science curricula in public schools.

NEUROSCIENCE

We have proposed that music is a window into higher brain function. These theoretical predictions from the trion model rest largely on the concept of the existence of a common, inherent internal neuronal language throughout the mammalian cortex at the columnar level, with music resonating with this language. This opens up an exciting program to investigate the neurophysiological basis of the Mozart effect not only in humans, but also in other mammals. Recent results by Fran Rauscher [4] are presented in Fig. 4.1, showing that rats following long-term exposure to the Mozart Sonata (K.448) have enhanced **spatial maze** performance, which lasts at least 4 hours after the last exposure to the music. This indicates that the Mozart effect might be made into a long-term effect. *However, I strongly advise parents not to play the Mozart Sonata in excessive amounts to their very young children with the expectation of increasing their reasoning abilities.* No relevant research has been done with infants, but such studies should definitely be done in a careful and scientific manner.

A recent study [5] with monkeys using a new analysis by Mark Bodner has provided the first neurophysiological experimental evidence for the symmetry

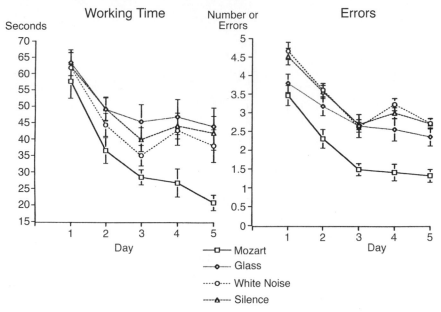

FIGURE 4.1   Behavior, working time, and number of errors for four groups of rats in a spatial maze after undergoing extensive listening conditions for months. The Mozart group of rats listened for 12 hours a day to the Mozart Sonata (K.448), the Glass group listened to the same piece of music by Philip Glass that was used as a control in the Mozart effect study (see Fig. 3.2), one group listened to **white noise**, and a fourth group listened to silence. The Mozart group shows daily improved performance. This experiment from the laboratory of Frances Rauscher has many important implications. From Rauscher *et al.* (1998).

relations of families of cortical firing patterns predicted by the trion model for the code or internal neural language for higher cortical function. I had proposed that cortical response to music, specifically that of Mozart, can be used as the "Rosetta Stone" for decoding the internal neural language of higher brain function in mammals. *There is probably no more important science project.* I suggest that Mark's results and new methods of analysis (see Chapters 16 and 17) will indeed lead to major breakthroughs.

CLINICAL

I am collaborating on four experiments, now in the early stages, to test whether the Mozart effect can be used in the treatment of neurological disorders of the cortex. Even short-term benefits can be of considerable interest, especially since

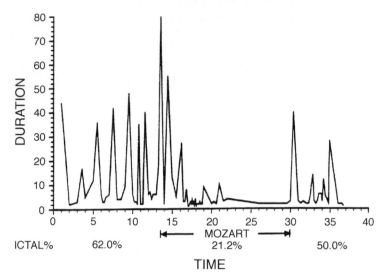

FIGURE 4.2   Duration of epileptic spiking events recorded in an electroencephalogram, showing a huge decrease while listening to the Mozart Sonata (K.448). This subject was in a coma. These experiments by John Hughes have enormous scientific interest and present significant clinical implications if the time of decrease of epileptic spiking can be lengthened through repeated exposure to the Mozart. From Hughes *et al.* (1998).

there are no detrimental side effects to listening to Mozart. The experiment [6] by John Hughes, Director of the Epilepsy Clinic at the University of Illinois at Chicago, is of enormous scientific significance and has considerable clinical potential. John played the Mozart Sonata (K.448) to epileptic patients who had many, usually repetitive focused discharges either when awake or in a coma. In 29 out of 36 cases, there were statistically significant decreases in this epileptic activity as measured in surface brain waves (see Chapter 6 on EEG brain imaging). Figure 4.2 shows the dramatic example of one patient in a coma. Clearly relaxation played no role here.

Very encouraging results [7] by Julene Johnson, from Carl Cotman's Brain Aging Institute, show enhanced spatial-temporal reasoning following listening to the Mozart Sonata (K.448) in a series of studies with an early Alzheimer disease subject. Julene found repeated enhancement after the Mozart listening condition and not after silence, nor after a popular piano piece familiar to the subject (this popular piano piece control was also used in John Hughes' epilepsy study with no effect).

Pilot studies of how listening to the Mozart Sonata (K.448) affects recovery of spatial-temporal motor skills following cerebral stroke are under way. The results were encouraging, but several features in our experimental design needed improvement. Matthew Peterson has created a software program that allows a small piano keyboard to serve as the motor skill device for the stroke patients and solves most of our design problems. This project will be considered later.

Williams syndrome [8] is a rare genetic brain disorder in which children are born with normal or even above normal music and language abilities. However, they are extremely poor in spatial-temporal reasoning, contrary to what would be expected in normal children. My colleague Howard Lenhoff told me about this and how it was strikingly demonstrated in his extremely charming and musically talented adult daughter Gloria. Howard convinced me that the study of children with Williams syndrome could reveal much about the brain. What interested me even more was the potential of improving their spatial-temporal reasoning through music training. Our pilot studies have convinced me that we must combine the music training with a simple version (MicroS.T.A.R.) of S.T.A.R. that is suitable for young children and primates (see the following).

Child Development

Music indeed plays a very special role in child development. Recent studies have demonstrated that sophisticated cognitive abilities are present in children as young as 5 months old. Similarly, musical abilities are evident in infants and neonates. Xiao Leng and I proposed that music may serve as a "pre-language" (with centers distinct from language centers in the cortex), available at an early age, which can access the inherent cortical spatial-temporal firing patterns and enhance the ability to perform spatial-temporal reasoning. It seems likely that well-designed experiments will be able to test whether the Mozart effect is present even for very young children. Whether there will be long-term enhancements is the big question. The crucial ingredient in such experiments is the ability to test enhanced spatial-temporal reasoning.

MicroS.T.A.R. is a version of the S.T.A.R. computer software now being developed by Peterson and Bodner for young children and primates to train them in spatial-temporal reasoning and to evaluate their spatial-temporal performance abilities. MicroS.T.A.R. will be an extremely useful tool, for example, in evaluating possible spatial-temporal reasoning enhancements in young children who listen to certain music for months. It is crucial to conduct these experiments, since state programs in Georgia and Florida are encouraging parents to have their very young children listen to classical music in order to improve their thinking abilities. State officials say that their programs are based on our research, yet they have never spoken with me! *Currently, there is no directly relevant research.* In several media interviews after these state programs were begun, I stated that the relevant scientific studies must be done. With the development of MicroS.T.A.R., I believe that these experiments can now be done properly.

PRIMATE EVOLUTION

The Mountcastle organization principle [9] gives the column as the basic neuronal network in mammalian cortex. This structured cortex yields an inherent repertoire of spatial-temporal firing patterns at the columnar level. These patterns can be strengthened by changes in connectivity through experience.

There are several possible evolutionary roles for this mammalian structured cortex. Clearly, the advantage of doing sophisticated reasoning is a good candidate. Kenneth Norris [10] has suggested that the very patterned group behavior (spatially and temporally) of spinner dolphins would be consistent with the consequences of a structured cortex. I think you will enjoy reading about Ken's research in Chapter 23.

The now established [11] presence of a Mozart effect in mammals other than humans allows for an exciting new way to examine the evolutionary development of the Mountcastle principle.

PHILOSOPHICAL

The philosophical consequences of the Mozart effect in humans are profound. We have only one cortex and it really cannot be "broken apart" into many separate intelligences, as evidenced by the fact that music can causally enhance reasoning. The philosophical consequences of having observed a Mozart effect in mammals might help bring about qualitative changes in our view of the reasoning capabilities of these animals.

We are now involved in a number of collaborative behavioral experiments to look for music preferences in primates, as well as to evaluate their spatial-temporal reasoning abilities when MicroS.T.A.R. is available. Perhaps the most famous gorilla in the world, Koko, will participate in our studies [12]. Koko uses a sign language vocabulary of over 600 words. Although Koko, who lives at the Gorilla Foundation in Woodside, California, has many talents and interests, her gorilla friend Michael is *exceptionally* talented in art. Figure 4.3 (see color insert) shows a painting by Michael. I would love to have any of Michael's paintings in my home. He paints quite often and, as you can see, in an outstanding manner. His art is clearly produced by higher brain functioning.

All of the concepts and results presented in this chapter will be elaborated on in later chapters.

Structured Brain and Symmetry

BRIEF GUIDE

Part II contains the more technical aspects of this book. I have tried hard to make all of it readable and accessible to everyone (with no equations). Lots of figures have been designed to help in this. However, Part II can be skipped or skimmed on first reading without losing the thread of my story that music is a window into higher brain function.

CHAPTER 5

Symmetry as a Common Theme

BRIEF GUIDE

If I had to sum up the entire book with one word, it would be symmetry. Symmetry applies to everything from music to art to nature to math to science to beauty and to life. My goal in this chapter is to introduce symmetry in some familiar ways and then give it a bit more formality. I suggest that this chapter at least be skimmed since it is so fundamental. In Chapter 8 I will present the reason why symmetry is so important to my story. *The role symmetry plays in our structured brain is the key to how we think, reason, and create.*

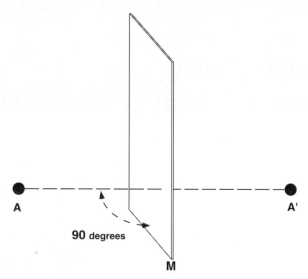

FIGURE 5.1   Mirror reflection of A into A', along the right angles made by the mirror M.

Perhaps the dominant theme of this book is the role of symmetry in higher brain function. We will examine it from many aspects, from the very familiar to the somewhat more abstract.

Symmetry is used in many ways and in all aspects of everyday life, as well as in art, music, math, architecture, philosophy, and science [1]. Thus everyone has some sense of the meanings of symmetric and symmetry. In the common-sense use of the words, symmetric means well balanced, and symmetry denotes the special relations that several parts have in building up the whole object that yields a form of beauty. The Greeks used these words to describe sculptures and music. I would like to examine some features of symmetry in a more precise manner as used in math and science. Symmetry is the crucial element in our belief that the structured brain we are born with has the innate ability to recognize symmetries, which forms a key component of how we think, reason, and create.

First, consider the mirror reflection of a point, as shown in Fig. 5.1. The distance from A to M along the right angle made by the mirror is the same as the distance from A' to M. This is all there is to it. Take any object you like and form its mirror reflection by proceeding to reflect it point by point. We know that for many objects we can immediately recognize its mirror reflection image, and in fact find that objects without mirror reflection symmetry are not as pleasing as those with "almost" perfect symmetry. It is fun to see a face as in Fig. 5.2 compared to what it would look like with exact mirror symmetries.

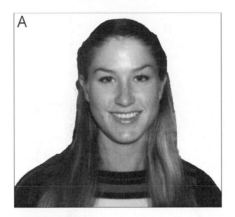

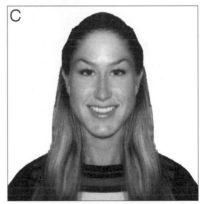

FIGURE 5.2   The face of my colleague Jill Hansen with and without exact mirror symmetry.

Another symmetry that we all are familiar with is rotation. Consider the star in the center of Fig. 5.3 and imagine a line running perpendicular through the page about which we can rotate the center star (called the **axis of rotation**). Without any detailed math, it is clear that we can rotate the figure through five different angles (either clockwise or counterclockwise) about the axis of rotation and still get a star figure that looks the same as the one we started with. Using math, we can calculate that these five rotation angles are integer multiples of 360 degrees/5 (with a 360 degree rotation being equal to a 0 degree rotation). [2]

Note the five mirror reflections M about the five lines joining each vertex of the star to the center. These symmetry operations also *take the star precisely to itself* as shown in Fig. 5.3. Together, the five rotations R with the five mirror

FIGURE 5.3   Symmetries of the star showing rotations R and mirror reflections M. Start with the top star labeled 1 and rotate it (R) as in the direction of the circular arrow until the dark segment matches that in the star labeled 2. If I remove the dark segments, then we see that star 1 has been rotated into star 2. Now go back to star 2 with the dark segment and mirror reflect (M) star 2 about the dotted line so that star 2 now matches star 3. If I remove the dark segments, then we see that star 2 has been mirror reflected into star 3. You can continue to alternate these R's and M's as indicated and get back to star 1.

reflections M taken in any order and any combination of these symmetry operations give back the same star (and form the higher math concept of symmetry group of operations on the star). Not only do we recognize such symmetries without any math knowledge, but we prefer objects with many symmetry operations in art, as in Fig. 5.4.

We recognize and like figures with symmetry, and we can also readily compare and recognize that two objects are precisely the same if one is, for example, mirror reflected, as in the example of a left and right hand in Fig. 5.5. In Chapter 19 I will return to this figure and discuss a fascinating experiment on patients with **phantom limbs** by V. S. Ramachandran [3], showing **plasticity** (the ability to be modified) in the brain with a clinical application. It will be relevant to our studies in Chapter 21.

There are other symmetries and symmetry operations that we recognize besides the spatial ones of rotation and mirror reflection. For example, consider the two sequences in Fig. 5.6. In sequence S_A, event A happens at the (**discrete**) time t_1, B at time t_2 and so on. In sequence S_R, R happens at time t_1 and so on. These are made equal by the symmetry operation T of going back in time or using time reversal (watching a video as it is slowly rewound).

FIGURE 5.4   Figures of snowflakes with lots of symmetries. These possess much beauty. From Weyl (1952).

We immediately recognize that the time sequence S_A is identical with S_R if we reverse its temporal order. I have deliberately used three different intuitive phrases (time reversal, reversal in time, and reverse temporal order) to denote the same precise symmetry operation in math and physics (time reversal T) in order to emphasize the innate nature of this operation in our experience.

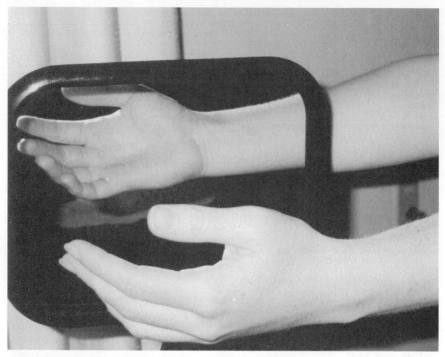

FIGURE 5.5   A left and right hand related by the symmetry operation of mirror reflection. This figure has great relevance in an amazing experiment on patients with phantom limbs by V. S. Ramachandran, which I will relate in Chapters 19 and 21.

We are always looking for symmetry relationships in space and time among patterns. This is not necessarily a conscious process, but one that is built into the structured brain (as I will show in Chapter 8). We naturally look for these

$$S_A: \quad A \rightarrow B \rightarrow G \rightarrow Y \rightarrow E \rightarrow R$$
$$\qquad t_1 \quad t_2 \quad t_3 \quad t_4 \quad t_5 \quad t_6$$

$$S_R: \quad R \rightarrow E \rightarrow Y \rightarrow G \rightarrow B \rightarrow A$$
$$\qquad t_1 \quad t_2 \quad t_3 \quad t_4 \quad t_5 \quad t_6$$

FIGURE 5.6   Two time sequences related by reversal in time. In sequence S_A, event A happens at the (discrete) time t_1, B at time t_2, and so on. In sequence S_R, R happens at time t_1 and so on. S_A and S_R are made equal by the symmetry operation T of going back in time.

FIGURE 5.7   Riders from the famous Etruscan Tomb of the Triclinium at Corneto. In this example
of broken symmetry, we see many small changes when comparing the left and right sides of this
artwork (including the lion, the horse, and the rider). This concept of broken symmetry is important in how the brain functions, as will be shown in Chapter 8. From Weyl (1952).

in nature, in art, in music, in math, in science, and in general when we think,
reason, and create. It is the ability to discern relationships and symmetries
among patterns and transform them in time sequences without the presence of
a physical image that forms the basis of the higher brain functions that we
denote as spatial-temporal reasoning.

> Another important and powerful concept in our model of higher brain function is
> "broken" symmetry, which occurs in nature, in art, and in physics. As noted by the
> renowned physicist Herman Weyl in his delightful book "Symmetry" [3] (outdated
> with respect to his brief remarks on the mirror reflection symmetry in nature):
>
> in contrast to the orient, occidental art, like life itself, is inclined to mitigate, to
> loosen, to modify, even to break strict symmetry. But seldom is asymmetry merely
> the absence of symmetry. Even in asymmetric designs one feels symmetry as the
> norm from which one deviates under the influence of forces of non-formal character.
> I think the riders from the famous Etruscan Tomb of the Triclinium at Corneto [see
> Fig. 5.7] provide a good example.

The concept of **broken symmetry** or almost perfect symmetry is important
in how our brains can recognize related patterns that perhaps are the common
basis for music and spatial-temporal reasoning. I will present this in detail in
Chapter 8.

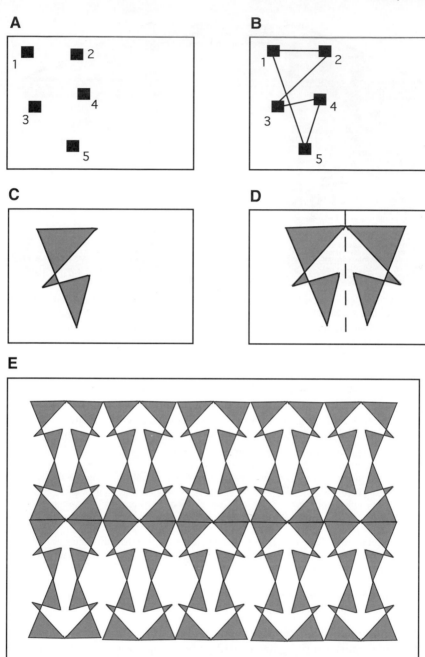

FIGURE 5.8 From random dots we can construct symmetry with beauty. A. Choose several dot positions at random. B. Connect them. C. Fill in. D. Do symmetry and unfolding operations to give E.

Let me conclude this chapter by noting a little discovery on symmetry and "beauty" that Matthew Peterson demonstrated to me (using the Drawing and Symmetry Program in his S.T.A.R. math software): Choose several dot positions at random as in Fig. 5.8A, connect and fill it in as in Figs. 5.8B–C, and then start doing symmetry and unfolding operations to give Fig. 5.8D–E.

I believe that Fig. 5.8 shows how adding symmetry to a random shape adds an attractiveness, and this in turn tells us something about how our brain is always searching for structure and symmetry, here in vision. (I believe this seemingly fuzzy statement can be tested, and will return to discuss how the brain searches for symmetry.) The same must be true in all our senses, in particular in music. Perhaps this is why human music can affect other mammals (see Fig. 4.1 and Chapter 18 for the results from Fran Rauscher's Mozart effect experiment with rats). It is biologically important for the highly auditory sensitive rat to be able to detect patterns in its auditory world.

I disagree with the remarks [4] by the famous neurolinguist Stephen Pinker, and strongly suggest that music is far from being an "accidental" feature in humans. In fact, human music can positively affect and resonate with the Mountcastle columnar design (Fig. 3.1) of the cortex of all mammals, as proven by Rauscher's experiment with rats [5]. *We have much to learn about the evolutionary role of music. The one sure thing is that it is not an accident and is not limited to humans.*

CHAPTER 6

Introduction to the Brain: Basic Brain Features and Brain Imaging

BRIEF GUIDE

I have included a very selected introduction to the brain focused on features that are of specific interest to this book. I apologize to those who find it too brief. The section on brain imaging contains some difficult material and can be skipped. It is included to give you some flavor of the many new and exciting imaging techniques, such as positron emission tomography (PET), functional magnetic resonance imaging (fMRI), and magnetoencephalography (MEG). All of these brain imaging techniques depend on powerful physics developments. As a physicist by training, I had fun *trying* to give you some idea of how these techniques work. The entire chapter can be skimmed (and certainly the brain imaging section) on first reading. Again, note that **bold** words or phrases are defined in the Glossary.

All our thoughts are the result of electrical communication among the tens of billions of neurons in our brains. The human brain, the most complicated machinery in our known universe, is just beginning to be understood. Here we summarize some features that will allow us to develop our model of higher brain function by making big but reasonable leaps from hard-core data. No model of the brain can currently be proven from even a large number of experiments. However, models can be disproven. Thus it is vital that models make predictions that can be tested experimentally. Our trion model has made a number of major predictions, and all tests to date have been supportive. I strongly believe that a model to guide our exploration of how the brain functions is absolutely necessary.

My fundamental guiding concept is that there are common principles that determine higher brain function in mammals and that symmetry plays a major role. Scales in space and time will be crucial, and the appropriate scale we want to look at will depend on the question we ask. For example, if I am trying to read this page and understand what I have written, I must look at it from a distance of about 30 centimeters (about 1 foot). If I look at the words with a microscope, I will see dots of ink; if I look at the page from 300 cm, I will see lines of fuzzy wiggles. I will be addressing the questions of how we think, reason, and create, and what are the appropriate spatial and temporal scales in the brain necessary to understand these questions.

NEURONS AND BRAIN ACTIVITY

Neurons are the basic building blocks of the brain [1]. We will be concentrating on the neocortex or cortex, which in terms of evolution is the newest part of the brain and the part most responsible for higher brain function. There are four main features of a typical neuron as seen in Fig. 6.1: (i) the cell body, (ii) the many branches or dendrites on which most input signals from other neurons arrive, terminating on the (iii) synapses or junctions, and (iv) the one axon that branches to carry the output electrical signal to other neurons.

Here it is useful to introduce the standard scientific notation where the superscript of 10 counts the number of zeroes after the 1; for example, 10^3 is 1000. The cortex contains some 10 billion (10,000,000,000 or 10^{10}) neurons. Each of these neurons has roughly 10,000 synapses receiving information, so there are roughly 10^{14} synapses in the cortex. This is a big number.

Some of the input signals excite a neuron and some inhibit it. If these inputs add up to a value more than the firing threshold of this neuron, it fires and sends an action potential signal out its one output axon. The output axon branches about 10,000 times and sends the information in the form of the action potential to 10,000 synapses on about 1000 other neurons.

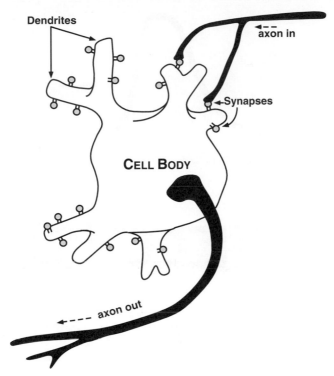

FIGURE 6.1   Main features of the neuron are shown in a highly schematic manner. The neuron is the fundamental cell of the brain. Electrical input signals (action potentials) from other neurons come in from their axons and terminate on the cell body or on the dendrites (branches) at the synapses or junctions (see Figs. 6.2 and 6.3). There are roughly 10,000 synapses on this neuron. Some of the input signals excite this neuron and some inhibit it. If these inputs add up in a time of roughly 0.02 second to a value more than the firing threshold of this neuron, it fires and sends an action potential signal in its one output axon.

The action potential is a simply amazing feat of nature. The output electrical shape, unique to a given neuron, travels *undiminished* down the axon and through its many branchings to the target synapses. The electrical properties of the axon have been compared to that of a copper cable and are considerably worse: the distance an electrical signal will travel before dissipation in the axon is much, much shorter than in the copper cable. Note that the carriers of electrical activity in the copper cable are tiny, fast **electrons**, whereas the carriers in the brain are heavy, slow **ions**. The miracle of propagation of the action potential takes place via the gates in the ion channels (Fig. 6.2) opening and closing in a marvelous manner, first letting sodium ions inside the axon and then potassium ions to reinforce the action potential in its path down the axon.

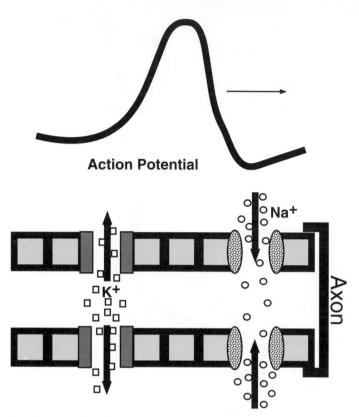

FIGURE 6.2 A simplified explanation of the action potential. (Top) The action potential is a shaped electrical activity that travels undiminished down the output axon. (Bottom) There is a higher concentration of sodium ions (Na+, with "+" meaning positive electrical charge) outside the axon and a higher potassium (K+) concentration inside. The electrical activity at the front of the action potential causes the Na+ ion channel gates in the axon membrane to open (briefly) and let more Na+ ions inside to reinforce the action potential. Some 0.001 second later the K+ ion channel gates open (briefly) to let K+ ions outside and maintain the shape of the action potential. An ion pump maintains the proper ion concentrations inside and outside.

An ion pump brings these ion concentrations back to normal after the action potential has passed by. The mathematics of this "miracle" were developed by A. L. Hodgkin and A. F. Huxley [2] some 60 years ago. Their work was perhaps the most successful interplay of theory and experiment in the history of neuroscience.

When the action potential reaches a synapse, the information is conveyed by **neurochemical** molecules or **neurotransmitters**, which are packaged in synaptic **vesicles** and emptied into an "empty" space that is a fraction of 0.0001 cm

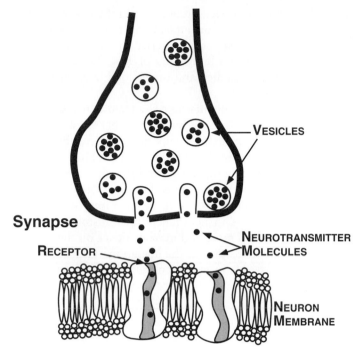

FIGURE 6.3   The synapse or junction between an incoming axon and the target neuron. A release of neurotransmitter occurs when an incoming action potential reaches the synapse. As shown, the neurotransmitter molecules (solid circles) are packaged in vesicles (big circles). There are two sources of fluctuation in the number of molecules of neurotransmitter released: the number of vesicles that are released and the number of molecules of neurotransmitter contained in each vesicle. The released neurotransmitter molecules move across to the membrane of the target neuron and open ion membranes, changing the electrical activity of the target neuron.

across (Fig. 6.3). Upon reaching the target neuron, these neurochemical transmitters alter the electrical state of the target neuron, either exciting it to make it more likely to "fire" and create an action potential, or inhibiting it to make it less likely to fire. The neuron sums its 10,000 inputs, and if it receives enough excitation (above a threshold amount) within 0.01 to 0.02 second, it fires and sends the action potential down its output axon.

There are two main types of neurons in the cortex: the **pyramidal neurons**, which tend to excite other neurons, and neurons that inhibit other neurons. Synapses are either excitatory or inhibitory depending on the type of transmitter released. Even though the action potential arriving at a specific synapse is always the same, the amount of neurochemical transmitter that is released upon arrival of the action potential varies or fluctuates. There is a **probabilistic** distribution of the number of vesicles released, and there is also a probabilistic distribution in the number of neurochemical transmitter molecules in the vesicles. This brings about a corresponding **fluctuation** in the change in electrical activity on the target neuron. Our knowledge of these fluctuations in the transmitter release was brilliantly studied and understood by Bernard Katz and his collaborators [3].

I heard about these synaptic fluctuations in a lecture by J. G. Taylor in 1972 and this aroused my interest. Here was something that I as a theoretical physicist could imagine to be of considerable importance in how the brain works. In the following year, 1973, I received a preprint from Bill Little that proved to be the seminal paper [4] in bringing the powerful techniques from **statistical physics** to brain theory [5]. R. Vasudevan and I [6] were then able to show that the physiological basis for some aspects of the equations in Little's model followed from these fluctuations in neurochemical transmission. Through the years, I have become aware of more and more evidence on the important roles that these synaptic fluctuations play in the operation of the brain. So, you can be sure that I will discuss this in several places in our journey through this book.

CORTEX

Although I focus in this book on the columnar picture of the cortex, it is important to introduce a few more general features. The most obvious feature is the six layers throughout the cortex as shown in Fig. 6.4. The roles of each layer are many and are intertwined vertically, but the general rules are known. For example, neurons in the layers near the upper cortical surface have long-range horizontal connections to other neurons. As envisioned by Mountcastle [7], the entire minicolumn, roughly a cylinder of 0.01 cm through the six layers of cortex, forms an irreducible processing unit. The minicolumns are connected in a horizontal direction to form the column, which is the basic neural network in the brain.

It is certainly worthwhile to show an actual picture of cortical neurons. The beautiful image in Fig. 6.5 is a stained section of cortex from the laboratory of Edward G. Jones. It is also helpful for readers to have an overall picture of the cortex and some of the subcortical systems. A schematic overview of the cortex is shown in Fig. 6.6.

In general, three orthogonal (at 90 degrees to each other) slices of the cortex are made to better view the brain's anatomy and function (Fig. 6.7A). Three subcortical systems of particular relevance are the **amygdala**, the **hippocampus**, and the **thalamus** (Fig. 6.7B). The amygdala [8] plays a crucial role in our emotions and emotional memories. The hippocampus [9] is essential in form-

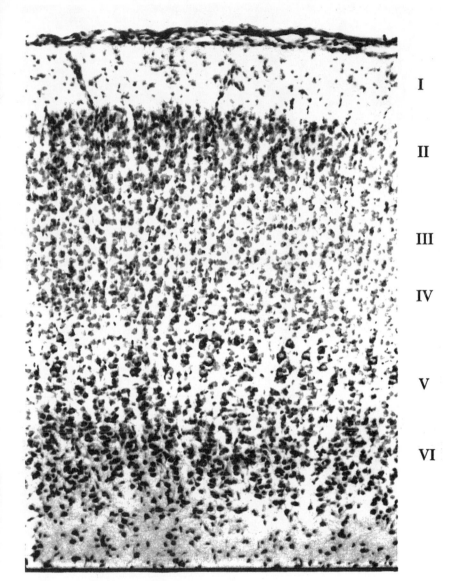

FIGURE 6.4   Layers of the cortex. These six layers are clearly shown in this section of the cortex stained to show the neurons. This photo is from the lab of Richard Robertson.

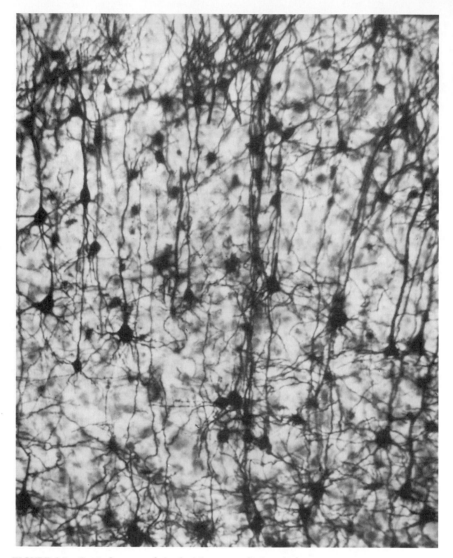

FIGURE 6.5   Cortical neurons from the laboratory of Edward Jones.

ing short-term memories and in their transformation into long-term storage. The thalamus [10] is the main gateway from our sensory inputs to the cortex. The **corpus collosum**, the large bundle of axons linking the left and right hemispheres of the cortex, is also shown in Fig. 6.7B.

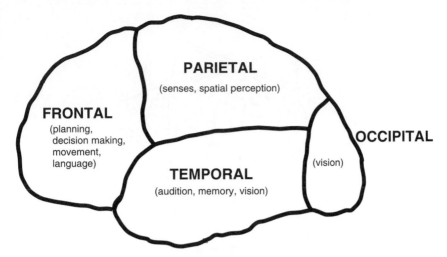

FRONTAL
(planning,
decision making,
movement,
language)

PARIETAL
(senses, spatial perception)

OCCIPITAL
(vision)

TEMPORAL
(audition, memory, vision)

FIGURE 6.6   Schematic figure of the cortex, showing the major divisions and some of their general functions.

Other subcortical systems involve the release of **neuromodulators** [11], which act on cortical neurons in a global manner in space and time, more so than the classic neurotransmitters [12] in the cortex. The large spatial distribution of two neuromodulators is shown in Fig. 6.8. These neuromodulators will be of great importance when we discuss our trion model of higher brain function in Chapters 8–10.

One of the most important and well-studied aspects of the cortex is how it is directly connected in terms of its huge number of neurons (10^{10} in humans) and roughly 10,000 times more synaptic connections. In contrast to the number of connections to the external world, there are many more internal cortical–cortical connections by a large factor. A very important concept is put forward by Braitenberg and Schuz [13] regarding the numerous cortical–cortical connections:

> [B]ut one thing is certain. Any sufficiently large portion of cortex is informed, either through direct fiber connections or indirectly by way of a few synapses, about the activity in the rest of the cortex. If there is no way of isolating pieces of the cortex from each other, the correct description of cortical information handling would seem to be one in terms of global states of the cortex. This . . . is quite irrelevant in present day neurophysiology, since global states cannot be observed with sufficient precision due to the limitation of recording techniques.

Thus it seems that we are faced with a paradox: it is necessary to understand global cortical states, but we cannot examine them with sufficient accuracy. I

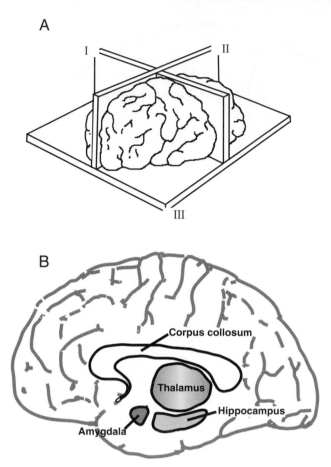

A

I   II

III

B

Corpus collosum

Thalamus

Hippocampus

Amygdala

FIGURE 6.7   (A) The three common orthogonal (at 90 degrees to each other) slices of cortex. (B) Schematic vertical cortex slice and a few of the many subcortical systems of relevance: hippocampus, thalamus, and amygdala. The thalamus is the main gateway from our sensory inputs to the cortex. Its many roles include attention, feedback loops from and to the cortex, and timing features. The amygdala plays a crucial role in our emotions and emotional memories. The hippocampus is essential in forming short-term memories and in their transformation into long-term storage. Also shown is the corpus collosum, the large bundle of axons linking the left and right hemispheres of the cortex.

propose that two developments will allow us to proceed. First, the new (and improved) brain imaging techniques described next do allow for the more accurate observation of larger regions of cortex. Second, the Mountcastle columnar principle of cortical organization (see Chapter 7) and our mathematical realization of it in the trion model (see Chapter 8) allow us to look at larger

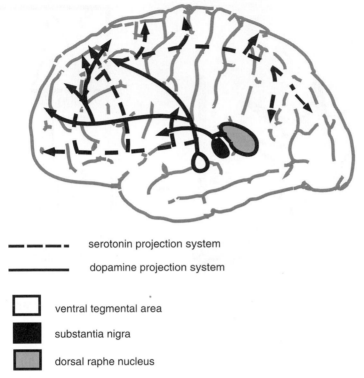

serotonin projection system

dopamine projection system

ventral tegmental area

substantia nigra

dorsal raphe nucleus

FIGURE 6.8   Schematic diagram showing two of the many important neuromodulators, dopamine and serotonin, originating in subcortical systems.

spatial and temporal scales than those for the single neuron. Using these tools, we can begin to seriously consider the global states of the cortex and to experimentally test these considerations to better understand human cognition.

BRAIN IMAGING

Although it is not necessary to understand in detail [14] how brain activity is monitored to follow the arguments in this book, I think some knowledge of the techniques will help you evaluate and put into perspective the large amount of new information that is being discovered. I expect that the biggest advances in science in the next 20 years will be in our understanding of how the brain works. Thus I will survey and compare the methods for monitoring and imaging mammalian brain activity: microelectrodes, EEG, MEG, PET, fMRI, and

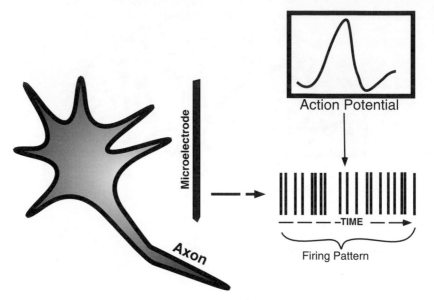

FIGURE 6.9   Schematic diagram showing the firing pattern of a single neuron using a microelectrode to observe the action potentials as a function of time.

optical recording. It is important to understand that many dramatic advances in technology coming from physics and computer science have made these six methods possible or have given new life to older ones (such as microelectrodes and EEG). These methods should be considered to be complementary, for each offers special features and windows into brain function and anatomy. Some experiments combine two of these techniques. I have tried to give you some sense of each technique without overwhelming you with the detailed physics. (One of the courses I most enjoyed teaching—I am now emeritus and no longer teach—was a senior-level undergraduate course in brain imaging for physics majors.)

MICROELECTRODES

The firing activity of single neurons can be monitored in the live behaving mammalian brain using **microelectrodes** (Fig. 6.9). The first use of more than one microelectrode to observe the firing of several neurons in the cortex was done by Marcel Verziano [15] in the late 1950s. Mike told me that when he first reported his new observations of possible circulation of firing activity among neurons at a neuroscience meeting, deriding comments ensued from the audience. This illustrates the difficulty in having new paradigms accepted in science. The use of arrays of microelectrodes is now a standard method of *directly* monitoring the firing behavior of networks of neurons in the cortex. I have had the privilege to collaborate in the analysis of multielectrode cortical data taken in the world-class laboratories of Joaquin Fuster at U.C. Los Angeles and of Jurgen Krueger at the University of Freiberg in Germany.

The microelectrode has been and remains absolutely invaluable in understanding mammalian brain function. However, it has its limitations. It is invasive and is used in the human brain only during operations where it is necessary, for example, to determine boundaries of speech areas of the cortex. It has become clearer to neuroscientists that larger networks of neurons than can be examined through arrays of microelectrodes also need to be studied. Luckily, other methods are now available to supplement and complement the microelectrode studies.

EEG

Surface arrays of electrodes can readily measure electrical activity of the brain in a completely noninvasive manner. **EEG** (or **electroencephalogram**) recordings are able to sample and measure electrical activity about 100 times a second, which is fine for the information we are interested in.

A surface electrode picks up the summed activity of several square centimeters of cortex. Thus EEG measures only concerted activity of large-scale groups of neurons and is therefore well suited to detect global cortical function. A few laboratories, such as that of our collaborator James Swanson at U.C. Irvine, now have the new technology with 128-electrode arrays (Fig. 6.10). This array is put in place and adjusted for recording in just a few minutes. A more common arrangement at present is the 19-electrode array shown schematically in Fig. 6.11.

Data analysis involves reduction into six **frequency bands** and the computation of the average amount of energy in these bands for a given mental task. A more powerful analysis method, called **coherence**, correlates the signals between neighboring electrodes (Fig. 6.11C). EEG coherence allows the experimenter to estimate the degree of coordination or synchrony of firing activity between two brain regions. Think of listening to a symphony orchestra: first listen to the violins, then the cellos, and then how they blend together. You are measuring the synchrony of the stringed instruments.

A breakthrough in our understanding of higher brain function, particularly in processing music, came some 10 years ago from the pioneering work of

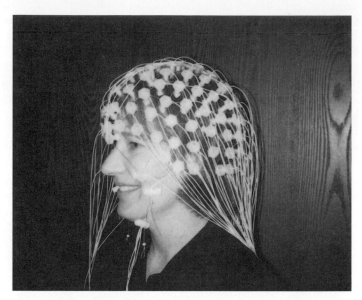

FIGURE 6.10   Array of 128 surface electrodes on my colleague Julene Johnson. The photograph was taken in the laboratory of James Swanson by our collaborator Michael Murias.

Hellmuth Petsche [16] at the University of Vienna. Petsche's lab used coherence analysis to quantify mental processing during music, chess, and other higher cognitive tasks.

The main contributions to the EEG measurements come from the (subthreshold for firing) electrical activity in the large dendritic branches of the cortical neurons rather than from the (above threshold for firing) action potentials communicating between neurons. While this might be considered a drawback in some experiments, it is a positive feature in the exciting collaborative experiments [17] that Fran Rauscher and I recently conducted with the University of Vienna laboratory to begin to examine the neurophysiological basis of the Mozart effect. Here we are concerned with the enhancing effect of listening to the Mozart Sonata (K.448) on subsequent (minutes later) spatial-temporal reasoning performance. Thus the subthreshold electrical activity is definitely of great interest.

MEG

MEG (**magnetoencephalogram**) measures the magnetic activity in the brain. This recent noninvasive technique holds great future promise. There are two

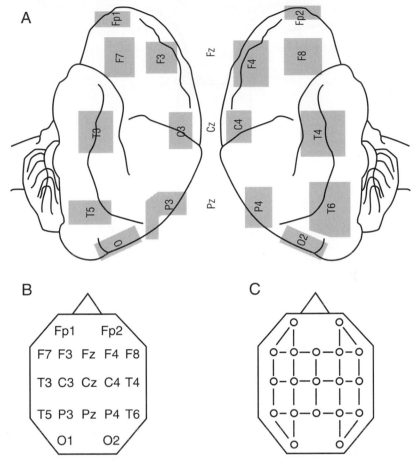

FIGURE 6.11   Nineteen surface electrode positions in the international 10–20 EEG system. (A) Location of the electrodes above the cortex. Fp, prefrontal; F, frontal; T, temporal; C, central; P, parietal; O, occipital cortical regions. (B) Schematic location of these electrodes. (C) The coherence or synchrony of cortical electrical brain wave activity is calculated between pairs of neighboring electrodes. This new coherence EEG technique is quite relevant for the collaborative experiments I will describe in our Mozart effect studies. From Sarnthein *et al.* (1997)

sources of magnetic activity in general: (i) alignment of atoms such as iron with intrinsic little bar magnet properties into arrays where these little magnets line up to give large magnetic fields, and (ii) change in motion of electrically charged atoms or electrons.

The **magnetic fields** in the brain are from the second source. The big problem is these magnetic fields in the brain are *supersmall,* thousands of billions

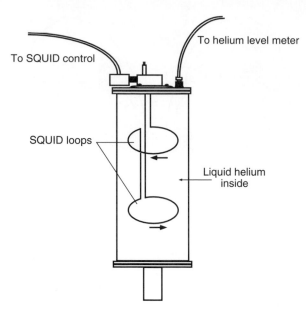

FIGURE 6.12   The SQUID (superconducting quantum interference device) is able to measure discrete and tiny amounts of magnetic fields that pass through it. The two superconducting loops circulate electrical current in opposite directions as shown. (The low temperature of the liquid helium maintains the wires in the superconducting state of no electrical resistance.) This device responds only to spatial differences in the magnetic fields going through the two nearby loops. This helps cut down the enormous background magnetic fields. For example, your heart produces tiny magnetic fields that are still 10,000 times larger than the magnetic fields from your brain activity that are to be measured.

times smaller than the magnetic fields from the earth. (It is known that birds detect the earth's magnetic field by using pieces of magnetic materials in their bodies as an aid in navigation. As you know from looking at a compass, magnetic materials tend to "point" in the direction of the magnetic fields they are in.) At considerable cost, the earth's magnetic field can be shielded out of the room where the MEG device is kept. The measurement of the brain's supertiny magnetic fields is a triumph of modern physics that uses tiny detectors called **SQUIDS,** which are based on some "miraculous" properties of **superconductors** (Fig. 6.12). Superconductors are materials that, when cooled to a low enough temperature, conduct electricity with no resistance. When they are made into a loop as in Fig. 6.12, they permit only certain "quantized" or discrete amounts of magnetic field though this loop, which then yields the measurement of these fields.

Unlike the EEG measurements, the MEG can accurately localize a source of brain activity related to a specific cognitive task. The future of MEG appears to

A   **B**

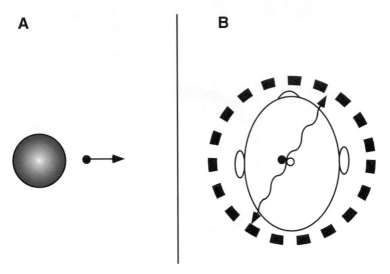

FIGURE 6.13   The PET principle. (A) The decay of radioactive oxygen, ^{15}O (8 protons plus 7 neutrons) gives off a positron (the anti-particle of an electron). (B) The positron stops in about 0.1 cm in the brain, and then annihilates with one of the many electrons there, giving off two photons in opposite directions, which are detected.

be extremely bright. The superconductors used in the present MEG SQUID detectors operate at standard very low temperatures (-260 degrees centigrade— water freezes at 0 degrees centigrade). New "high"-temperature superconductors (-150 degrees centigrade) might make the measurement of the brain's tiny magnetic fields much easier. My colleague Bill Little, who revolutionized brain theory (see Chapter 8), is the physicist whose theories in the 1960s paved the way for the searches and discoveries of the present high-temperature superconductors, which may one day lead to the "holy grail" of room temperature ($+20$ degrees centigrade) superconductors [18].

PET

The very powerful but invasive **positron emission tomography** or **PET** relies on the radioactive decay of certain atoms that give off positrons. A **positron** is the anti-particle of the electron, and when it "closely" encounters an electron, they destroy (or annihilate) each other giving off two high-energy light particles or **photons** (Fig. 6.13). When emitted from the radioactive atom, the positron has an amount of energy that allows it to move roughly 0.1 cm before stopping and annihilating. This limits the accuracy of locating the source of the positron.

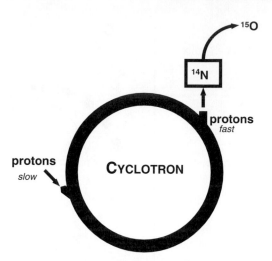

FIGURE 6.14 The cyclotron (a relatively small device, a few feet in diameter, as compared to high-energy accelerators, which are miles in diameter) accelerates protons to fast speeds (but only low energies, according to elementary particle physics). A fast proton hits a nitrogen (^{14}N, 7 protons plus 7 neutrons) to form radioactive oxygen, ^{15}O, which decays with a 2-minute (half) life into a positron (and ^{15}N, 7 protons plus 8 neutrons, which is stable). If we start with 32 ^{15}O atoms, then after 12 minutes there would be (on the average) none left. This gives an idea of how fast the experimenters must work to make the radioactive molecules from the ^{15}O atoms, inject this into the PET scan subject, and perform the measurements shown in Fig. 6.13. It also shows why the radioactivity from the ^{15}O injection is rapidly gone from the subject.

The basic idea of PET is to employ atoms that are normally used by the brain, but to render them radioactive so that they emit positrons. For example, the most common scheme at present is related to blood flow in the brain in response to increased local firing activity induced by some behavioral experiment. Now it is important to use radioactively labeled atoms that decay rapidly so that the subject need not take a high dose. This means that you need to have a **cyclotron** nearby to make the labeled atoms, as shown in Fig. 6.14. Consider the radioactive atom oxygen ^{15}O, where 15 refers to the number of neutrons plus the number of protons in the oxygen central core or nucleus. Oxygen always has 8 protons, thus ^{15}O has 8 protons and 7 neutrons. The radioactive ^{15}O must then be chemically bound into a molecule, for example, an oxygen, water, or carbon dioxide molecule, and quickly used.

We can expect the development of new and better PET scanners that utilize better high-energy photon detectors and further advances in sophisticated data analysis methods. Together, these tools will produce the brain images and extract more quantitative measures of the brain activity related to the relevant higher brain function.

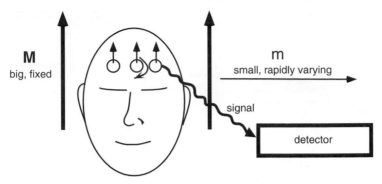

FIGURE 6.15   A simple schematic of MRI and fMRI. A very large magnetic field causes the (angular momenta or spin, denoted by arrows, of the nuclei of) atoms to align themselves in the direction of the magnetic field. A smaller time-varying magnetic field then allows these atoms to (precess like a top and) give off signals that identify them. The directions of the big magnetic fields are changed many times a second to accurately image different "slices" of the brain. The energy associated with the changes in magetic field is given off in sound, which you hear as a loud "ping." (These pings posed a problem for us to solve, as I will discuss.)

fMRI and MRI

Magnetic resonance imaging (**MRI**) and the more recent functional MRI, **fMRI**, are powerful and noninvasive imaging methods that utilize quite sophisticated magnetic field manipulations to determine the location of specific atoms in the brain. MRI yields extremely accurate measures of neuroanatomical features of the brain, and fMRI gives functional images of brain activity related to increased blood flow during a behavioral task. Figure 6.15 gives a simple picture of how these manipulations of the fields give off the detected signal.

MRI brain images give the highest accuracy of brain anatomy that can now be achieved. It is now being used in conjuction with PET, as shown in Fig. 6.16 (see color insert). Mark Bodner and I are now collaborating with Orhan Nalcioglu and Tugan Muftuler at U.C. Irvine in an extremely exciting fMRI study of the Mozart effect [19].

Optical Recording

Optical recording is an extremely promising technique that gives very good accuracy in space and time in monitoring brain activity, primarily in nonhuman mammals. It was developed over many years in many laboratories [20]. I suspect that there will continue to be breakthroughs in this brain imaging

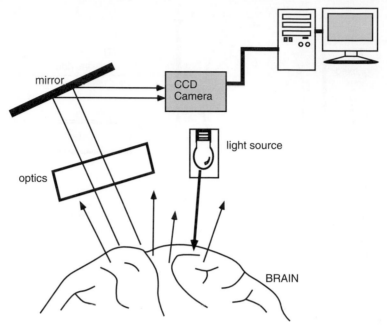

FIGURE 6.17   An optical recording scheme. The amount of reflected light in the cortex that is then detected depends on several (secondary) properties of the brain activity. This is a very powerful technique. Mark Bodner is planning to make and compare optical recordings while primates are listening to the Mozart Sonata (K.448) versus control music.

technique. Figure 6.17 is a schematic diagram of this powerful method. The amount of reflected light depends on several (secondary) properties of the brain activity.

In the next chapter, I present a beautiful picture from the laboratory of Ron Frostig of rat whisker activity, illustrating the functional structured activity that mirrors the dramatic neuroanatomical structure. Ron has pioneered the technique of thinning the skull covering the rat cortex, so that optical imaging can be done through the skull.

I expect that all of these imaging techniques will undergo technical advances in the next 10 years. Many of them are complementary to each other and will be used together more and more [21]. I always tell young college science and engineering students that I believe that brain imaging is a very exciting and growing field to go into for their careers.

Mountcastle Theory of Mammalian Cortex: Internal Neural Language of Higher Brain Function

BRIEF GUIDE

Vernon Mountcastle's organizational principle of mammalian cortex is the key to my entire story. The structured brain of Mountcastle leads to a highly structured spatial-temporal internal neural language for higher brain function. My trion model in Chapter 8 is a mathematical realization of Mountcastle's principle. The trion model is the guide for all our behavioral and neurophysiological experiments concerning music and higher brain functions such as math. This chapter may be skimmed on first reading.

Vernon Mountcastle [1] proposed that the well-established **cortical column** [2] is the basic network in the cortex and is composed of small irreducible processing units called **minicolumns**. A simple pinwheel representation [3] of the minicolumns in the column shown in Fig. 7.1 seems to represent the data [4]. Mountcastle proposed that the column has the capability of being excited into complex spatial-temporal firing patterns. The assumption is that *higher* mammalian brain functions involve the creation and transformation of such complex spatial-temporal firing patterns. (This is in contrast to a cortical language or **code**, which involves sets of neurons firing with high frequency that might be used in emergencies such as when you see a lion running at you.)

Vernon Mountcastle is one of my personal heroes. He is a giant in his fundamental and pioneering experimental discoveries of the columnar nature of specific areas of cortex that preceded the Nobel Prize-winning work of David Hubel and Tortsen Wiesel in the visual cortex. In his seminal columnar organizational principle of mammalian cortex, Vernon put forth, in my opinion, the key idea that will lead to our understanding of higher brain function. My research is based on my mathematical realization of his work.

In his seminal paper of 1978, Mountcastle generalized the existing data and proposed his columnar organizational principle for the functioning of mammalian cortex: The cortex is functionally organized into columns roughly 0.07 cm in diameter (and 0.2 cm deep through the six layers) consisting of 1000 to 10,000 heavily interconnected neurons. The column is defined by its subcortical inputs and its patterns of functional response. For example, all the neurons in a column in the visual cortex respond maximally to stimuli presented in the same part of the visual field. The column is regarded as the fundamental neuronal network in the cortex (Fig. 7.1). Each column is subdivided into processing units called minicolumns, each of which is about 0.01 cm in diameter. The neurons in a given minicolumn in the primary visual cortex will respond maximally to bar stimuli presented at a specific orientation.

Much further research is necessary to establish the Mountcastle principle for all of the mammalian cortex. I assume that the Mountcastle principle is true and ask what are the consequences.

In the Mountcastle model, the columns have the capability of being excited into complex spatial-temporal firing patterns of the minicolumns. The code for higher brain function involves the creation and transformation of such complex patterns among columns over large regions of cortex, as shown in Fig. 7.2. Thus there are two cortical spatial scales beyond the single neuron and smaller than **cortical areas**: the column, with a scale of 0.07 cm, and the minicolumn, with a scale of 0.01 cm.

There is considerable evidence supporting Mountcastle's ideas. I suggest that this evidence will continue to be found at an even more rapid rate. In general, I think this will be due to two factors. First, as the new techniques described in Chapter 6 are further perfected, it will be easier to determine spatial and temporal structure and function in the cortex. Second, as more and more evidence for the Mountcastle model of mammalian cortex accumulates, more neuroscientists will be drawn to these investigations.

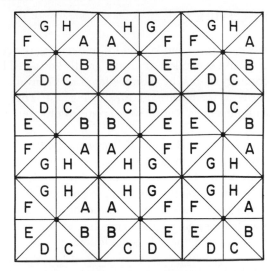

FIGURE 7.1 Highly schematic representation of the Mountcastle columnar principle of the cortex, which is the basis of our mathematical model of higher brain function. Each square represents a column of neurons, roughly 0.07 cm in dimension, which is assumed to be the fundamental network in mammalian cortex. Consider these columns to comprise all six layers of the cortex as shown in Fig. 6.4. The triangles represent the minicolumns, which are Mountcastle's irreducible processing units, roughly 0.01 cm in diameter. The neurons in a given minicolumn in the (primary) visual cortex will respond maximally to bar stimuli presented at a specific orientation. I represent the general minicolumn labels by these capital letters. Much further research is necessary to establish the Mountcastle principle for all of the mammalian cortex.

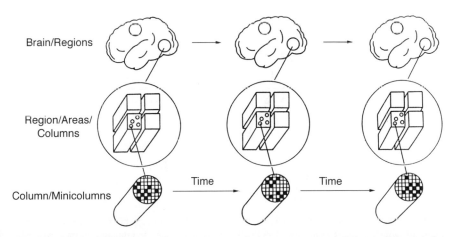

FIGURE 7.2 Highly schematic firing patterns in the cortex over space and time following the Mountcastle spatial-temporal code. Many regions of the cortex are involved in any higher brain function.

SPATIAL STRUCTURE

The pioneering work of Hubel and Wiesel [5] in detailing the columnar structure of visual cortex has been followed up and greatly advanced by many workers. Optical recording results by Bonhoeffer and Grinvald show a truly remarkable similarity to the idealized cortex in Fig. 7.1. They found that the orientation minicolumns in cat cortex were arranged precisely in pinwheellike structures [6].

Erich Harth, Arnold Scheibel, and I [7] presented a number of additional anatomical, physiological, and theoretical arguments for the minicolumn being composed of roughly 30 to 100 neurons (which corresponds to the Mountcastle spatial scale of 0.01 cm). I present one of these anatomical examples in Figs. 7.3 and 7.4. Although we knew that none of the arguments by itself was convincing, together we felt they gave a good guideline to our basic scale for higher brain function in the cortex. Other examples follow.

Excellent candidates for the anatomical basis of the Mountcastle minicolumns are the **dendritic bundles** (Fig. 7.3), which have been well established by

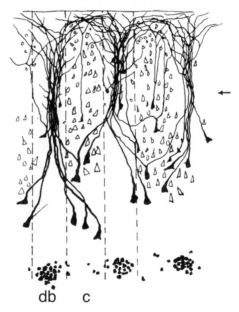

FIGURE 7.3   Somewhat schematized drawing of cat cortex, showing the organization of vertical dendritic bundles. The major vertical (apical) dendrites of many pyramidal neurons, especially from deep in layer 5, ascend in closely organized groups. Apical dendrites from the higher layers may join in the bundles. This drawing is from the laboratory of Arnold Scheibel.

many investigators. Kathleen Roney, Arne Scheibel, and I [8] wrote a review article in 1979 on dendritic bundles, since they have been found throughout the mammalian brain and are unquestionably fundamental units in the brain's functioning. However, no physiological experiments to determine their role have been performed. As shown in Fig. 7.3, the major vertical or apical dendrites of many pyramidal neurons ascend from the lower layers of the cortex to the upper layers in these closely organized bundles.

Two amazing and detailed closeup views of these dendritic bundles as observed in **scanning electron microphotographs** from Scheibel's lab are shown in Fig. 7.4. These dendritic bundles are clearly of the appropriate size and spacing to be the anatomical basis of the minicolumns. Furthermore, it seems very likely that because of the direct contact between neighboring dendrites over considerable distances, they can carry out the direct electrical averaging needed for the cooperative effect (see the following discussion), which must be met if they are the irreducible processing units envisioned by Mountcastle. Thus far, no one has conducted the extremely difficult experiments to test these ideas.

Another elegant anatomical demonstration was found by Herbert Killackey in rat **somatosensory** cortex of a spatial structure of roughly 0.01 cm. Figure 7.5 shows the segmented sensory representation or cortical map of an entire rat body. When someone touches your nose, a part of your somatosensory cortex corresponding to your nose responds to the touch. (Note that Herb is well known for his study of the neuroanatomy of rat whiskers, shown in more detail in Fig. 7.6. Just like a cat, rats have whiskers that they use to tell them of the world around them when it is dark.)

One of the ways to investigate the spatial-temporal aspects is through optical recording experiments (see Fig. 6.17). These optical methods can be combined with neuroanatomical methods to show both function and structure in a dramatically convincing way, as shown in Fig. 7.6 (see color insert) from Ron Frostig's laboratory. This depicts the rat (somatosensory) cortex, showing the structure and function corresponding to the 3 × 3 array of whiskers (which are part of Fig. 7.5) [9]. Only the peak activity regions are shown in Fig. 7.6. Other results by Ron show the widespread optical activity in a striking time-dependent manner.

Related to these spatial scales is the structured connectivity between neurons and groups of neurons [10]. Gilbert [11] has shown a clustering of synapses from an axon at spacings of about 0.01 cm. So, here again, we see the spatial scale of the minicolumn. Gilbert [12] has also shown long-range lateral axons connecting different columns in primary visual cortex via neurons in minicolumns having the same orientation "specificity." Rockland [13] has found very structured connectivity projecting from one cortical area back to the primary visual cortex. Other results show that connectivity from one cortical area to

FIGURE 7.4   Scanning electron microphotographs of dendritic bundles in the spinal cord of the rat. Dendrite surfaces are in close contact. Original magnification: (A) 1900×, scale bar = 0.001 cm; (B) 4000×, scale bar = 0.0005 cm. From the lab of Arnold Scheibel.

another over large distances is via specific (columnar) patches. I will discuss some generalization of these data in our trion model of higher brain function in Chapters 8–10.

This leads me to further discussion of the concept of a functional unit, along with the ideas of **cooperativity** and structured connectivity. As proposed by

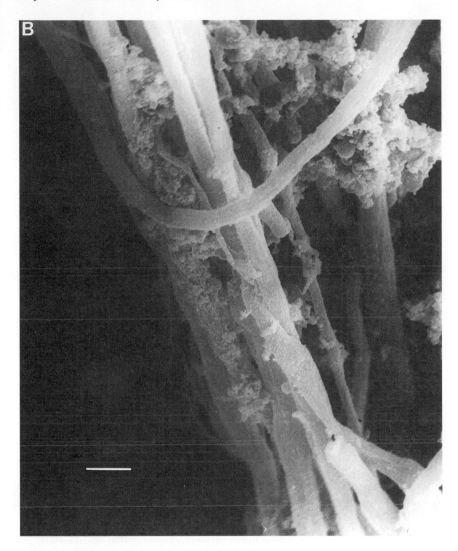

Mountcastle, the minicolumn is an irreducible functional processing unit, not simply a group of neurons with very similar response properties. The powerful ideas of cooperativity borrowed from physical spin systems by Little in his seminal model of neural networks dynamics help us understand the idea of a functional unit. The **nonlinear** features play a crucial role, so that the response of a functional unit is *not* simply the linear sum of the individual neuronal responses.

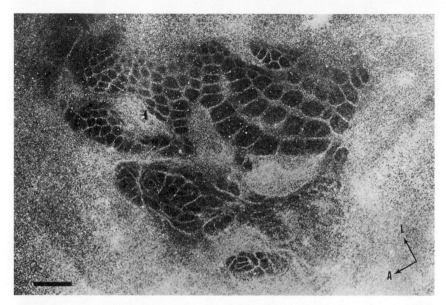

FIGURE 7.5   Microphotograph of a flattened section of layer 6 of rat (somatosensory) cortex shown by staining. This is an entire body representation, in which the lower three segments reading from left to right are the cortical representations of the rat lower lip, forepaw, and hindpaw, respectively. The scale bar is 0.05 cm, so the dark patches have a spatial scale of roughly 0.01 cm. These structures are highly reproducible from one rat preparation to another. From the laboratory of Herbert Killackey.

As noted earlier, we showed that a minimum of roughly 50 neurons is necessary for this cooperativity. It is certainly not necessary or expected that each minicolumn have the same number of neurons for the minicolumn to be a "useful" concept. Further, we note the structured connectivity that permits the notion of these "units"—minicolumn, column, and cortical area—to be called functional cooperative units in a dynamical processing sense: (i) the heavy interconnections vertically (excitatory and inhibitory) among the neurons through the cortical layers form the basis for the minicolumn; (ii) the (neurons in the) minicolumns are connected to neighboring minicolumns in the same column through horizontal connections in a weaker manner; and (iii) the long-range connections between distant columns as seen above are still highly specific and yet still weaker in strength. *Thus it seems quite reasonable to think of (at least) three spatial scales of cooperativity defining the functional units of minicolumn, column, and cortical area.*

In addition to these scales, there are of course smaller ones associated with the neuron, synapse, and receptor, and larger ones for cortical systems (such as the visual, auditory, and motor systems, each consisting of several cortical areas) and the entire cortex. These spatial scales are discussed by Churchland and Sejnowski [14]. Next I will discuss various temporal scales and their possible relationships to the spatial scales.

TEMPORAL SCALES RELATED TO
SPATIAL SCALES

There are many temporal scales in the brain, just as there are many spatial scales. These temporal scales range from those associated with a receptor configurational change of some 0.0001 sec to the **circadian rhythm** of roughly 24 hours or 100,000 seconds (sec). As shown in Fig. 7.7, we can make some *rough* correspondence between temporal scales and spatial ones. However, this becomes *very approximate* as we consider timescales longer than a few 0.001 sec. There are the various frequencies in the 40 to 3 cycles/sec (or hertz, Hz) range (or time scales—1/frequency—of 0.025 to 0.3 sec) found in EEG recordings. As recently shown, neuronal spike correlations in cortex extending up to several centimeters show firing in synchrony at 40 Hz to 10 Hz, or at temporal scales of 0.025 to 0.1 sec. *It is this region of temporal scales of 0.025 sec and greater that I associate with spatial scales of the minicolumn and larger.*

Thus for our discussion of higher brain function, the temporal scale of 0.025 sec is the minimum that we will deal with directly. Now, Xiao Leng and I [15] considered higher brain function as involving timescales lasting some tens of seconds up to some minutes. Thus, if we take 0.025 sec to be our basic time step τ, then 4 minutes of music mental rehearsal would be the huge number 10,000 τ. We will see in Chapter 11 that mental rehearsals of music of duration roughly 10,000 τ and involving much of the cortex can be done with the remarkable accuracy of about 1%. We suggested that perhaps there exist a number of timescales between 1 sec and 1 day that are associated with higher brain function and that form the physiological basis of such temporal accuracy.

As shown in Fig. 7.7, there are a number of scales between the ones for the minicolumn (about 100 neurons) and the column (about 10,000 neurons) and the entire cortex (about 10 billion neurons) that are involved in higher brain function. Similarly, we suggest in Fig. 7.7, that there are a number of temporal scales between those of 0.025 to 0.250 sec or 1 to 10 τ that are familiar and the 10,000 τ that is necessary for higher brain function. One role of these intermediate timescales might be to reset and coordinate the sophisticated spatial-temporal firing patterns over large areas or over the entire cortex.

The origins of such **ultradian** (less than a day) **rhythms**, as well as their full consequences, are not understood. One way to account for the maintenance of

Unit	Number	Spatial scale (cm)	Temporal scale (sec)
synapse	10^{14}	0.0001	0.001
neuron	10^{10}	0.0002	0.001
minicolumn	10^8	0.01	0.02
column	10^6	0.07	0.25
			**2
area	10^2	3	**20
			**200
system	10	10	**2,000
			**20,000
cortex	1	30	**100,000 (1 day)

Left-margin connectors between structures (number of the above structure that occur in the one below):

- synapse → neuron: 10^4 (=10,000)
- neuron → minicolumn: 10^2
- minicolumn → column: 10^2
- column → area: 10^3
- area → system: 10
- system → cortex: 10

FIGURE 7.7 Very rough spatial and temporal scales for various structures in the cortex. The number on the left between structures represents the number of the above structure that occur in the one below. For example, there are 10^2 (or 100) neurons in a minicolumn. The spatial scales for the minicolumn and larger should be considered along the cortical surface after it is unfolded and flattened out. We consider the spatial and temporal scales of 0.01 cm and 0.025 sec and larger, respectively, to be those we explicitly include in our model of higher brain function. The temporal scales marked with asterisks are new proposed scales associated with higher brain function and may be associated with spatial scales of the column and larger.

extremely specific spatial-temporal patterns (see Chapter 11 for the remarkably accurate mental rehearsals of music) is to invoke "orchestration" by a central clock or pacemaker. The existence of intrinsic pacemakers in brains has been known for some time, and the best studied are the circadian (roughly 24-hour) pacemakers localized in a variety of animals in a particular brain region [16].

To concretely examine the potential consequences of these ultradian rhythms in higher brain function, we will introduce the concept of such temporal periodicity in various neuromodulators along with various spatial scales.

Specific spatial and temporal scales that we hypothesize and attribute to neuromodulators might come about through the interactions of several actual neuromodulators. Further, it is very likely that other controlling factors contribute to these multiple temporal scales.

EVIDENCE FOR TEMPORAL SCALES BETWEEN 1 SECOND AND 1 DAY

Here I present a few varied arguments supporting the idea of timescales in the brain, and their function longer than 1 sec and less than 1 day. I believe that unless their presence and significance are taken seriously, they will not be well studied.

The idea of a series of timescales was first expressed clearly to me by Elliot Montroll. Elliot, a renowned physicist who had made outstanding contributions to a number of fields, including biology, had recently accepted a Distinguished Professorship in Physical Sciences (for one quarter each year) at U.C. Irvine. Elliot, Herb Killackey, Norman Weinberger, and I formed a research unit in 1981 on "Cooperativity in Brain Function." Herb, a neuroanatomist, Norm, a neurophysiologist, and Elliot and I, both theorists, were interested in higher brain function in mammalian cortex. One day I was discussing looking for a specific temporal scale associated with higher brain function. Elliot, using his incredible insight and research experience in physical and biological systems, said that if there was one such scale, he fully expected (from his experience with nonlinear systems) that there should be a simple *series* of such scales. (I think that our research unit would have expanded and become permanent were it not for the untimely death of Elliot in 1983.)

Some 6 years later, Leslie Brothers and I [17] (as described in Chapter 11) found some remarkable results in the reproducibility of the temporal duration of the mental rehearsals of pieces of music by professional musicians. For pieces of several minutes' duration, the variation in temporal duration was on the order of a percent. Thus when Xiao and I were developing our trion model of higher brain function, these mental rehearsal results, along with the earlier remarks of Elliot, led us to introduce three new timescales of roughly 2, 20, and 200 sec by simply extrapolating smaller cortical timescales of 0.025 and 0.250 sec. Adding the additional scales of 2000 and 20,000 sec, this gives us the temporal scales in the brain less than the diurnal 24 hours or 100,000 seconds proposed in Fig. 7.7. These temporal scales are simply guidelines (to within factors of 2) to be used in organizing experimental searches and theoretical investigations. I believe, following Elliot's prescient suggestion, that it is important to look for the possibility of such a temporal series. The clinical consequences might be enormous if they exist (see Chapter 21). I will now present some reports that are supportive of these speculative ideas.

Ernst Poppel [18], in an article entitled "The Measurement of Music and the Cerebral Clock: A New Theory," introduced how important tempo is to music by quoting the famous conductor Bruno Walter:

> "If I was not sure of the correct tempo of a musical phrase or episode for a long period of time, suddenly, as from the depths of my inner being, a decision occurred to me. Like in a moment of enlightenment, the right tempo appeared, and I had a feeling of security that freed me of doubt, and in most cases, this remained forever."

Poppel then asks that if tempo is so fundamental, how is it one can find the right tempo and maintain it once found? He then presents a model of a "brain-clock." A series of relevant behavioral experiments that he performed on spoken language gave some evidence for a 3-sec timescale for processing in the brain. Poppel reported this 3-sec period to be stable across cultures, languages, and centuries. An example he gives is for the reader to recite Sonnet 18 by William Shakespeare and have the reading timed:

> Shall I compare thee to a summer's day?
> Thou art more lovely and more temperate.
> Rough winds do shake the darling buds of May.
> And summer's lease hath all too short a date:
>
> Sometime too hot the eve of heaven shines.
> And often is his gold complexion dimm'd.
> And everyfair from fair some time declines.
> By chance, or nature's changing course, untrimm'd:
>
> But the eternal summer shall not fade
> Nor lose possession of that fair thou ow'st.
> Nor shall Death brag thou wand'rest in his shade.
> When in eternal lines to time thou grow'st.
>
> So long as men can breathe or eyes can see,
> So long lives this, and this gives life to thee.

As noted by Poppel, during recitation, each spoken line in this Shakespeare sonnet lasts about 3 sec.

Mark Bodner [19] in his analysis of primate cortical data taken during short-term memory tasks, found striking results in which families of symmetric temporal firing patterns of single neurons were identified. This will be presented in detail in Chapter 16. The relevant feature for my discussion now is that the dominant temporal family of symmetric patterns was 1.8 sec in length. Well within a factor of 2, this timescale is compatible with the 3-sec behavioral timescale found by Poppel.

A much longer behavioral timescale of multiples of 45 minutes in primate behavior has been reported by Bowden and collaborators [20]. Day-long observations of solitary and social behavior of pairs of (adult male) rhesus monkeys were made and analyzed for temporal structure. While the researchers found no sharp peaks, cyclic behavior was found.

A study in the lab of J. Justice [21] examined the concentration of the neuromodulator dopamine in the rat brain (using **microdialysis** techniques). They found a very large and significant day–night circadian variation. I suggest that similar studies be dedicated to looking for a neurophysiological basis of the 45-minute behavioral timescale by searching for variations in neuromodulators. The neuromodulator levels must be monitored about every 15 minutes.

The finding that some neuromodulators (such as dopamine or serotonin) have temporal variations between 30 minutes and several hours might lead to major scientific and clinical breakthroughs. I will return to this in Chapter 21.

CHAPTER 8

Trion Model and Symmetries

BRIEF GUIDE

This is the most abstract material in the book. It traces my 25 years of scientific investigation into brain theory. The resultant trion model can only be a guide into the complexities of the cortex. However, it has led to new concepts and insights into how we think, reason, and create, which have led to behavioral and neurophysiological experiments testing the predictions from the model. Thus far all the results from these experiments have been supportive of the model. You may skip this chapter, but it would be better if you skimmed it (once and perhaps a second time later). The material is not simple, but I present it in a readable manner (no equations) and still maintain all the important features. I do not recommend that this chapter be studied in detail before you finish the book.

HISTORY

Understanding how the human brain works poses some of the most interesting and fundamental challenges in science, both experimentally and theoretically. In the early days of brain theory, there were at any time a relatively small number of individuals working in semi-isolation; their work was scattered over a relatively large number of journals. Not only was there insufficient cross-referencing by these workers, but many were forced to "bootleg" their research in brain theory, devoting most of their time to work in their original fields (ranging across mathematics, physics, biology, engineering, computer science, and psychology). Starting around 1983, there has been enormous growth in brain theory and its subsequent complete integration into the world-class neuroscience laboratories. One evening in the summer of 1987, my friend and brain theory colleague Guenther Palm and I were discussing this history over a couple of beers in my house in Laguna Beach overlooking the Pacific Ocean. It occurred to us that it was important to document brain theory and make the classic scattered articles available by collecting them in a reprint volume. The resultant 1988 volume [1] of 44 reprinted articles starts with the famous math foundation articles of Alan Turing in 1937 and of Warren McCulloch and Walter Pitts in 1943 and ends in 1982. Certainly one of the most insightful ideas of this period was the simple, ingenious, and now famous mechanism of learning and memory through synaptic (see Fig. 6.3) modification that was put forward by Donald Hebb in 1949 [2] :

A NEUROPHYSIOLOGICAL POSTULATE
Let us assume that the persistence or repetition of a reverberatory activity (or "trace") tends to induce lasting cellular changes that add to its stability. The assumption can be perhaps stated as follows: When an axon of cell A is near enough to excite a cell B and repeatedly or persistently takes part in firing it, some growth process or metabolic chance takes place in one or both of the cells such that A's efficiency, as one of the cells firing B, is increased.

This is the basis for what is commonly called the **Hebb synapse** or the **Hebb learning rule.** (Note that it is common in the study of the brain to refer to a neuron as a cell.) The crucial feature is the time correlation of input to the neuron and firing of the neuron. I will call any generalization of this a Hebb learning rule, even when groups of neurons are involved, as for our trion model.

An illustrative schematic understanding (which I heard posed by Guenther Stent some 20 years ago) of this Hebb learning rule is shown in Fig. 8.1. I want to stress how far ahead of his time Hebb was. He used his synaptic learning rule to predict the growth of assemblies of neurons, and to explain and explore the formation of concepts related to higher brain function. Although brain theorists immediately began to use some form of the Hebb learning rule in their models, it was only some 10 years ago that the first experimental evidence for the Hebb

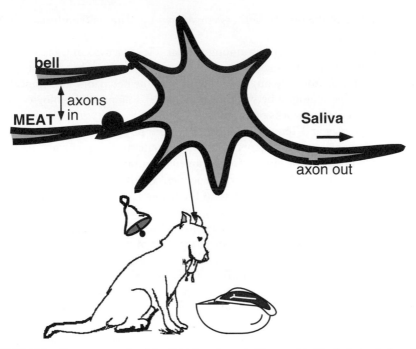

FIGURE 8.1   Cartoon example of the Hebb learning rule illustrated in "Pavlov's dog," who sali-
vates at the sight of meat. Pavlov rang a bell while the dog was salivating at the sight of the meat.
After several such pairings of stimuli, the dog would salivate when it heard the bell in the absence
of the meat. This figure represents the neurophysiological basis of this behavioral experiment
within the neuron shown. As the meat causes the neuron to fire (and the dog to salivate), the bell
input reaches the neuron in the appropriate time window to cause its synapse to be strengthened
by the Hebb learning rule. As a result, the input from the bell strengthens enough to be able to fire
the neuron in the absence of the meat input.

synapse was found. The precise rules and mechanisms of synaptic change or
plasticity are still being determined.

Starting in the 1950s there was great progress in physics in understanding
cooperative phenomena involving systems of strongly interacting particles.
*This idea of cooperativity in a system is that new behavior is observed that was not
seen in the parts or is simply inferred from the sum of the parts of the system.* For
example, there was the highly successful theory of superconductivity (see text
associated with Fig. 6.12) by John Bardeen, Leon Cooper, and John Schrieffer.
These three received the Noble Prize in Physics in 1972. Cooper made the
switch to neurobiology and is now a world renowned brain theorist. Two other
Nobel Laureates who made highly successful moves to brain theory from physiology are Francis Crick and Gerald Edelman. It is not surprising that the

understanding of the human brain is considered by many as the ultimate challenge in science.

The effect of the interactions among the particles in a system was to allow a **cooperative state** (such as superconductivity) with a relatively ordered structure and behavior from the huge number of possible behaviors. It is appealing then to consider analogies between these physical systems and biological systems, in particular networks of neurons.

In 1954, Cragg and Temperly [3] brought from physics the ideas of cooperative phenomena among systems of atoms to generate magnetism. The concepts of a temperature or fluctuation parameter T, an interaction between pairs of atoms, and a probability function (dependent on the ratio of the interaction divided by T in determining the state of the material) were all introduced into brain theory. They suggested the neuronal analogy of cooperativity in determining the dynamics of a network of neurons. Although they had no biological analogies for the interaction and T, and they did not develop their ideas mathematically, their work presented many important ideas.

Some 20 years later, William Little (the "father" of high-temperature superconductivity), unaware of Cragg and Temperly's work, developed his seminal mathematical model [4] based on the spin system model used in understanding magnetism. The firing or not firing of a neuron (see the action potential firing of a neuron in Fig. 6.2) was analogous to the up and down states of the atom (Fig. 8.2).

Thus here was an exciting full mathematical model that opened new vistas in studying brain behavior in *quantitative* detail. After Bill sent me a copy of his paper, I immediately saw the potential for showing the physiological basis for the "temperature" T and the probability function in the model. As noted in the Prologue, I had recently heard a lecture about the fluctuations in the release of the neurochemicals at the synapse between the input axon and the target neuron as demonstrated by Bernard Katz (see Fig. 6.3). Fortunately, my friend and colleague R. Vasudevan was visiting the University of Southern California when I got Bill's paper. Using my intuition and Vasu's impressive skills in mathematics, we were able to derive [5] the temperature T and the probability function for neuronal firing in Little's model from the observed fluctuations in synaptic transmission.

Then followed the most inspiring and influential time in my 25-year career in brain theory, working directly with Bill on the learning and memory properties of his model of networks of neurons. Bill and I [6] made a mathematical version of the Hebb learning rule (shown in Fig. 8.1) that was tailored to Bill's model (see Fig. 8.2). This allowed us [7] to make considerable progress and show that the memory storage capacity of the network was related to the number of synapses rather than the smaller number of neurons (each neuron has many synapses). Recall that there are 10^{14} synapses in the cortex versus 10^{10}

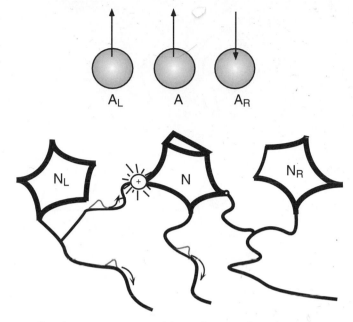

FIGURE 8.2   Bill Little's neuron system model in analogy to a physical spin system. At the top we see three atoms, each having its spin or rotation (**angular momentum**) shown by the arrow. The up arrow represents a clockwise rotation and the down arrow represents counterclockwise rotation. There is an attractive interaction between atoms A and A_L due to their spins being in the same direction, and likewise a repulsive interaction between atoms A and A_R due to their spins being in the opposite direction. Bill introduced the neural analogy in which spin up corresponds to the neuron firing (in a specific time window) and spin down corresponds to the neuron not firing. This is represented in the bottom part of the figure by having neurons N and N_L firing (see the action potentials traveling down their axons), and N_R not firing (no action potential).

neurons. Although 10^{10} sounds like an enormous number, I just read that you can buy a memory (hard drive) disk for your home computer with a memory capacity of 10^{10} (bytes).

Although this important memory storage result was established in principle, it seemed to me [8] that a physiological realization required that groups or assemblies of neurons, rather than individual neurons, be the appropriate units conveying the processing of information in the cortex. As shown in Fig. 8.3, this was to take place via time sequences of firings of these assemblies.

In the same year that my paper on these time sequences in Fig. 8.3 appeared [9], Mountcastle's columnar organization principle for cortex was published [10] (I had known of Mountcastle's paper). Mountcastle's paper convinced me that I was on the right track and that the assemblies in my Fig. 8.3 were his

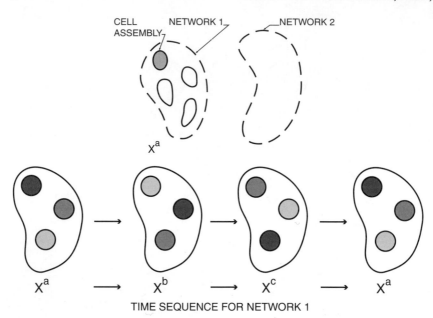

TIME SEQUENCE FOR NETWORK 1

FIGURE 8.3   Time sequences of firings of neuron assemblies in networks in the cortex, as envisioned by me in 1978 to give maximum memory storage capacity. The number of dots in one of the circles represents the level of neurons firing. My idea was that it was not the firing of individual neurons that represented the code or language of the cortex but rather the firing levels of these groups (or Mountcastle minicolumns). From Shaw (1978).

minicolumns and the networks were his columns. My graduate student Kathleen Roney and I then worked hard on developing the mathematical consequences of this concept. We developed the concept of a **statistical factor g** that would take into account the internal features of an idealized minicolumn and allow us to consider it as a single entity having three firing states [11]. This g would be an extremely important ingredient of the trion model, which made the system stable. Later in this chapter we will see a calculation that is relevant to the neuropathology of Alzheimer disease in which g plays the important role in calculating what happens to short-term memory as neurons die in this horrible mental disorder.

Together with noted neuroanatomist Arne Scheibel, Kathleen and I wrote a comprehensive review paper on dendritic bundles [12] (see Figs. 7.3 and 7.4). (As is not uncommon, the graduate student, Kathleen, did most of the work.) We presented these dendritic bundles as the potential anatomical bases of the physiological minicolumns. Yet the physiological function of these intriguing bundles remains a mystery. This paper convinced me that I was moving into the right field: we had over fifteen hundred requests for reprints.

There were still many possible ways to move toward a mathematical realization of Mountcastle's columnar organizational principle of cortex with the minicolumn as the irreducible processing unit and the cortical column as the fundamental neural network. The crucial step for me occurred in June, 1980, when I was browsing through the recent weekly *Physical Review Letters* (containing the latest and hottest results in physics) and saw the remarkable paper by Michael Fisher and Walter Selke [13]. They solved a seemingly simple variation of the physical spin model of Fig. 8.2 and found an amazingly huge, sophisticated, and structured number of possible stable configurations of spins. This is illustrated in Fig. 8.4.

The number of stable configurations in these physical models is related to the memory capacity of our neural model. There were three essential features of the Fisher and Selke results as I later saw it: (i) The fundamental unit in Fig. 8.4 was a layer of spins rather than the individual spins. (This would be analogous to the Mountcastle minicolumns.) (ii) There were two fundamental interactions (in one spatial direction), a short-range attractive interaction V between neighboring spins and a slightly longer range repulsive interaction W with a *very specific ratio of the strength of V to that of W. The presence of symmetry was dominant.* (By analogy, I took the interactions between minicolumns as having first an attractive interaction followed in time by a quite specific repulsive one.) (iii) The fluctuations were essential in producing the large number of stable configurations. (The presence of fluctuations was already built into Bill Little's model.)

It took me over three years to put together all the pieces of the puzzle to come up with the successful trion model. The final ideas fit together when I was visiting my good friend and colleague George Patera at the University of Montreal. Numerous discussions with George, one of the world's leading experts on symmetries in physical systems, provided the missing links.

Thus I wrote down the trion model as a structured mathematical realization of Mountcastle's organizational principle. It was developed starting from Little's neural network analogy to the physical spin system, and was modified in a direction inspired by the structured spin system model results of Fisher and Selke. As promised, this book will not include the equations, but I will present a pictorial description of the model and the results of 14 years of analyzing it.

TRION MODEL

I assumed that each minicolumn had three possible firing states [14]. This was the next level of sophistication from a single neuron that could fire or not fire.

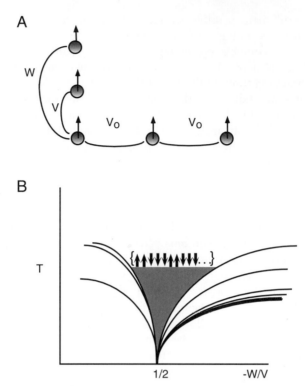

FIGURE 8.4   Fisher and Selke's structured spin model. (A) In addition to the spin interactions V_o between neighboring atoms (as in Fig. 8.2) in the horizontal direction, they introduced additional spin interactions V and W in the vertical direction, where W was repulsive if the spins were in the same direction. (B) The V_o interaction aligned atoms in horizontal layers (thick arrows) below and the competing attractive and repulsive V and W allowed for an amazing richness in possible states of this physical spin system shown. The brackets show one such state in terms of the spins of alternating layers of atoms. This richness occurred only near the ratio of W/V equal to 0.5. Further, the stability of these states as seen by the size increases as the temperature or fluctuation parameter T increases. When I saw this amazing result, I knew how I should start to construct my trion model.

The trion in Fig. 8.5 represents an idealized *distinguishable* minicolumn or roughly 100 neurons. (By distinguishable, I mean that each minicolumn in the cortex can, *in principle*, be effectively labeled through its response.) The trion has *three* levels of firing activity S for the entire minicolumn (hence I came up with the name trion).

In our cortical column of interconnected trions, *each trion* can have one of three possible firing states, S, with respect to the average. We also use a gray scale (Fig. 8.5) or a color scale for S (as in Fig. 9.14):

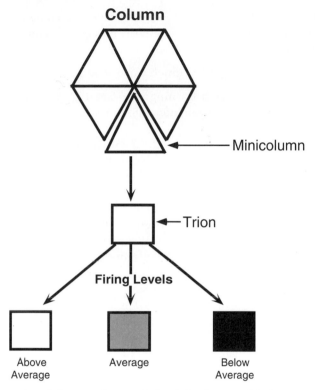

FIGURE 8.5   I identified a minicolumn with the idealized trion and the basic network column as in the Mountcastle organizational principle of the mammalian cortex. As shown, the trion has three levels of firing S: above average (white), S equal to 1 (or +); average (gray), S equal to 0; and below average (black), S equal to −1 (or −).

Above average:	S equals + or 1	gray scale = white, color = red
Average:	S equals 0	gray scale = gray, color = yellow
Below average:	S equals − or −1	gray scale − black, color = blue

The trion states are updated in discrete time steps τ. I have given arguments for the reality of a discrete time step τ for firing and that τ should be roughly 0.05 sec (to within a factor of 2). The firing state of the column of trions at a time n times τ or $n\tau$ depends on the two [15] previous time steps $(n − 1)\tau$ and $(n − 2)\tau$. The interactions V at $(n − 1)\tau$ are attractive and those W at $(n − 2)\tau$ are repulsive and specifically related to each other.

The trion column equations P(S) for the firing S are probabilistic as in Little's model, with the temperature factor T being dependent on the random nature of the synaptic transmission (see Chapter 6). The model determines only the chance of an evident happening. For example, when you flip a coin, there is a probability P of 0.5 for heads and a P of 0.5 for tails happening on any flip. A factor g(S), noted earlier, took into account the number of neurons internal to the idealized minicolumn by having

$$g(0)/g(+/-) \text{ much larger than } 1$$

(more on this soon). The Hebb learning rule (see Fig. 8.1) determined the modification of strength of the trion interactions V and W, dependent on firing history of the column, or "experience."

As soon as I returned home from Montreal with the brand new trion model, I presented it to my colleague Dennis Silverman in the U.C. Irvine Physics Department. Dennis, being a computational expert, programmed the model to look for the memory patterns. (Dennis and I did a lot of good work together.) The repertoire of memory patterns is found by evolving all possible initial states S (of the first two time steps τ) by always choosing the S at the next τ that has the largest probability P(S), or most probable path. We took six trions in our column, which meant that there are (3^{12}) more than 500,000 [16] possible initial states to follow until repeating spatial-temporal patterns or **memory patterns** (**MPs**) are found. The computer started printing out all the memory patterns for the first choice of interactions. These initial results were like winning at Las Vegas—1804 MPs appeared in this repertoire! *We had indeed hit the jackpot.*

Together with my graduate student John Pearson, we then studied the learning properties of this repertoire of memory patterns. *We saw that each of these memory patterns could be enhanced via the Hebb learning rule to a large cycling probability P(S), and indeed they could correctly be called memory patterns.* We then named these memory patterns (or magic patterns), since they alone and not an arbitrary pattern could "learn" via the Hebb rule. Thus the MPs are the inherent memory patterns of the trion model. I was convinced that the trion model was a major advance in modeling higher brain function. The published results [17] appeared in 1985.

In a full probabilistic or **Monte Carlo calculation**, as shown in Fig. 8.6, the possibility of *not* following the largest probability is allowed. The roulette ball will go into the smaller boxes, but fewer times than into the largest box.

I was extremely lucky to continue after John Pearson to have a series of truly outstanding students working with me on investigating further properties of the trion model: among the best and brightest and dedicated were Xiaodan Leng, John McGrann, and Krishna Shenoy.

NATURAL SEQUENCES

In a Monte Carlo evolution, the MPs evolve in natural sequences from one to another (Fig. 8.7). These time evolutions are generated from the trion model

FIGURE 8.6   Roulette analogy for a Monte Carlo or full probabilistic calculation of time evolutions of the trion model. The probabilities P(S) for the three firing levels for each trion at a given time step are determined by the dynamics of the trion model and are represented in the roulette wheel by the size of the respective box. The actual choice is decided by which box the rotating roulette ball falls into. The larger the box, the more likely the ball will fall into it. Thus, although the ball is more likely to fall into the white box in this example, it could go into the gray box or even the black box. In contrast to this Monte Carlo evolution, the MPs or memory patterns are found by always choosing the largest P(S) and following the evolution until a spatial-temporal pattern keeps repeating.

by a computer. Two distinct types of Monte Carlo evolution [18] are seen in Fig. 8.7, the **sequential mode** and the **creative mode**. They are related to the temperature parameter T, and I will return to them in Chapter 9.

We found two striking features regarding the fluctuation or temperature parameter T in the trion model [19] (Fig. 8.8): (i) As T varies, there exists a series of "transitions" at precise values, giving new repertoires of MPs. (ii) Near a transition in a Monte Carlo calculation, the time evolution wanders back and forth between related sets of these MPs (in what I define as the creative mode in Chapter 9), in contrast to the more structured sequential evolutions or sequential modes that appear far from a transition. This latter feature will help us quantify our concepts of sequential and creative modes. Further, Xiao Leng and I suggested that the fluctuation parameter T can vary in a real cortical network via the action of various neuromodulators.

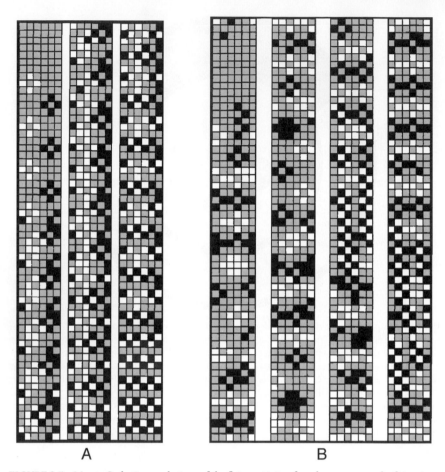

A   B

FIGURE 8.7   Monte Carlo *time* evolutions of the firing activity of a columnar network of six trions as generated by a computer, giving examples of (A) the sequential mode and (B) the creative mode (see Chapter 9). Each square in a given row represents the firing levels of a trion at that time step τ. The grey scale white, grey and black represent the firing levels S = +, 0, or − as in Fig. 8.5. The time steps (rows) are consecutively ordered, beginning at the top of the column at the left and continuing from the bottom of that column to the top of the next column, and so on. Each horizontal row represents a ring of interconnected trions, so that the sixth square wraps around to meet the first as in Fig. 8.5. (A) There are seven different MPs or memory patterns that cycle two or more times. This is an example of a sequential evolution of the MPs and it has high symmetry in the connections and low fluctuations (low T). (B) This Monte Carlo evolution has connections similar to that in A but with a small breaking of the symmetry, and a T that is near the transition shown in Fig. 8.8. This is an example of a creative evolution in that specific MPs appear and reappear. It is these creative evolutions that when mapped onto music give our striking results (see Chapter 9).

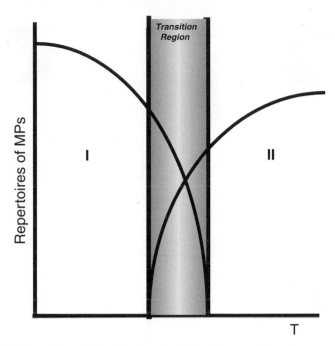

FIGURE 8.8   Repertoires of MPs and regions I and II, and the transition region connecting them, as a function of the fluctuation parameter T. The sequential mode evolution in Fig. 8.7A is in the region I, and the creative mode evolution in Fig. 8.7B is in the transition region. Xiao Leng and I proposed that neuromodulators could change T from one region to another.

Figure 8.7A presents, qualitatively, the concept of **natural sequences of MPs**. For a more quantitative depiction, I present the evidence [20] for these natural sequences in Fig. 8.9, where starting from a single MP, 1000 Monte Carlo evolutions are followed to see which MPs are evolved to next. This can be repeated for each MP to develop the natural sequences of how the MPs evolve over time. These natural sequences can be modified by experience through the Hebb learning rule.

This result of inherent or natural sequences of MPs is a major result. It will be vital when I discuss music, spatial-temporal reasoning, and inherent movement motor patterns that are observed in the human fetus (see Chapter 19).

LEARNING BY SELECTION

Consider learning an MP using the Hebb learning rule (see Fig. 8.1), multiplied by our **Hebb learning coefficient ϵ**. The example of learning an MP is shown

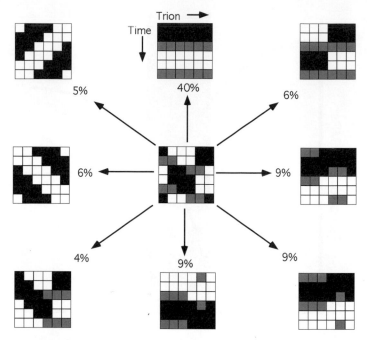

FIGURE 8.9 Natural sequences of Monte Carlo calculations starting with the MP in the center. The numbers at the end of the arrows give the percentage of 1000 Monte Carlo calculations that go to the eight other MPs (including all spatial rotations). Shown here are only those MPs that are accessed with percentages greater than 3%. These relations can be substantially modified through learning. By repeating these calculations starting from other MPs, we see the details of *series of natural or inherent sequences of MPs that are embedded in the trion model*. This is a major result. From McGrann *et al.* (1994)

in Fig. 8.10, where we plot the probability of cycling P_C versus ϵ. The precise symmetry in the V's and W's among the trions are now slightly modified by the Hebb learning so that there is broken symmetry.

This small symmetry breaking (small ϵ) seen in Fig. 8.10 was then shown [21] to form the basis for an *extremely rapid* **selectional learning** in contrast to a much slower fine-tuning of the parameters necessary for what is called **instructional learning**. (Both are probably necessary to understand behavior.) The powerful concept of learning by selection was presented by Gerald Edelman [22] in analogy to his Nobel-winning studies of selection in the immune system (Fig. 8.11).

I believe that Edelman's concept is correct, but that selectional learning is realized in the cortex *not* as in his explicit model through selection of groups of neurons, but rather through the selection of MPs from the inherent repertoire

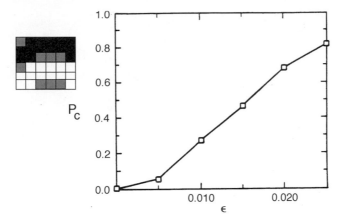

FIGURE 8.10   Learning an MP through the Hebb learning rule (see Fig. 8.1). The MP shown on the left is used along with the Hebb rule multiplied by the Hebb learning coefficient ϵ to modify the initial couplings between trions, which give the repertoire of MPs. The cycling probability P_C to remain in this MP is shown to become quite large for even small values of ϵ. (This striking example of learning is particularly enhanced by having T near the transition region in Fig. 8.8.) From Shenoy et al. (1993)

we are born with. The extremely rapid selectional learning process must be present in the brain, since we can, for example, remember a name and phone number together after hearing them only once. Of course, whether they go into long-term memory storage in the brain depends on other factors.

In the next section, I show that the symmetry breaking in the Hebb learning forms the basis for the recognition of the symmetries among the MPs present in a repertoire. I suggest that this is the basis for higher brain function.

SYMMETRY OPERATIONS AS THE BASIS OF HIGHER BRAIN FUNCTION

Now I want to present the key features of symmetry in the trion model. I believe these ideas will be crucial once we finally understand higher brain function.

Having made the choice of parameters, the repertoire of MPs or memory states is found as follows: For a given initial firing state, follow the procedure of always choosing the S for each trion that has the largest probability P(S) or most probable path. Then the time evolution rapidly goes into a repeating spatial-temporal pattern or MP. An example of a repertoire with 155 MPs [23] is shown in Fig. 8.12.

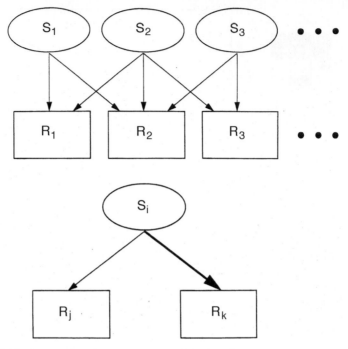

FIGURE 8.11   Learning by selection. Input stimuli S_1, S_2, and S_3 excite various responses R in the cortex. The large repertoire of responses is inherent to the cortex (even without experience) of the newborn. *Through experience and thereby learning, a stimulus will elicit predominately one of these responses and can do so very rapidly.* Krishna Shenoy showed that the trion model has this selectional learning.

There are just 34 separate MPs shown in Fig. 8.12, since we can group them together into ones related by spatially rotating the patterns as shown in Fig. 8.13. This grouping of MPs according to symmetries can be carried further and put on a more formal basis. Let us call the series of operations Γ (gamma), which temporally evolves an MP according to its most probable path for its cycle length and returns the MP to precisely itself. Then a very important property is "readily" demonstrated [24]:

> Consider a symmetry operator α (see Chapter 5) inherent in the brain's operations Γ, for example, rotation or mirror reflection. Then α operating on a memory pattern MP is αMP. The big deal is that αMP must also be an MP or memory pattern. Thus there exist families of MPs related by symmetries, which we call symmetry family groups.

We expect for our structured connectivity in the trion model that there will be a number of symmetry operators α that will characterize a repertoire of MPs or memory patterns [25]. Among those that have been reported are:

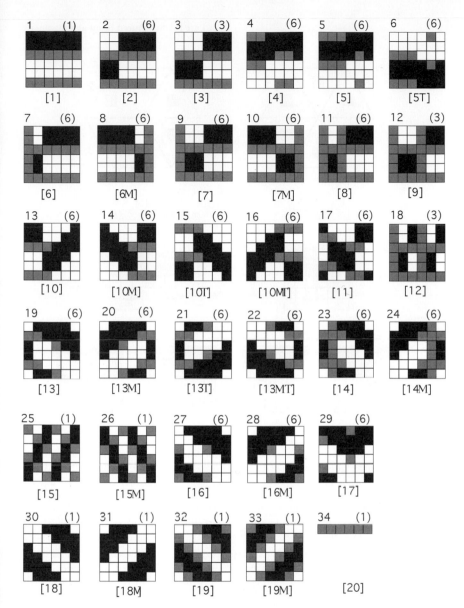

FIGURE 8.12 Repertoire of 155 MPs from a given set of connections among the six trions. The most probable path with the largest P(S), in evolving all possible (roughly 500,000) initial states until repeating patterns (the MPs) is obtained. Each square represents a trion with three levels of firing activity as in Fig. 8.5. Each horizontal row represents a ring of interconnected trions (so that the sixth square wraps around to the first) and time evolves downward. There are a total of 155 MPs that can be completely classified by their distinct spatial rotations (see Fig. 8.13) into 34 groups of MPs shown here. The group number is listed on the top left corner, while the number of MPs in each group is given in parentheses on the top right (**cyclically rotate** the MP so that the first column is the second, etc.; if the MP is not a temporal rotation of any of the other elements in the group, it is considered distinct). These 34 MPs are further classified, below each MP, into 20 symmetry groups according to the additional symmetries of mirror reflection M (reflection of trion number about a line separating two trions), time reversal T, and a combination of M and T. An explicit example is shown in Fig. 8.14. In a Monte Carlo calculation, these MPs would flow from one to another. From McGrann *et al.* (1994)

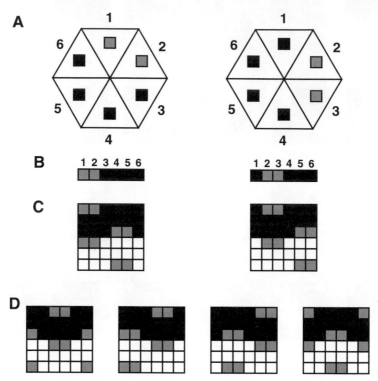

FIGURE 8.13   Spatial rotations of an MP from Fig. 8.12. (A) On the left is a cortical network of six trions (triangles) with the firing level in the square directly placed in the numbered trion at one time step. On the right is a spatially rotated form of the firing levels on the left. (B) Place the six firing levels in A in the forms shown here. Each now represents the first time step for the six trions explicitly numbered above in the MPs shown in C. (C) The MP on the right is a spatial rotation of the MP on the left: Rotate the entire pattern on the left so that the entire first column with six time steps goes into the second column, the second into the third, . . . , and the sixth into the first. Below are the other spatial rotations. All six of these MPs are distinct. We denote these six distinct MPs by a representative one as shown in Fig. 8.12.

R: spatial rotation among the *distinguishable* trions
M: mirror reflection
T: time reversal operation
C: interchanges firing levels S and −S (white and black in Fig. 8.5 or red and blue in Fig. 9.14)

Examples of MPs related by M and T are shown in Fig. 8.14. In general, a product of two of these symmetry operators α is also an α, for example, MT as shown here.

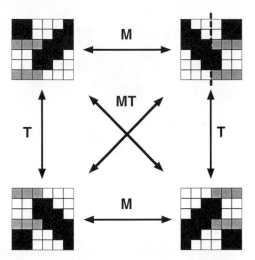

FIGURE 8.14   An explicit example of the symmetry relations among the MPs in the symmetry group [10] in Fig. 8.12 according to M, T, and MT. The 34 MPs are further classified, below each MP, into 20 symmetry groups according to the additional symmetries of mirror reflection M (reflection of trion number about a line separating two trions as shown in the upper right MP), time reversal T, and a combination MT.

These MPs, when operated on by an operator α equal to C (interchanging S and −S), just give a *temporal rotation* of the MP that is not considered as a distinct MP (Fig. 8.15.) There are repertoires in the trion model for which C operating on an MP gives distinct MPs. The operator C will be seen to be crucial when we look at Mark Bodner's analysis of actual primate cortical data.

The 34 MPs shown in Fig. 8.12 can be placed into 20 symmetry family groups. *This concept of symmetry family groups in the repertoire of a single cortical column will form the fundamental building blocks of a cortical language and grammar as we build a higher level of cortical architecture from coupled columns.*

There are 1804 MPs in the repertoire given by the connections [26] that determined the Monte Carlo evolutions in Fig. 8.7. These 1804 MPs can be placed into 73 symmetry family groups. This repertoire proved to be especially interesting when mapped onto music and onto robotic motion (see Chapter 9).

As I will present next (as shown by John McGrann), *the big deal with these symmetry family groups is that after an MP is enhanced by the Hebb learning rule ("through experience"), a trion columnar network can recognize the other members of this MP's symmetry family group.*

Xiao Leng and I proposed that perhaps this built-in ability of the structured cortex to recognize patterns related by symmetries was the elemental operation

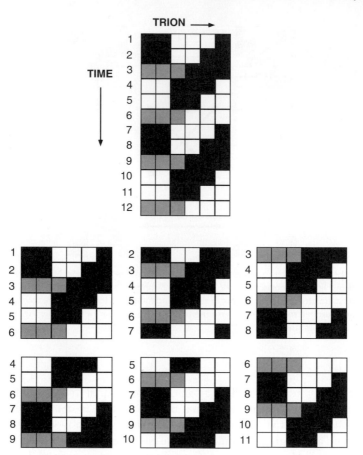

FIGURE 8.15 Temporal rotations of an MP. If we are looking at an isolated (not coupled to other MPs in other cortical columns) MP or memory pattern, it does not matter which time step is numbered as 1 or 2 or 3, etc. So, these six temporally rotated MPs are the same MP. However, when I discuss the coupling of several columns together, we will see that the relative temporal rotations of coupled MPs (see Fig. 8.22) in these columns are quite important.

for higher brain functions involved in spatial-temporal reasoning and processing of music. I suspect that there must be additional general symmetries to be discovered, especially when several columnar networks are coupled together. However, again let me stress that the trion model is only supposed to give us hints about the real cortex and what to look for.

RECOGNITION OF ROTATION AND TIME REVERSAL

Here I discuss the recognition of spatially rotated and time-reversed objects in the trion model [27]. *This recognition of symmetry is built into the highly structured trion model.* Consider a simplified example in which a specific visual object, for example, my favorite animal, a rhino, is represented in the cortex by one of the MPs. Rotated rhinos are represented by rotations of the MP of the rhino as in Fig. 8.16.

The rhino seen in a position facing us is learned or enhanced with the Hebb rule and thus the symmetry among the connections is broken by a small amount. When a rotated rhino (in a position other than facing us) is seen, the rotated rhino MP evolves in a Monte Carlo calculation into the MP for the rhino facing us, thereby identifying it as a rhino; the number of time steps to evolve is linearly related to the amount of rotation, in agreement with experiment (Fig. 8.17).

A similar scenario is considered for recognition of time-reversed MPs, as shown in Fig. 8.18. Here we do not give an explicit physical representation for the abstract MPs, although the mappings onto music and robotic motion in Chapter 9 are relevant.

My colleagues and I suggested that these "built-in" recognitions of MPs related by symmetries constitute the basic operations in the cortex for higher brain function. I suggest that we are all constantly looking for patterns and relationships even when we are not conscious of this, and even when we are not sure what to do with the results. *This search for relationships in patterns in space and time and their related symmetries is inherent in the mammalian cortex.* We need to recognize this, understand it fully, and then exploit it properly in educating our children to think, reason, and create.

INHERENT CORTICAL LANGUAGE AND GRAMMAR

I want to explicitly consider the idea that

> *there is an internal neural language and grammar that are common throughout the cortex and common to mammals.*

Although this is a very strong hypothesis, it seems to me to be a very reasonable one. Consider an alternative that it is not common throughout the cortex in a person. This would be like having one cortical area "speaking Chinese," another

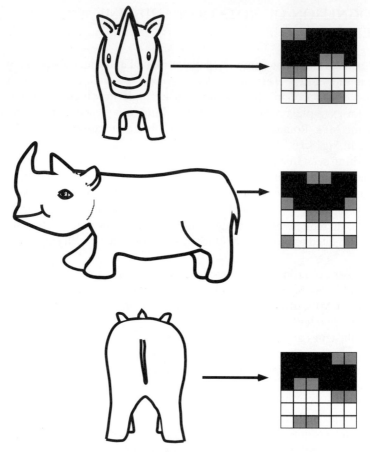

FIGURE 8.16   Rhino and two spatially rotated views of the rhino as schematically represented in the cortex by an MP and two of its spatially rotated family members.

one "speaking Spanish," another one "speaking English," and so on. This seems to be extremely inefficient and unworkable. I believe that not only does my hypothesis make evolutionary sense (see Chapter 23), but that it is also testable. Furthermore, as Fran Rauscher and I proposed [28],

> *Perhaps the cortex's response to music is the "Rosetta Stone" for the "code" or internal language of higher brain function.*

Let us consider what my colleagues and I have learned from the trion model. We have in mind that the MPs in a repertoire from a cortical column of trions are "words." Thus the simple repertoire in Fig. 8.11 has 155 MPs and thus 155

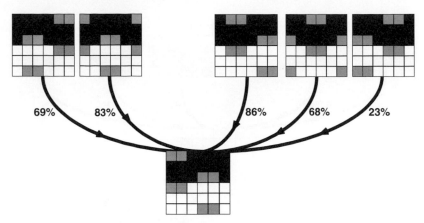

FIGURE 8.17   Monte Carlo (1000 runs for 50 time steps) results from the recognition of rotated rhinos (MPs) starting in each of the five rotated MPs (and then searching for the bottom MP within the 50 time steps) after enhancing this (bottom) MP with the Hebb learning rule as in Fig. 8.10. The percentage of runs evolving to the learned MP are shown for a specific amount of learning and can be further increased. (You can see the small fluctuations in percent between the twice-rotated patterns with 68% and 69%, or between the once-rotated patterns with 83% and 86%.) These percentages give the probabilities that a given rotated pattern will be recognized in the trion model. From McGrann et al. (1994)

words. Note that all of these 155 words consist of combinations of three temporal patterns for the individual trions a, b, and c and their temporal rotations as shown in Fig. 8.19.

It would be of great interest to be able to determine the repertoire in Fig. 8.12 starting from this "alphabet" a, b, and c. However, I have not been smart enough to do this. So far our results come from computer computations of the model. We did find that this same alphabet holds for the repertoire with the same connections among the trions for any number of trions greater than 3 (up to 9 trions, which was as far as we could compute). A small part of the repertoire for 9 trions in a column is shown in Fig. 8.20.

An inherent repertoire of 1804 MPs [29] or words results from the connections among trions in Fig. 8.7. A much larger number of letters comprise the alphabet for this repertoire. The take home message is that when we search for an "alphabet" in actual cortical data, we should use the concepts and not the explicit details to guide our search.

Now consider a higher-level architecture of cortical columns so that we might look at putting words together to make phrases. Our recent and ongoing trion model computer calculations show the presence of an inherent cortical grammar [30]:

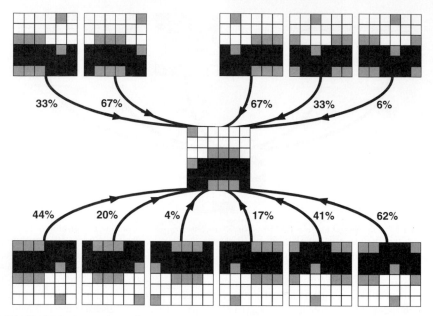

FIGURE 8.18   Recognition of time-reversed and spatially rotated MPs (see Fig. 8.17 for details) in Monte Carlo calculations after learning the center MP. The top MPs are related to the learned MP by spatial rotations and to the bottom MPs by the symmetry operation of time reversal T. From McGrann *et al.* (1994)

Only certain MPs or words "fit" together and only in specific spatial
and temporal orders.

We are still in the early stages of this project, so I cannot give you more than a glimpse into what we are finding. I also will tell you how we were led to these results and what special assumptions we made to create a specific situation that we could study. Again, let me stress that these results should be considered as suggesting the direction for appropriate experiments to test our predictions. *The main point is that the trion model does contain a language and a grammar, but the details are for guidance.*

Our initial goal was to understand if we might enhance the reliability of maintaining an MP or word in active short-term memory by coupling several columns together. This followed our elaboration of a suggestion of the great mathematician and computer pioneer John von Neumann [31] in his 1956 paper on how to get reliable behavior from unreliable components. We could couple four columns together in a ringlike manner and let the connections between minicolumns be determined by a Hebb learning rule as in Fig. 8.21. Guided by experiment [32], the couplings we allow are from each labeled trion

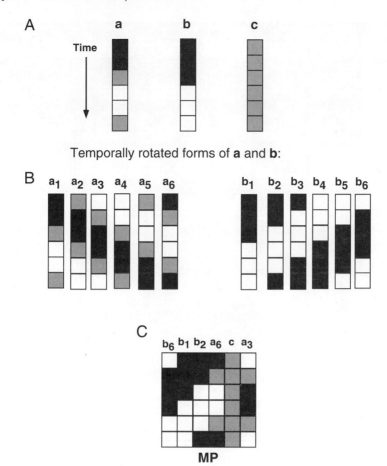

FIGURE 8.19   (A) The three temporal sequences a, b, c for a trion are defined as "letters." (B) The temporal rotations of a and b. The sequence a_2 is gotten from a_1 by temporal rotation, so that the top square in a_1 goes to the bottom square in a_2 and all the other squares in a_1 move up one to form a_2. Together with c, the sequences in B form the entire repertoire of MPs in Fig. 8.12. (C) An explicit example.

in a column to the same labeled trion in a coupled column. The connections within each of the columns are the same as those that give us the repertoire of MPs in Fig. 8.12.

I suggest that there is a very rapid Hebb rule [33] between these trions that is responsible for short-term memory, as when you remember the name and phone number of someone you have just met. Whether this information goes into long-term memory storage or is soon forgotten depends on other factors.

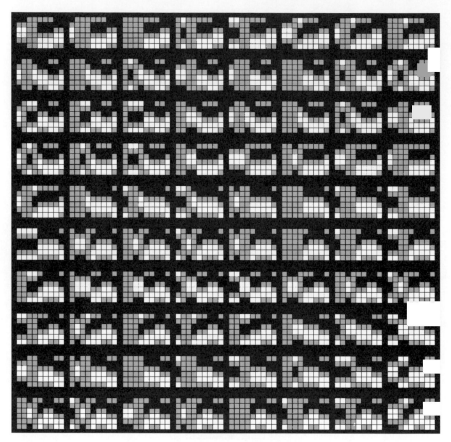

FIGURE 8.20   A small part of the huge repertoire for nine trions in a column having the same connections among the trions as in Fig. 8.12. The same three "letters" a, b, and c in Fig. 8.19 make up all the MPs or words in the entire repertoire. This is from unpublished work done with John Pearson.

RELIABLE MEMORY FOR A SINGLE MP IN COUPLED COLUMNS

We found striking results for the system of four coupled columns in Fig. 8.21 with the same MP or word in each column: only for specific temporal phases between the MPs in different columns can large values of P_L be obtained. P_L is the probability of these MPs remaining for one cycle in the system of coupled columns. An example is shown in Fig. 8.22.

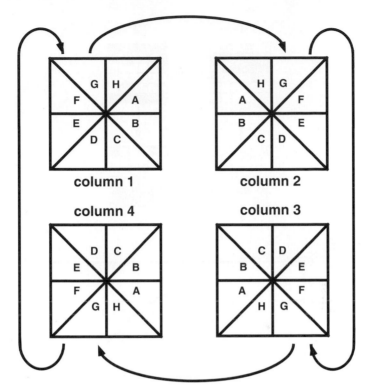

FIGURE 8.21   Four cortical columns coupled clockwise in a ring. The couplings are from each labeled trion in a column to the same labeled trion in the coupled column. The couplings between the *G* trions are explicitly shown. The strengths of these couplings are determined by a Hebb rule between the MPs. We imagine that there is a very rapid Hebb rule between these trions that is responsible for short-term memory, as when you remember the name and phone number of someone you have just met.

These results show a dramatic increase in P_L as a function of ϵ_c for the representative example in which there are temporal phase differences between the same inherent patterns in connected columns. *For the cases in which there are no temporal phase differences, there is essentially no learning.* Note that for practical short-term memory purposes it is likely that not all the columns need maintain the pattern.

Then we generalized these results to consider the same reliability criterion in having different MPs or words in the connected columns. This would allow us to seriously investigate the proposal that Xiao Leng and I had made years before that a common inherent columnar language throughout the cortex results from the Mountcastle columnar principle:

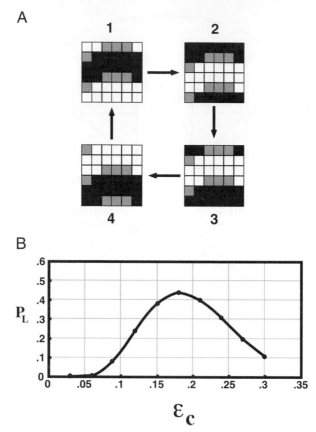

FIGURE 8.22   Example of rapid short-term learning of a word or MP in the four coupled columns in Fig. 8.21 by a Hebb learning rule. Here the same word or MP is in each column. Only when we allow temporal rotations in different columns can this word be learned. (A) The appropriate set of temporal rotations or temporal phase differences that can be learned for the four MPs. (B) Plot of P_L for the MPs in A versus the rapid Hebb learning parameter ϵ_c between the trions in different columns in Fig. 8.21.

If there was to be a language, there must be rules and thus a grammar.

So, now we had a concrete means of looking for the trion language and grammar.

DIFFERENT MPS IN EACH COLUMN YIELDING A CORTICAL LANGUAGE

Now we consider different MPs in each column and investigate the conditions under which the global firing probabilities P_L are greatly enhanced. We indeed find temporal phase and spatial rotations under which a large number of combinations of MPs satisfy this enhancement condition. My outstanding summer student Chris Figge developed a very nice software program to search through all possible temporal rotations and spatial rotations among a chosen four coupled MPs. An example of his results is presented in Fig. 8.23, in which P_L is enhanced.

There are combinations of MPs that do not satisfy this condition of large P_L for any possible temporal phase and spatial rotations. An example is presented in Fig. 8.24.

It turns out that the order of the different MPs in the ring configuration (Fig. 8.21) also makes a big difference. Meredith Crosby, Jill Hansen, Syndi Vuong, and I just found this result, illustrated in Fig. 8.25.

I am extremely pleased with these results, which are very supportive of an inherent cortical language having a grammar with specific built-in rules. My colleagues and I will be investigating this in much more detail. We strongly suspect that the symmetry families will play a very big role in the grammar.

ALZHEIMER DISEASE MODEL OF DEGENERATIVE SHORT-TERM MEMORY

Now I present a version of the calculation in Fig. 8.22 as a simple model for degenerative short-term memory loss [34] as in Alzheimer disease. Here I let the ratio of $g(S)$s,

$$g(0)/g(+/-) \text{ much larger than } 1$$

decrease from the value 500 usually used. This decrease represents a decrease in the number of neurons in a trion, which is our idealized minicolumn. As $g(0)/g(+/-)$ decreases, we expect a decrease in the reliability of short-term memory in our model. Further, as the equivalent number of neurons in the trion goes below a number roughly equal to 30, we expect the functional cooperative behavior to dramatically fail [35].

We let $g(0)/g(+/-)$ decrease in one trion in one of the four connected columns in Fig. 8.21. The resulting values of P_L versus $g(0)/g(+/-)$ are shown in Fig. 8.26. As expected, there is a slow decrease in P_L as $g(0)/g(+/-)$ decreases, until a value of roughly 40, at which time a sharp decrease in P_L occurs. This value of $g(0)/g(+/-)$ roughly corresponds to the number of neurons equal to 30 in the minicolumn represented by this degenerating trion. The number 30 roughly represents the minimum number of neurons in the minicolumn for functional cooperativity to exist [36].

Thus the results for our simple model of short-term memory loss in Alzheimer disease predict that there are two stages. First there is an early slow rate of

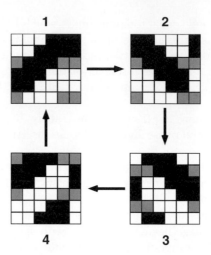

FIGURE 8.23 Example of four different MPs or words that can be learned together in the order shown. See Fig. 8.22 for details. The temporal phase differences and spatial rotations shown are those that gave the highest learning P_L.

memory loss as neurons degenerate, and then a very rapid loss when the number of neurons in our trion or minicolumn fall roughly below the number 30. The two stages of memory loss agree nicely with clinical data on Alzheimer

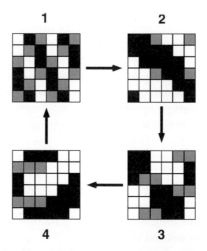

FIGURE 8.24 An example of four MPs or words that could not be learned in our model for any choice of temporal rotations or spatial rotations. See Fig. 8.22 for details.

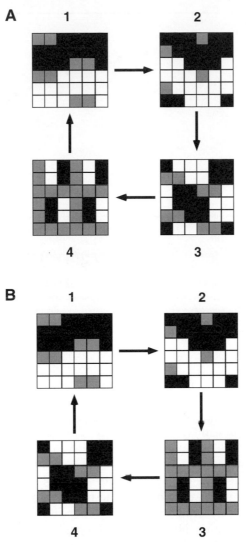

FIGURE 8.25   The order of MPs or words matters. (A) An example of the order of four MPs with large P_L. (B) Now invert the order of the third and fourth words in A. The P_L obtained is much less than for the order in A. See Fig. 8.22 for details.

disease. Although the prediction of 30 neurons cannot be easily tested, it gives another consistency check on our model. I consider our calculations of Alzheimer disease to be another confirmation that we are on the right track in our model of higher brain function.

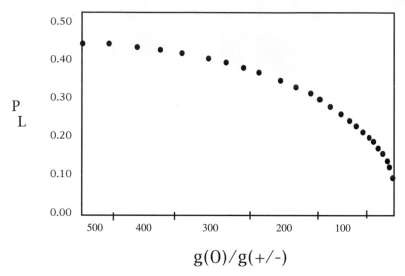

FIGURE 8.26   Reliability or short-term memory as measured by P_L as $g(0)/g(+/-)$ decreases in a simple model for Alzheimer disease. This is the example shown in the coupled columnar trion system in Fig. 8.22. The decrease in $g(0)/g(+/-)$ is related to a decrease in the number of neurons in a minicolumn.

SIGNIFICANCE OF CORTICAL GRAMMAR

I want to briefly summarize these results, since I think that the concepts will prove to have great significance. They may influence a range of disciplines, from neurophysiology to philosophy to evolution to the building of a **thinking machine** (see Chapter 22).

Von Neumann discussed, in a mathematical analysis, the building of reliable organisms from unreliable components in terms of **multiplexing** the basic components. We have presented a specific calculation that combines the von Neumann multiplexing with Hebb intercolumnar couplings to achieve dramatically increased firing reliability. The potential relevance extends from that of a model for the neuropathology of memory loss in Alzheimer disease to that of an inherent common cortical language with a built-in grammar.

Using the Hebb learning rule, we found dramatic enhancement in short-term memory as measured by P_L resulting from temporal phase differences (see Fig. 8.22) for the same MP firing patterns or words in the connected cortical columns. This suggests the possibility that the circulation of the MPs among the columns in a manner in which they causally feed into each other is a key ingredient for the enhancement. Experimental evidence for the presence of families of temporally structured firing patterns in cortical neurons during short-term memory was found by Mark Bodner (see Chapter 15). His new SYMMETRIC analysis method, based on families of patterns related by symmetries, bins the spike train data in time and firing level as in the trion model, thus allowing a possible comparison between experiment and theory.

The striking results in Fig. 8.22 with the same MP in each column are extended to the situation in which different MPs or words are in the four coupled cortical columns. We found that, in general, large enhancements of short-term memory for the entire system can be achieved only for specific temporal phases and spatial rotations (see Fig. 8.23). Not all combinations of MPs or words could be enhanced for any combination of temporal phases and spatial rotations, as shown in Fig. 8.24. Furthermore, the order of the MPs or words matters, as illustrated in Fig. 8.25. I am sure that symmetry plays a major role here.

These results are an exciting glimpse of an inherent internal cortical language with a built-in grammar. As noted previously, I view the temporal patterns for the individual trions as letters in an alphabet, and the resultant MPs as cortical "words" dependent on the connectivity among the trions in a column. Now for cortical columns coupled through the Hebb learning rule, we are able to build reliable short-term memory patterns with different words in each column for specific temporal phases and spatial rotations, but not for all combinations of such words. This is a manifestation of an inherent internal cortical grammar resulting from the structured Mountcastle columnar principle.

Much more work on the trion model, both computationally and then analytically, is necessary before more detailed features of the proposed cortical language and grammar can be discerned. However, testable neurophysiological predictions can be made. I suggest searching for a temporal "alphabet" at the minicolumn level, which is common throughout the cortex. This involves not only the appropriate behavioral experiments, but also the appropriate analyses of the resultant cortical data, now being done by Mark Bodner.

It has been stressed that the neural basis of human language is a very important and very difficult pursuit. It is clear that this human language has an innate grammar [37]. It is still unclear whether human language systems in the cortex are the result of a qualitative departure from the general mammalian cortical design, or a less radical specialization with origins present in lower mammals [38]. I suggest that our findings of the presence of an inherent mammalian cortical language with a built-in grammar give strong support for the second hypothesis. *I believe that our human language and grammar has its origins in the common cortical internal language and grammar coming from the Mountcastle columnar principle for mammalian cortex.*

I will make only a few remarks about the effects of music on language. I have repeatedly been asked whether I thought the Mozart effect—the enhancement

of spatial-temporal reasoning from prior listening to the Mozart Sonata for Two
Pianos in D Major (K.448)—could be generalized to enhancing language abilities. I am now much less hesitant about this. Based on the recent trion model
results on an inherent cortical language and grammar, I believe that there
should be some important effects, but the relevant experiments must be carefully thought out. It may show up in a more obvious form as a secondary result
of the music training that enhances spatial-temporal reasoning on a long-term
basis (see Fig. 3.3). I just have not thought enough about this issue to present
more detailed remarks at this time. However, I do intend to consider these ideas
much more seriously now.

I hope that you have gotten a general sense of how I have used our trion
model calculations to gain crucial insight into how the brain works. In the next
two chapters I will show how music can influence how we think, reason, and
create. I will present the experimental tests starting in Chapter 11.

CHAPTER 9

Trion Music: Reasoning and Creativity

In this chapter, I explain how we not only got the insight that music can be used as a window into higher brain function, but made the prediction that music training could enhance spatial-temporal reasoning. This followed from the mapping of trion model firing pattern evolutions onto music. I introduce the concepts of sequential reasoning and creative reasoning within our model. Then, since the trion model has been shown in Chapter 8 to give an inherent common cortical language and grammar, I present several diverse examples of other applications of the trion model evolutions in understanding brain function (dance, visual art, speech recognition, and text recognition). I think that these all add support to our program. This chapter is important and can be skimmed, but not skipped.

Everyone always asks how I got into doing research on music and its influences on thinking and reasoning. It was totally by accident! About 10 years ago, I met an expert here at U.C. Irvine in computer electronic music, Eric Wright. After talking with Eric, my graduate student Xiaodan Leng and I decided that it would be an interesting idea to map or translate our trion model computer evolutions onto music. Xiao and I had been thinking about how these spatial-temporal trion patterns represent cortical thought processes (as noted in the following). In addition to the visual representations on the computer screen, we figured that we might gain further insight by listening to these patterns evolve in time. Before I discuss the results and implications of Xiao's dramatic and startling mappings, I want to distinguish the two important types of trion evolutions in Fig. 9.1 that Xiao and I [1] called sequential and creative modes. I have repeated this figure from Chapter 8 since it is so relevant to developing our ideas of these two quite different yet complementary types of trion model evolutions.

SEQUENTIAL VERSUS CREATIVE MODES

We are all aware of various moods such as being elated, emotional, sad, happy, and so on. It is generally believed that the subcortical brain regions, through their interactions with the cortex via the role of the many neuromodulators (see, for example, Fig. 6.8), control and express moods. Although these neuro-modulators are indeed explicitly present in our model of higher brain function (see Chapter 10), I will not be dealing explicitly with moods in this book, so I will not attempt to define them. However, I will need to provide a concise *neural* definition or description of what I mean by sequential and creative modes for the sake of our discussion. Further, these terms, especially creativity, have *many* possible descriptions. There are two types of Monte Carlo evolutions that we will identify as the sequential mode and the creative mode:

> *The sequential mode corresponds to a precise evolution of the memory patterns (MPs) (Fig. 9.1A) and has been used in our studies of memory and spatial-temporal reasoning.*

With only somewhat different parameters than used for studying memory and sequential reasoning,

> *The creative mode generates a much more flowing and intriguing series of patterns (Fig. 9.1B).*

Let me first attempt to justify these descriptions of sequential and creative modes in terms of relevance to human behavior, and then be more specific about our neural definitions. I do not wish to get involved with a very difficult

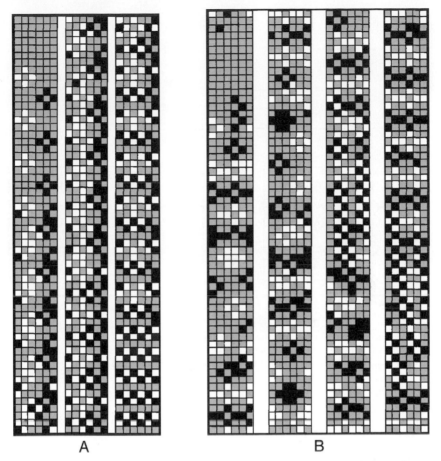

A   B

FIGURE 9.1   Two distinct yet complementary trion model Monte Carlo evolutions. The time steps (rows) are consecutively ordered, beginning at the top of the column at the left and continuing from the bottom of that column to the top of the next column, and so on. (A) Sequential mode and (B) creative mode in the trion model as presented in Fig. 8.7. Note how the diamond pattern starting at time step 8 in A can be seen to appear and reappear in several spatially rotated forms in B.

semantic problem (clearly, there are numerous publications dealing with the definition of creativity). Thus I will give some brief, restrictive ideas on creative thought, contrasting it with sequential thought.

Consider a specific problem to be solved, for example, in mathematics, engineering, sculpture, or music composition. I will also want to apply our terminology to much more ordinary problems that we all have to solve in life.

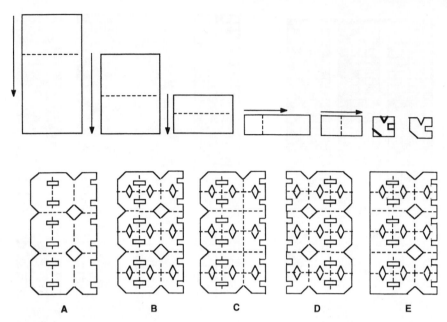

FIGURE 9.2   Example of the sequential type of spatial-temporal reasoning in the paper folding & cutting (PF&C) tasks we used in the Mozart effect experiments (modified from the Stanford-Binet tests). Depicted is a piece of paper before it was folded and cut (top left figure). The dashed lines and straight arrows represent the location of the folds, and the solid lines represent cuts. Subjects had to choose which of the five choices the paper would look like when unfolded. (This is one of the more difficult items.)

Contrast the two necessary yet distinct and complementary methods of solution as (A) the sequential method and (B) the creative method:

(A) If the problem you have to solve is a slight variation of a quite familiar type (even if it is very difficult), then perhaps the method of solution involves a fairly prescribed sequential series of mental computations, which I call a sequential solution. For example, consider the **paper folding and cutting (PF&C)** tasks used in the Mozart effect experiments (Fig. 9.2) [2].

(B) If a sequential solution to the problem at hand is not clear, *then the mental processes in the creative solution involve rapidly picking out a potential solution from perhaps an enormous number, as in the middle or end of a chess game.* Unlike present computer chess programs that sequentially examine all possibilities, in a short time a Master chess player [3] comes up with one or a few potential solutions without even being aware or fully conscious of the mental process used in finding them. These solutions are complementary in that it is usually necessary to sequentially examine a creative solution for validity of the details.

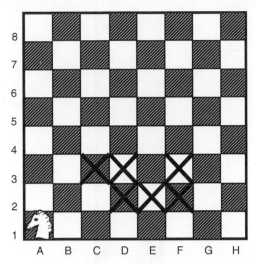

FIGURE 9.3   Creative spatial-temporal chess task devised for us by chess Grand Master Jonathan Yedidia. The chess knight (or horse) can move one square horizontally or one square vertically, and then one square on the diagonal. Thus, the knight on square A1 can move to square B3 or square C2. The task is to move the knight from its starting position on A1 to H1 without landing on the squares that have X's. Since there are several possible choices of moves at each step that could lead to a correct solution, we define this task as creative, unlike the sequential task in Fig. 9.2, which has only one correct answer at each (time) step. (The least number of moves gets the highest score.)

A simple example of a creative spatial-temporal task in chess (to be used in our experiments) was devised for us by our Grand Master chess consultant Jonathan Yedidia (Fig. 9.3).

Consider now the sequential and creative modes in our Monte Carlo evolutions as in Fig. 9.1. In Fig. 9.1A, the fluctuation or temperature T value is outside the transition region in Fig. 9.4, leading to a Monte Carlo calculation in which the MPs evolve in some natural sequences in what we define as the sequential mode. There will be a number of such sequences for each MP with different probabilities. Further, there are specific relationships (or symmetries) among these MPs that we are now studying. In Fig. 9.1B, there is a fluctuation T value near the transition in Fig. 9.4 that leads to a Monte Carlo in which MPs appear and reappear in what we define as the creative mode.

It is as if the MPs evolve in related but novel ways in the creative mode and in related but more prescribed ways in the sequential mode. It is these creative evolutions that, when mapped onto music, gave Xiao her striking results.

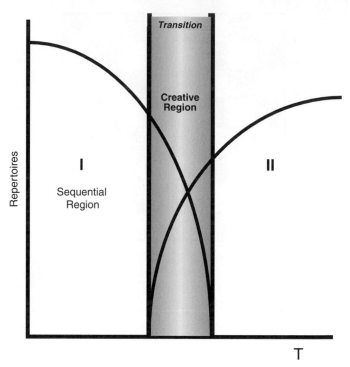

FIGURE 9.4   Sequential and creative regions as a function of fluctuation parameter T as in Fig. 8.8. Repertoires and transition regions are shown. We proposed that neuromodulators could change T from one region to another.

These columnar trion network descriptions are useful for considering the neural bases of *both* sequential reasoning and creative reasoning.

When fluctuation parameter T is in the transition region in Fig. 9.4, the Monte Carlo evolutions are in the creative mode as compared to the sequential mode, when the T value is outside this transition region. Both modes are crucial to and complementary in our discussion of higher brain function.

The key idea is that Xiao Leng and I [4] proposed that specific neuromodulators can induce this change in T and thus cause this important change in thought processes in the same columnar networks, allowing the processes to go back and forth from the sequential to the creative mode. In particular, we suggested that the neuromodulator **serotonin** might be involved here [5]. I will return to this point later, and discuss the role that listening to specific music might play in enhancing sequential and creative spatial-temporal reasoning.

I will propose that the Mozart effect experiments were primarily dealing with sequential reasoning. Further, since the creative–transition region in Fig. 9.4 is a smaller range in T than the sequential region in T, it might be harder to access and it might be highly individual. Thus, the type of "classical" music needed to enhance the creative process might be highly individual. I am now working on a precise experimental design to test this proposal.

Now let us examine Xiao's trion model music.

MAPPING OF MONTE CARLO EVOLUTIONS ONTO MUSIC

We proposed that the trion model patterns represent a candidate for the internal language of the brain, that is, that they explain how one part of the brain communicates with the other parts.

Xiao Leng mapped the Monte Carlo evolutions of the model, or translated this internal language of the brain, into music [6]. Although her mappings of Monte Carlo evolutions of the sequential mode type in Fig. 9.1A were very interesting, the results were striking when the Monte Carlo evolutions of the creative mode type in Fig. 9.1B were mapped onto pitches and instruments to produce music.

There are many, many possible choices of mappings! As Xiao demonstrated, they generate good approximations to different recognizable (Western and Eastern) human styles of music. *None of her mappings involved detailed tuning of detailed parameters.* One of the three mappings published in the initial study is shown in Fig. 9.5. It should be emphasized that pitches and instruments were the only two elements that were varied from one time step to the next (all other parameters, such as the length of the discrete time step and the volume, are constant throughout each piece of music presented).

The trion music was created by taking a specific trion evolution as in Fig. 9.1B and mapping it onto music as in Fig. 9.5. Then her sophisticated software program gave the resultant computer instructions through a **MIDI** (Music Instrument Digital Interface) to an electronic music synthesizer (Fig. 9.6).

By the way, in 1988, when Xiao was starting to study the trion music as part of her Ph.D. thesis research, I had no funding for equipment. She purchased the necessary (expensive) computer from her own savings.

COMPOSING TRION MUSIC VARIATIONS ON A THEME

A further important feature of Xiao's trion music is that *variations on a theme could be composed in her software since any given MP can be enhanced through the Hebb learning rule.*

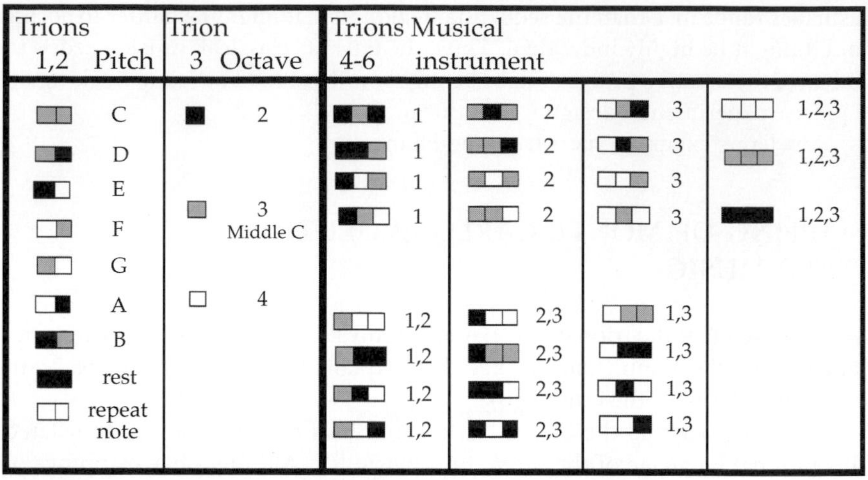

Trions 1,2 Pitch	Trion 3 Octave	Trions 4-6 Musical instrument			
C	■ 2	1	2	3	1,2,3
D		1	2	3	1,2,3
E	▨ 3 Middle C	1	2	3	
F		1	2	3	1,2,3
G	□ 4				
A		1,2	2,3	1,3	
B		1,2	2,3	1,3	
rest		1,2	2,3	1,3	
repeat note		1,2	2,3	1,3	

FIGURE 9.5   Mapping the trion model onto music. This is an example of a mapping by Xiao Leng onto pitches and instruments for each time step of a six-trion Monte Carlo evolution. Trions 1 and 2 together give the pitch, trion 3 gives the octave, and trions 4–6 give the combinations of instruments.

So, for example, if you liked the sound of the "diamond pattern" MP in Fig. 9.1A using a particular mapping as in Fig. 9.5, then Xiao's program could then enhance this MP, leading to a slightly modified set of connections among the trions. A resultant Monte Carlo (Fig. 9.7) is seen to have the diamond MP appear and reappear in the original and in spatially rotated family members. The mapping of this Monte Carlo evolution onto music gives a variation on the diamond theme. Since everyone has music preferences, Xiao's software would even allow a person who is completely untrained in music, such as myself, to compose music of interest.

TRION MUSIC AND GENERAL FEATURES OF MUSIC

The resulting trion music was so striking and unlike what we expected that Xiao and I made the bold proposals [7] that led to this book. Let me summarize the fundamental basis for the trion model music results and how this basis is compatible with some important general features of music that are relevant to higher brain function.

I propose that humans start with the basic Mountcastle columnar structure in the cortex at birth, which gives rise to a huge repertoire of inherent spatial-

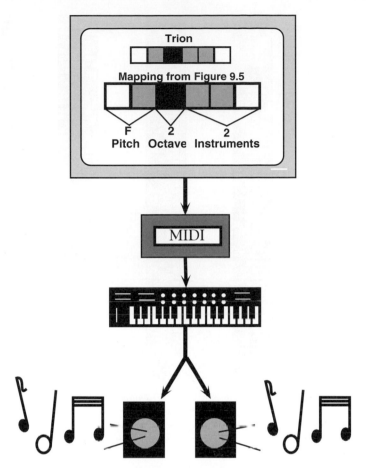

FIGURE 9.6   Schematic production of trion music starting with a Monte Carlo as in Fig. 9.1B and using the mapping in Fig. 9.5 through computer instructions to assign instructions to the MIDI and then to an electronic music synthesizer.

temporal firing patterns. These patterns can be excited, they evolve from one to another in natural sequences that are related to each other by certain symmetries, and they can be readily learned in a selective manner. I discussed all of these features in Chapter 8. Keeping these features in mind, we will now consider their compatibility with the following features of music.

(i) Music composition, performance, and listening all involve the evolution of this inherent repertoire of spatial-temporal memory patterns (MPs in the trion model) coming from the Mountcastle columnar structure of cortex. It is the creative genius of a composer such as Mozart or the brilliance of a conduc-

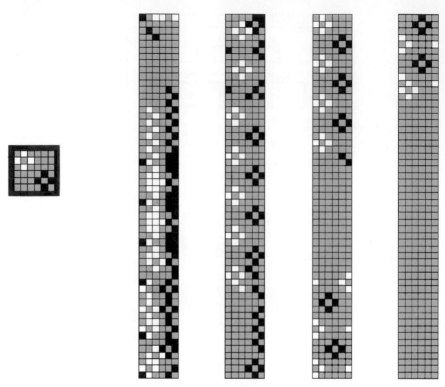

FIGURE 9.7   Variation on the Diamond Theme. The "diamond" MP on the left, when mapped onto music by Xiao, produces a theme. The Hebb learning rule is used to enhance the occurrence of this MP (and related ones) and produce the trion evolution on the right. When mapped, this trion evolution produces a music composition that we call a "Variation on the Diamond Theme."

tor such as George Szell that produces a magnificent performance that involves higher brain function at its highest level. *I suggest that what is involved here is the perfect use of these inherent spatial-temporal patterns common to mammalian cortex. It is not only the patterns, but also their symmetry family members and the inherent natural sequences of these pattens that are used in brilliant music. As listeners, we need only appreciate the result of having these inherent patterns and their natural sequences excited in our brains.* We can all appreciate music, even though few of us can compose it, and very few in history have even approached the genius of Mozart in composing music. As we have seen, Xiao's different mappings of the same Monte Carlo evolution gave different recognizable human styles of music (Western and Eastern). This then is consistent with the universal appreciation of music.

(ii) *The assumption that this inherent repertoire of patterns and their sequences is essentially present at birth is perhaps a necessary condition to understanding the appreciation of music (and particular pieces of music) by the infant.* In addition, there are inherent structures in the brain that are devoted to music, just as there are such structures for human language. Further, these structures are accessible for use from birth without any learning. In this sense, we might consider music as a sort of "pre-language" [8]. I believe this is necessary if we are to understand the fascinating behavioral experiments in Chapter 21 by Carol Krumhansl [9] with 4-month-old infants.

(iii) Again, the fact that millions of people over centuries have been captivated by certain composers and specific pieces of music speaks to the common universality of the repertoires of inherent spatial-temporal patterns.

(iv) The enormous memory capacity of musicians and certain musical savants [10] is indeed paradoxical. The storage and recall of a symphony note by note would be staggering. However, following the insight from our Monte Carlo evolutions and their mappings onto music, *we propose that it is not only these inherent patterns with their families related by specific symmetries that are utilized in the composition, but the natural sequences of these patterns as well that allow this enormous memory capacity for certain music, such as that of Mozart.* Although this does not answer the paradox completely, it does give some important insight into the solution.

(v) We have tried to understand the *incredible precision to 1% in time duration of repeated mental rehearsals of a piece of music* [11] by introducing the new timescales of seconds to minutes that are associated with the periodicities of "neuromodulators," which perhaps could "reset" the accuracy of firing patterns across cortex. This important phenomenon is explored in detail in Chapter 11.

(vi) An initial glimpse into the marvelous creativity involved in the composition of music can be discerned in the trion model example "Variation on the Diamond Theme" presented in Fig. 9.7.

If our trion model of the Mountcastle columnar principle gives a viable picture of the inherent common internal language (and grammar) of cortex, then it must make some useful contact with other art forms (not just music) as well as other brain functions. Indeed, this is the case, and I will now present some simple examples.

MAPPING TRION EVOLUTIONS ONTO DANCE AND MOTION

The first contact that our trion model made with dance was through my long-time friend Janice Plastino, Professor of Dance here at U.C. Irvine. In 1991, Jan received the prestigious National Dance Association Scholar of the Year Award, which gave her the opportunity to have a new dance choreography performed at the national meeting in San Francisco. Jan's choreography was a "Structured Improvisation" based on one of Xiao's trion music compositions. Jan explained the basic essence of the trion model of the brain and the trion music, and then the dance was performed by 8 dancers from U.C. Irvine.

Shortly thereafter, I read an article in the *Los Angeles Times* about Margo Apostolos, who had recovered from cancer and now ran marathons. What intrigued me was that she was a Professor of Dance at the University of Southern California and her research specialty was doing choreography with big robot arms. She was the originator of this marvelous idea of mixing robots and humans in dance performance. I phoned her and suggested that she, Xiao, and I might collaborate on using the trion evolutions to instruct the computer in controlling movements of the big robot arms. Margo readily agreed and we set about to perform this fun experiment. It was done through a straightforward mapping onto the motion of the arm through its shoulder, elbow, and wrist (ignoring the motion of the fingers). Thus, with the evolution of one column of six trions as in Fig. 9.1B, we assigned two trions to control the motion of each of the three joints, as shown in Fig. 9.8.

The robot arm "danced" to the trion patterns and was accompanied by Xiao's trion music from the same Monte Carlo evolutions. The human eye could follow the visual robotic motions—the visual patterns of the trion evolutions—and listen to the trion music. The robotic movement appeared to be very closely matched to the trion patterns both visually and audially. Although strictly subjective, Margo judged that "the robot did in fact move in a dancelike fashion to the music." A videotape was made for further analysis. Again, Margo concluded that: "Specific movements in the videotape reveal an almost humanlike aspect to the motion. That is, the resemblance to movement programmed by a human choreographer was quite apparent. During the trion experiment, much of the robot movement appeared to be free-flowing rather than strictly governed by the **Cartesian coordinate system.**"

The next venture into trion-controlled movement was done by one of my talented summer undergraduate research students, Sharad Shanbhag [12]. Here, the ideas and mappings were very similar to that done with Margo and the robot arm, only Sharad programmed the movement of a two-dimensional arm on a computer screen using the mapping in Fig. 9.8. The goal of Sharad's project was to characterize the many interesting possible movements generated from a given repertoire of trion MPs. An example of Sharad's results is shown in Fig. 9.9.

The basic idea I had was that since the MPs can be *rapidly enhanced in a selective manner through the Hebb learning rule,* perhaps the trion model might be used to control robotic motion in novel situations in space missions on, for

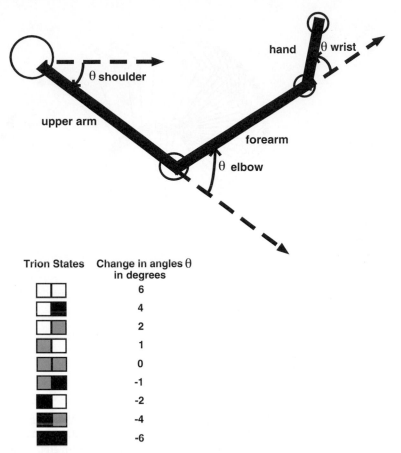

FIGURE 9.8   Trion states and corresponding changes in motion in joint angles θ of shoulder, elbow, and wrist for robotic motion. The trion creative evolutions in Fig. 9.1B were used to control the robot arm. Two trions, as shown, control the motion of each of the three joints.

example, Mars. Sharad and I only scratched the "surface" of this project, but I believe it holds much promise.

Two other projects of considerable technological promise, trion mapping onto speech and text recognition, are discussed next. Each of these studies would need considerable resources to test our proposals that they could produce useful technological devices. Our studies showed that the trion model had something useful to say in each of these projects. However, to produce a useful device, it must be better than existing ones in at least some crucial aspects. I would not know if this is the case without much further study.

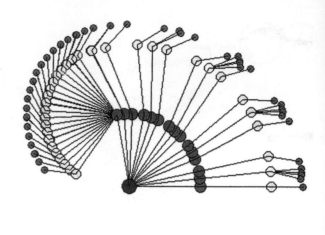

FIGURE 9.9   An example of a trion model evolution (on the left) mapped (using Fig. 9.8) onto a computer-simulated arm motion by Sharad Shanbhag. The time evolution of arm motion on the right starts with the lower horizontal segment.

TRION MODEL RECOGNITION AND SYNTHESIS OF SPEECH

Annette Ostling, another of my outstanding undergraduate summer students, achieved major results [13] during her 10-week stay in 1993. Using a very versatile commercial software package, she developed a program that analyzed spoken words into a small number (nine) of frequency bands. Annette determined a trionlike three-level rating in 0.025-sec time bins that could "recognize" these words. Her program then would reconstruct the recognizable spoken word from these relatively few trionlike parameters. All this was done with the able advice of Bob Atmur. Bob, an electronic technician in the U.C. Irvine Physics Department, had worked on speech recognition for the U.S. Army. The design of Annette's software program is shown in Fig. 9.10.

Annette achieved success to some degree with almost all the words that were reconstructed. Figure 9.11 shows the comparisons of original waveforms (as spoken by Annette) with her reconstructed ones for the two words "yet" and "yellow." The reconstructed speech produced was in general crude. However, the words spoken by the computer were clearly discernible. We concluded that a more robust and clear sound production could easily be produced with further optimization.

Trion Sampling

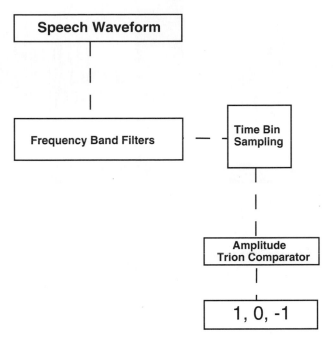

FIGURE 9.10 Annette Ostling's speech analysis. Her spoken words were recorded and analyzed by her software program first into nine frequency bands for discrete time bins of 0.025 sec. Then the resultant frequency band amplitudes determined a trionlike three-level rating in the 0.025-sec time bins that could "recognize" these words. Her program could then reconstruct the recognizable spoken word from these relatively few trionlike parameters.

WRITTEN TEXT RECOGNITION

The written text recognition project was the Ph.D. research of Milind Sardesai [14]. It was based on some ideas developed by David Horn and me [15] on the structure of visual cortex, and then very nicely implemented by Milind using the trion model. Following the **feature detector** Nobel Prize-winning work of Hubel and Wiesel [16], David and I proposed the presence of neurons in visual cortex that detected angles between lines (vertices) (Fig. 9.12). Milind then developed software that could recognize most printed letters (Fig. 9.13).

In the case of ambiguities, Milind used a mapping onto trion model patterns along with Hebb learning by selection to eliminate most of these ambiguities [17]. Although quite encouraging, much additional research and development

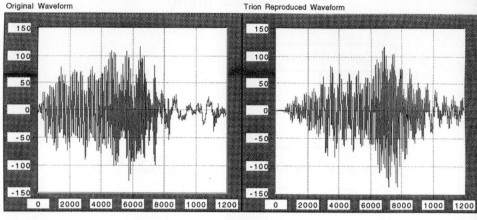

YET

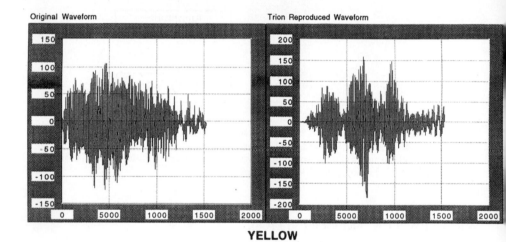

YELLOW

FIGURE 9.11   Waveform comparisons of original and reconstructed words for "yet" and "yellow" by Annette Ostling. Amplitude (vertical axis) is shown versus time (horizontal axis) in units of 0.001 sec.

would be necessary to tell if Milind's results could be advanced to a commercially useful device.

The main take home message of the successful research projects of Sharad, Annette, and Milind is that the trion model had some powerful and useful results that were relevant to these quite varied higher brain functions of sophisticated motor movement, speech recognition and production, and text recog-

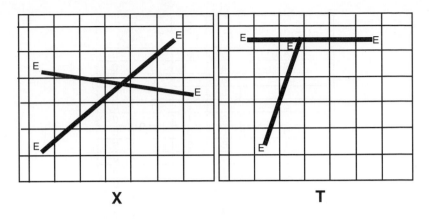

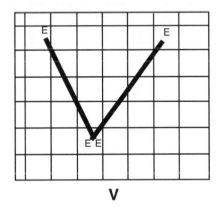

FIGURE 9.12   Types of feature detector neurons in visual cortical areas known (E) and proposed (V, T, and X) that would be excited by these three stimuli. For each stimulus, a grid is given to represent a schematic **visual** or **receptive field** with small regions R. There are the classic (Hubel and Wiesel) orientation-specific neurons for bars in a given region, R, of your visual field. E neurons detect bars ending in this R. V, T, and X neurons were proposed by David Horn and myself and used by Milind Sardesai in his written text recognition. V neurons detect V's of various wedge angles, X neurons detect line crossings, and T neurons detect a line stopping on another line as shown. Also shown are examples of visual presentations of V, T, and X stimuli and the features in each that would excite E neurons in the cortex. Courtesy of Milind Sardesai.

nition. I believe that these results provide major tests of the trion model, which we have proposed as a model for the internal neural language that is common throughout the cortex. Thus I consider these positive results to be very supportive of our ideas.

Letter	E	V	T	X
A	6	5	2	0
B	8	11	1	0
C	6	2	0	0
D	8	6	0	0
E	7	2	1	0
F	5	1	1	0
H	6	0	2	0
I	6	0	2	0
J	8	2	1	0
L	4	1	0	0
M	8	3	0	0
N	6	2	0	0
P	6	2	1	0
T	4	0	1	0
U	6	2	0	0
V	4	1	0	0
W	8	3	0	0
X	4	0	0	1
Y	6	3	0	0
Z	6	2	0	0

FIGURE 9.13   Detection of printed letters by software written by Milind Sardesai using E, V, T, and X neurons. Note that there are several ambiguities that cannot be distinguished by these classifications. Milind distinguished these ambiguities by mappings onto trion model evolutions.

Now, let's look at some visual art representations of the trion model in this same spirit.

TRION MODEL VISUAL ART

Xiao Leng made no attempt to produce visual art forms from the trion model. Our first thought of this possible relevance came when Xiao and I were meeting with Margo in a diner discussing our mapping of Xiao's trion patterns to control the robotic arm. In addition to the Monte Carlo evolutions from a single cortical column of trions, Xiao was showing Margo some of the Monte Carlo evolutions of three coupled columns (see Chapter 10). Our waiter looked at Xiao's two pictures and immediately said, "Wow, that one looks like Indian belt designs." Since then, numerous viewers have agreed with his statement. One of Xiao's Monte Carlo evolutions [18] is shown in Fig. 9.14 (see color insert).

I would like to tie together the varied applications of the trion model in this chapter with some insightful comments by the late giant of brain theory, David Marr. In his classic book "Vision," he said [19]:

Let us look at the the range of perspectives that must be satisfied before one can be said, from a human and scientific perspective, to have understood visual perception. First, and I think foremost, there is the perspective of the plain man. He knows what it is to see, and unless the bones of one's arguments and theories roughly correspond to what this person knows to be true at first hand, one will probably be wrong.... Second, there is the perspective of the brain scientists, the physiologists and anatomists who know a great deal about how the nervous system is built and how parts of it behave.... And the same argument applies to the experimental psychologist. On the other hand, someone ... with a small home computer ... wants the explanation ... telling him what to program.... He doesn't want to know about rhodopsin, or the lateral geniculate nucleus, or inhibitory interneurons. He wants to know how to program vision.

It is in this spirit that it is crucial to see if my ideas about music and other higher brain functions make sense on all three of David Marr's points. Clearly, my colleagues and I are at the very beginning of this endeavor, which started with Xiao's work, to use music as a window to understand how we think, reason, and create, and to enhance these abilities.

Trion Model of Higher Brain Function: Prediction that Music Enhances Spatial-Temporal Reasoning

BRIEF GUIDE

I generalize the trion model from the previous two chapters. The role of neuromodulators is introduced in a highly schematic manner. Then I address the prediction that music can enhance spatial-temporal reasoning. This chapter is meant to be readable by everyone, however, it does contain theoretical concepts.

I have described the theoretical results relevant to music and other higher brain functions obtained from a *single* and from *four* coupled columns of trions. The latter has given us the first hints of an inherent grammar that results from the structured Mountcastle columnar principle for mammalian cortex. I believe that these results on the neural grammar are major ones. I will return later to these ideas, in particular the role of *symmetry*, to help decode the internal

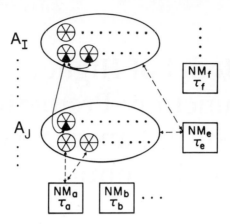

FIGURE 10.1   Highly schematic diagram of our trion model for higher brain function. The circles represent cortical columns and the pie wedges represent minicolumns or our idealized trions. The ovals represent cortical areas A_I and the solid arrows represent connections between (neurons in) minicolumns with similar modalities, represented by shaded minicolumns (such as orientation response) in the same area as well as different areas (see Fig. 8.21). The squares represent neuro-modulators (NM) and are proposed by us to have various periodic timescales τ of seconds up to hours (see Fig. 7.7), as well as various spatial scales. NM_a and NM_e have spatial scales at the columnar and cortical area sizes, respectively.

spatial-temporal code for higher brain function. I want to generalize the trion model and propose that the concepts presented in Chapters 8 and 9 should hold true under a wider range of assumptions.

First I consider a general schematic diagram of the trion model of higher brain function put forth by Xiao Leng and me (Fig. 10.1) [1]. Consider a system of interacting cortical areas, each composed of interacting cortical column trion networks. The interactions between columns consists of connections between (neurons in) minicolumns with similar modalities, represented by shaded mini-columns (such as orientation response in the same cortical area as well as different areas). These intercolumnar connections between minicolumns are in general taken to be roughly an order of magnitude less than those in the same column.

Our highly schematic treatment of neuromodulation will follow the spatial and temporal scales introduced in Fig. 7.7. The temporal scales range from 0.025 sec up to 24 hours, and spatial scales from a single column to a cortical area. We implement this role at, for example, the columnar scale by having them modulate either a common threshold for firing for a column or the fluc-tuation temperature parameter T.

The incredible precision in the temporal reproducibility of music mental rehearsal of music performance (see Chapter 11) led us to propose a series of new neuronal timescales in higher brain function from seconds to minutes in order to "reset" the phases of the sophisticated spatial-temporal firing patterns in the cortex (as in Fig. 7.2). Just as there exists a series of spatial scales from the single neuron to the 10^{10} neurons in the cortex (see Fig. 7.7), we proposed that there are a series of temporal scales from the single neuron timescale of 0.001 sec to the higher brain function timescale of up to the diurnal rhythm of a day, or 100,000 seconds.

We implement these timescales in our model of higher brain function through periodicities of "neuromodulators" that control the firing threshold and the fluctuation parameter T of the cortical column networks in the trion model. The resulting spatial-temporal patterns represent the higher brain function of the internal language of the brain, that is, how it communicates with itself when performing higher cognitive processes. It is understood that one crucial role of these neuromodulators is to signal the importance or emotional content of an external situation that a person is experiencing.

I propose that in addition to the time-dependent release of neuromodulators in response to external stimuli, there are series of natural periodic rhythmic variations.

As presented in Chapter 9, these neuromodulators [2], through control of the fluctuation parameter T, change the trion model evolutions back and forth from the sequential mode to the creative mode.

I suggest that the concepts, ideas, and predictions from the trion model will hold under much more neurobiologically realistic conditions. For example:

(i) We have shown [3] that allowing a breaking of symmetry of 20% for the connections among the trions reduces the number of MPs in the repertoire from 1804 to 883, still a very large number. *This demonstrates the robustness of the model.*

(ii) For simplicity, the trion model assumes that there are three levels of firing for the minicolumn. However, real cortical data may require more than three levels to adequately understand the cortical language for higher brain function. We have readily generalized the trion model to five levels of firing for the minicolumn. Further, instead of having the column of minicolumns connected in the ringlike structure of Fig. 7.1, Dennis Silverman and I considered a two-dimensional array. A Monte Carlo evolution with both of these features, five levels of firing and a 7 × 7 array of minicolumns in the column was calculated by Dennis [4].

(iii) All the minicolumns or trions in a column need not have the same number of constituent neurons [5]. This is clearly shown in Fig. 8.26, where the factor $g(0)/g(+/-)$ related to the number of neurons was allowed to decrease in one trion in a column. A large decrease was required before it changed the behavior of the system of connected columns.

The bases for our generalization of music to other similar higher brain functions rest on the concepts that (a) they share the same built-in Mountcastle columnar neural language (and grammar) in terms of inherent spatial-temporal firing patterns and (b) all higher brain functions utilize many of the same cortical areas.

These inherent spatial-temporal patterns correspond to the concrete information for the specific higher brain function configured in appropriate "chunks" (for example, five or more piece configurations in chess or themes in music). The evolutions in natural sequences (related by certain symmetries) correspond to analysis of this information both sequentially and creatively (see Fig. 9.1). *Further, although each different higher brain function will crucially depend on specific different cortical areas and systems, I suggest that many of the "higher" cortical areas are involved in each higher brain function at some important level.* The EEG coherence studies of Petsche [6] and his collaborators clearly show this. Different mappings or translations will be involved in each higher brain function, with much more complex mappings than we have used for the music mapping shown in Chapter 9. *It is the internal neural language of the brain that is the same for the various higher brain functions.*

Clearly, human memory is still not well understood by neuroscientists. However, it is also clearly not too soon to investigate the higher brain functions of thinking, reasoning, and creating, all of which involve memory. As I have presented in this chapter and Chapters 8 and 9, in our trion model, *the MPs or memory patterns in the brain are the basic building blocks of higher brain function. It is an inherent ability of the cortex to use the symmetric families of these MPs to recognize related patterns, and the inherent natural temporal sequences of the MPs that are the crucial concepts. Again, I stress that our program is to investigate higher brain function using music as a window.*

If I had to summarize Part II in one word, it would of course be "symmetry." I suggest that a more realistic understanding of the cortex would still involve an inherent and highly structured Mountcastle-like anatomy involving symmetry. This in turn would yield an inherent internal language and grammar for mammalian cortex in which the ability to recognize symmetries in spatial-temporal patterns is built-in. This is why symmetry is part of our thinking, reasoning, creativity, music, and ideals of beauty.

Now I turn to the crucial behavioral and neurophysiological experiments that not only have tested, but fortunately have supported and extended, our theoretical ideas.

Tests of Predictions in Human Behavior

BRIEF GUIDE

The four chapters in Part III contain all the details of the dramatic behavioral experiments that I have done with humans involving music. This does not include those behavioral experiments relevant to neuropathologies or those with animals, which I will present in later chapters. All of this material should be readable by everyone, except for one section in Chapter 13, which, as I will point out, is more technical and can be skimmed.

Tests of Predictions in Human Behavior

CHAPTER 11

Highly Accurate Mental Rehearsals: Correlation with Top Performance in Sports

---

BRIEF GUIDE

This material on the remarkable temporal reproducibility of mental rehearsals contains some of my favorite stories. It is meant to be interesting, entertaining, and readable, especially to anyone who follows sports. I hope you might even consider doing several of these simple experiments to follow up on some of my ideas.

Leslie Brothers and I [1] argued that standard laboratory experiments, in which neural responses are measured within the half-second or so after the presentation of a stimulus, do not probe some of the most interesting features of higher brain function. We offered the analogy that it is more sensible to study the musical characteristics of a violin by playing the sorts of musical sequences that the violin is specifically designed to beautifully produce rather than to scrape a bow across the strings in a random manner. Extending this analogy to understanding higher brain function, we suggest that *it is important to focus on the high end of the range of cognitive tasks, by examining the performances of professionals in highly trained demanding tasks.*

It is with this goal in mind that I acknowledge the seminal role that the late Frieda Belinfante had in this story. She was a simply amazing lady, an accomplished conductor and cellist who is a legend in her homeland of Holland. In the 1930s she founded a chamber music group in Amsterdam, and became (perhaps) the first woman conductor of an all-professional orchestra anywhere in the world. When Holland was invaded by Germany in 1940, Frieda began counterfeiting non-Jewish identification cards for Jewish acquaintances. The effort became a large covert operation. In 1943, to keep the operation from being exposed, Frieda and her resistance colleagues blew up the document room of Amsterdam's City Hall. Her operation was later infiltrated and destroyed. Frieda was only one of two who escaped. Illegally crossing borders on foot in the winter, she crossed the mountains to Switzerland in 1944. After the war, she returned to Amsterdam.

On a lighter note, Frieda once told me the following story. Just before blowing up City Hall, the operation needed funds and so she went to her friend Mr. Heineken, head of the Heineken Brewery, and asked for some money. He replied that he could not support her operation, but that he could buy her cello from her, which he did. After the war ended and Frieda returned to Amsterdam, Heineken gave Frieda her cello back.

Frieda moved to southern California in 1947. Here she made many major contributions in bringing music to Orange County. She was my daughter Robin's cello teacher, which was how I met her and developed our friendship. She died at the age of 90 in 1995.

Frieda often spoke to me about the accurate timing in the mental rehearsal (MR) of music. It was part of her normal rehearsal routine to mentally "conduct," in silence with eyes closed, a piece of music that she was preparing for performance with her orchestra. *She would mentally image the members of the orchestra performing and mentally hear them play while she mentally conducted.*

Mental rehearsal is an extremely high level brain function that is routinely performed, for example, by many musicians, dancers, athletes, pilots, and surgeons. Anecdotally, and in some controlled studies, these MRs are known to complement actual rehearsals of the highly skilled task in improving performance [2]. It is also known that the temporal duration of actual performances, for example, of a piece of music by the same group or same conductor, is highly reproducible. Of course, there is lots of feedback during an actual performance, which makes these results not of special interest in understanding higher brain function. However, Frieda said that the durations D of the MRs could be highly reproducible. In this situation, there is no external feedback, and thus reproducible D's for the high-level MRs could be of enormous interest in brain science, because lower-level MRs of cognitive tasks show substantial variation in temporal duration.

The significance of this is that the D's *must* be highly reproducible for the Mountcastle code of higher brain function to be *viable*. Otherwise, the columnar spatial-temporal patterns in our trion model would get fuzzier and wash out during a 1-minute reasoning process without sensory input. Thus, testing Frieda's statements would be my first experimental test of the trion model. One cannot prove a brain theory model with one such test (or even several), but we could disprove the trion model with a negative result in the MR experiments.

My collaborator Leslie and I proposed that

all higher brain function of substantial difficulty for sustained time of greater than a few seconds requires extremely accurate timing for the organized firing of groups of neurons over large regions of cortex.

We then set out to test this with our MR experiments. We found that the MRs of musical performance of several minutes' duration can be highly reproducible, with D's varying by less than 1% [3]. These remarkable results pose fundamental neurophysiological problems: It is necessary to understand the underlying neuronal bases for this accuracy without sensory input or feedback. Also, these results present a powerful constraint on neuronal models of brain function. In particular, our trion model survived its first experimental test. Further, we suggested that our results on the MRs may provide an extremely useful behavioral correlate for high-level performance. (Our interesting but inconclusive attempts to test this further prediction in sports are presented in the following.)

We tested these ideas by looking at Frieda's durations of MRs while she was preparing for a symphony orchestra performance. Consider a variation V in the average time duration $\overline{D}$ (the average is denoted by "bar") of a series of MR trials as

$$V \text{ equals } \sigma/\overline{D}$$

where σ is a measure of variation of D in the trials and is further explained in Chapter 13. It is this **normalized or scaled quantity** V that I can compare to other experiments and to theoretical expectations. Frieda's results are shown in Table 11.1.

I then asked my colleague Jan Plastino (see Chapter 9) if she could help Leslie Brothers and me get some dancers as subjects. Again, it is fairly standard for dancers to do MRs in addition to their actual rehearsals as they get ready for a dance production. The results $\overline{D}$ for three dancers were remarkably reproducible [4]. The fourth dancer performed MRs on a 6-minute piece and her $\overline{D}$ was not as accurate. Six minutes is a long time to dance, and this dancer said

TABLE 11.1   Reproducibility of MR orchestra performances by the conductor Frieda Belinfante. $\overline{D}$ is the average of the times D of the MRs, σ is a measure of variations in the D's, and V is simply the ratio $\sigma/\overline{D}$. In the final stages of rehearsal as compared to the early stages, the V for each movement has decreased from about 3% to about 1.5%. The size of these V's is remarkably small.

	Early stages			Final stages		
	$\overline{D}$ (sec)	σ (sec)	V (%)	$\overline{D}$ (sec)	σ (sec)	V (%)
First movement	146	4	2.7	160.5	2.5	1.6
Second movement	113	4	3.5	121.5	1.5	1.2
Third movement	212	8	3.8	234	4	1.7

afterward that the MR experience was fatiguing and that she noted difficulty in maintaining her concentration.

These results were dramatic, but were all self-reporting, that is, the subjects recorded their own MR data for the durations in a notebook and gave them to us. A controlled experiment was needed to confirm these results.

The next subjects were highly trained adult (male) musicians. Each did a series of mental rehearsals of one or more pieces of familiar music in our laboratory. Each had previously used mental rehearsals, with eyes closed and imaging the performance *both* visually and audially, as a means of practicing, in addition to the actual rehearsal while playing his instrument. Table 11.2 shows the MR data for subjects rs and et [5]. They started a stopwatch at the beginning of the MR and stopped it at the end of the MR. The face of the stopwatch was

TABLE 11.2   Extremely accurate reproducibility of MR of music by two highly trained adult (male) musicians, rs and et. The number of MRs is given as the number of **trials**.

rs: Mental rehearsals playing the trumpet

Music	Number of trials	$\overline{D}$ (sec)	σ (sec)	V (%)
F.J. Haydn trumpet	3	51.25	0.51	1.00
solo from "Trumpet Concerto"	3	57.73	0.26	0.44

et: Mental rehearsals playing percussion

Music	Number of trials	$\overline{D}$ (sec)	σ (sec)	V (%)
"Sweet Lullaby" (own composition)	3	90.72	0.84	0.92

TABLE 11.3   *Remarkable reproducibility* of mental imaging (MI) data by an 11-year-old girl. She mentally imaged the block in her bedroom and counted as the visualized second hand moved. *This is a very high level cognitive task.*

	Trial	D (sec)	$\overline{D}$ (sec)	σ (sec)	V (%)
Counting to 50	1	49.12			
	2	49.12			
	3	49.01	49.08	0.05	0.11
Counting to 100	1	99.03			
	2	99.22			
	3	99.28	99.18	0.11	0.11

covered and the time was not seen by the subject. We would record the temporal duration D of the MR and reset the stopwatch. They were able to obtain V's of less than 1% in pieces having lasting from 40 to 90 sec.

Another subject, jl, is an 11-year-old girl with an IQ over 150. She is exceptional at a number of higher brain functions, including chess, music, math, and languages. During our experiment with jl [6], she was asked to count both to 50 and to 100 with her eyes closed. Each task was performed three times. She pressed a computer key when she started her **mental imaging** (MI), and again at the finish of the MI so that the temporal durations were directly recorded on the computer. She told us that she did her counting by mentally imaging the clock in her bedroom and counting as the visualized second hand moved. I leave it to you to verify that this is a very high level cognitive task! These remarkable results are shown in Table 11.3.

These findings appear to be paradoxical in relation to other observations. For one thing, our subjects' superaccurate performances seem to contradict both intuitive and experimentally determined notions of timing capabilities. For example, a study by Michon [7] of 12 normal subjects practiced in estimating time durations showed an average error of 28% in estimating a 10-sec interval. Second, the amount of variability in our subjects' performances (less than 2% for durations of 3 minutes or less) is far less than the roughly 10% variability that an individual neuron shows in its response to a stimulus in a neurophysiological experiment [8]. *These results demonstrate smaller temporal variability in extensive and sophisticated brain activity than in the individual components.*

I suggest that the striking mental rehearsal and mental imaging data in Tables 11.1–11.3 impose a profound constraint on the underlying neurophysiological behavior of the brain. Billions of neurons (or millions of cortical minicolumns, the basic Mountcastle spatial scale; see Fig. 7.7) are undoubtedly involved in these very high level tasks (see, for example, the EEG correlation studies of Petsche [9] when his subjects perform mental rehearsals of music performance). These MR and MI data are for durations of at least 50 sec. *The V's for our subjects were as low as 0.1%.* This should be contrasted with the well-known large temporal variability of the spike train response in an individual cortical neuron to a sensory stimulus.

Thus, in these higher-level brain functions, we are observing extensive neuronal activity patterns with considerably less variability than found in their individual components. It is necessary to understand the underlying neuronal bases for this apparently paradoxical accuracy in the spatial-temporal activity of billions of neurons occurring over minutes without sensory input. *These results were necessary to ensure the viability of the Mountcastle code for higher brain function.* In turn, these results were also necessary for the viability of the trion model (which has a built-in time step) and its relevance to understanding the neuronal basis of some aspects of music. Of course, these results do not rule out other neuronal models, but provide a very powerful constraint.

As mentioned earlier, mental rehearsals are often used by top-level musicians, dancers, athletes, surgeons, and pilots to improve their performance. Studies have documented the value of these mental rehearsals in achieving this result. We speculated that the temporal reproducibility of the MRs over several trials would provide a predictor of the actual behavioral level of performance: Small V's should indicate that a subsequent actual performance would be at a high level. I set out to test this. Before describing this long endeavor, I want to describe some self-reporting data that are relevant to a highly accurate internal clock in the brain that could play a role in the data we obtained.

INTERNAL CLOCK

The existence of an accurate and *accessible* clock in the human central nervous system is suggested by data on timed self-awakening. Though the ability to accurately self-awaken has been known for some time, formal studies have yielded only a few good instances of it. With some exceptions, less-than-impressive performances have been reported in the literature [10]. One reason seems to be that the sleep lab setting, with all its paraphernalia, disrupts the sleeper's performance. Another is that often subjects have been recruited without regard to whether they were accurate self-awakeners at home. Such studies have shown, however, that for the individuals that could produce accurate timed awakening in the lab, repeated awakening, checking, and returning to sleep was not the mechanism responsible, nor were environmental cues.

We conducted a test of self-awakening on my colleague Virginia Trimble of the U.C. Irvine Physics Department, who is a self-reported accurate awakener. Virginia is a renowned astrophysicist with a truly phenomenal memory, and is

TABLE 11.4   Timed self-awakenings of Virginia Trimble. The asterisk indicates that her alarm was miss-set. Her average ΔT/T was 1.4%, which is a remarkable result. Note the range of bedtimes and of planned awakening times, which reduces the possibility that timing was influenced by external factors.

Bedtime (P.M.)	Planned awakening time (A.M.)	Actual awakening time (A.M.)	ΔT (min)	T (min)	ΔT/T (%)
11:30	6:45	6:40	5	435	1.1
10:00	6:45	6:45	<1	525	<0.2
11:40	7:30	7:28	2	478	0.4
10:00	6:20*	6:30	10	500	2.0
10:30	5:37	5:25	12	427	2.8
9:30	5:30	5:25	5	480	1.0
10:35	6:00	6:00	<1	445	<0.2
11:00	7:00	6:55	5	480	1.0
9:23	5:30	5:20	10	487	2.1
9:20	6:00	5:55	5	520	1.0
9:30	5:30	5:10	20	480	4.2
10:15	6:00	5:52	8	465	1.7
9:30	6:00	5:58	2	510	0.4

the author of numerous review articles in many areas of astrophysics. I remember asking her about some details on her famous review paper on dark matter (apparently only a small percentage of the matter in the universe is observable, hence the term dark matter), which contained over 600 references. She knew (and could evaluate) all of the main points of these references. Leslie and I felt that Virginia would be a good candidate to test for accurate self-awakening.

On thirteen nights in September, 1988, Virginia recorded her lights out time, her planned awakening time, and her actual awakening time. Note that results in Table 11.4 show that planned awakening times varied, thus reducing the possibility that environmental cues determined the awakening times. The striking finding is that Virginia's behavior is extremely accurate in the time domain, showing an average error of less than 2% in matching the actual duration of sleep to the planned duration. *This performance suggests the operation in the brain of a continuously accessed clock.*

How are these results in Table 11.4 possible? That clocks may exist in many animal brains—perhaps implemented in a variety of ways—is suggested by the extremely accurate navigation performance of insects. Sun–compass direction is expressed by honeybees [11] in the waggle dance describing food location: since the sun's position changes continuously, the dance must vary as well in order to maintain accuracy. Honeybees are able to update the dance continuously while remaining in darkness, an ability that would seem to depend on a "continuously consulted clock." Such clocks can apparently be read to an accuracy of 8 minutes per day, or about 0.5% accuracy.

As noted in Chapter 7, one way to account for the maintenance of extremely specific spatial-temporal patterns is to invoke "orchestration" by a central clock or pacemaker. The existence of intrinsic pacemakers in brains has been known for some time. Best studied are the circadian (roughly 24-hour) pacemakers localized in the brain of a variety of animals [12]. I introduced earlier the concept of many temporal scales in the brain between that of one second and the circadian period (see Fig. 7.7). In Chapter 21 I will discuss how this may relate to the clinical treatment of mental disorders.

Now I turn to a series of *noncontrolled* experiments that I have had a lot of fun with.

HIGH-LEVEL PERFORMANCE IN SPORTS AND MR TIME DURATION REPRODUCIBILITY

Leslie Brothers and I speculated that the temporal reproducibility of the MRs over several trials might provide a predictor of the actual behavioral level of performance: Small V's should indicate that a subsequent actual performance would be high level. I decided to test this idea in sports for which there was a quantitative measure of performance. Let us call the entire program **quantitative MR** or **QMR**.

Just imagine the consequences if I was able to show that this idea is correct:

Consider a coach knowing which of his players would be in the "zone" for the next game where they would perform far above their average performance by employing our QMR.

I knew that the famous world record holder and dominant 400-meter hurdler Edwin Moses (who, by the way, has a university degree in physics) worked out on the U.C. Irvine track. Clearly, running hurdles involves accurate timing. So I walked out to the track one afternoon and looked around for Moses. Not seeing him, I asked another athlete if he knew Moses' schedule, telling him briefly what I had in mind. This athlete, Daniel Young, had been a world-class 110-meter high hurdler. He told me that I really should try out my ideas on the high hurdles, and he was just the person to work with the QMR program.

The 10 high hurdles are 107 cm high, placing an extreme premium on form and timing. As Daniel emphasized, unlike other track events, where you must react to your competitors' moves, the 110-meter high hurdles is a performance where you must not change your stride in between hurdles from what you had

TABLE 11.5   Results of Daniel Young's MRs for the 110-meter high hurdles. Not only were the $\overline{D}$'s approaching world-class performance times, but the variations V were decreasing.

Date (1991)	Number of trials	$\overline{D}$ (sec)	σ (sec)	V (%)
6/6	8	17.14	2.21	12.8
6/7	8	15.21	1.40	9.2
6/8	6	15.08	1.06	7.0
6/13	9	14.10	0.82	5.8
6/17	10	13.64	0.33	2.4
6/19	7	13.51	0.72	5.3

planned. Daniel had just missed being on the U.S. Olympic team in 1984, was injured in 1988, and was starting to train for the 1992 Olympics. He had regularly used MRs in his training, and was eager to test my ideas on the reproducibility of the temporal durations correlating with performance. His goals were not only to make the Olympic team in 1992, but to run the 110-meter high hurdles in a world record time (less than 12.9 seconds).

The data for Daniel's MRs for a two-week period are shown in Table 11.5. These results were very encouraging: Not only was the average duration $\overline{D}$ approaching the world-class performance times that Daniel was working toward on the track, but the variations V were decreasing. On the track, Daniel was doing 2 and 3 hurdles, working up toward the whole 10 hurdles. This was in addition to his sprinting workouts. He also did some MRs on these smaller segments, which were also very encouraging.

Unfortunately, Daniel sustained a serious leg injury during training that forced him to abandon any comeback to competitive form. However, he and I both felt that his brief experience with the QMR program was quite encouraging. Further, we had discovered two very important points that should be explicitly included in the QMR program. We decided to apply our modified QMR program to **free throws in basketball**. Daniel was a decent basketball player with above average free throw ability, so he became the subject.

Table 11.6 presents the results of our free throw experiment. Daniel and I thought that these initial results were very good. We worked out several important features:

(i) It was important to differentiate between MRs as visualized by Daniel *from outside* his body and his visualization from his perspective outward. *It was only when he visualized outward that his D's were accurate.* (We later confirmed this with other subjects.)

TABLE 11.6   Results of Daniel Young for basketball free throws. Included are the number of free throws made out of 100 actual attempts on four occasions. Comparison to the MR $\overline{D}$'s are the average duration times on three occasions when I timed his actual free throws.

Date (1992)	Number of trials	$\overline{D}$ (sec)	σ (sec)	V (%)
7/21	10	6.71	0.96	14.3
7/21	Perform free throws (10 sets of 10): Made 66 of 100			
7/22	10	6.36	1.21	19.1
7/25	10	6.19	0.33	5.3
7/27	10	5.92	0.33	5.6
7/28	10	4.42	0.41	9.7
7/28	Perform free throws (10 sets of 10): Made 74 of 100			
7/28	Timed actual free throws: $\overline{D}$ equal to 3.43			
7/28	10	4.36	0.44	10.1
7/31	10	3.18	0.44	13.8
7/31	Peform free throws (10 sets of 10): Made 74 of 100			
7/31	10	2.89	0.24	6.9
7/31	Perform free throws (10 sets of 10): Made 79 of 100			
	Timed actual free throws: $\overline{D}$ equal to 3.09			
8/2	10	3.40	0.14	4.1

(ii) Using a camcorder, I took a video of Daniel's best performances for him to view before doing MRs. Keeping feature (i) in mind, I stood on a chair behind him to try to get the video perspective we wanted.

(iii) It was useful for Daniel to note responses during a MR, for example, "good routine, clear vision to basket, made shot," or "lost focus, did not see ball in the air or go through," or "lost focus and regained it, made shot."

(iv) We started having Daniel do a set of three MRs following a "poor" set of 10 actual free throws (see Table 11.6). It seemed that this improved his percentage made on the next set of 10.

We felt that we had the details of our QMR program well worked out and that we were ready to seriously try it out "Big Time" with a National Basketball Association (NBA) team. It seemed that the ideal situation would be to work with professional, highly motivated athletes who had been practicing their free throws daily for many years. If we succeeded, it was clear to us that the relatively little personal attention we gave the NBA players could not be the reason for their improved performance, but the details of our QMR program. Poor free throw performance by even some of the superstars continues to plague almost every NBA team. We believe that our QMR program could enhance the free throw performance of those athletes who were able to do MRs, especially in the clutch situations at the end of close games.

I had been a Los Angeles Lakers fan since I came to California over 30 years ago, following Jerry West and Elgin Baylor, two of the all-time basketball greats. Thus I wrote to "my hero" Jerry West, who was now the Laker General Manager:

Mr. Jerry West, General Manager June 9, 1993
Los Angeles Lakers
PO Box 10
Inglewood CA 90306

Dear Mr. West:

My research team and I have developed a program which we believe will substantially improve the free throwing percentage during games. It involves doing mental rehearsals of the free throws with our new quantitative measure of these rehearsals. I would like to meet with you to discuss our pilot studies and show you the data which support our ideas and detail the program we wish to work with the Lakers on.

I would very much like to work with the Lakers this coming season to prove our program works. I will not contact any other team unless you do not wish to work with us. I have chosen the Lakers to contact first since a) I have been a Lakers fan for over 30 years, and b) I consider you one of the smartest men in basketball, on and off the court.

I understand that the Draft is coming up at the end of June and you will be extremely busy then. I could meet with you next Wednesday or Thursday at your convenience. It will not take much time to explain our program.
I look forward to hearing from you.
Best wishes,
Gordon Shaw
Professor of Physics

To my delight, in July I had a message on my voice-mail from Jerry West saying that I should contact the new Lakers head coach Randy Pfund. An NBA summer league for rookies and tryouts was being held on the U.C. Irvine campus, and Daniel and I arranged to meet with Randy Pfund there. Our meeting went very well and he proposed that Daniel and I should go to Hawaii in September to work with the Lakers in their training camp. It remained for him to work out the details. This was very exciting for an old sports fan like me.

However, it did not happen. We had a few subsequent, encouraging phone conversations with Randy, but our "tryout" with the Lakers fell through. Daniel left Irvine for an opportunity in Colorado, and I have not heard from him since. Two years later in June 1995, I wrote a somewhat more detailed letter to every head coach in the NBA about our QMR program. I got no positive response from any team. The response from then Laker head coach Del Harris read: "Gordon, Thanks for your note but our staff has great coaches including West,

Magic, Coop, etc. Del H." Since our research program detailed in this book has expanded in such a successful manner that I no longer have the time to pursue our QMR program, I bequeath the details in this chapter for others to pursue. I still believe in its potential for success.

One final point should be investigated. After Daniel left, I started working with two basketball neophytes on the QMR program, my colleague Fran Rauscher and my lab research assistant Wendy Dennis. Franny and Wendy added a new feature to the mental rehearsals by preceding them with listening to "our" Mozart Sonata for Two Pianos in D Major (K.448) (see Chapter 12). There was a hint in their data that there might be an *optimum delay period of some minutes between the listening condition and the MRs* for giving an enhancement in the mental rehearsal timings. An undergraduate student, Dinoo Daewer, is starting to investigate this in a related experiment.

This discussion illustrates a general feature of my research: The idea in question to be tested may indeed prove to be correct, however, I am just not clever enough to come up with a good enough experimental design. Thus, even years later, I may return to the original idea with a new way to investigate it. I will never stop believing that there is much more to learn about higher brain function from the work started some 10 years ago by Leslie Brothers and me on these accurate mental rehearsals. Perhaps after reading this chapter, someone else will be able to clearly show the correlation of this ability to do accurate mental rehearsals with the enhancement of the actual performance.

Listening to Mozart Sonata (K.448) Enhances Spatial-Temporal Reasoning: The "Mozart Effect"

BRIEF GUIDE

I have been asked many questions about the fascinating and dramatic experimental finding of the Mozart effect. Of course, I don't have all the answers you would like to hear, but I will address some questions in this chapter (such as how we chose this particular Mozart sonata) and other questions later on.

As I described in the Prologue, I hired Frances Rauscher in August, 1992, to be my postdoctoral research associate. The daughter of two professors of music at the Manhattan School of Music, Franny started on her career as a concert cellist at the age of 3. She abandoned this first love at the age of 24, and to follow her second love, she went to Columbia University to get her B.S. and Ph.D. in experimental psychology.

Immediately after arrival in my lab, Franny set out to test the predictions of Xiao Leng and myself that music training for young children would act as exercise for higher brain function, in particular spatial-temporal reasoning. I describe this dramatically successful story in Chapter 13. However, it became clear that with our extremely limited resources, this study would take years. One day in December, 1992, Franny and I were sitting in the lab discussing long-range strategy when we realized that if music training might yield a long-term enhancement of spatial-temporal reasoning, then perhaps even listening to music might produce a short-term enhancement! This seemed like a great idea, since by using U.C. Irvine college students as subjects we could quickly and cheaply do the experiment to test this hypothesis.

We decided to use three listening conditions: silence, a relaxation tape, and a selection by Mozart. (I devote a section of Chapter 13 to discuss in general the designing of experiments and analyzing the data.) It was clear to us that we should use Mozart. As I discussed in Chapters 9 and 10, Xiao and I had the idea that specific music might optimally "resonate" (Fig. 12.1) with the inherent internal neural language resulting from the structured Mountcastle columnar principle of mammalian cortex.

Mozart began composing at the age of three. Later on, it is reported that *he would sometimes write down music composed entirely in his head and then not change one note.* The magic genius of Mozart perhaps displayed a supreme use of the inherent internal cortical language in his music. The Mountcastle cortical language resulting from the columnar structure has (i) families of spatial-temporal memory firing patterns related by symmetries and used in higher brain function and (ii) natural sequences of these patterns. The details of these features (as seen in the trion model) are not known. Nor do we know what in Mozart's music, and what other music, gives the enhancements that Franny and I found in spatial-temporal reasoning. I describe an ambitious neurophysiological project in Chapters 16 and 17, using Mozart's genius to help answer these questions and to help decode this inherent Mountcastle language in mammalian cortex.

CHOOSING THE MOZART SONATA FOR TWO PIANOS IN D MAJOR (K.448)

The choice of the specific Mozart composition that we were to use was left to Franny's expertise. As she describes it:

> We [Franny and composer friend, now husband, Danny] picked that Mozart Sonata because it is composed of a limited number of musical motives which appear in symmetry a number of times. It's an extremely organized composition. The fact that

FIGURE 12.1   Highly simplified, but familiar example of **resonance**. When you push someone on a swing, you must take into account the period of the swing. If you want your push to add to the motion, not subtract from it, the temporal phase of your push is crucial. If you do this properly, your pushes resonate with the swing and keep building the amplitude of the swing. Children immediately grasp these concepts. When I talk about the music of Mozart resonating with the inherent neural structure of the cortex, I envision enormously sophisticated spatial-temporal processes throughout the cortex, about which we know little. See Chapter 15 on EEGs and the Mozart effect and our suggested experiment to test this resonance concept.

it's a two piano sonata made it even more appealing, because there are more opportunities for the motives to evolve from one piano to the next. Basically, we just listened to tons of compositions, and this one seemed the most appropriate—cerebral.

After some days, Franny came in and proceeded to play the CD of the Mozart Sonata for Two Pianos in D Major (K.448) as recorded by Murray Perahia and Radu Lupu. It seemed perfect to me: "intellectual," complex, and riveting. It remains so after the *innumerable* times I have heard it over the past 6 years, never boring, always profound (to my untrained musical sense).

As noted by Mozart biographer Alfred Einstein [1] regarding the Mozart Sonata (K.448):

> This work is gallant from beginning to end; it has the form and the thematic material of an ideal sinfonia for an opera buff; no cloud obscures its gaiety. But the art with which the two parts are made completely equal, the play of the dialogue, the delicacy and refinement of the figuration, the feeling for sonority in the combination and explorations of the different registers of the two instruments—all of these things exhibit such mastery that this apparently "superficial" and entertaining work is at the same time one of the most profound and mature of all Mozart's compositions.

In hindsight, I believe that there is something extremely special about this Mozart Sonata (K.448), and in particular the first movement. Other music (by Mozart or Bach or others) might give comparable dramatic effects over such a range of experiments that I will describe. However, since there are such enhancing effects on the brains of humans [2] and of rats [3], Mark Bodner, John Hughes, and I believe that this first movement offers a "gold mine" in learning about higher brain function if we are smart enough to analyze it in an appropriate manner.

THE MOZART EFFECT EXPERIMENT

The human subjects approval by the U.C. Irvine review committee was rapid, since our simple experimental design using college-age students as subjects was passed without a lengthy full-board review. Students in psychology classes receive some class credit if they volunteer for an approved experiment. So Franny and our outstanding undergraduate lab assistant Katherine Ky were soon collecting data. Each student was given three sets of standard IQ spatial reasoning tasks [4]: each task was preceded by 10 minutes of (i) the Mozart Sonata for Two Pianos in D Major (K.448), (ii) a relaxation tape, or (iii) silence. Thirty-six students participated in all three listening conditions. Immediately after each listening condition, the student was tested on one of three spatial tasks from the Stanford-Binet intelligence tests [5] namely paper folding & cutting (PF&C), pattern analysis, and matrices.

Franny and Kathy finished the experiment with the 36 subjects at the end of February, 1993. Franny then entered all the data into the computer and analyzed it statistically. As agreed upon, only then did we look at the dramatic results. We found that the students did much better in the spatial reasoning after listening to the first 10 minutes of the Mozart Sonata (K.448) than after listening to silence or to the relaxation tape. As Franny puts it, "we expected a positive result, but we were extremely pleased by the size and statistical significance of our results." The results were statistically significant to a probability p less than 0.01 (see Chapter 13 for a discussion of what this p value means).

The scientific significance of our results was that it was the first proof of a causal enhancement of reasoning from music.

The design allowed us to conclude that the enhancing effect of the Mozart listening condition does not last much beyond the 10- to 15-minute period during which the subjects were engaged in each spatial task (since the enhancement did not carry over to the next task). Pulse rates were taken before and after each listening condition, which allowed us to exclude arousal as an obvious cause.

We began writing up a manuscript for publication in a scientific journal. At the next **Helmholtz Club** meeting, I told my friend and colleague V.S. Ramachandran [6] about our results. Rama enthusiastically replied that this was a dramatic result that should be submitted to the prestigious British journal *Nature*.

We completed the manuscript and sent it off to *Nature*'s London office for review. *Nature* has two levels of peer review: the first is a quick response indicating whether the content is of large and broad interest, and the second is the more detailed review. We survived both and were informed that *Nature* would publish a shortened version (in which we were to remove our theory that led to the experiment and would give a possible neuroscientific basis for our results). We followed these instructions in our rewriting and then waited for the paper to appear. One stipulation of *Nature* is that there can be no publicity prior to publication, so Franny and I carefully avoided any publicity. We were informed that the publication date was October 13, 1993. We grew concerned when a number of reporters called prior to this date, however, we were assured that *Nature* had sent a press release and that news stories would be held up (embargoed) until the date of publication.

Although Franny and I expected a large response, we were really overwhelmed by the worldwide interest (see Fig. 1.1). The media soon called our experiment the "Mozart effect." The idea that listening to this Mozart Sonata (K.448) could make you smarter, even if only for 10–15 minutes, had captured everyone's interest.

We would later note a further very important result. As shown (Fig. 12.2) in our subsequent analysis of the results from the *Nature* paper [7], the dominant enhancement came from the PF&C task, the only task that *explicitly* requires spatial-temporal reasoning. This was predicted by Xiao Leng and myself [8] in 1991.

OUR FOLLOW-UP MOZART EFFECT EXPERIMENT

In addition to our preschool music-training experiments (see Chapter 13) in progress at that time, we set about in 1994 to design a new experiment to

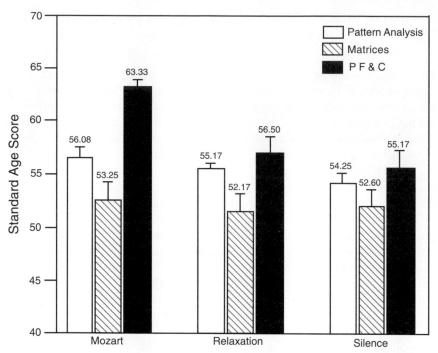

FIGURE 12.2   Subsequent analysis of the *Nature* paper findings showing that the main enhancement came from the Mozart Sonata listening condition followed by the PF&C tasks. The PF&C task explicitly requires spatial-temporal reasoning, whereas the other two spatial tasks, pattern analysis and matrices, do not have this temporal requirement and, as predicted, were not enhanced. The results were statistically significant to a probability p less than 0.01 (see Chapter 13 for a discussion of what this p value means).

reconfirm and further explore the details of the Mozart effect. Our analysis in Fig. 12.2 convinced Franny, Kathy, and me that we should concentrate on the PF&C task illustrated in Fig. 9.2

Theoretically, of the three tasks from the Stanford-Binet test used in our first experiment (PF&C, pattern analysis, and matrices) only the PF&C explicitly tested spatial-temporal reasoning, and experimentally the dominant effect in Fig. 12.2 came from this task. Thus we made 80 of our own PF&C items for this follow-up five-day experiment.

Seventy-nine UC Irvine students participated for five consecutive days. It is easy to get students to come *once,* since they get class credit if they volunteer. However, to get them to come more than once, we decided to pay them, and they had to complete all five days to get their money.

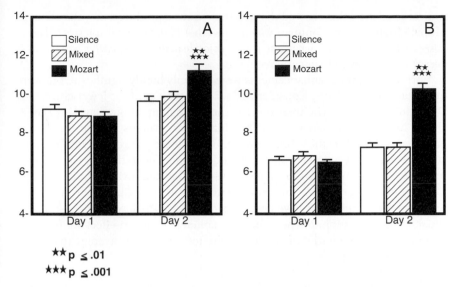

$\star\star$ p $\leq$ .01
$\star\star\star$ p $\leq$ .001

FIGURE 12.3   (A) Mean number of PF&C items answered correctly out of 16 by the Silence, Mixed, and Mozart groups for Days 1–2. The Mozart group's improvement from Day 1 to Day 2 was significant (p less than 0.001) and was significantly greater than that of the Silence and Mixed groups on Day 2 (p less than 0.01). No other differences were significant. (B) Same as A only for those subjects scoring 8 or fewer on Day 1. Note the dramatic increase from Day 1 to Day 2 of 62% for the Mozart group versus 14% for the Silence group and 11% for the Mixed group. From Rauscher *et al.* (1995).

All 79 students got 16 PF&C items on Day 1. (We also tested them on short-term memory items.) We graded the PF&C exams that evening, and matched grades in sets of three. Then each set was randomly divided into our three groups—the Mozart group, the Silence group, and the Mixed group. Each group was then tested in a separate room for the remaining days. On each of Days 2–4, the Silence group sat in silence for 10 minutes and were then tested with 16 new PF&C items; the Mozart group listened to the first 10 minutes of Mozart's Sonata (K.448) and were tested with the same 16 PF&C items as the Silence group. The Mixed group listened to 10 minutes of something different every day. On Day 2 they heard a **minimalist** work "Music with Changing Parts" by Philip Glass; on Day 3 they heard an audiotaped story; and on Day 4 they heard a British-style dance (trance) piece. They were tested on the same PF&C items as the other groups after each of these conditions. The Philip Glass piece was very repetitive in melody and the British dance piece was very repetitive in rhythm, which is why they were used as controls.

The dramatic results [9] for Days 1 and 2 are shown in Fig. 12.3. Thus, in addition to reproducing the original findings of the Mozart enhancement with respect to silence, this showed that repetitive music produced no enhancement of spatial-temporal reasoning. *I would stress that Philip Glass is a respected composer and there are times when one would enjoy listening to repetitive music, but it doesn't enhance spatial-temporal reasoning.*

Furthermore, these enhancements were not only highly significant, but were quantitatively *very large*. Consider the subjects who got 8 or fewer correct on Day 1 in Fig. 12.3A. The increases for these subgroups from Day 1 to Day 2, shown in Fig. 12.3B, were 62% for the Mozart group versus 14% for the Silence group and 11% for the Mixed group. Now these are not below average students—all University of California students must be in the top 10% of their respective high school classes. Thus, I suspect that the "priming" effect of the Mozart Sonata (K.448) on the neural pathways in cortex involved in spatial-temporal reasoning might have even larger effects on "below average" subjects. It would be interesting to repeat the EEG coherence Mozart effect studies [10] presented in Chapter 15 with students who test well below average in spatial-temporal reasoning.

The results of the PF&C tasks continued to improve on subsequent days, with the Mozart group always doing best. However, here we ran into what is called a **ceiling effect**, namely, a substantial number of students were getting 15 or 16 of the 16 PF&C items correct. Thus, since it is not possible to do better on the test, the full enhancing effect of listening to the Mozart could not be evaluated. The Silence group scores continued to be lower than those of the Mozart group, but the magnitude of the difference decreased. The Mixed group's scores remained significantly below those of the other groups. The immediate improvement of the Mozart group's scores was due to listening to the music, whereas the improvement of the Silence group's scores was probably the outcome of a learning curve. The inclusion of more difficult items would flatten this learning curve, remove the ceiling effect, and determine if the Mozart group's scores continue to improve relative to controls in subsequent days. An important question that arises is whether repeated listening to the Mozart Sonata (K.448) increases the short-term enhancement from 10–15 minutes to a longer time. I believe that improvements both in magnitude of enhancement and in time of this enhancement will occur, justifying more difficult, but necessary experiments (more on this in Chapter 18).

On Day 5, the Mixed group was divided into two new groups with equal means and distributions, based on their Day 1 memory items. The two groups were separated; one listened to the same Mozart Sonata (K.448), and the other group heard nothing. Immediately afterward, we issued both groups the same 16 new [11] memory items, which were difficult to memorize using a rhythmic pattern (for example, M 9 ! B 2 ? N %). This was quite important since it is well known anecdotally that the use of music or rhythmic patterns is a great aid for memorization of material. For example, when I first learned to sail, I was taught the very useful rhyme "There is no red port left," so I can always recall that the left side of the boat is called the port side and the appropriate light on that side is red (versus green for the right or starboard side).

Each item was presented for 5 seconds, and the students were to write down what they remembered in the correct order. As predicted, the Silence (mean score equal to 7.85) and the Mozart (mean score equal to 7.54) groups did not differ significantly. This demonstrated that the Mozart listening condition enhanced spatial-temporal reasoning and did not cause a general arousal that in turn enhanced general brain function. For further elaboration on this and for suggestions for future experiments, Franny and I [12] wrote a paper entitled "Key Components of the Mozart Effect." For example, we suggested that the maximum enhancement of spatial-temporal reasoning might occur some minutes after listening to the Mozart Sonata, rather than immediately after listening.

An amusing detail of this study was that the NBC Dateline TV show wanted to do a report on our research, but the producer, Betsy Kovetas, did not want a staged reenactment. So we said, naively, come film a live experiment. The film crews recorded all aspects of the experiment, including our nightly grading of the exams. Of course, we were a bit nervous, but it all worked out well and we got the dramatic results shown in Fig. 12.3.

FURTHER STUDIES

Clearly, many questions are raised by these two studies. Perhaps the question most asked is what other pieces of music will yield the enhancements in spatial-temporal reasoning generated by the Mozart Sonata (K.448)? (We suggest trying the highly structured music of J.S. Bach.) Other questions are what is there in the music that causes this enhancement? What other higher brain functions might be similarly enhanced? What are the optimum listening conditions (length of time and delay time from the end of listening) for subsequent enhancement of spatial-temporal reasoning? Can the enhancements be made to last? None of these questions has an adequate answer at this time, but I will speculate on all of them in later chapters. My postdoctoral research colleague Amy Graziano is planning a program to investigate a number of these questions. Talking with Francis Crick recently (once again at a Helmholtz Club meeting), I suggested, half seriously, that what is needed is a **Mozart effect meter**—a device that would measure the priming effects of music on reasoning in a reliable, robust manner. Yet such a device may be possible if we can identify the proper task and use EEG brain wave or fMRI imaging measurements.

Relevant to these questions, there are four recent Mozart effect experimental results that I will present in later chapters: the EEG coherence studies in collaboration with the University of Vienna [13]; the rat studies [14] in Fran

Rauscher's lab at the University of Wisconsin, Oshkosh; the epilepsy studies [15] in John Hughes' lab at the University of Illinois, Chicago; and the Alzheimer disease studies [16] by Julene Johnson in Carl Cotman's lab at U.C. Irvine. In addition, there are the just started but dramatic fMRI studies [17] in Orhan Nalcioglu's lab at Irvine. Each of these extremely important studies may add crucial support and further understanding of the Mozart effect. We are still at the beginning of this quest.

CHAPTER 13

Music Training Enhances Spatial-Temporal Reasoning in Preschool Children

BRIEF GUIDE

I present all the details of the striking Preschool study with three-year-old children that demonstrated that piano keyboard training enhances spatial-temporal reasoning in contrast to other control training. *These effects last long enough to have major educational implications.* The publicity associated with these results has been even greater than with the Mozart effect results. Clearly these findings are of strong interest to parents and educators, as well as scientists. I have included an important but technical section on Testing, Probability, Statistics, and Experimental Design. This section may be skimmed.

Xiao Leng and I started getting some publicity about our predictions [1] by early 1992. The following *Los Angeles Times* article was written by Kristina Lindgren [2]:

Tuning Up Brains
Early Musical Training May Enhance a Child's Mental Ability

Early musical training, even as early as age 3, may enhance a child's overall mental ability, UC Irvine brain researchers said. It has long been known that infants recognize and respond to music and that appreciation for works by composers such as Bach and Mozart transcends generations, geography, and culture. The reason, the team of UCI scientists believe, is that humans are born with certain brain cells that respond to musical sounds. These neurons fire in patterns that can be expanded as a sort of "prelanguage" to perform ever more complex interactions—even before the brain has developed verbal language skills, UCI physicist Gordon Shaw said. And this ability may well bolster higher level thinking skills. "We don't believe that by taking violin lessons you're going to become Albert Einstein," said Shaw . . . "On the other hand, we think that this ability is going to be a very useful tool in any kind of higher brain activity. So, music training amounts to exercising not muscles, but brain cells." To prove the thesis, he said, fellow researchers plan to test preschool music students . . . and track them over time to see how they develop in other areas.

As a result of this (and related) publicity, a few local preschools that already had music programs contacted me and said they were interested in participating in our study. This was very fortunate since I had previously tried calling several preschools without an introduction, and I quickly learned that this front door approach did not work. I would say to the director that I was a professor of physics and wanted to do a study to test our prediction that music training could enhance children's reasoning. The standard incredulous response was "You are who, and you want to do what?" It was also crucial that the schools that contacted me already had music programs under way, since I had just enough funding to hire a postdoctoral researcher in psychology to do a preliminary (pilot) experiment, but not enough to provide all the training (and controls) we would later need if things looked promising.

After a nationwide search, I was fortunate in hiring Frances Rauscher in August, 1992. Immediately after Franny joined my lab at U.C. Irvine, she set about conducting a first pilot experiment to test the very specific prediction of Xiao Leng and myself that music training at a young age would enhance the child's ability to do spatial-temporal reasoning.

In describing the southern California preschools that we worked with in this chapter and the elementary schools in Chapter 14, I have used symbols instead of their names. However, we have established a long-term relationship with the 95th St. Elementary School in Los Angeles, which I will always identify as such. This school is our "Lab" and has become accustomed to the frequent and favorable TV publicity.

PILOT STUDY

Five children from each of two schools participated in this small pilot study. All ten participants were female, and at the start of the study they ranged in age from 3 years and 1 month to 3 years and 11 months. One school, OCC, was an inner-city daycare center and the other, CS, was a school for the arts. The number of children in the study was quite small, and we did not have appropriate control groups (with random assignment into the groups) nor **blind** (to the hypothesis) testing, but we had an experiment!

Music training would be started after Franny did the first round of testing. Children in the below-average demographic OCC daycare received 30 minutes of group singing each day. Children in the above-average demographic CS school for the arts received weekly 15-minute private piano keyboard lessons and presumably practiced at home. All the children were then retested at the end of the 6 months of music training.

Franny gave the children the Performance subtest of the **Wechsler Preschool and Primary Scale of Intelligence—Revised** (WPPSI-R) [3] when they were admitted to their schools. The Object Assembly test presents the child with pieces of a puzzle (Fig. 13.1A) arranged in a standardized form, and the child is required to fit the pieces together in the correct meaningful whole within a specified time limit. This tests spatial-temporal reasoning, because it required forming a mental image of the completed object and rotating the puzzle pieces to match the image. Performance was facilitated by putting the pieces together in particular orders, thus defining the spatial-temporal nature of the task.

The other five WPPSI-R tasks measured spatial recognition that required matching, classifying, and recognizing similarities among displayed objects. Sequential order was not relevant. Four of these tasks were used. An example of a spatial recognition task is shown in Fig. 13.1B.

Xiao and I had predicted that it would be spatial-temporal reasoning that would be enhanced by music training and not spatial recognition. Basically, a child is constantly being presented with situations that require **spatial recognition,** so any enhancements from limited music training would not make a big difference. On the other hand, music training directly involves patterns developing in space and time and evolving an internal mental image. These processes are also used in reasoning, but are not used much by the young child. It seemed to us that even limited music training would make a difference in the child's spatial-temporal reasoning performance. (Additional features of the advantages of a particular kind of music training will be discussed later in the book.)

Before presenting the results, I want to briefly introduce some important concepts and details about experiments. I hope this will enable concerned readers of this book who have not seen such material before to begin to read relevant articles in scientific journals with understanding and some ability to evaluate the findings for themselves. A few times during my 35 years as a professor of physics, I would teach a course for nonmajors about important technical topics that the students would read about in the media, with the idea in mind of giving them the background to evaluate for themselves what the conflicting experts were telling them. It is with this in mind that I proceed.

A

Before

After

B

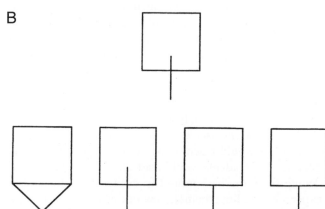

GENERAL REMARKS ON TESTING, PROBABILITY, STATISTICS, AND EXPERIMENTAL DESIGN

The following discussion will be too simple for an expert and too detailed for the nonexpert, but I feel that it is useful and necessary.

The testing and scoring procedures of the WPPSI-R tasks are well prescribed by the developers [4]. **Raw scores** for each task used were converted to **scaled scores** appropriate to the exact age of the child, calibrated at three-month intervals, using the WPPSI-R tables. The distribution of scaled scores was designed to have a **mean** of 10 and a **standard deviation** σ of 3. Thus if a child initially has a scaled test score of 10.2, the child is slightly above average. If the same child has a scaled score of 10.9 after 6 months of some sort of training, it means that they kept up with the raw score increase that was expected as they got older, and further increased the scaled score by 0.7. However, the 0.7 scaled score increase is not large (compared to σ). To get an idea of what a standard deviation means, consider a test given to lots of children. If the test is well designed, the distribution in scores will be **bell-shaped** (or **gaussian**), as shown in Fig. 13.2. Here half or 50% of the children score above the mean and half or 50% below the mean. The σ measures how fast this bell curve decreases. The number of children scoring greater than 1 σ from the mean (on either side of) is about 16%, the number scoring greater than 2 σ is about 2%, and greater than 3 σ is 0.1%.

Statistical analyses are done on test results of groups of children to determine if the results of training are statistically significant. It is possible even for the previous small difference of 0.7 to be statistically significant if the number n of children in the study was very large. A measure of this quantity is the **standard error s**, where the square of s (s $\times$ s or s^2) equals the square of σ divided by n, or [5]

$$s \text{ equals } \sigma/ \text{ square root of } n$$

So, if our σ is 3 as for the WPPSI-R tasks, and we had a difference between groups of children before group training of 0.7, we must have an s much smaller than 0.7 to have any chance of getting statistically significant results. If there

---

FIGURE 13.1   (A) Schematic representation of the Object Assembly task requiring spatial-temporal reasoning. The child arranges pieces of a puzzle to create a meaningful whole. (B) Schematic representation of the Geometric Design task requiring spatial recognition. The child points to the bottom-row figure that matches the figure in the top row.

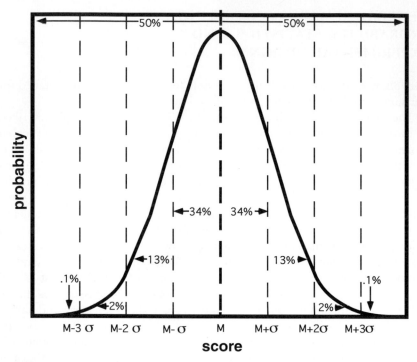

FIGURE 13.2   Example of how test scores of a large number of children in a study are distributed in a bell-shaped or gaussian probability curve. Fifty percent of the children have test scores above the mean and 50% are below the mean. The standard deviation σ measures how fast this curve decreases from the mean value. The number of children scoring greater than 1 σ from the mean is about 16%, the number scoring greater than 2 σ is about 2%, and greater than 3 σ is about 0.1%. So, if your child scores 1 σ above the mean, he or she is in the top 16%.

were 900 children (the square root of 900 equals 30) in our study, the standard error s would be $\sigma/30$, equal to 3/30 or 0.1, which indeed is much less than the 0.7 result of training. In the case of an experiment with 16 children (the square root of 16 equals 4), the standard error would be ¾ or 0.75, which is greater than our 0.7 result of training. Thus we should expect that a real statistical analysis of the large group results would be statistically significant and that of the small group would not be significant. The effects of statistical fluctuations are less with the larger group.

A probability p is determined and *it is standard to say that the results of a study are statistically significant only if p is smaller than 0.05.* A p value of 0.05 (or $1/_{20}$) means that if one repeated the exact same experiment 20 times (and there were no systematic errors), 1 of the 20 experiments would give the results of the study totally by chance, not due to the training. A good eyeball measure of whether a result of an experiment might be statistically significant is whether the "before" and "after" results differ by more than 3 standard errors. Experimenters sometimes represent their results with "stars": 1 star if p is less than 0.05, 2 stars if p is less than 0.01, and 3 stars if p is less than 0.001.

Much caution needs to be used when evaluating experimental results: *I like to see a big effect clearly evident, in addition to seeing the statistical significance.* This is because there may be many possible **systematic errors** in any experiment in addition to the **statistical error**. Consider doing a series of 10,000 flips of a coin. We would expect to get roughly 5000 heads and 5000 tails since it should be equally probable to get a heads or a tails on each flip. If we got 8000 heads and 2000 tails, we would know that this coin must be abnormally weighted to give us a large systematic error. This is because the statistical errors can be calculated and would be about 1% or 100 flips. The difference of 8000 from the expected 5000 heads is 3000 heads, which is 30 times the statistical error. If we had done only 10 flips and had 8 heads and 2 tails, this can readily happen by chance since the statistical error for the 10 flips would be about 30% or 3 heads.

These systematic errors either must be estimated or directly measured and accounted for in the experimental design. In a standard physics experiment, the scientists may spend years determining their systematic errors. This is especially difficult in human behavioral experiments, but it can be done.

Consider what has been called the **Westinghouse effect**. This occurs when a teacher turns on additional lights in her class before a test, and that causes the students to pay more attention and they improve by, say, 4% over an identical situation with no additional lights. We could imagine a number of such generalized Westinghouse effects, extraneous to the heart of the experiment, that could influence assessments to see if specific training influenced performance. What should a serious scientist do, especially if resources are limited? It is clearly impossible even to list all the possible Westinghouse effects, let alone come up with an experimental design to take them into account. Usually, one or two control groups (to take into account the effect of additional training or attention, known as the **Hawthorn effect**) are used. Thus there will always be effects that cannot be directly accounted for in having control groups. *These effects will introduce what are called systematic errors.*

In analogy to what is done in physics experiments, one can do a number of separate small experiments to determine the sizes (magnitudes) of these Westinghouse effects or systematic errors that you are aware of, or one could look in the published literature for similar such measurements. Then one uses some data along with these measurements to estimate the Westinghouse effects. Then, by combining these errors in a standard manner, one can calculate an overall systematic error in addition to the statistical error. For example, in addition to our light bulb systematic error of 4%, suppose there is a second Westinghouse systematic type error of 3%. In the simplest situation, these errors would combine; the combined error squared equals the sum of the 4% error squared plus the 3% error squared, giving a combined systematic error of 5% ($3 \times 3 + 4 \times 4$ equals $9 + 16$ equals 25 equals 5×5.)

Another way to average out some of these unknown factors is to do a long-term study (say, for at least three years) involving a large number of (for our case) schools in rural and urban areas as well as among advantaged and disadvantaged populations (**demographics**) throughout the country. In fact, this is an absolute necessity if the results are to have significant influence on educational reform.

RESULTS OF PILOT STUDY

To return to our pilot study, the enhancements of the spatial-temporal Object Assembly task were *huge* and, just as predicted, no enhancement was found in the spatial-recognition tasks (Fig. 13.3). The use of the standardized, age-calibrated WPPSI-R tests allowed this determination.

Even though we could put stars on these results (since they were statistically significant), because the number of children in the groups was so small and because we had no control groups, we would not submit them for publication in a scientific journal. However, we were extremely excited about these large enhancements, especially since they occurred precisely as predicted for the spatial-temporal task and not for the spatial-recognition task. Next, we set about lining up funding and preschools to participate in our expanded study.

PRESCHOOL STUDY

It turned out to be quite easy to get preschools interested in our new study. Bonnie Grice had a daily morning program of classical music on radio station KUSC in Los Angeles. On December 14, 1992, Bonnie held a live interview with Xiao, Franny, and me on our research studies "Music Is Exercise for Higher Brain Function." I had long been a great fan of Bonnie, who went beyond the usual classical music format and discussed matters of general interest with style and thought. (By the way, although Bonnie had many fans, she was later fired because her programs were not standard enough for many listeners.)

Bonnie started our interview with the Symphony Number 1 by Mozart, which he composed at the age of eight. Xiao, Franny, and I had great fun in our one-hour interview, in which we included a request for preschools with lower- and middle-income students to participate in our upcoming study. We ex-

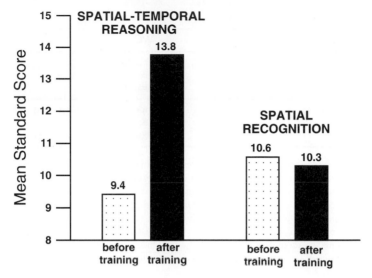

FIGURE 13.3   Combined results of the pilot study of children at OCC and CS preschools as measured by the age-calibrated WPPSI-R tasks. Children in the below average demographic OCC daycare received 30 minutes of group singing each day. Children in the above average demographic CS school for the arts received weekly 15-minute private piano keyboard lessons and presumably practiced at home. All the children were tested before training and then retested at the end of the 6 months of music training. Note the huge increase in the spatial-temporal task performance after music training and no change in performance for the spatial recognition task, just as predicted.

plained that we would bring our own music instructors into the preschools at no cost to them. As Franny emphasized, "And in this way we can really control the amount and the type of training that they receive." We discussed the testing that we would conduct and details of the research program. By the end of the next day, I had 20 phone calls from preschools wanting to participate. We narrowed these preschools down to two with average demographics, LB and NC. We later added another preschool (SA) in the second year of the study.

A total of 111 children were in our program over the two years. Thirty-three children withdrew from the preschools during the course of the study, and were not included in the analyses. The children who withdrew were fairly evenly distributed among the experimental groups. This left 78 children, 42 boys and 36 girls, for analysis. All children were of normal intelligence. The participants ranged in age from 3 years, 0 months to 4 years, 9 months at the start of the study.

Only three children were left-handed. Left-handedness has been anecdotally linked to spatial-temporal reasoning. This might make sense since a left-hander probably would make more use of the right hemisphere of her cortex, which is linked to spatial-temporal reasoning. Both Franny and I are left-handed, and

Lessons given at each preschool

School year	LB	WC	SA
1993–1994	Keyboard & No Lessons	Keyboard & No Lessons	—
1994–1995	Computer & Singing	Computer & Singing	Keyboard & Computer

FIGURE 13.4   Experimental design showing preschools and treatment groups. Seventy-eight children of diverse ethnicity and normal intelligence (42 males and 36 females) participated. The data were collected over two years from three preschools. SA participated in 1994–1995 only, and did not contribute to the No Lessons or Singing groups. No group differed significantly prior to training. LB and NC received lessons once per week for eight months; SA received lessons twice per week for six months. No statistically significant difference in our testing results was found for number of lessons, so these data could be safely combined in the final analysis. For clarity, we referred to the interval between testing periods as six months.

we are always interested in the performance of left-handers. When I was active in elementary particle physics, I organized conferences every two years. In the 1977 conference, I took a survey of the 320 physicists and found that 18% were left-handed, which is higher than the 10% found for the general population.

The two-year design of the study [6] is shown in Fig. 13.4. We provided 34 children, the Keyboard group, with private piano keyboard lessons and group singing sessions, and assigned the remaining children to one of three groups: Singing, Computer, and No Lessons. The Singing group (10 children) took part in the same singing activities as the Keyboard group. The Computer group (20 children) received private computer lessons matched in length and number to the piano keyboard lessons. The No Lessons group (14 children) did not receive any training. None of the children had prior music lessons or computer lessons, and parental involvement was minimal.

All children in participating classrooms whose parents consented took part in the study. Children from the SA preschool were randomly assigned to either the Keyboard or the Computer groups (see Fig. 13.4). The logistics of classroom schedules influenced group assignment in the other two preschools. Because the preschools assigned children to classrooms according to age, the children in the No Lessons group were older than the children in the other three groups (4 years, 1 month to 4 years, 9 months versus 3 years, 0 months to 3 years, 11 months, respectively). Our assignments were necessary to keep classes intact, to optimize sample size, and to avoid singling out children for participation in one treatment group over another. It is important to note, however, that the children's test scores were standardized by age, and no significant differences were found between groups prior to training.

We provided piano keyboard lessons rather than lessons on some other instrument because the keyboard gives a visual linear representation of the spatial relationships between pitches. We felt that coupling visual information with aural information might assist the neural pattern development that is relevant to spatial-temporal operations. Further support for using the keyboard came from our pilot study. We had no information regarding other instruments. We recruited professional instructors from the Irvine Conservatory of Music to provide the preschool lessons using inexpensive electronic piano keyboards arranged on child-sized tables. The 10-minute private keyboard lessons consisted of performance exercises derived from traditional approaches. The children studied pitch intervals, fine motor coordination, fingering techniques, sight reading, music notation, and playing from memory. After six months, all the children were able to perform basic primer-level melodies and *very simple* melodies by Beethoven and Mozart.

The preschools reserved an hour each day for keyboard practice. My lab assistant Wendy Dennis was only able to observe these practice sessions infrequently. The children did practice, but we have no quantitative details.

Because many classes in the three schools already included some group singing activities, the Singing group was included to standardize these activities and to determine if such singing instruction would produce an effect in the absence of piano keyboard instruction, as indicated by the pilot study. The 30-minute singing sessions, led by our music instructors, were held five days a week. Songs included popular children's tunes and folk melodies.

Our inclusion of a Computer group was intended to control for the expected benefits of being in the keyboard group, namely, the motor and visual coordination provided by the keyboard instruction, the personal attention, and the child's engagement with the activity. A professional computer instructor brought a personal home computer to the preschools for the 10-minute private lessons. The children were taught to open entertaining, age-appropriate, commercial software programs by copying simple computer commands. Most of the children mastered this after one month. The software was designed to teach reading and simple arithmetic skills. Letter recognition varied for each student. Some children could identify many letters at the start, whereas most children could identify 8 to 10 letters after three months. The children also learned sentence structure by completing sentences such as "I am thankful for. . . ." Counting skills and number recognition were also taught. On average, children were able to count three objects after one month and six objects after three months. The lessons did not involve use of the desktop mouse or software programs that centrally featured music.

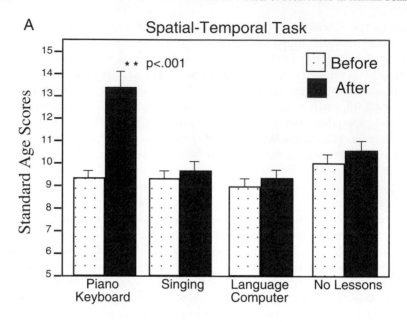

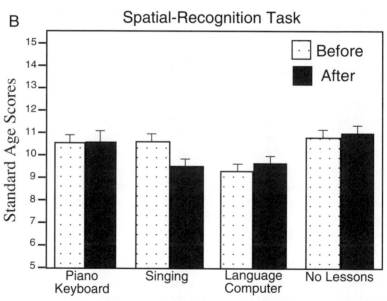

FIGURE 13.5   (A) Means for the OA standard age scores with standard errors are plotted measuring spatial-temporal reasoning for the Keyboard, Singing, Computer, and No Lessons groups before and after lessons. The Keyboard group improved significantly following lessons, whereas the other groups did not. (B) The spatial-recognition score means with standard errors for the four groups before and after lessons. No groups improved significantly. (The drop in spatial-recognition scores for the Singing group is not statistically significant.) From Rauscher *et al.* (1997)

The No Lessons group controlled for task artifacts; a particular task score may improve because the children enjoy it more with age, rather than as a function of training.

As in the pilot study, prior to training we tested all the children's spatial reasoning with four tasks from the WPPSI-R intelligence test. Children were tested individually at the preschools. As shown in Fig. 13.1A, in the Object Assembly task, which measured spatial-temporal skill, the child arranged pieces of a puzzle to create a meaningful whole. The spatial-recognition tasks required matching, classifying, and recognizing similarities among displayed objects. Sequential order was not relevant. Children were retested on all tasks after six to eight months of lessons. The No Lessons group was retested at the same time as the other children.

Testing during the first year was performed by Franny. During the second year, testing was performed by research assistants who were **blind** both to the hypothesis of the experiment and to group assignment, so that no bias could be introduced in any way. Analysis conducted on these two sets of data showed no differences in results, so the data could be combined for the final analysis. All tasks were independently scored by two researchers blind to condition assignment.

Figure 13.5A shows how each of the four different types of training affect spatial-temporal abilities by presenting the before and after training Object Assembly (OA) mean scores. This figure reveals that music training for the Keyboard group produced a *dramatic* overall increase in OA scores (as evidenced by a pretraining mean of 9.79 and a posttraining mean of 13.41), whereas none of the other training groups showed any appreciable change. To verify the obvious difference, a statistical analysis was performed on the change in scores with respect to the four training groups. As expected, this analysis produced highly significant differences between the four groups.

Analysis of the children's scores on the other tests (Geometric Design, Block Design, and Animal Pegs) showed that spatial recognition did not change significantly after lessons (Fig. 13.5B).

The OA scores of the Singing, Computer, and No Lessons groups did not improve significantly, nor did their scores on the spatial-recognition tasks. The lack of significant improvement of the Singing group on the OA task (mean of 9.80 before and 10.10 after) suggests that either a more structured singing program is required or that experience with a musical instrument, with its visual and motor representation of spatial-temporal relations between sequences of pitches, may be crucial to the effect. We could rule out the possibility, however, that the group singing contributed to the enhancement of spatial-temporal reasoning found for the Keyboard group. We suspect that the significant improvement found in the pilot study by the inner-city children at OCC who received group singing may have been due to the school's demographic composition. What this means is that if children start out with low

No. of Subjects   No. of Subjects

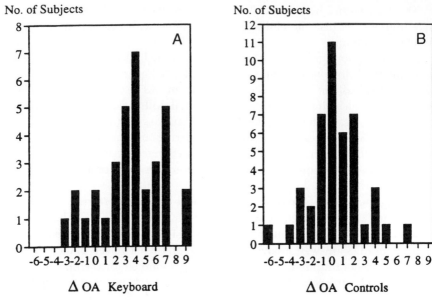

FIGURE 13.6   (A) Plot of OA scores after lessons minus OA scores before lessons (ΔOA) for the 34 children in the Keyboard group. (B) The corresponding plot for the 44 children in the combined three control groups. As expected, the changes in B center at 0. The changes in A center at about 4. There is a dramatic shift from the control groups to the Keyboard group. *This clearly shows how large the enhancement is and how many of the children benefited from the piano lessons.* From Rauscher et al. (1997)

enough skills, any special attention may give them a big boost. Clearly, this must be studied further.

The stability of the Computer group's OA scores (mean of 9.25 before lessons versus 9.60 after lessons) rules out attention, motivation, and motor coordination as primary contributors to the Keyboard group's improvement. This, we believe, is a *substantial* finding given the captivating nature of the animated images used in the computer training. Finally, the OA scores of the No Lessons group did not improve significantly after eight months (mean of 10.50 before versus 11.00 after). This indicates that the Keyboard group's improvement was not due to task artifacts.

To convey the dramatic extent of the Keyboard group's improvement on the OA task, we plotted the results of scores after treatment minus scores before treatment (ΔOA) (Fig. 13.6A). *Twenty-four of the 34 children, or 71%, improved by 3 or more points* (recall that the WPPSI-R's σ's are all equal to 3), as compared to the expected 5 or 6 children (16%) according to the gaussian model (see Fig. 13.2) if these results were due to random changes. Figure 13.6B shows the results for the three combined control groups. Only six of these 44 children (14%) improved by 3 or more points.

The magnitude of the improvement in spatial-temporal reasoning from music training was greater than one standard deviation, equivalent to an increase from a starting point near the 50th percentile on the WPPSI-R standardized test to above the 85th percentile. This is a very significant result.

Memory researchers differentiate between **short-term and long-term memory** [7]. Long-term memory, lasting hours or longer, is associated with enduring synaptic changes. To determine if the enhancement found in this study was long term, we compared the ΔOA scores of the children who were tested one day or more after their last keyboard lesson to those of the children who were tested less than one day afterward. We found no significant difference. *The enhancement on the OA spatial-temporal task from piano keyboard training lasted at least three days, and so is considered by memory researcher standards to be long term.*

Our previous findings of enhanced short-term (lasting roughly 10 to 15 minutes) spatial-temporal reasoning in college students after listening to the Mozart Sonata suggest that music can prime regions of cortex that are responsible for spatial-temporal reasoning. (I will describe the EEG coherence study of this short-term enhancement in Chapter 15.) *The long-term enhancement of spatial-temporal reasoning found in this piano training study of at least three days represents an increase by more than a factor of 100 in time over the previous Mozart effect listening experiments.* This study suggests that music training, unlike listening, produces long-term modifications in underlying neural circuitry in regions not primarily concerned with music but rather with spatial-temporal reasoning. However, a long-term enhancement of spatial-temporal reasoning simply from listening over longer periods of time must be considered a possibility, especially following Fran Rauscher's experiment with the Mozart group of rats, who improved their learning ability in a spatial maze [8].

The precise duration of the enhancement and the possible existence of a **critical period** need to be examined. The idea of a critical period is that there are certain time windows in a child's development when certain higher brain functions are best learned. For example, it is known that it is easiest to learn a foreign language when you are young. An exploration of the aspects of music training that are responsible for the enhancement must be undertaken, so that the optimum training method can be identified. Further research is necessary to identify other spatial-temporal reasoning tasks that may be enhanced by music training.

It has been clearly documented that young students have difficulty understanding the concepts of proportion that are heavily used in math and science, and that *no successful program has been developed to teach proportional math in the school system* [9]. We predicted that an enhanced ability to evolve temporal sequences of spatial patterns as a result of music training will lead to an enhanced conceptual mastering of proportional math.

The bottom line, however, is that parents and educators want to see that, indeed, improved spatial-temporal reasoning leads to improved learning of math and science. As stressed in Part I, Wendy Boettcher and I [10], some five years ago, anticipated that to truly optimize the effects of enhanced spatial-temporal abilities (induced by the music training) new methods of teaching math must be developed. Matthew Peterson and I set out to accomplish this over four years ago. Through his creativity and enormous effort, Matthew has produced the highly successful Spatial-Temporal Animation Reasoning (S.T.A.R.) software, which is discussed in Chapter 14.

CHAPTER 14

Music Training Plus Spatial-Temporal Training Equals Improved Math

BRIEF GUIDE

The dramatic results presented in this chapter are of major educational interest. The 2nd grade children who took piano keyboard lessons and S.T.A.R. lessons were able to learn proportional math concepts. The findings are of great importance because proportional math is usually introduced during the 6th grade and has proven enormously difficult to teach most children using the usual language-analytic methods. Not only is proportional math crucial for all college-level science, but it is a first academic hurdle that requires the children to grasp the underlying concepts before they can master the material. Rote learning does not work. All the material here should be readable to everyone.

Xiao Leng and I predicted, based on the mathematical trion model of the cortex, that early music training would enhance spatial-temporal reasoning. As I presented in Chapter 13, Fran Rauscher and our team demonstrated that preschool children given six months of piano keyboard lessons improved dramatically on spatial-temporal reasoning while children in appropriate control groups did not improve. We then predicted that the enhanced spatial-temporal reasoning from this training could lead to enhanced learning of specific math concepts, in particular proportional math, which is notoriously difficult to teach using the usual language-analytic methods (see Chapter 2).

An educational study [1] of 45 countries and 500,000 students has shown that the U.S. ranks below average in mathematics. Specifically, U.S. students are below average in geometry and proportional reasoning, which will harm their understanding of specific science concepts. These deficiencies carry over to poor performance in college-level math and science.

Traditionally, proportional math is taught using language-analytic methods, with ratios and fractions leading to the comparison of ratios or proportional math in 6th through 8th grade [2]. Spatial-temporal, or ST, methods play a hands-on role in early childhood learning of math concepts using, for example, blocks. Computer software programs are also useful for introducing ST methods. However, ST reasoning is for the most part neglected: (1) neither the use of building toys nor computer programs approach is carried far enough in depth, in purpose, or in the full use of the young child's ST capabilities, and (2) they are dropped out when the child is considered "ready" to go on to the presumably more appropriate and powerful language-analytic methods. I contend that these are major flaws in our educational system.

Over four years ago Matthew Peterson and I set about to develop computer software that would teach young children these difficult math concepts using spatial-temporal reasoning based on our ideas from the trion model about higher brain function (presented in Chapters 8–10). Basically, there is an *innate* ability in mammalian cortex to apply spatial-temporal reasoning through the use of symmetries to transform patterns in space and time without an explicit external image. Music training can enhance the basic cortical "hardware" for this spatial-temporal reasoning.

Because it is such a relevant statement (by such an eminent scientist), I will repeat the quotation from Richard Feynman in Chapter 2. Feynman described the interplay of spatial-temporal and language-analytic approaches as a mysterious process that we can all recognize:

> It's like asking a centipede which leg comes after which—it happens quickly, and I'm not exactly sure what flashes and things go on in the head. I do know it's a crazy mixture of partially solved equations and some kind of visual picture of what the equation is saying is happening, but not as well separated as the words I'm using. . . . Strange! I don't understand how it is that we can write mathematical expressions and calculate what the thing is going to do without being able to picture it.

If this ability to visually understand a concept is so important to a Nobel Laureate physicist, it must be important to all of us. In particular, I strongly propose that it is crucial to a child learning a new concept in math and science.

About five years ago, Matthew Peterson, then an undergraduate, came into my office and asked if he could work with me on our research on music and the brain (he had seen the articles I put on the wall outside my lab). It took me no time at all to decide that Matthew was truly exceptional in many aspects: for starters, he had a triple major in engineering, biology, and Chinese. After helping with several other projects, his main and long-term project became the development of the ST math software, which evolved to become S.T.A.R. Matthew created and developed the first version of S.T.A.R. (see Matthew's enclosed CD Demo) in his "spare time" (by getting up at 5 A.M.) as he worked on his Ph.D. thesis in visual neuroscience at U.C. Berkeley.

What I present now is the strikingly successful use of S.T.A.R. in a study by Amy Graziano, Matthew, and myself [3] involving 237 2nd grade children. Further, as predicted, children given piano keyboard training along with S.T.A.R. scored significantly higher on proportional math and fractions than did children given a control training along with S.T.A.R. These results were readily measured using the companion Evaluation Program (S.T.A.R. E.P.). The training time necessary for children to reach a high level of performance on S.T.A.R. is extremely rapid (see Fig. 2.5). This suggests that, as predicted, we are tapping into fundamental cortical processes of spatial-temporal reasoning. Matthew and I suggest that this spatial-temporal approach is easily generalized to teach other math and science concepts in a complementary manner to traditional language-analytic methods, and can be used at a much younger age.

The S.T.A.R. E.P. is designed to evaluate the learning of symmetries, fractions, and proportional math, and it replaces the Wechsler tasks as a measure of ST reasoning in our studies. The Wechsler tasks [4] (see Chapter 13), used in the Preschool study, were from the Wechsler Preschool and Primary Scale of Intelligence-Revised [4] (WPPSI-R), which can be used for children from ages three to seven years. The Wechsler Intelligence Scale for Children-Third Edition [5] (WISC-III) can be used for children from six to sixteen years. For the Preschool study with three-year-old children, the Wechsler tasks served as an appropriate post-test evaluation, in particular, the Object Assembly task provided an age-appropriate measure of ST reasoning. However, for this study with older grade-school children, the Wechsler scales present some *serious* limitations. We therefore decided to use WISC-III scores only as a baseline measurement of ST reasoning, rather than as a pre/post evaluation. Our reasons for using the Wechsler tasks in this capacity, rather than as they were used in the Preschool study, are as follows:

(i)   Administration of the WPPSI-R or WISC-III spatial tasks requires trained and skilled testers.

(ii)   The tests must be given one-on-one and require 1–2 hours per child (including the scoring).

(iii) A certain proficiency in English is necessary for children to understand the test instructions; it is therefore difficult to administer these tasks to non-English speaking populations (unlike the previous version of the WISC, the WISC-III does not have, for example, a Spanish version).

(iv) Because knowledge of English is a factor in test administration, using English language training as a control may confound results from the Wechsler tasks.

(v)   The basic spatial operations required to master performance of these Wechsler tasks do not include the full range of ST operations, such as symmetry operations, which we believe are enhanced by the piano keyboard training.

(vi) The Wechsler tasks do not assess the math skills, such as fractions and proportional math, which are particularly relevant to enhanced ST reasoning.

Because of these reasons, when we set about to develop the new S.T.A.R. software to teach math, we also had in mind developing the S.T.A.R. E.P. as a replacement for the Wechsler tasks.

The first version of Matthew's ST math software required lots of animation and was very "labor-intensive" in developing the scenes to teach symmetries and proportional math. Laura Cheung, Amy Graziano, and Krista Hahn spent many hours getting this pilot version ready and successfully testing it on young children ranging in age from three to six years old. (For the three-year-olds, we had a touch screen so they did not have to be able to use a mouse.) These children loved our ST math software and were readily able to do all the tasks: Several features of our unpublished results are definitely worth reporting here:

1. The three-year-olds were immediately able to recognize rotated objects: they needed no training. It would be interesting to try this with even younger children. Our trion model suggests that this is one of the inherent built-in cortical operations and thus should be able to be done by *very* young children.

2. Five-year-old children readily learned the proportional math problems we had related to filling up objects.

3. One of the large problems in teaching children math and assessing what they knew or learned is to capture their interest and maintain their attention. This is especially truly for neurologically challenged children. In particular, we had a number of five- and six-year-old children with attention disorder deficit try our math software. Not only could they do the tasks, but they all wanted to keep on playing with it and were not bored after 10 minutes. I will come back to this important point in Chapter 21.

FIGURE 4.3 Painting by Koko's gorilla friend Michael. Michael paints regularly. Courtesy of The Gorilla Foundation/Ron Cohn.

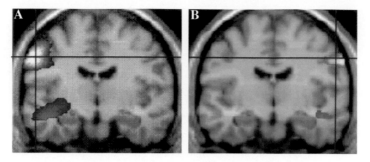

FIGURE 6.16 (A) PET scans of a subject listening for particular words shown in cortical slice from MRI scans. (B) The subject is listening for particular accents. These data clearly show that the cortex is processing words mainly in the left hemisphere and accents mainly in the right hemisphere. This figure is from the lab of Mark Mandelkern and Steven Berman.

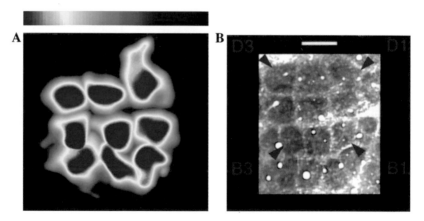

FIGURE 7.6 Structure and function corresponding to the 3 × 3 array of whiskers from rat (somatosensory) cortex prepared in Ron Frostig's laboratory. (A) Activity from nine whiskers optically imaged through the (thinned) skull, coming from activity changes in veins flowing out of these areas. Only the peak activity regions are shown. (B) Photo of (cytochrome oxidase) staining of the same nine whisker representations in cortical layer 4. The scale bar for both is 0.05 cm. From Masino *et al.* (1993). Copyright © 1993, National Academy of Sciences, U.S.A.

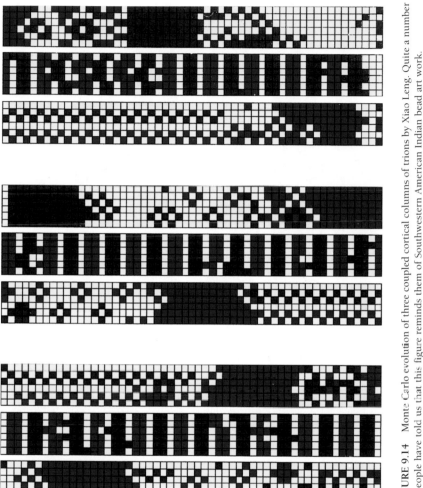

FIGURE 9.14 Monte Carlo evolution of three coupled cortical columns of trions by Xiao Leng. Quite a number of people have told us that this figure reminds them of Southwestern American Indian bead art work.

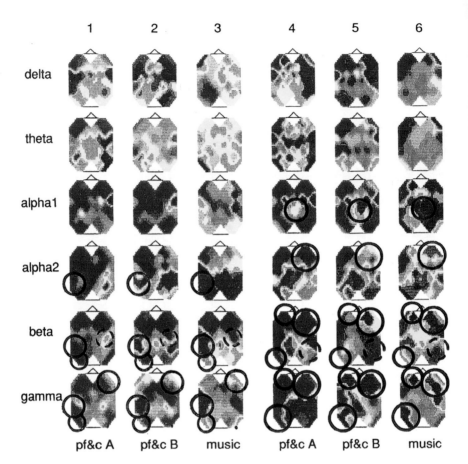

FIGURE 15.2 EEG coherence patterns during Sessions A and B for two subjects (UW, columns 1–3, and VS, columns 4–6). Coherence values are calculated with respect to a baseline condition. The magnitude of the coherence changes is color coded with increases (red) and decreases (blue) and **interpolated** between electrode pairs (see Fig. 6.11). Rows denote the frequency bands. **Subject UW:** Column 1. Coherence patterns during the PF&C tasks in Session A. Column 2. Coherence patterns during PF&C tasks in Session B. Important differences have been circled; increases from Session A to B (more red in column 2) are solid circles and decreases are dotted circles. Column 3. Coherence patterns in Session B while listening to the Mozart Sonata prior to solving the PF&C tasks. The circles have also been drawn to guide the eye. The patterns for the PF&C tasks in column 2 look like a superposition of patterns for the PF&C task in column 1 and those in column 3. **Subject VS:** The reading of these columns 4–6 is the same as in columns 1–3. Note that the location of the circles turned out to be very close to those in columns 4–6 for subject UW. From Sarnthein *et al.* (1997).

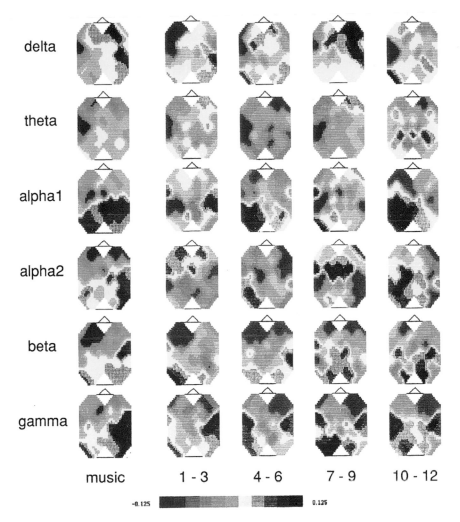

FIGURE 15.3 EEG coherence patterns of subject JJ during and after listening to the Mozart Sonata (K.488). Column 1 shows the coherence patterns while listening to the first 10 minutes of the sonata. Columns 2–5 show the patterns for four subsequent periods of 3 minutes each. Note the long-lasting effect of the Mozart listening condition on the subsequent relaxation period, where many of the features of the patterns remain similar throughout all five columns. Another very interesting feature is that the temporal oscillations occur on the order of minutes. From Sarnthein *et al.* (1997).

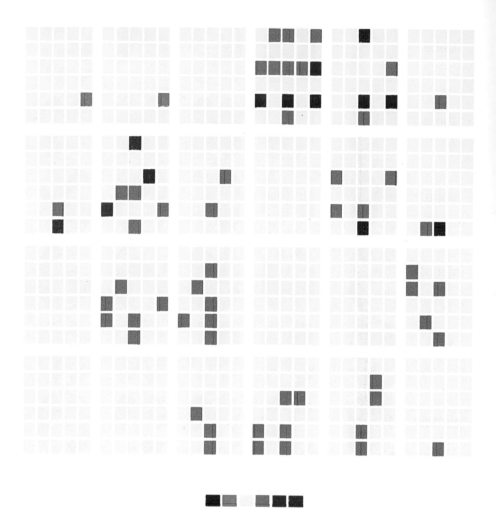

FIGURE 16.6 Analysis of multielectrode data from the visual cortex. There are six levels of firing (as shown in the color bar), with red being the highest level of firing down to purple as the lowest for each 0.025-sec time bin. The spatial arrangement of squares in the 5 × 6 array corresponds to the multielectrode array in the cortex. The temporal evolution is shown as a series of snapshots: 24 frames covering a time span of 0.6 sec starting at the uniform light stimulus onset (the stimulus was on for the entire time shown). Time increases from left to right and then from top to bottom. The data were averaged over 40 presentations of a uniform white light. Note that the activity builds up and dies down repeatedly with a period of about three time steps. The spatial-temporal distributions are not simply a temporal modulation of a spatial pattern. Further, the distributions (not shown here) depend on the nature of the stimulus in a sophisticated manner. From Shaw *et al.* (1993).

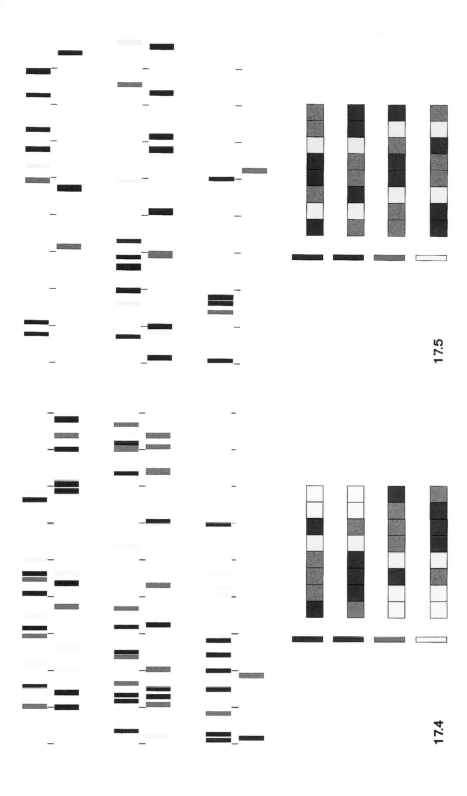

17.5

17.4

FIGURE 18.3 Photo of Koko pushing one of the six buttons on the GUI. The GUI is connected to a computer, which plays a selection of music in response to the push of that button and records all the relevant data for analysis. The connections to the computer from the GUI buttons could be readily adjusted to change which button played which piece of music. Courtesy of The Gorilla Foundation/Ron Cohn.

FIGURE 17.4 Temporal occurrence of the 8-time-step (each step is 0.15 sec) SAC family of patterns during simultaneous recording from two neurons while listening to music for three minutes. (Bottom) As in Fig. 16.10, there are the direct pattern (and its temporal rotations all denoted by the vertical red bar) and the C symmetry (denoted by the dark blue bar), the T symmetry (denoted by the green bar), and the CT symmetry (denoted by the yellow bar) family members. Matches on 7 out of 8 (or better) symbols must be found to be shown. (Top) SAC family of patterns. Time starts in the upper left row, increases to the right, and then repeats in each of the next two rows. The results for 1 neuron are shown above the time hash marks, and those for the other neuron are below the hash marks. The width of a bar increases as its pattern continues on beyond the 8 time steps of the pattern. I qualitatively note that the occurrence of red-green (or green-red) pairs seems to pop out for each neuron and between neurons.

FIGURE 17.5 The occurrence of a second SAC family of patterns in the same spike train data from the two neurons as in Fig. 17.4. See Fig. 17.4 for all details. (Bottom) Family of patterns. (Top) Occurrence of the family members in the neuron data. It appears that this second SAC family would fall in place between the first family occurrences in Fig. 17.4.

Clearly we were on the right track, but a new approach was needed to speed up the development by going to an **object-oriented platform** (underpinning) for our software. This platform would allow numerous variations of a task to be readily obtained, which is exactly what we needed. Matthew found such a software platform called Metropolis. Our project required not only great creativity in how we present our math concepts, but now a quite sophisticated ability in this object-oriented computer programming. At this point, the progress of our project rested almost entirely on Matthew.

FIRST VERSION OF S.T.A.R.

Matthew's first version of S.T.A.R. used in this study is language free. In it, a friendly, cute animal, the penguin JiJi (designed by Matthew's wife Elsa), is the character in a video game that (racially mixed) boys and girls liked and identified with. The instructions and material are introduced through interactive computer animation, although during training our professional computer instructors did provide introductory remarks and were always present to answer questions. To maintain interest, the tasks and settings change throughout the course of S.T.A.R. Music is not used; however, sound effects are part of the software.

S.T.A.R. takes children through two stages. The first stage is a multi-level spatial-temporal training in the form of various games. These games develop skill and confidence in transforming multiple mental images in space and time. For this study, the transformations were limited to (a sequential time series of) the following symmetry operations applied to two-dimensional figures: folding and unfolding around multiple axes in the plane of the computer screen, rotations around the axis at 90 degrees to the screen, 180 degree flips around the axes in the plane of the screen, and translations of this plane (Fig. 14.1, A–C).

The second stage consists of games that challenge children to apply their developed spatial-temporal skills to solve math and science problems. For this study we limited the problems to fractions and proportions. Again, this stage is language free and does not require children to perform numerical calculations (Fig. 14.1, D and E).

Each level within both stages begins with an introduction. All introductions have the following characteristics: (i) For each question, there is one correct answer out of three or four possible choices. (ii) There is no penalty for incorrect responses. (iii) Visual feedback is provided that indicates whether or not the child's response is correct, and why the response is correct or incorrect. (iv) For each question, children are allowed as many attempts as are necessary before arriving at the correct answer. (v) For each attempt at any given question, the answer choices and the order of choices remain the same.

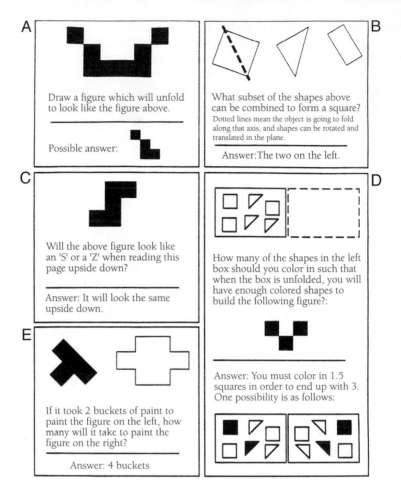

FIGURE 14.1   Some (less difficult) examples of concepts presented in Matthew Peterson's first version of the S.T.A.R. software. The software does not include the verbal instructions shown here. Children quickly learned what was expected from each question without instructions. A, B, and C are training problems; D and E apply spatial-temporal reasoning to proportional math and fractions. From Graziano *et al.* (1999a)

After the introduction, the game proper begins for each level. Each question consists of one correct answer, taken at random from a set of correct answers for that question, and two to three wrong answers, taken at random from a set of incorrect answers. Thus, two children working independently on the same question could have two different sets of correct/incorrect answers to choose from. This randomization minimized any memory component and helped maintain children's interest when they re-played the same level. It also prevented children from copying answers from other children.

As in the introductions, visual feedback is given that indicates whether or not the child's response is correct, and why the response is correct or incorrect. However, unlike the introductions, points are given for correct responses, whereas incorrect or slow responses result in either a reduction in points or a return to the beginning of the level. The ongoing score for each child is displayed in real time, and the final score for each game is recorded in a file for each child.

At present, the scores for each game are also entered on a graph for that game for each child. The children quickly learned how to read the graphs since they were eager to keep track of their scores and progress. I regret to note that many college students have trouble understanding graphs.

PILOT STUDY

One hundred and two 2nd grade children from two Orange County schools (IR and SA) were involved in a one-month Pilot study to determine the general effectiveness of the S.T.A.R. software. Ages ranged from 6 years, 8 months to 8 years, 5 months.

School SA is considered to be a below-average demographics school. We selected two classes from SA to receive training, and for logistical reasons one class received S.T.A.R. training (Math group with 20 children) while the other class received English language training on the computer (English group with 20 children). Both classes had the same amount of very basic computer lessons at school, approximately once per month, and none of the children had received training similar to S.T.A.R. A third group (No Lesson group with 62 children) was taken from the above-average demographics school IR.

The purpose of this Pilot study was: (1) to test the hypothesis that the Math group would perform better than the English group or the No Lesson group on a post-training assessment of ST reasoning, and (2) to fine-tune both the first level of the training stage and the proportions level of the applications stage of S.T.A.R.

The Math and English groups from school SA each received training twice a week, in 50-minute class sessions for nine sessions. We provided two professional computer instructors who taught both groups. The lessons were given in the school computer lab on 14 Mac computers that were adequate to run S.T.A.R. Since there were 20 children in each group, more than half of the children might be sharing a computer at any time.

The Math group was taught using the first two levels of stage one in the S.T.A.R. software. The English group was taught using age-appropriate, friendly, commercial software programs designed to teach reading, spelling, and writing.

All three experimental groups were tested on their spatial reasoning with three tasks from the Performance subtest of WISC-III. As noted earlier, WISC-III tasks were used to establish baselines for ST reasoning rather than to measure individual improvements with our one month of training. Children were tested individually at their schools. The Math and English groups were tested prior to the start of training.

The Stanford Achievement Test, ninth edition (Stanford 9), is a nationally calibrated test in reading, writing, and math, now used by the entire state of California. The test is administered to students in grades 2 through 11. We used average math scores on the Stanford 9 from schools SA and IR as baseline measurements to confirm the below-average and above-average achievements of SA and IR, respectively, also confirmed by the WISC-III results.

Results from the Stanford 9 confirm that school SA is below average in math while school IR is above average. Second graders from SA ranked in the 27th percentile in math as compared to a nationally selected group, and second graders from IR ranked in the 67th percentile. Pretesting with the WISC-III ST tasks was useful in that it verified that children from the below-average demographic schools LA and SA were indeed performing below national norms in ST reasoning. WISC-III pretesting also verified that children from the above-average demographic school IR were performing above the national norms.

All three experimental groups were given a Pilot Assessment test at the end of training for the Math and English groups. Our Pilot Assessment was composed of 25 questions to test the ST concepts and proportional math presented in the pilot version of S.T.A.R. However, the format of the Assessment was different from that of S.T.A.R. For example, the penguin JiJi in S.T.A.R. was not used in the Pilot Assessment. In addition, the filling process for proportional math problems in S.T.A.R. used fuel cells, whereas the Assessment used trucks. The details of the Pilot Assessment problems were also different from those in S.T.A.R.

The experimenter gave the Pilot Assessment to an entire 20-student class using color transparencies on an overhead projector. The Assessment started with a 10-minute verbal introduction, in which students interacted with the experimenter while doing sample questions. These questions were explicit examples explaining each concept in detail using the transparencies. The test questions were presented in the same way. Each child was given a test book, which contained a separate answer page for each introductory question and for each of the 25 test questions. Each answer page contained four graphic choices, only one of which was the correct answer, and these choices correspond exactly with the four choices presented on each color transparency.

The results of the Pilot Study Assessment Test are given in Fig. 14.2. I note that the distribution of the results on each of the 25 test questions showed that the English and No Lesson groups understood the nature of the questions and

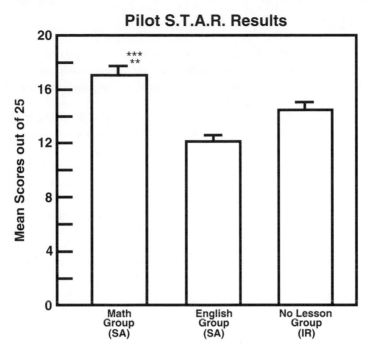

FIGURE 14.2   Results of the Pilot Study Assessment Test after one month of training with S.T.A.R. The Math group scored 36% higher than the control English group from the same below-average demographic school SA. This difference is significant to p less than 0.001. The Math group also scored 14% higher (significant to p less than 0.01) than the No Lesson group from the above-average demographic school IR. From Graziano *et al.* (1999a)

performed significantly above chance. The results demonstrate the effectiveness of S.T.A.R. in teaching the math concepts given in Fig. 14.1. The Math group scored a striking 36% higher than the control English group. These two groups are from the below-average demographic school SA. The Math group also scored 14% higher than the No Lesson control group from the above-average demographic school IR.

I suggest that these results in Fig. 14.2 with 2nd grade children have enormous potential significance. In just one month, S.T.A.R. training effectively *leveled the playing field,* in the math we tested on, between the below-average-performing children in school SA and the above-average-performing children in school IR. This included proportional math. This point is big news because math educators have been looking for ways, using language-analytic methods, to improve proportional math performance in 6th and 8th grade middle-class children and have not succeeded [6]. There is a long way to go, but we are well on our way. Please see Fig. 23.2 regarding what I mean by leveling the playing field.

MAIN STUDY

We worked with 170 2nd graders from the inner-city 95th St. Elementary School in Los Angeles in a four-month study designed to explore how piano keyboard training, versus an appropriate control, in conjunction with S.T.A.R., affected students' performance in math.

I described in Chapter 2 my fortuitous meeting with Linda Rodgers, a teacher from the 95th St. School. The M.I.N.D. Institute has a long-term relationship with this school and it is now our Lab for trying out our new innovations in math education through music training combined with S.T.A.R. training. Everyone who visits the 95th St. School is tremendously impressed with what the children in our program are accomplishing. As I was writing this page I could not resist putting in these qualitative observations. BBC's "Tomorrow's World" did a 6-minute TV piece on our program here that was shown in England in June, 1998. The children's enthusiasm for music and math came through in a marvelous manner, and I received over 30 phone calls and letters from England.

Thirty-four students withdrew from the school during the course of the study and were not included in the analyses. The students who withdrew were fairly evenly distributed among the experimental groups. This left 136 children, 67 boys and 69 girls, ranging in age from 6 years, 8 months to 8 years, 10 months at the time of pretesting. Seventy-six of the children were of Hispanic origin, 59 were African-American, and 1 was Caucasian.

The 95th St. School is considered to be a below-average demographics school, as well as below average in academic achievement. The main experimental groups were drawn from five 2nd grade classes. The logistics of school scheduling influenced group assignment. Class 1 received piano keyboard training and S.T.A.R. training (Piano-ST group) for four months. Class 2 received English language training on the computer and S.T.A.R. (English-ST group) for four months. Class 3 was randomly and evenly divided between the Piano-ST and English-ST groups. There were a total of 26 children in the Piano-ST group and 29 in the English-ST group. The No Lesson group (with 28 children) comprised students from classes 4 and 5.

In addition to the main experimental groups, we worked with three groups from classes 6, 7, and 8 that received S.T.A.R. training only, for different amounts of time. The ST-3 group (17 children) received training for three months, the ST-2 group (20 children) for two months, and the ST-1 group (16 children) for one month. *None of the children had prior music lessons or computer lessons, and parental involvement was minimal.*

All lessons took place at the 95th St. School in the same classroom and were conducted in the morning. The Piano-ST and English-ST groups each received S.T.A.R. training twice a week in 31 hour-long sessions for four months. During the same four-month period, the Piano-ST group received group piano lessons, and the English-ST group received group English lessons on the computer, three times a week in 42 hour-long sessions.

Because of the logistics of class scheduling, the Piano-ST group was divided into two subgroups of 17 and 9 children, respectively. The English-ST group was also divided into two subgroups, of 19 and 10 children, respectively. S.T.A.R. lessons for the Piano-ST and English-ST groups were conducted separately with three classes of 19, 16, and 20.

The three ST groups also received S.T.A.R. training twice a week in hour-long sessions for the following number of months and lessons: ST-3 had 22 lessons in three months, ST-2 had 17 lessons in two months, and ST-1 had 7 lessons in one month.

The Piano-ST group was our main experimental group. The English language training on computers given to the English-ST group controlled for the motor and visual coordination provided by the piano keyboard, personal attention, time away from normal classroom activity, and the child's engagement with the activity. The No Lesson group offered a baseline comparison for the S.T.A.R. Evaluation Program.

The three ST groups allowed us to begin evaluating the S.T.A.R. training software. We were able to compare performance on the S.T.A.R. E.P. after four months, three months, two months, and one month of training, and with the performance of the No Lesson group.

The proposed role of our piano instruction was to enhance the neural "hardware" in the cortex for spatial-temporal reasoning. As noted in Chapter 13, we focused on piano keyboard lessons rather than lessons on other instruments because the keyboard gives a visual-linear representation of the spatial relationships between pitches. This is not true, for example, with string instruments, where pitch is not fixed. It is therefore easier to use the piano to teach important musical concepts such as intervallic relationships, which concern the distance between notes. Furthermore, we feel that coupling visual information with aural information might assist the neural pattern development that is relevant to ST operations. Keyboard instruments are also optimal for our purposes because they are available in electronic form, designed for use in group lessons.

Piano keyboard lessons were designed, supervised, and conducted by Amy Graziano, with the very able assistant teacher Miyoung Kim. We used two teacher consoles, each linked to ten electronic piano keyboards. The keyboards were placed on child-sized tables, four per table, with the tables arranged in a generally square configuration.

For the purposes of this study, Amy developed an instructional methodology derived from several standard music education systems. Based on results from the Mozart effect experiments, we predicted that a listening component added to standard piano lessons would further enhance ST reasoning. Thus, each lesson began with up to 10 minutes of listening to piano music. We focused on

Mozart piano sonatas, because experimental data are available only for the effect of Mozart's Piano Sonata for Two Pianos in D Major (K.448) on the enhancement of ST reasoning. During piano instruction, children were taught basic musical concepts: finger number associations, clef signs, rhythmic values, and how to identify letter names on the staff and on the keyboard. They learned to read and play simple melodies for right hand alone (RH), left hand alone (LH), and hands together.

After four months, all children were able to identify treble and bass clefs, count combinations of note values, and read letter names in RH C position from the staff, and identify them on the keyboard. All 26 students were able to play simple melodies for RH and LH, separately and together, in LH F position and RH C position. All 26 were able to count the note values in the melodies they played. Fifteen of the 26 Piano-ST children were also able to read and play RH G position and LH C position after four months.

English language lessons were conducted by Tina Earl, a highly professional computer instructor, who served this role in the Preschool study. The assistant piano teacher also served as assistant teacher to our computer instructor, since the software used was readily understood and not difficult to teach. Lessons were conducted on 20 Power Mac computers, which we supplied. The computers were placed on child-sized tables, three per table, with the tables arranged along two adjacent walls of the room. Each child worked on a separate computer. Each lesson was conducted by the two teachers, with the entire class on computers for the whole 60 minutes.

Age-appropriate, friendly, commercial software programs designed to teach reading, pronunciation, spelling, and sentence structure were used. After four months, most children were able to spell and pronounce approximately 30 vocabulary words, and to use them in written sentences. Prior to training, on average the children were not able to perform these tasks.

Training with S.T.A.R. proceeded as described earlier. All lessons were conducted by Tina and an assistant on the same computers used for English language training. Each child worked on a separate computer, except for one game level, where two students competed at the same computer.

All 55 children in the Piano-ST and English-ST groups completed all levels of S.T.A.R. However, approximately half the children needed extra help from the instructor to pass the last three levels. The remainder of the students completed the final level with no help or prompting. Tina estimates that four to six additional lessons would have been sufficient to allow the children who needed help to finish on their own.

All 37 children in the ST-3 and ST-2 groups completed all levels of S.T.A.R. However, their pass criterion was lower than that for the Piano-ST and English-ST groups. The ST-3 and ST-2 groups were required to pass levels three, four, and five only once versus three times for Piano-ST and English-ST groups. ST-3 and ST-2 had only one day with level six, the final level, and were not required to pass it. The ST-1 group completed level one with the three-pass criterion, then were introduced to all remaining levels, except the final one. They were not required to pass any level after the first.

As in the Pilot study, we used three tasks from the WISC-III as a pretraining baseline of ST reasoning (Object Assembly, Block Design, and Picture Arrangement). Children were tested one to two months prior to training.

The S.T.A.R. Evaluation Program has two parts: a one-hour introduction session for children who have not had the S.T.A.R. training, and the testing session itself. One hundred twenty-seven of the 136 children were tested with the E.P. testing session; 7 of the No Lesson group and 2 of the Piano-ST group were absent on testing days and so were not tested. The No Lesson group, which also received the one-hour introduction session, was retested a second time with the E.P. one month after taking the test for the first time. For all groups, the E.P. was administered by our computer instructor, who gave verbal instructions on how to answer each type of question. She was available at all times to address any difficulties a student might have.

The S.T.A.R. E.P. is composed of 44 nonverbal questions of the types shown in Fig. 14.1: 3 questions of type A, 10 of type B, 11 of type C, and 16 of types D and E. Four additional questions deal with other aspects of spatial-temporal symmetry. Each type of question is introduced with a demonstration in which the software gives solutions to two examples of that type. Most questions on the test are multiple choice with four choices, only one of which is correct. However, there are also other formats, such as questions that require students to draw something on the computer, and questions that require students to select the appropriate subset of answer choices that best makes up the solution. After selecting a solution, students are able to change their answer choice before going on to the next question.

The No Lesson group was given the one-hour introduction session and the E.P. on two consecutive days. During the introduction, students are taught basic concepts of symmetry and given physical demonstrations of ST operations such as rotation, folding, and unfolding. Students are then guided through selected parts of S.T.A.R. in order to experience interacting with the computer in the ways required of them during the E.P.

The results of the S.T.A.R. E.P. from the four-month Main study at the 95th St. School, given in Fig. 14.3, are dramatic, showing the benefit of piano training in conjunction with S.T.A.R. training.

> The Piano-ST group scored 15% higher than the control English-ST group overall on the 44 questions, *and a striking 27% better on the 16 questions devoted to fractions and proportional math.*

Note that the last piano lesson for the Piano-ST group was given six days before the testing on the Math Video Game E.P. Both Piano-ST and English-ST groups (which received S.T.A.R. training) performed over 100% better than the No

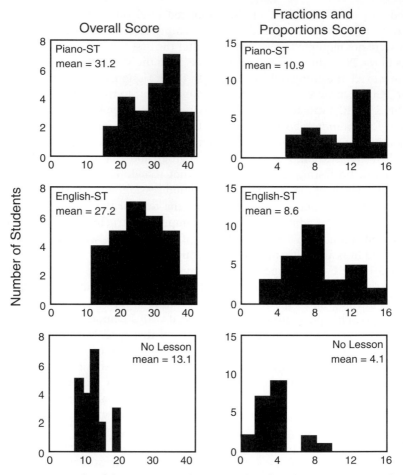

FIGURE 14.3   Results of the S.T.A.R. E.P. showing number of children versus score on the E.P. after four months of training. The left side shows scores from the entire E.P. The Piano-ST and English-ST groups each scored over 100% higher than the No Lesson group. The Piano-ST group scored 15% higher (with a p less than 0.05) than the English-ST group. The right side shows scores from the subset of questions on the E.P. dealing specifically with fractions and proportional math. Again, Piano-ST and English-ST groups each scored over 100% higher than the No Lesson group. The Piano-ST group scored a striking 27% higher (with a p less than 0.05) than the English-ST group. From Graziano *et al.* (1999a)

Lesson group from the same school. All groups performed far above chance level, which is a score of 7.17 out of 44 questions.

These results [7] (Fig. 14.3) showing the enhanced math performance of the Piano-ST group as compared to the English-ST group, are especially dramatic since there were only four months of piano keyboard training. Unlike the ex-

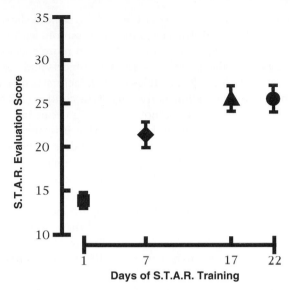

FIGURE 14.4   Results of the S.T.A.R. E.P. testing math concepts as a function of the number of S.T.A.R. training lessons that each group of 2nd grade children had. This shows how rapidly they master the ST training. Each data point represents the average score of a different group on the E.P. The E.P. consists of the test plus one day (1-hour lesson) of ST training for those children who had no previous ST training from us. Thus the No Lesson group (square) had one day of ST training. Group ST-1 (diamond) had 7 days of ST training, ST-2 (triangle) had 17 days of training, and ST-3 (circle) had 22 days of training. Chance performance was a score 7.17. As shown in Fig. 14.3, piano keyboard training further enhances math performance. From Graziano *et al.* (1999a)

tremely rapid learning curve for S.T.A.R. training shown in Fig. 14.4, we expect (as discussed later) that the enhancement in math will grow with years of piano training. The three ST groups show a striking learning curve when results from the S.T.A.R. E.P. are plotted against number of lessons (Fig. 14.4). The curve rises sharply from the No Lesson group to ST-1, becomes more shallow between ST-1 and ST-2, and then levels off after ST-2.

In addition to these quantitative results, interviews with the homeroom teachers revealed qualitative improvements in several relevant academic areas. The teacher of S.T.A.R. at school SA during the Pilot study reported that four of five significantly below-average students caught up and understood numbers better after the month of training. Teachers of the Piano-ST group in the Main study at the 95th St. School reported better attention and concentration abilities in almost all the piano students. Perhaps the most interesting qualitative observation was how few lessons were necessary for these below-average 2nd graders to master the sophisticated spatial-temporal reasoning tasks in S.T.A.R.

An important educational question is whether or not time spent at piano (or the English control) and S.T.A.R. lessons interfered with normal classroom instruction. Interviews with teachers at the 95th St. School show that the additional instruction did not distract or diminish classroom learning. Instead, it facilitated a more carefully planned curriculum and more effective time management. Teachers were able to cover all normal subjects and lessons and still have time for piano and S.T.A.R. The roles of such factors as motivation, interest, self-esteem, and determination on the part of the child as well as the teacher are clearly vital. However, they are not sufficient in learning difficult math concepts such as proportional math. I contend that it is our spatial-temporal approach that has broken this barrier for many children to learn proportional math. It is the child's understanding of proportional math that produces self-esteem not the other way around. I will return to this discussion in more detail in Chapter 23. We have shown here that ST methods in the nonverbal S.T.A.R. allow children to better learn fractions and proportional math. In particular, children from disadvantaged backgrounds learned these concepts at an earlier age than normally done in the public schools. This is significant given the fact that these concepts are known to be extremely difficult to teach using standard language-analytic methods. In addition, the results presented here indicate that piano keyboard training, in conjunction with S.T.A.R. training, further enhances the learning of fractions and proportional math. The next step is to demonstrate that these conceptual understandings can lead to better performance on language-analytic assessments, such as standard math word problems.

An important question to ask is why piano lessons may have helped the learning of fractions and proportional math. Our previous research [8] indicates that piano lessons specifically enhance ST reasoning. Since proportional thinking relies on ST reasoning, it follows that piano lessons, through an enhancement of ST reasoning, may lead to better fraction and proportional math thinking skills. The learning of music emphasizes thinking in space and time. We have already discussed why piano lessons, in particular, emphasize the spatial dimensions of music: with the keyboard, students have a clear visual representation of auditory space.

Other reasons why music may enhance ST reasoning and proportional math are:

(i)   When children learn intervallic relationships (the distance between two notes), they are learning spatial relationships.

(ii) When children learn rhythm, they are learning ratios, fractions, and proportions—an eighth note is half of a quarter note, which is half of a half note, which is half of a whole note; an eighth note is to a quarter note as a half note is to a whole note, and so on.

(iii) Playing an instrument has a temporal element, so children learn to think ahead. For example, a child will need to be playing one note while at the same time looking at the next note on the page and determining where to place his or her fingers. Ultimately, students learn to

look ahead in the written music for whole patterns of notes—ascend-
ing, descending, repetitive, even symmetrical patterns. They learn to
determine what they will play next, before they start playing it.

(iv)   Music listening also has a temporal element. When children are familiar
with a piece, they can think ahead and anticipate what they will hear next.

The performing of music exercises ST reasoning and proportional thinking
using auditory, visual, and sensory-motor modalities. We stress that piano keyboard lessons in combination with S.T.A.R., which specifically teaches proportional math through the visual mode, is a powerful educational tool.

The ST methods in S.T.A.R. can be extended to almost all math at all levels.
As an example, the use of symmetries in ST methods has been used successfully
by Xiao Leng in analyzing the behavior of equations for a pre-calculus course
that she teaches at Pasadena City College. *Thus, the use of spatial-temporal
methods to enhance understanding of math is not limited to disadvantaged and/or
very young students.*

In addition to the teaching of math, we expect that these ST methods can be
successfully extended to teaching all branches of science, since most scientists
and mathematicians rely heavily on this ST faculty. However, despite its prevalence in the pursuit of science, ST reasoning is almost completely absent from
our current educational system. One level in Matthew's latest version of S.T.A.R.
for 2nd grade children deals with building figures from components in which
the figures are ozone molecules. This should be very useful when these children
study chemistry in higher grades.

As noted earlier, the most interesting qualitative observation was how
quickly the children mastered the sophisticated ST reasoning tasks in S.T.A.R..
For example, all children in both Piano-ST and English-ST groups passed the
first level of stage one before the fourth lesson. In order to pass, each child was
required to achieve 320 points on each of three different trials of level one (each
child had four to six trials of level one per lesson). This can be compared to the
actual performance of a dozen university science researchers, the majority of
whom did not achieve more than 200 points on either of two trials.

I believe that this rapid learning of the concepts taught in S.T.A.R. gives
considerable support to the strong predictions of the trion model: (i) that the
elemental operations inherent in the cortex are the symmetry operations and
(ii) that they form the basis for higher brain functions of ST reasoning. If this
trion model prediction was incorrect, we would expect that the time necessary
for 2nd graders to master the sequences would be much longer. This suggests
that a study to quantitatively determine the time required to achieve a successful criterion on a level of S.T.A.R. versus that of an appropriate control would
be of neuroscientific interest.

The long-term enhancement (*lasting at least 6 days after the final piano lesson*) of performance for the Piano-ST group over that of the English-ST group

in fractions and proportional math suggests a neurophysiological experiment: In analogy to the EEG coherence study of the Mozart effect [9] presented in Chapter 15, I suggest that possible priming through listening to the Mozart Sonata (K.448) just prior to training with the S.T.A.R. be investigated in EEG coherence studies.

Another area that should be investigated is how the many different methods of music instruction appropriate for group settings [10] affect ST reasoning and math performance. Some of these methods may work better than others for specifically enhancing ST reasoning, and/or may work more efficiently in a public school setting. For example, if a particular music training program gives 60% as large an enhancement in math performance with only 10% of the cost of a different program, then it would make sense for a school to consider the less expensive program. It is also of enormous interest, regardless of such cost factors, to know which music training programs [11] are the best for enhancing ST abilities. Amy Graziano, Matthew Peterson, and I [12] have designed a protocol on how to use any existing music training program to quickly address these crucial questions, as well as which music training program. The key component of our proposal rests on the rapid learning curve seen in Fig. 14.4. I will return to this idea later.

It is interesting to note that a general trend can be observed in the Stanford 9 results for below-average schools in Orange County, California: Math scores that are below average at 2nd grade tend to decrease as grade level increases. This may be due to the fact that the Stanford 9 does not test for fractions and proportional math on the 2nd grade level, but does so for higher grades (as children begin to learn these more difficult math concepts their performance seems to decrease). Thus some parts of the Stanford 9 math test for higher grades might serve as an appropriate standardized evaluation of achievement in fractions and proportional math as taught in S.T.A.R. *However, the music and S.T.A.R. training must first be integrated into the standard math language-analytic word problems. We are now doing this in our program in the 95th St. School.*

The M.I.N.D. Institute has proposed that a pilot study be done with several other schools, followed by a large, standardized three-year study. This project would investigate enhanced performance in math concepts due to a combination of piano keyboard training and spatial-temporal training that is integrated into the standard math word problems. Measurements of ST reasoning, proportional math, and general math achievement can be obtained from S.T.A.R. E.P. and from new tests made from standardized tests used for older children. *It is absolutely crucial that the results presented in this chapter be duplicated in programs anywhere using our protocol.* I will present some details of our proposal in a later chapter. Success of this large study would help revolutionize the learning of math and science by all children.

PART IV

Tests from Brain Imaging and Animal Studies

BRIEF GUIDE

The exciting results and proposed studies that I present in Part IV are crucial to a better understanding of higher brain function. You have seen the trion model described in Part II and its behavioral predictions successfully tested in Part III. However, the detailed *scientific* understanding of what is happening in the brain must be studied. Not only do we want to confirm that we are proceeding on the right track, but as we learn more about what is happening at the neurophysiological level, we will be better able to design behavioral studies that may lead to practical educational and clinical applications.

CHAPTER 15

EEG and fMRI Studies of the Mozart Effect

BRIEF GUIDE

In this chapter I present surface brain wave EEG studies done at the University of Vienna. The results were dramatic and gave the first neurophysiological support for the Mozart effect. I wrote this material to be readable, but it is technical and can be skimmed. The visually striking figures need to be studied to be understood. The first dramatic results for fMRI studies of the Mozart effect are also discussed.

In 1994, Fran Rauscher and I were invited by Hellmuth Petsche to attend a symposium on "Music and the Brain" that he had organized in Vienna. Hellmuth is a pioneer in studying the neurophysiological basis of higher brain function, not just as a sensory response to a brief stimulus. His long-term research [1] using EEG coherence methods (see Chapter 6) to study music represents seminal and landmark work. Thus, we accepted immediately. Franny had visited Vienna many times in her previous career as a touring concert cellist, and Vienna was her favorite city. Not only was the symposium extremely stimulating, but it provided a compelling setting to fully understand the experiments of Hellmuth and his collaborators, and for them to understand ours. It was a natural conclusion that we should collaborate on an EEG coherence study of the Mozart effect as a first experiment to investigate its neurophysiological basis.

Astrid vonStein, a dynamic young postdoctoral researcher in the lab of Petsche and Peter Rappelsberger, volunteered to fit this side project into her busy research schedule, at least to try on one subject. So Franny and I sent Astrid the two sets of PF&C tasks (see Fig. 9.2) along with the Mozart Sonata (K.448) and the protocol we used in the follow-up study described in Chapter 12. Astrid would use a tape of a short story in German for the control listening condition. Not long after, Astrid sent an e-mail message saying that the results with her first subject were extremely exciting. However, she had no time to test further subjects in our Mozart effect EEG experiments, particularly owing to the necessary lengthy analysis. Luckily, her fiancé (now husband), Johannes Sarnthein, had recently gotten his Ph.D. in theoretical physics and was in the process of switching careers to one in neuroscience. Johannes would take over our joint experiment.

An EEG, as noted in Chapter 6, records the summed electrical output of large regions of the underlying brain [2]. This brain activity varies in a "slow" wave manner as compared to the fast action potential of individual neuronal firing. The dominant source is electrical activity from the dendrites (not from the action potentials). This is exactly suited to our examination of the Mozart effect, since we expect that listening to the Mozart Sonata (K.448) "primes" the relevant neural pathways for the subsequent spatial-temporal reasoning tasks. So, the **firing subthreshold** (for producing the neuronal action potentials) dendritic activity would be expected to be crucial!

The EEG coherence analysis is designed to measure the degree of synchrony between the activity of two brain regions from two scalp surface electrodes during a specific higher brain function task as compared to a testing condition. This was perfect for examining the Mozart effect. All pairs of electrodes can be examined, or just neighboring (or local) pairs as in this experiment. This local coherence has the big advantage of giving a great color-coded brain imaging representation of what happens during the behavioral task. You will see that our results are quite visually striking and demonstrate the first evidence for the neurophysiological basis of the Mozart effect.

The experiment took place in two sessions for each subject, the time interval between sessions A and B ranging from a few hours up to several weeks. As in the (follow-up) Mozart effect behavioral experiment [3], subjects solved two sets of 16 PF&C items (see Fig. 9.2), which tests spatial-temporal reasoning. In

TABLE 15.1   Subject information along with test scores on the 16 PF&C items in the EEG coherence study of the Mozart effect. Session A is after listening to a story and Session B is after listening to the Mozart Sonata (K.448). The average score in Session A is 11.5 and that in Session B is 13.1 (an asterisk indicates that the score was not recorded and so her scores are not included in these averages).

Subjects	Age/sex	Musical experience	Profession	Scores A	B
UW	26 f	Serious cellist	Engineering	15	16
JJ	30 f	Serious flutist	Psychology	*	13
VS	26 f	Some piano	Architecture	11	15
ME	26 f	None	Mathematics	15	10
UK	28 f	None	Computer science	15	15
AvS	34 f	Some cello	Medicine	8	10
BK	21 f	Some piano	Psychology	5	13

Session A, subjects listened to a story spoken in their native language and then solved the 16 PF&C items of the first set, taking about 1 minute per item. In Session B, the procedure was repeated with the second PF&C set after listening to the Mozart Sonata (K.448) instead of the text.

Particulars of the seven subjects are shown in Table 15.1, along with their scores on the PF&C tasks. We did not attempt to duplicate the behavioral experiment results with only seven subjects, but their scores are worth discussing. Possibly because of their professional training, three of the subjects obtained particularly high scores in the first session, leaving no room for significant enhancement in Session B. Further, it was shown in Fig. 12.3 in the behavioral experiment that subjects with low initial scores improved the most after listening to the Mozart Sonata (K.448). We see in Table 15.1 that our present subjects did improve from an average of 11.5 in Session A to 13.1 in Session B. Another interesting point is that although participants in the behavioral experiments did not have musical training, this EEG experiment was carried out in Vienna, where musically naive subjects are difficult to find.

The EEG recording of the brain electrical data is analyzed in a sophisticated but standard manner that yields the output of the slow electrical waves in six frequency bands:

delta (1.5–3.5 cycles/sec or Hz)
theta (4.0–6.5 Hz)
alpha1 (7.0–9.0 Hz)
alpha2 (9.5–12.5 Hz)
beta (13.0–18.0 Hz)
gamma (18.5–31.5 Hz)

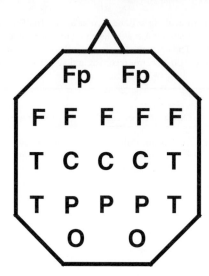

FIGURE 15.1 Highly schematic diagram of the cortex, showing frontal (F), temporal (T), central (C), parietal (P), and occipital (O) regions. Fp is the prefrontal region. The triangle at the front represents the nose. These are the same regions described in Chapter 6 in somewhat more detail.

Both the amplitude (or size) of the waves and their coherence patterns are determined. The amplitude and coherence patterns during the PF&C tasks were *highly reproducible* for the 16 items *within each session*. This was true for each of our seven subjects. This is a very reassuring result, for both the stability of the experiment and the robustness of the brain activity during the PF&C tasks in a session. We will focus on the coherence brain patterns, since they are measuring the neurophysiological quantities of most interest to us. For orientation, Fig. 15.1 shows a highly schematic designation of the cortical regions.

A dramatic result found by Astrid and Johannes [4] was that in three of the seven subjects, right frontal and left temporal-parietal coherence activity (between neighboring electrodes) induced during the listening to the Mozart Sonata (K.448) carried over to the spatial-temporal PF&C tasks. This can be seen in Fig. 15.2 (see color insert), where results of the subjects UW and VS are given. Note the reproducibility of the gross features in columns 1 and 2 for UW for the PF&C tasks in Sessions A and B, respectively. Important differences between these columns have been circled; solid circles indicate coherence increases and dashed circles indicate decreases. The same circles have been drawn in column 3 for the listening to the Mozart Sonata.

Now observe that the circled patterns in column 2 appear to be a superposition of those in columns 1 and 3. In other words, the overall coherence patterns of the PF&C task after listening to the Mozart Sonata appear as a superposition of the patterns of the PF&C task after listening to text and the pattern while listening to the Mozart Sonata. This effect is also seen for subject VS in columns 4–6. *There is a carryover from the listening to the Mozart Sonata (K.448) to the subsequent spatial-temporal PF&C task. It was readily seen in three of the seven subjects.*

We then examined the duration of this carryover. In an additional session (not involving the PF&C tasks), subject JJ again listened to the first 10 minutes of the Mozart Sonata (K.448) and the EEG recordings were continued for the next 12 minutes [5]. The first column in Fig. 15.3 (see color insert) shows the coherence pattern during the listening to the music. The following four columns show the patterns that were found during the subsequent relaxation, each period lasting about 3 minutes. *This is neurophysiological evidence that the effects of listening to the Mozart Sonata last for at least 12 minutes, which is roughly the time that Franny and I had found from the first behavioral experiment.*

These results are an extremely promising first glimpse into the neurophysiological basis for the Mozart effect. Clearly the usual remark holds: additional research needs to be done. We are now collaborating with groups at U.C. Irvine, U.C.L.A., and the University of Vienna to examine this carryover effect with a number of subjects, contrasting the effect of the Mozart Sonata with control music. *This new project will be of huge importance in testing our prediction that the Mozart Sonata (K.448) is resonating with the inherent Mountcastle cortical language of higher brain function. The EEG coherence for the Mozart then should last considerably longer than that for control music.*

The state-of-the-art 128-electrode EEG device (see Fig. 6.10) from James Swanson's lab at Irvine is being used. Another important aspect of Fig. 15.3 is the oscillations that occur on the order of minutes, which we will investigate. I emphasized in Chapter 7 the possibility that such time scales may exist.

Mark Bodner and I are collaborating with Orhan Naclioglu and Tugan Muftuler in an analogous fMRI experiment. Compared to an EEG, functional MRI brain imaging experiments give a much more spatially localized picture of what is happening in the brain during a behavioral task. However, the EEG coherence studies give the crucial synchronization of brain activity in neighboring regions. Thus these two noninvasive approaches complement each other.

Our fMRI experiment has an interesting aspect. As the magnetic fields in the magnets (see Fig. 6.15) are changed so they can image different "slices" in the brain, a very loud "ping" sound emerges (from the changing currents in the magnets dissipating energy, which emerges as these sounds). These pings are so loud and frequent (up to 30 times per second as the direction of the large magnetic field is changed) that they must be blocked out somehow. Cho [6] has recently demonstrated that the unmodified pings modify the fMRI imaging in auditory, motor, and visual cortical areas. The ping noise is serious in fMRI as compared to in MRI (which determines anatomy), since the signals to be measured result from subtle changes in oxygen flow in the brain due to the stimulus being studied. For our experiment, we also need to bring the music to the subject. The nontrivial (*it cannot contain any magnetic materials*) device we were able to afford consists of a commercial headset with the rest of the interface built by Jim Kelley. It does not totally block out the pings, but considerably reduces them in loudness.

We have just collected the first fMRI data [7] relevant to the Mozart effect, and they look extremely interesting. All four subjects listening to control music gave statistically significant signals only in the auditory cortex. In all four, the Mozart Sonata (K.448) generated substantial and highly significant signals in the frontal cortex. The results from the next set of subjects will be of tremendous interest.

I think that this synchrony feature of EEG coherence is beautifully illustrated in recent studies by Johannes Sarnthein [8] on short-term memory. Although human memory has been very well studied, Johannes was able for the first time to determine the cortical regions synchronized during *active* short-term (or working) memory [9]. He found that short-term memory involves synchronization between prefrontal and specific other cortical regions, all in the low-frequency theta (4–7 Hz) brain activity. I will return to his results in Chapter 16. Now I turn to the relevant animal studies that add a crucial and dramatic dimension to our story.

CHAPTER 16

Symmetry in Primate Higher Brain Function

BRIEF GUIDE

The material, experiments, and analysis in this chapter are readable but technical. Large parts may be skimmed. It represents for me almost 20 years of planning and preliminary studies leading to the present results of Mark Bodner, which give strong, detailed support for the trion model. The book's key concept of symmetry is truly present in the neurophysiological data.

In Part II, I presented details about our structured trion model of the cortex, which led to the prediction that early music training could act as exercise to enhance higher brain functions, in particular spatial-temporal reasoning. The resultant behavioral experiments presented in Part III gave dramatic results in support of this prediction. A large piece of our whole program is testing the trion model and understanding the behavioral results at the neuronal level. The EEG coherence and fMRI studies of the Mozart effect in Chapter 15 gave the first evidence for a neurophysiological basis. This chapter presents our experiments to more directly test the trion model at the neuronal level. I will first give some history leading up to Mark Bodner's exciting results.

HISTORY

VISUAL ILLUSIONS AND NEUROPHYSIOLOGY

In 1980, George Patera at the University of Montreal and I started thinking about ways to design both sensory experiments with humans and neurophysiological experiments with animals to test some of the early ideas that I had presented in 1978 [1] (see Fig. 8.3). The basic idea, following the Mountcastle columnar principle [2], is that the processing capabilities of the cortex are much greater than previously measured and involve the flow of firing activity among the minicolumns within the column. George is one of the world's leading experts on the mathematics of symmetries and their use in scientific problems. I had the good fortune to collaborate with George on some problems in high-energy physics and now I was to put his expertise to good use in my studies of the brain. *One of the most important skills that one learns in physics is the extreme importance of how one views data.* By properly binning (organizing and sorting) prospective data and using George's powerful insights on symmetry, we got some important first results on how to design relevant experiments to test these ideas concerning Mountcastle's columnar principle of the cortex. We considered sets of discrete quantities, obtained by choosing appropriate bin sizes for the stimuli and the expected cortical responses.

George and I decided to present these results as an abstract ("Dynamics of Firing Patterns in the Visual Cortex") at the 11th Annual Society of Neuroscience Meeting in 1981 [3]. Although our poster presentation contained some excellent ideas and was well received, my artwork was not up to the high style standards that are the norm. Since then, all posters that I have been an author on have been put together by colleagues and students, who have done a much better job of preparing them artistically.

I wanted to test some of our ideas so I started discussing them with neuroscience colleagues here at U.C. Irvine. Someone suggested that I talk to an extremely bright young post-doc at Cal Tech, V. S. Ramachandran. I arranged a meeting and was quite surprised when Rama told how he first met me almost 15 years previously in Madras, India. That was during a 10-week visit I made there to the Mathematical Institute of Sciences, whose founder and director was my friend Alladi Ramakrishnan. In turns out that Alladi is Rama's uncle. Rama came up with a very clever way to perform a relevant experiment in **apparent motion** to test the ideas I presented to him. Since he was just about to move to Irvine as a researcher in cognitive sciences, we were able to quickly carry it out.

Consider a series of spots separated in space and time. If presented visually to an observer with some reasonable spacings and time ordering (Fig. 16.1A), the observer will see an apparent motion of the spots that is remarkably similar to that of real motion. In fact, the two may be indistinguishable, as in a movie, or an animal running fast behind a picket fence, where a time sequence of stationary frames gives rise to the illusion of smooth continuous motion. The identity of an object moving on the screen is constantly preserved in spite of the fact that it is being sampled intermittently.

Our experiment [4] was designed to see how this illusion of continuity is achieved. We wanted to distinguish whether the gaps are "tolerated" by the brain because of its limited resolving abilities combined in space and time, or whether there is an actual perceptual filling-in of the gaps between discrete presentations. The latter possibility was the one predicted by the model [5] I presented to Rama.

As shown in Fig. 16.1A, the basic stimulus as presented on a personal computer was a vertical column of seven closely spaced dots, presented as a temporal sequence of discrete positions starting from 1 and ending in 8 and repeated. The time between successive presentations (which I call t_s) of the columns of dots was a constant in a given set of observations, but changed from values of 0.050 to 0.200 sec. As known from previous experiments for the shorter times t_s, the motion looked continuous. Next, one position (Fig. 16.1B), was left out of the time sequence. Again for shorter t_s, from 0.50 to 0.75 sec, the motion appeared continuous. *Even when the subjects were told that a gap was in fact present, they were unable to point to the column that had been skipped.*

To make the effect even more striking, we used a slightly modified version. Instead of completely skipping position 5, we presented a partial column of two dots as in Fig. 16.1C. This would be a more critical test of filling-in. The observers were asked to judge whether they noticed any difference between upper and lower segments of the columns of moving dots. They were provided with a fixation point in the center of the screen and were instructed to keep fixated on the point and avoid tracking the columns. *None of the observers could see anything odd.*

If the time t_s was increased to 0.125 sec or greater, the illusion was broken. Also, if we presented only positions 4, 5, and 6 (in the repeated loop), the illusion was broken. A sequence of at least two complete columns on either side of the partial column is necessary for the filling-in illusion to occur. This of course implied that the visual system in the brain must be integrating spatial information over several time frames and the result of this computation influences the spatial perception of the temporally subsequent frames. It was a

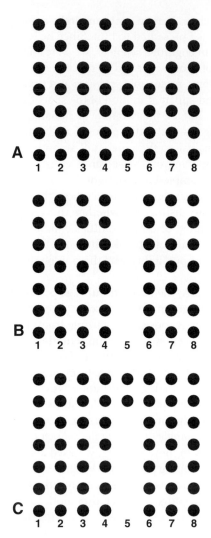

FIGURE 16.1   Design of experiment showing interpolation in apparent motion. (A) The vertical columns of dots are presented sequentially at the position shown in the time order shown by the numbers. Only one column is shown at a time. (B) The same as in A but at time 5 the screen is blank. (C) Same as in B, but two dots are shown rather than none at time 5. If the time between presentations of the dots is appropriate, all three sequences, A–C, look continuous and no difference among them is seen.

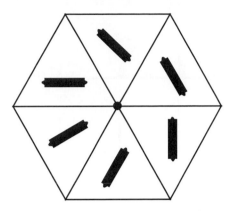

FIGURE 16.2   Highly schematic cortical column in primary visual cortex. The bar "/" represents the minicolumn where the neurons respond maximally to this orientation or angle of the bar. This structure was discovered in the pioneering experiments by Hubel and Wiesel (1977). More recently, this structure has been seen in optical recording experiments that show a number of such columns in one image.

delight to work with Rama, who has gone on to become a world-renowned leader in beautifully designed and executed experiments in behavioral neuro-science [6].

The next step was to look for the neurophysiological basis of such apparent motion illusions. I was able to get my neurophysiologist friend Pat Rinaldi to do the relevant experiment in her lab. She was willing to work on this unfunded project even though study of the visual cortex was outside her direct expertise. This is the usual "catch 22" in science: It is extremely difficult to get funding for neuroscience research from government sources without any data, so any truly new study must be done unofficially or with "borrowed" funds from other funded projects. Thus Pat, my graduate student in brain theory, John Pearson, and I set out to do the experiment.

As shown by Hubel and Wiesel in their classic Nobel Prize-winning experiments [7], the **primary visual cortex** (or cortical area 17 or V1) contains neurons in the cortical minicolumns that respond maximally in their firing rate to small bars presented at specific angles in a given part of the visual field [8]. The Mountcastle-type columnar structure (see Fig. 7.1) for the primary visual cortex is shown in Fig. 16.2, where the bar tilted like "/" represents the minicolumn that responds maximally to this orientation or angle.

First, we determined the optimum orientation of a light bar of the neuron being monitored by a microelectrode (see Fig. 6.9). Denoting this orientation by the vertical bar |, we presented temporal sequences (about a central point) on a computer screen of this bar and/or bars oriented at angles of 45 degrees

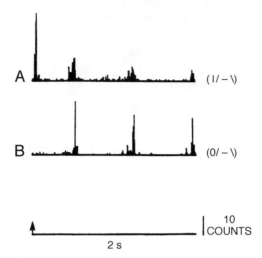

FIGURE 16.3　Neuronal firing data in response to the sequences of oriented bar stimuli presentations shown on the right (orientations are shown relative to the optimal one designated as | or vertical). As in Fig. 16.2, only one bar is shown at a time. (A) The clockwise sequence is repeated 30 times. (B) Same as A with the | bar omitted. Note the dramatic sharpening as well as the greatly increased peak firing response of the secondary peaks. From Shaw *et al.* (1983).

(/), 90 degrees (—), and 135 degrees (\ ) to this optimal orientation. We then presented sequences to an anesthetized cat that gave the illusion of continuous rotation about a point to a human (Rama and I had also done this rotation illusion with our human observers). We found a number of very interesting results [9].

Sharpening and increased peak response. A dramatic sharpening, as well as greatly increased peak firing response, is seen in Fig. 16.3 when the optimum stimulus | is omitted from the sequence | / — \ (repeated 30 times).

Dependence on order of presentation. Note the striking change in Fig. 16.4 when the order of presentation of the sequences of bar stimuli were changed from clockwise (| / — \) to counterclockwise (| \ — /). When the "random" sequence | ? ? ? (? denotes that these orientations were varied randomly) was presented, no structure was seen.

Possible "filling-in". A hint that there is a possible "filling-in" occurring is shown in Fig. 16.5 when the optimum oriented bar is omitted.

These results were very encouraging and intriguing. In particular, the "filling-in" was confirmed in more cases, and could be evidence for the neurophysiological basis for the apparent motion illusion seen in human observers with the same stimuli sequences. It was clear to us that more sophisticated experiments needed to be done. For example, we had not been

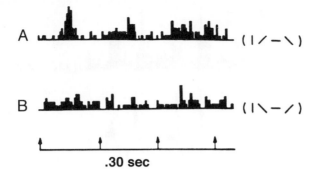

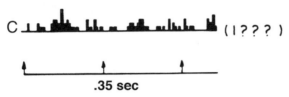

FIGURE 16.4   Another example similar to that in Fig. 16.3 showing the dependence on order. (A) Neuronal response to the clockwise sequence of bar presentations | / — \ . (B) Same as A, with a counterclockwise sequence | \ — / of bar presentations. Note the striking difference between the neuronal responses in A and B. (C) The "random" sequence | ? ? ? (? denotes that these orientations were varied randomly) was presented and no structure was seen in the neuronal responses. From Shaw *et al.* (1983).

monitoring a single neuron in each of these cases, but two or three neurons. It would be very useful to "isolate" a single neuron in each recording. This was just our first series of experiments. We started a second series of experiments [10], but we soon ran out of resources, ending this project. Nonetheless, I think that there was much more to learn here.

The next step in my quest to experimentally search for the code or neural language of the brain came after I had some substantial theoretical results from our studies of the trion model.

PATTERNS IN CORTICAL DATA

Now I had a better idea what to look for in cortical data: *A method of binning the data in time bins and also into levels of firing, as in the trion model, was what*

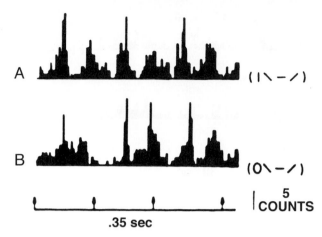

FIGURE 16.5 An example of a possible filling-in is seen in the neuronal responses. (A) The neuronal responses to a clockwise presentation of bar stimuli. (B) Same as in A with the | bar omitted. A hint of this filling-in is seen. From Shaw *et al.* (1983).

I would pursue. Here we would want to examine multielectrode data. A collaboration developed with Jurgen Kruger, a very dedicated and talented neurophysiologist from the University of Freiberg, who had published some multielectrode data [11] that he would let us analyze with our new methods. With the help of Ad Aertsen, a brain theorist from the Max-Planck Institute in Tubingen (a lovely college town in Germany where I sometimes went to work with my friend Guenther Palm), Dennis Silverman and I began our new analysis.

"Decoding" the brain's neural language is, I believe, the biggest challenge in science. The role of brain theory is crucial since understanding the brain totally from a bottom-up approach is just too difficult. On an almost trivial level of comparison, imagine trying to understand how your television set works by measuring some electrical parameters in the circuits of the TV. Our modest but important goal was to distinguish among four possible types of brain theory models using Kruger's data.

An important key to distinguishing between the various neural models of cortical function is to simultaneously observe the firing of a number of neurons in the cortex. Brain theory models of cortical function contrast *widely* in their basic assumptions concerning the code of information processing. I will distinguish among four codes:

1. A very localized spatial code with "grandmother" neurons as a limiting case [12]. A grandmother neuron is a single neuron or small group of neurons that can identify your grandmother.

2. A distributed spatial code, including the quite popular random-spin models [13].

3. A localized spatial-temporal code in a manner suggested by the Mountcastle organizational principle for the cortical column, embodying activity patterns moderately localized in space and time, as in our trion model.

4. A distributed spatial-temporal code [14] such as in the large cell assemblies envisioned by Hebb (in his famous book [15] that put forth his synaptic learning rule, shown in Fig. 8.1). Here the activity moves from large assembly to large assembly.

The results that I now describe for our analysis of Kruger's data give evidence for a spatial-temporal code (model types 3 and 4) as opposed to a pure spatial code (types 1 and 2). *This means the code cannot be separated into a spatial part times a temporal part. The spatial and temporal components of the code are inexorably intertwined.* I believe that this result is already helping us to understand the role of music in increasing our ability to think and reason. Specifically, it should help us begin to understand, from a basic neurobiological point of view, why the relatively simple control music did not enhance subsequent spatial-temporal reasoning in our Mozart effect experiments. In other words, these results may imply that rhythm alone or melody alone cannot be the key factor in reasoning enhancement.

As I have stated throughout this book, I think that the key to understanding the code of higher cortical processing involves looking simultaneously at the appropriate spatial and temporal separations; suggested scales are roughly 0.01 cm and 0.050 sec, respectively. At too large a scale, all structure in the firing patterns will be washed out, whereas at too fine a scale, one will be lost in a morass of detail and fluctuations. With this in mind, we employ here a new type of analysis for data from multielectrode recordings that will readily enable us to observe spatial-temporal structure in the response of the observed cortical network. We believe that our new analysis can be executed extremely fast (since it binned the data) and is thus suitable for interactive use (in real time) during multielectrode recording experiments. This analysis could be modified for use in human EEGs.

Kruger's experiments were made with 30 microelectrodes (a 5 × 6 array with 0.16-cm spacing, corresponding roughly to the minicolumn scale) in the primary visual cortex of monkeys. Among the stimuli applied repeatedly were sequences of large colored fields (red, green, or white) turned on and off, with each phase lasting 2 sec. For each electrode, we determined the time course of firing in bins of 0.025 sec to each of the color stimuli, averaged over several presentations. Then a division of the firing into six firing levels along with a statistical method of determining the probability of attaining such levels of

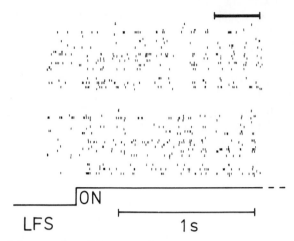

FIGURE 16.7   Spike trains from all 30 neurons during two presentations of a white light stimulus. Each firing is shown as a short vertical dot. The two stripes of dots represent the firings during the two presentations of the stimulus. The data shown start before the onstart of the stimulus and last until 1.3 sec after the stimulus is on. In the time span marked by the horizontal bar at the upper right, clear oscillations in firing occur. However, in these two trials, they are out of phase and hence these oscillations would cancel when the results from the two presentations are added. From Shaw *et al.* (1993).

firing was developed. Thus the statistics devised mainly by Dennis Silverman were already built explicitly into this new analysis [16].

Figure 16.6 (see color insert) shows the results of analyzing Kruger's data with Dennis's analysis in an arrangement corresponding to that of the 5 × 6 electrode array. The temporal evolution is shown in 24 time steps of 0.025 sec each. There are several nice results:

(i)   The activity builds up and dies down repeatedly (in the whole array) with a period of about three time steps.
(ii) The spatial-temporal distributions are not simply a temporal modulation of a spatial pattern.
(iii) The spatial-temporal distributions depend on the nature of the stimulus in a nontrivial manner (not shown here).

The average over several stimulus repetitions was taken to improve the statistics and to approximate the sampling of more neurons in postulated, somewhat localized assemblies. Though this was reasonable for the analysis presented in Fig. 16.6 for the first 0.6 sec after the start of the stimulus, it is not as adequate for longer times. This is strongly demonstrated in Fig. 16.7, where the detailed firing responses of all 30 neurons are shown for the entire 2 sec for two stimulus presentations. The detailed structure that appears after 1 sec tends to be washed out by averaging. The lesson is that the neural language or code of the brain undoubtedly has more structure than we usually observe.

We concluded that the stimulus-driven neuronal activity in a region of monkey visual cortex about the size of a cortical column displays synchronous, oscillatory behavior. The spatial-temporal patterns determined from our new analysis are layer and stimulus dependent, "build up and die down" rhythmically with periods of 0.07 to 0.1 sec, and cannot be factorized into separate spatial and temporal components. These results gave evidence for a spatial-temporal code as opposed to a purely spatial code. I want to stress that the search for a code with a temporal component in cortical data, including recording from more than one microelectrode, has a long and very instructive history [17], from which I have learned a lot.

These results were very encouraging and we suggested that the new type of spatial-temporal analysis presented here might be modified for use in multisite human EEG recordings. Here one would average slow-wave amplitudes for each electrode over the time bins. The levels of activity for each site could be determined by the deviations in each time bin from the average.

The final step in this personal "history" was the analysis of EEG data taken in the lab of Ken Tachicki from humans doing mental rehearsals of music. An undergraduate student Jemmy Chen and I started looking for repeating patterns in space and time in these data. I turned to the trion model and used a three-level analysis of the EEG data. Jemmy and I indeed found some intriguing results, as illustrated in Fig. 16.8. It was clear that we were seeing interesting spatial-temporal patterns that repeated, and Jemmy determined from a simple statistical analysis that these features were not simply fluctuations. However, I knew that there were some missing ingredients.

The key to further progress came when Mark Bodner and I went back to the trion model. *We realized that the method of looking for spatial-temporal patterns that Jemmy and I had used must be changed to include family members related by symmetries.* Now the story shifts to Mark's dramatic program and results, which would be explicitly supportive of the trion model predictions.

I first met Mark in 1991 while he was still a graduate student in physics at U.C.L.A. He was completing his well-regarded thesis in theoretical physics on the very mathematical string theory, which is concerned with combining all the fundamental forces in nature using sophisticated symmetries. Mark had decided that his other love was neuroscience and that he would switch fields. Having read the "Brain Theory Reprint Volume" as well as a paper on symmetries in brain theory that I had co-authored [18], Mark came to see me at U.C. Irvine to discuss his plans. I was immediately taken with this highly motivated and exceptionally intelligent scientist. We began a collaboration that has continued and grown in depth and scope, capitalizing on our common appreciation

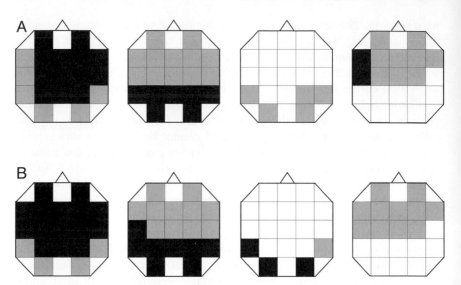

FIGURE 16.8   Example of repeating spatial-temporal patterns found by Jemmy Chen and me in human EEG data during mental rehearsal of music. We used three levels of electrical activity as measured from an average activity in 0.05-sec bins. White represents above-average, grey represents average, and black represents below-average activity. (A) The activity in the 19 electrodes is displayed in an array representing the physical location of the electrodes in each of the four time bins, with time increasing from left to right. (B) A spatial-temporal pattern found at a different time in the EEG recording than that in A, but still quite similar. This is only meant to give a qualitative feeling for the repeating patterns we were seeing in the data.

of what we felt was the enormous yet neglected role of symmetry in the brain. Mark is now a faculty member in the Medical School at UCLA working with Joaquin Fuster.

SYMMETRIC ANALYSIS

In Chapter 8, I presented all the relevant details of the trion model. In particular, I showed that structure in the basic cortical column of trions gave a large repertoire of memory patterns that could be excited. These memory states were readily enhanced through learning, and evolved in natural sequences. Most relevant was that these MPs had family members related by symmetries. In the trion model, these symmetry families of MPs allowed the cortex to recognize relationships among patterns and formed the neural basis for higher brain function. Mark Bodner and I concluded that the next step in looking for patterns in cortical data should explicitly include families of symmetry firing patterns. This was to be the crucial missing component.

As discussed in Chapter 8, for our structured connectivity in the trion model I expect that there will be a number of **symmetry operators** α that will characterize a repertoire of memory patterns. Among the symmetry operators that we have found in the trion model are:

R: spatial rotation among the *distinguishable* trions
M: mirror reflection
T: time reversal operation
C: interchanges firing levels S and −S

Examples of MPs related by M and T were shown in Fig. 8.14. In general, a product of two of these symmetry operators α is also an α.

In addition to these symmetries, there are the temporal rotations of the MPs shown in Fig. 8.15. In an evolution of any MP, it could start at any time step in the pattern, so this must be allowed for in the analysis of the cortical data.

If these R, M, T, C, and temporal rotation symmetries (or others that would be discovered) were symmetries in how our brain functions, then if a spatial-temporal memory pattern is discovered, it must have family members related by these symmetries. This is the hypothesis that Mark and I would test.

The data to be analyzed were time series of spikes or action potentials recorded from a single neuron. So, in the new analysis that Mark and I named the **SYMMETRIC analysis**, we would include just the temporal symmetries T, C, CT, and temporal rotations. When we later looked at spatial arrays of electrodes, for example, in EEG recordings, M would be included [19].

The initial cortical data were taken by the neurophysiologist Yong-Di Zhou [20], who works in the lab of Joaquin Fuster at U.C.L.A. Joaquin has brilliantly pioneered the neurophysiological study of primate memory behavior [21]. I believe that our understanding of the full extent of primates' higher brain function capabilities will be of enormous benefit to humankind and will cause a dramatic shift in our philosophical conception of these intelligent primates.

A SYMMETRIC analysis was done of single neuron spike trains recorded from the **parietal** cortex of monkeys performing a short-term memory task. The task consisted of a sample period during which one of two 3-cm-diameter rods was available to the monkey for touch, but was not seen visually. These rods were equal in all aspects except for their surface features, which for one rod consisted of horizontal ridges and for the other vertical ridges.

The sample period was followed by a memory period of 12 sec, during which the monkey was to retain the information of which rod had been presented.

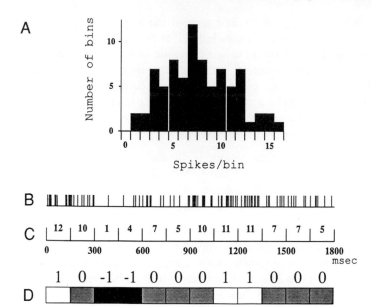

FIGURE 16.9   Example of a spike train during the 12-sec memory period. Time is divided into 0.15-sec bins for a total of 80 bins. (A) The number of time bins having a given number of spikes per bin is shown. The three firing levels are chosen so the bins having 11 or more spikes are mapped to a 1 or above-average firing, bins having 5 to 10 spikes are mapped to 0 or average firing, and bins having 4 or fewer spikes are mapped to −1 or below-average firing. (B) A 1.8-sec segment of the spike train. (C) The spike train segment in B is divided into the 0.15-sec bins and the number of spikes is shown. (D) A sequence of 1's, 0's, and −1's is obtained from the mapping of C using A. Then the 1's are grey scaled coded to white, the 0's to grey, and the −1's to black (as in the trion model). From Bodner et al. (1997).

Following the memory period, both rods were presented for touch, again out of sight. If the monkey pulled the rod matching the sample, it was rewarded. An intertrial baseline period of 12 sec preceded the presentation of each stimulus to be remembered.

The relevant steps of the SYMMETRIC analysis are as follows [22]:

1. Time was first divided into bins of equal duration and a graph was generated of the number of spikes appearing in the various bins (Fig. 16.9, A and B).

2. Based on the results of 1, upper and lower partitions were chosen so that the activity in each bin fell into one of three firing levels (just as in the trion model) depending on the number of spikes in that bin (Fig. 16.9C). The temporal activity of the spike train was then mapped into a sequence of 1's, 0's,

and -1's using the following mapping (Fig. 16.9D): (i) bins containing a number of spikes equal to or greater than the number set by the upper partition were mapped to 1 or above-average firing; (ii) bins containing fewer spikes than the upper partition number, but a greater or equal number to the one designated by the lower partition, were mapped to 0 or average firing; and (iii) bins containing fewer spikes than the number designated by the lower partition were mapped to -1 or below-average firing. A bin size of 0.15 sec was selected for several reasons. In particular, this seems to be the appropriate time bin for memory data found in human EEG coherence studies by Johannes Sarnthein [23].

3. A search for specific pattern templates P was performed on the mapped spike sequences. The templates used for the search were obtained directly from the mapped spike trains. Included in the searching were the family members related to P by C, T, CT, and all their temporal rotations. Since we are only looking at single-neuron spike trains rather than the output of minicolumns (with many hundreds of neurons), we allowed for statistical fluctuations by requiring a match to the template or family members of 80% of the pattern. For the results presented in Fig. 16.10, the family was 12 time steps long. We required matches for 10 of the 12 steps or 82%.

The statistical significance of the occurrence of a pattern in a particular spike train was determined in several ways. For example, that train was randomly shuffled 1000 times, and the number of matches was determined in each of these shuffled versions using the same criteria as in the original data. In this manner, a distribution of the number of matches was obtained and it could be determined if the number of matches found in the original data was due to chance within a probability less than 0.05 (see Chapter 12).

Ten different neurons with 221 memory trials were analyzed. The statistically significant symmetry pattern family, shown in Fig. 16.10A, was identified in the neurons during the memory task described earlier. *It was significant only when the entire family was included in the analysis.* The symmetry pattern family is 1.8 sec in duration, corresponding to 12 symbols obtained from the mapped activity of twelve 0.15-sec time bins.

The symmetry pattern family members repeat in most cases in intervals throughout the memory period, as shown in Figs. 16.10B and 16.10C. It is important to note again that for any given neuron, individual pattern family members might not meet the criterion for statistical significance, whereas the presence of the entire symmetry family itself is significant. Furthermore, this particular symmetry family was significant primarily while the monkey was retaining information in short-term memory and not in the times between the memory trials. This is consistent with the trion model's idea that symmetry family patterns represent memory states.

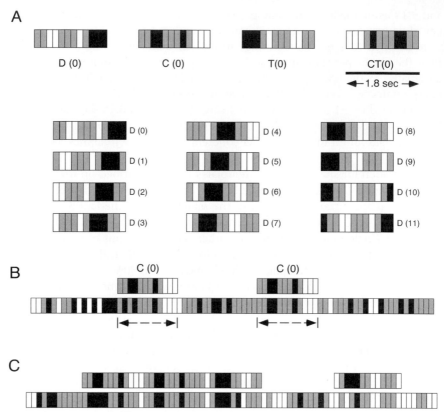

FIGURE 16.10 Family of symmetric firing patterns found during a memory task. This family was statistically significant in data from 10 neurons for 221 memory tasks. It was significant only when the entire family was included in the analysis. (A) Family of symmetric patterns. The designation of D(0), where (. . .) represents the temporal rotations, as the family representative is arbitrary. C(0) is the pattern obtained from D(0) by C symmetry, that is, by interchanging white and black, T(0) is obtained from D(0) by time reversal, and CT(0) is obtained from D(0) by the combined symmetry operation of C and T. The 12 temporal rotations D(. . .) of D are shown. There are analogous ones for C(. . .), T(. . .), and CT(. . .), not shown, in this symmetry pattern family. (B) A representative memory spike train mapped in the SYMMETRIC analysis for its entire 80 time bins. Above it are the family patterns C(0), which occur twice. (C) Another memory spike train similar to that in B in which the symmetry pattern family members occur for more than half of the 12 sec. From Bodner *et al.* (1997).

Clearly, more research needs to be done. However, I think these cortical memory results showing symmetric families are of great significance. They not only support the trion model at the neuronal level, where it might be excused if these symmetry pattern family members had not been found, but also open up the possibility of actually decoding the internal cortical language for higher brain function. I will describe this extremely ambitious but realistic program in the next chapter. It has sometimes been stated that understanding human memory is the "holy grail" in neuroscience. I suggest that understanding memory is crucial, but it is only the first step in understanding how we think, reason, and create, which I consider to be the most important problem in science.

CHAPTER 17

Musical Structure of the Internal Neural Language of the Brain: Using Music as the Rosetta Stone to Help Decode this Internal Language

BRIEF GUIDE

Here I present some extremely ambitious goals and concepts, namely, to decode the internal cortical language for higher brain function. I discuss mainly ideas and research to be done, along with some preliminary results. This chapter is meant to be entirely readable.

In this chapter I present the next major conceptual step in our unified research program "music as a window into higher brain function."

Step I was to map the time evolutions of the trion model onto music, as a way to represent, in principle, how we think and reason and create. Xiao Leng's trion music produced recognizable human styles of music. This led to the realization that music was exciting the internal common cortical language in other higher brain functions, in particular spatial-temporal reasoning. Xiao and I then predicted that music could enhance spatial-temporal reasoning.

Step II consisted of the dramatically successful behavioral studies of the Mozart effect (the college student studies, Rauscher's rat study, the Hughes epilepsy study, and Johnson's Alzheimer Disease study) and the music training (with preschool and 2nd grade children), all of which supported the results of Step I. The EEG coherence studies by Sarnthein provided the first neurophysiological basis for the Mozart effect. The recent fMRI studies of the Mozart effect from Nalcioglu's lab are extremely promising.

Step III was the SYMMETRIC analysis by Bodner (Chapter 16), with the primate memory data showing the clear presence of families of symmetric firing patterns, just as predicted by the trion model.

Step IV was the trion model calculations from coupled cortical columns (Chapter 8), which gave further insight into the nature and rules of the cortical language and grammar.

Step V, presented here, is to begin to map the primate memory data as analyzed by Mark Bodner onto music, and to use the results of the Mozart priming data along with the insights from the trion model to begin to *decode the cortical language for higher brain function*.

This goal of decoding the internal cortical language for higher brain function is obviously an extremely ambitious one. If it was presented by itself, it would sound at best premature. However, Mark and I propose to take all of the foregoing results seriously and use them in devising a way to begin to attack what is perhaps the most important problem in science.

So, let me begin. Keep in mind that I have no clear-cut way to solve this problem of decoding the cortical language, only some directions. However, these ideas are all very focused. If you asked me what my main scientific strengths were, I would say that it is my ability to focus on a goal and to design tests of my ideas.

The goal here is one that Xiao Leng and I talked about 10 years ago. As soon as Xiao had gotten her major results from mapping the trion model evolutions onto music, we had the idea of combining mapping of real cortical data onto music along with insight from the trion model to begin to understand higher brain function. Not enough of the pieces were in place, so it remained an idea for some years. You might well ask why we would want to map the cortical data onto music. What do we expect to learn? One answer is that just as with Xiao's results from the trion music 10 years ago, we got unexpected insight, so let's see what happens with the cortical music. I will present what I believe are better answers as we continue.

MAPPING CORTICAL DATA ONTO MUSIC

Three years ago Mark Bodner started his SYMMETRIC analysis of the primate memory data. As a result, Xiao wrote our first computer program to take the SYMMETRIC three-level analysis of Mark's spike trains during the memory tasks and map them onto music. As discussed in Chapter 9, there were many ways to map the trion evolutions onto music. Similarly, there are many possible mappings for the cortical data onto music. Since Mark's analysis involved data from one electrode, it seemed reasonable to use a simple music contour mapping for each time bin:

Cortical firing level	Musical mapping
Above average or 1	Go up n notes
Average or 0	Hold note
Below average or -1	Go down m notes

The user would choose the integers n and m (usually I would take n and m both equal to one or both equal to two), the starting note, the length of the time bin, and the musical instrument(s) to be used by the synthesizer. We could then listen to music (see the analogous case for trion music in Fig. 9.6) from the three-level analysis of the memory data from Chapter 16. An example of the mapped cortical music is given in Fig. 17.1.

This musical example (and others from Mark's analysis) sounded very pleasing to all who listened. Perhaps this was not terribly surprising since these memory data had been shown to contain recurring members from a family of symmetric firing patterns. On the other hand, these data were taken in parietal cortex during a memory task having nothing to do with music or the auditory cortex. Was there something deeper here? Yes!

Amy Graziano and Miyoung Kim (both researchers in my lab who are music experts) made the important observation that the family symmetries of C, T, and CT in Fig. 16.10A had precise musical analogies. They suggested that these analogies might provide a crucial link between the trion model of higher brain function and the nature of music in higher cortex function. The analogies represent standard relationships found in different Western musical styles and genres, for example, in classical music of the eighteenth and nineteenth centuries. This standard musical terminology, which corresponds to primate memory data symmetry relationships, is shown in Fig. 17.2.

A further analogy with music that Mark and I noted came from examining the temporal rotations of the SYMMETRIC family in Fig. 16.9A. The 12 temporal rotations can be grouped into **musical motives.** Here we consider two motives to be the same if they have the same musical contour as illustrated in Fig. 17.3.

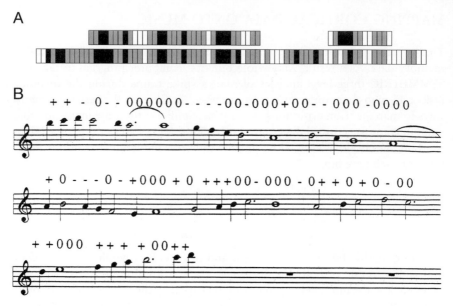

FIGURE 17.1   Example of mapping cortical memory data onto music. (A) The spike train SYM-METRIC analysis from Fig. 16.9C in which the symmetry pattern family members in Fig. 16.9A occur for more than half of the 12 sec. (B) Using Xiao Leng's mapping scheme (with n and m equal to one), A becomes the score shown. It was played by the computer and synthesizer (see the analogous case for trion music in Fig. 9.6).

FIRING SEQUENCE	MUSICAL ANALOGY
P	Pattern
C	Inversion
T	Retrograde
CT	Retrograde Inversion

FIGURE 17.2   Example of comparison of family members found in cortical data from Fig. 16.9A related by symmetries C, T, and CT with their corresponding musical analogs.

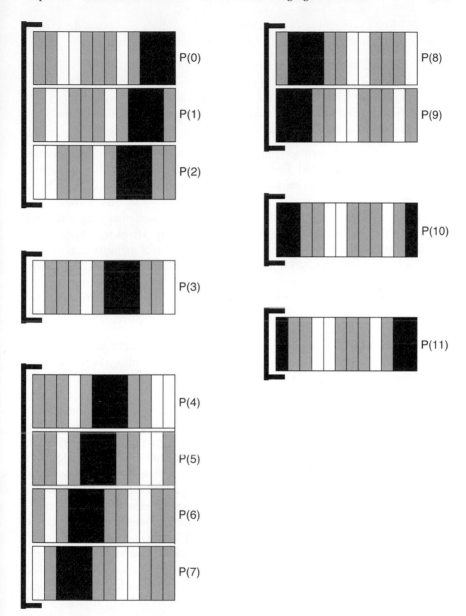

FIGURE 17.3 Example of temporal rotations of the cortical memory data SYMMETRIC patterns from Fig. 16.9A and their grouping into music motives. We consider two motives to be the same if they have the same musical contour.

So, our first examination of the SYMMETRIC analysis of cortical data firing patterns (SAC patterns) in terms of music was quite promising:

(i)   The SAC memory data when mapped onto music is pleasing.
(ii)   The SAC family symmetries of C, T, and CT have the musical analogs of inversion, retrograde, and retrograde inversion, respectively.
(iii) The temporal rotations of each SAC pattern can be grouped into analogs of musical motives.

Further sophistication even for the mapping onto music of the single-neuron SAC data is being considered. For example, specific rules for putting a **musical meter** into the mapping can be done. Again, the procedure is not unique, but a few such possibilities can readily be included in future versions of Xiao's program. Other possible features could be written into a music mapping computer program of the SAC data, which we call **MSAC**. Amy, Miyoung, Mark, and I considered the following possibility: Could MSAC of real memory data be distinguished musically from MSAC of randomized data in a statistically significant manner? We gave some thought and effort to such a program, but concluded that much more work was needed before we could draw a conclusion about its feasibility. If such an MSAC program were feasible, however, it would be extremely interesting.

Now consider SAC data from several electrodes. The recent experiments in Joaquin Fuster's lab at U.C.L.A. involved simultaneous recordings from four neurons (spaced at distances compatible with being in different minicolumns). Not only are these cortical data being collected during short-term memory tasks, but they allow the possibility of collecting data during other higher brain functions.

Our SAC analysis now turned to these multielectrode data from prefrontal cortex, certainly one of the highest thought areas of the cortex [1]. With the excellent programming skills of Roger Gabriel, a computer science major, and ideas from Mark and Miyoung, we obtained a very nice visual display of the occurrence of symmetry family members during cortical recordings. Again, we were exploring new ideas and new territory looking for results that, if interesting, we would then examine in a quantitative manner. Two such representative displays in Figs. 17.4 (see color insert) and 17.5 (see color insert) convinced me that we were onto something exciting that we could pursue quantitatively. Each figure shows the occurrences of one SAC family in two neurons recorded simultaneously during a higher brain function for 3 minutes. The temporal sequences look intriguing and give me the "gee whiz" feeling that here is a glimpse into the cortical code for higher brain function.

For a long time I stared at the sequences of patterns in Fig. 17.4. For example, the occurrence of red-green (or green-red) pairs seems to pop out for each neuron and between neurons. (These are the pattern and its time-reversed family member.) Most of the occurrences of the second SAC family in Fig. 17.5 would fall in place between the first family occurrences in Fig. 17.4. Such representative qualitative results convinced Mark and me that we had found something very exciting that must be examined in a quantitative manner.

We are now in the process of setting up a large computer program to systematically search for statistically significant sequences from one to four SAC families across several neurons recorded simultaneously during a higher brain function. For example, we intend to analyze cortical data while a monkey is listening to the Mozart Sonata (K.448) versus other music. Phil Davis, a summer student from Brown University, began this formidable task in 1998 and made good progress.

I now return from this proposed quantitative analysis to the proposed qualitative musical mapping of the SAC data (MSAC) from several neurons recorded simultaneously during a higher brain function such as listening to music. What I have in mind is that as we listen to the music produced from the cortical data, under certain choices of the MSAC parameters and during a particular higher brain task, the music will sound very "orchestrated." Think of the various string, brass, woodwind, and percussion sections of this well-known orchestra warming up before the famous conductor comes on stage. The musicians and sections are doing their own musical exercises. Then the conductor appears and the first piece of music is played. Everything comes together in a marvelous way and we hear magnificent music. If I had never seen a concert and were just listening to this sequence of auditory events, it would sound like the sudden cooperative change in behavior that I described in Chapter 8 that happens in physical and biological systems. So, this is what I would be listening for as the MSAC brain music unfolds in time. Under certain circumstances, the music would undergo a cooperative change to a much more pleasing and orchestrated sound. Then I (and my colleagues doing all the work) would say "aha!"— something interesting here must be examined.

I strongly believe that before we begin to decode the neural language of higher brain function, all possible means of attacking this enormous problem must be pursued. It is not simply a straightforward matter of systematically examining various possibilities. The brain is far too complicated for such an unimaginative approach. I suggest that our qualitative MSAC approach will add a very useful component to the arsenal of approaches, which would include our quantitative SAC analysis.

ANALYSIS OF THE MOZART SONATA FOR TWO PIANOS IN D MAJOR (K.448)

I will briefly discuss an obvious third approach in our quest to decode the neural language of higher brain function. As many people ask me during my talks about music as a window into higher brain function, what is there in the

Mozart Sonata (K.448) that enhances spatial-temporal reasoning? I used to jokingly say that if I knew the answer to their question, I would be on my way to Stockholm to accept a Nobel Prize. Now, I say that we are working on it. Of course, this we includes a few dedicated colleagues with the appropriate musical and neuroscience expertise.

I was extremely fortunate to meet Frank Ticheli, an acclaimed composer on the faculty of the famous School of Music at the University of Southern California. Recently, I was giving a talk to a group of artists and scientists [2] that meets regularly at the stunning home of Mary Lyons in Newport Beach. When I played the Mozart Sonata (K.448) for a few minutes during my talk, I could see that Frank was actually analyzing the music. Frank had asked himself the above question of what is so special about this music and had begun to investigate it right then. It was clear to me that I wanted Frank on our research team, and he accepted my invitation. Just as I have stressed that a variety of powerful approaches are needed to investigate higher brain function, similarly experts in a variety of disciplines are needed in this exciting quest.

Mark Bodner and I are now meeting with Frank to go over his very detailed and powerful analysis of the musical structure of the first movement of the Mozart Sonata (K.448) in terms of patterns and symmetries and sequences of patterns. Frank's analysis of the first movement is a time line of the 195 measures, extending 200 cm in length and containing seven different features that he has identified.

Just as Mark and I had used the trion model predictions to successfully guide the SAC analysis of the cortical data, the three of us intend to use Frank's analysis to guide our future analyses. The trion model suggests that certain symmetries and sequences of patterns are present in the code for higher brain function. I am convinced that the Mozart Sonata analysis will reveal crucial details about symmetries and sequences of patterns to use as we compare the SAC analysis of cortical data. These data will include EEG and fMRI recordings from humans and multielectrode recordings from monkeys while listening to the Mozart Sonata (K.448).

Clearly we are in the early stages of looking to the magical genius of Mozart to gain insight into the secrets of higher brain function. John Hughes and a colleague in Chicago have recently devised and applied a very sophisticated temporal analysis of the sound properties of a large number of recordings of Mozart piano pieces as well as those of other composers. These unpublished results show some very interesting features, and more work is in progress. John's analysis complements that being done by Mark, Frank, and myself.

John has a very nice descriptive insight [3] into the Mozart effect: "The superorganization of the cerebral cortex would seem to resonate with the superior architecture of Mozart's music." I agree precisely with this statement. It is not that Mozart's music is structured, but that the structure corresponds resonantly with the structure of mammalian cortex as put forward by Vernon Mountcastle. This is of course a concept that must and will be tested.

I am very optimistic that by combining the following five complementary elements we will make progress in our quest to understand the neural code of higher brain function:

(i)   The insight gained from the trion model (Chapter 8) into the cortical language and grammar.

(ii)   The SAC analysis of the cortical data recorded from multielectrodes or from EEG.

(iii)   The music from MSAC analysis of these data.

(iv)   The detailed musical analysis of the first movement of the Mozart Sonata for Two Pianos in D Major (K.448).

(v)   The use of powerful symmetry approaches from math theory.

This brings up a story from 10 years ago. Xiao Leng and I had met with Joaquin Fuster in his lab at U.C.L.A. to discuss implementing what we thought was an exciting idea. We had new methods of analyzing cortical data and some ideas from the trion model about what to look for in the data. For individual trions, Xiao and I realized that (as detailed in Chapter 8) there should be a set of temporal patterns or "cortical letters" that formed the "alphabet" that made up the spatial-temporal memory patterns for the cortical column language. We expected that this same alphabet was used throughout the cortex.

Joaquin was a pioneer in primate neurophysiological studies involving higher brain function (recall the memory tasks described in Chapter 16). Usually neuroscientists measure the first second or less of the neuronal response to physical stimuli. I suggested that this response probably did not involve the code for higher brain function (for example, if a lion is chasing you, it is neither necessary nor wise for your brain to do sophisticated calculations). So Xiao and I proposed that we might analyze Joaquin's cortical data from the 12-sec memory tasks, looking for patterns suggested by the trion model. Then if some candidate "cortical letters" were found, we could try to identify trion model parameters that would give such cortical letters. The trion model would then be used to *predict* all the rest of the cortical letters of the alphabet and repertoire of memory patterns. Well, we had a fruitful discussion, but concluded that we were not ready for such an ambitious program.

Ten years later, Mark and I and our colleagues are now ready to begin to explicitly include the trion model in our program to decode the language for higher brain function. This story illustrates the comment I made at the end of Chapter 11 when I remarked that I will store ideas in my mind for years until a new idea or result makes it worthwhile to reinvestigate a scientific study. It also illustrates my belief that a model of the brain must make testable predictions, otherwise it is useless.

CHAPTER 18

Animal Behavior While Listening to Music and Doing Higher Brain Functions

BRIEF GUIDE

The material in this chapter is extremely important to our understanding how music enhances spatial-temporal reasoning and math in children. This is because in animal studies, there is no confounding language-analytic reasoning nor cultural biases to consider. I greatly enjoy investigating the varied and marvelous higher brain function capabilities of animals. I refer you back to the lovely abstract painting by the gorilla Michael in Chapter 4. All the material in this chapter is readable. I hope you find it interesting, informative, and fun.

The understanding of human higher brain function must involve behavioral and neurophysiological studies of higher brain function in other animals. The reliability of animal studies is not confounded by language-analytic reasoning or the cultural biases that can distort human studies. I will show how both of these factors are very important. Since this book is based on the Mountcastle organizational principle of mammalian cortex, I will limit my discussion to mammals and their response to human music, as well as studies of their higher brain functions. I will include anecdotes, behavioral observations, and controlled studies. [1]

My friend Wiebke Aschenborn produces documentary stories for German TV. During a recent visit to California, Wiebke showed me her latest video (in progress) of a woman, Fiona, living with her family on the island Islay in Scotland, who devotes herself to helping seals survive the encroaching competition with fishermen. Here is Fiona's story as told to me by Wiebke and shown on the video.

> Fiona is a musician and one day she played her violin right at the beach, just by herself. Fiona noticed that seals would swim up to her, stick their heads out of the water and listen to her. From then on she has been playing to them a lot of times. Sometimes she also takes a little boat out to a nearby small island to play her violin to the seals. She knows by now which kind of music they like. They like slow melodic songs, no fast tunes like Scottish jigs. (Fiona composes music for the seals and she records it in her little studio at home.) The longer she plays for them, the more seals come around to listen to her. Once she starts to play something like Scottish jigs, they disappear fast. She also raises sick and abandoned seals [see Fig. 18.1]. They live in her salt water tubs for about 2–3 months and swim in a little tank for a few hours each day. Seals she has raised tend to stay in the bay where Fiona lives. They always come back to check things out and to listen to her play her violin. Each seal looks differently and Fiona is able to recognize the ones she has cared for. Seals are very shy animals, but with Fiona and her violin, they seem to forget their shyness.

Let me relate another animal story from Costa Rica. When my wife Lorna and I were vacationing in Costa Rica with our friends Arnold and Bonnie Hano in 1993, we spent a few days at a resort hotel owned by John Fraser and located in a tropical forest area along the Pacific Coast. One of the attractions here are the numerous howler monkeys that live in this area. Howlers always seem to be on the move. They frequently howl at each other and the sound is not at all musical. Thus I was quite surprised when I overheard Fraser telling some visitors that whenever he played classical music on his hi-fi system, many howler monkeys would appear outside his room and quietly listen for tens of minutes. Upon my questioning him, he could recall no especially favorite pieces that attracted the monkeys.

Some colleagues and I plan to visit this area and do some controlled experiments to see if the howler monkeys have specific preferences for classical music. In the meantime Matthew Peterson, Mark Bodner, Lori Oliver (from the Gorilla Foundation), and I arranged to do an exploratory (pilot) study with Phyllis

FIGURE 18.1   Fiona with one of the seals she was caring for before releasing it. Courtesy of George and Fiona Middleton.

Dolhinow and her graduate student Allisa Carter. A colony of langur monkeys has been studied at U.C. Berkeley by Phyllis and other faculty for some years. Our experiment was designed to see if these monkeys had a preference for the Mozart Sonata (K.448) used in our Mozart effect studies versus the Philip Glass minimalist music selection used as a control. Our simple langur experimental design is shown in Fig. 18.2.

We collected quite a few hours of data over many days spread out over several months. We recorded with two camcorders, one positioned to monitor the langurs' behavior in response to the listening conditions in each of their two enclosures. The listening conditions for the Mozart Sonata (K.448), the Glass composition, and silence were presented in random sequences for 10 minutes each through a boombox. The videos were later played back with the sound off (so as not to bias the analysis), and Lori and Allisa would stop the playback once a minute and record all relevant behavior of the langurs. In particular, we were interested in the number of langurs in the enclosure nearest to the music as a function of time. The monkeys showed no preference or obvious behavior change during the playing of the Mozart Sonata versus the Glass selection versus silence [2]. These results are quite relevant for the

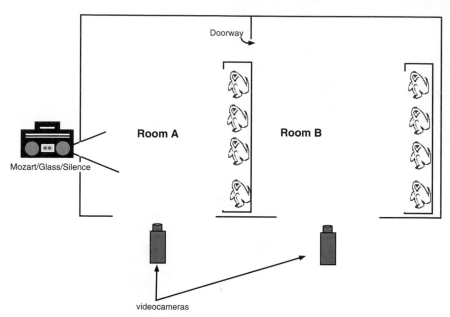

FIGURE 18.2 Design of our langur monkey music preference experiment. A boombox played either 10 minutes of the Mozart Sonata (K.448) or 10 minutes of a Philip Glass piece of music or was off for 10 minutes. (The sound level for the two music listening conditions was calibrated using the gadget built by Jim Kelley, described in Chapter 1 in the experiment with the research mathematicians.) These listening conditions would be presented in a different order on different days and repeated twice for an hour. Two camcorders were placed to monitor the langur behavior in each of the two connecting enclosures.

remarkable rat behavioral studies done by Fran Rauscher [3], as they would rule against any simple music preference being the responsible agent.

Our experimental design is so simple and so portable that we want to repeat this experiment in a more natural setting with other primates. There is a colony of bonobos at the nearby San Diego Zoo, one of the finest zoos with the most natural settings in the world. Bonobos are closely related to chimpanzees and humans, and are amazingly humanlike in looks and behavior [4]. For example, they walk upright, have sex face to face, and are not limited in time to specific menstrual periods. It has been reported that they will use sex to settle disputes. I am in the process of submitting a research proposal to the San Diego Zoo to conduct a version of the langur music preference experiment in the more natural bonobo setting.

In addition to examining group behavior, it is also common to do behavioral experiments with a single subject. The idea with a single subject is that the experiment can be done again and again under very controlled and reproducible conditions, thus single-subject studies can be extremely valuable. Perhaps the most famous single subject studies in neuroscience are with HM [5], an adult human male who, because of numerous and dangerous epileptic seizures, underwent the radical surgical procedure of bilaterally removing his hippocampus. It solved his epileptic problem, but destroyed his ability to retain any new memories. (Bilateral removal of the hippocampus is no longer done.) The number of research papers written on HM is huge and the data are immensely valuable.

As I emphasized in Chapter 11, although much can be learned from subjects with deficits like HM, I strongly believe the exceptionally talented must also be studied, especially if we are to understand higher brain function. I view memory as a building block for higher brain function. So, I had in mind a fun experiment involving a primate with exceptional training and abilities, Koko the famous gorilla, who knows and uses about 600 words in sign language. Koko has even made the cover of *National Geographic* twice [6].

I wrote to Penny Paterson, director of the Gorilla Foundation where Koko lives with her gorilla friends Michael and Ndume. I and Mark Bodner and Matthew Peterson proposed an experiment in which Koko would push buttons on a **GUI** (**gorilla user interface**) (which Jim Kelley named and built). The GUI would be connected to a computer that would play different selections of music in response to pushing the buttons, and record all the relevant data for analysis. Matthew would develop the appropriate software. Our experiment was approved, and an extremely bright young assistant at the Gorilla Foundation, Lori Oliver, was assigned to work with us. Figure 18.3 (see color insert) shows Koko playing with our experiment and pushing the buttons on the GUI.

We had six quite different selections of (nonvocal) music, ranging from Mozart and Vivaldi to Latin music and Philip Glass. At first Koko would push the GUI buttons as shown in Fig. 18.3. However, she got bored with the setup before we collected enough data. Because Koko has a lot of toys, this was not too surprising. My initial design was that the music played only as long as the button was being pushed (since long button pushes would give us significant data quickly). In hindsight, that was not such a good idea: I would not want to have to keep pushing a button to hear music. So Matthew reprogrammed his software to give 30 sec of music for each button push. Button pushes during the 30-sec music presentation were not counted. Again, Koko tired of this before we got sufficient data to determine if she had a preference. The next step was to reward her for button pushes through a food treat. I could not locate a commercial feeding device, so my whiz summer student Chris Figge built one (Fig. 18.4). The idea was that the food rewards would keep Koko interested in pushing the buttons. Presumably, she would continue to push the button that gave a particular piece of music if she had a preference. Again, Lori observed that Koko got bored.

FIGURE 18.4   Photo of Chris Figge holding his gorilla feeder, which was activated by the computer to give a food treat when Koko pushed a button on the GUI.

Penny had told us that Koko was never as interested in music as was Michael. In fact, Michael supposedly liked to listen to opera, in particular recordings by the great tenor Luciano Pavarotti. (Remember the abstract painting by Michael in Fig. 4.3?) So we tried working with Michael. It turns out that Michael is extremely curious and extremely strong. He got two fingers through the fence mesh (see Fig. 18.3) and disabled our device. Another time our device malfunctioned. Thus Michael got frustrated and bored, and we never got enough data with Michael or later with Ndume to actually determine if they had music preferences.

We still intend to work with Koko, Michael, and Ndume, but now the goals will be to study their spatial-temporal reasoning and math abilities, and then to see if the Mozart Sonata (K.448) will prime these reasoning abilities. You may be startled to see me writing of math abilities in primates, but I will explain myself shortly. First, I want to present the amazing and profound Mozart effect results that Fran Rauscher collected from her rats.

MOZART EFFECT WITH RATS

My postdoctoral fellow Fran Rauscher had left my lab to become a professor in the Psychology Department at the University of Wisconsin, Oshkosh, with her own lab and research program. About two years ago, Franny told me that she was going to do a Mozart effect experiment with rats. As you now know from reading this much of my book, I love to speculate, and the Mountcastle columnar principle of cortical organization and function applies to *mammalian* cortex. However, I was taken aback by her bold idea. I encouraged her to do it, but I did not really expect her to succeed in getting positive results.

Franny exposed groups of rats to one of four auditory conditions: (1) the first movement of the Mozart Sonata (K.448), (2) the opening of Philip Glass' "Music with Changing Parts," (3) silence, and (4) white noise (sounds like a buzzing hum). Figure 18.5 shows Franny with one of her Mozart rats. Unlike the Mozart effect experiments with college students who listened to an auditory condition for 10 minutes prior to testing on a spatial-temporal task, the rats were exposed to the auditory condition for 12 *hours a day,* starting at 3 weeks before birth and continuing for 60 days after birth. The rats were then tested in a standard spatial maze (Fig. 18.6).

Fran's results [7] are shown in Fig. 18.7. All four groups of rats start out on Day 1 by having roughly the same time to do the spatial-temporal task of going through the spatial maze and making the same number of errors (wrong choices of direction). This seems to rule out various classes of unknown systematic error contributions. As we can see, the Mozart rats do better and better on succeeding days, with the effects getting larger and the statistical significance getting greater. She is continuing these experiments, and is now looking for neuroanatomical effects of the dramatic results shown in Fig. 18.7. In the process, she has replicated her earlier results.

For a number of reasons, I believe that Rauscher's results have profound scientific and philosophical significance:

1. *The timescale for the enhancement of the Mozart effect is now at least 4 hours.* The rats were tested each day about 4 hours after the auditory condition ended. No attempt was made in her experiment to see how long the increased learning of the spatial-temporal task lasts. This timescale is at least a factor of 10 longer than the time for the enhancement that we had with the college students in 1993 [8]. This is a startling finding since it is usually thought that

FIGURE 18.5   Fran Rauscher with one of the rats that had listened extensively to the Mozart Sonata (K.448) while being raised. Courtesy of Frances Rauscher.

there must be *active participation* to enhance a behavior. (For example, we gave piano keyboard lessons to preschool children in our successful experiment [9] to get long-term enhancement—lasting for days—of their spatial-temporal reasoning abilities.) This certainly makes it of enormous significance to see if such enhancements can be accomplished with shorter exposure times to the Mozart Sonata (less than 12 hours a day), and to see how long the enhanced ability to learn a spatial-temporal task lasts.

> *I would urge extreme caution at this time to parents. They should not give their infants such long listening exposure to the Mozart Sonata as Rauscher did with her rats (see Chapter 19).*

2. These results totally rule out the possibility that some cultural or peer pressure effects play any role in the Mozart effect.

3. Rauscher's results provide very strong support for the Mountcastle columnar principle for the organization and function of mammalian cortex. I suggest that this is not only a profound scientific result, but also a philosophical

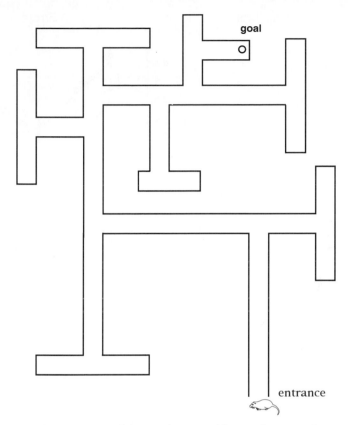

FIGURE 18.6   Schematic version of the spatial maze used by Rauscher to test the rats after long-term exposure to auditory stimuli. The rats were tested on their ability to learn this spatial-temporal task over a period of 5 days.

one. Here we have the magic genius of Mozart dramatically enhancing the ability of rats to learn and reason.

4. Explicit in Rauscher's results is the establishment of an **animal model** for the Mozart effect. It is clear from point 3 that the proper experiments should allow the further elaboration of both the behavior and neurophysiological bases of the Mozart effect in other mammals, in particular primates. This should prove to be of enormous significance in our understanding of how we humans think, reason, and create and how we can enhance these abilities.

Next I will present selected studies to illustrate the abilities of primates to do spatial-temporal reasoning and math. Recognition of these higher brain

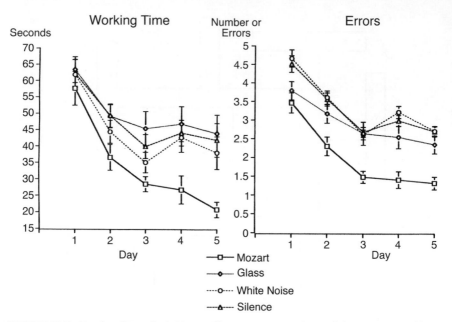

FIGURE 18.7 Results of Rauscher's Mozart effect experiment with rats. (A) Average times (three trials each day) for the four groups of rats to do the spatial-temporal task of the maze in Fig. 18.5. (B) Same as A for the average number of errors (wrong choices). We see that the Mozart rats learn this task better than the other groups of rats with each succeeding day. The rats were tested each day about 4 hours after the auditory condition ended. From Rausher et al. (1998).

function capabilities in primates [10] will be of key importance in planning the most useful Mozart effect experiments.

SPATIAL-TEMPORAL AND MATH ABILITIES OF PRIMATES

I want to present the results of several recent experiments that demonstrate that the spatial-temporal reasoning and math capabilities of primates are much greater than might have been expected. You will see that the use of the term math is warranted. I believe these results are all consistent with our trion model of higher brain function, and my colleagues and I intend to put these results and ideas to great use.

A recent study has dramatically and convincingly demonstrated that rhesus monkeys understand, can use, and can generalize the math concept of "number." In an elegant experiment, Brannon and Terrance [11] first showed that rhesus monkeys could order sets of visual stimuli that consist of 1 element, 2 elements, 3 elements, and 4 elements in terms of the number of elements. An example of such sets of objects is shown in Fig. 18.8A. The authors showed that the rhesus ability does not depend, for example, on the size, color, shape, or position of the objects. Then they tested the monkeys on sets of objects that have 5, 6, 7, 8, or 9 elements (Fig. 18.8B) without new training with these larger numbers. Again the monkeys ordered these sets in terms of the number of objects in the sets.

It has been proposed that human language-analytic methods must be used in the use of numbers beyond the number 3. This experiment completely overturns such notions. Since these monkeys do not know our number system, they must be using patterns in some profound way. I suggest that they are using their spatial-temporal reasoning abilities. A test of this idea might examine whether there is a Mozart effect that primes their ability to order sets of objects according to number.

A fascinating experiment has shown that primates have some ability to add and subtract numbers of objects. This experiment [12] is a version of the marvelous one done by Wynn [13] with 5-month-old human infants, which I describe in Chapter 19. Obviously, these infants are not using language-analytic methods at this age, and I would suggest that they must be using spatial-temporal reasoning as must the primates in this analogous experiment. The primate experiment [14] is amazing to me because it was carried out in the wild! The experiments were done with *wild* rhesus monkeys living on the island of Cay Santiago, Puerto Rico. The experimental data "were obtained *opportunistically*" wherever the adult monkeys remained in one position for a sufficiently long time for the experimenters to present their series of stimuli, which were eggplants placed in a similar setup (see Chapter 19). *The monkeys, as did the 5-month-old children in Wynn's experiment [15], looked longer at situations in which the numbers of objects involved incorrect addition or subtraction.*

Moving on to another gifted primate, an elegant experiment has shown that macaque monkeys can do sophisticated spatial-temporal mazes on a computer. In this experiment, done at the University of Tohuku in Sendai, Japan [16], monkeys were taught to do a checkerboard maze with each hand moving a cursor. The cursor movements on the screen, the details of the maze, and the positions of obstacles could all be changed, thus allowing all sorts of higher brain function to be investigated. Mark Bodner and I saw this poster presentation at the 24th Annual Meeting of the Society of Neuroscience held in Los Angeles in November 1998. The monkeys had to think several moves ahead in space and time and had to change strategies as the maze was changed. Mark asked the presenter about how the monkeys were rewarded for performing these tasks. He stated that the monkeys enjoyed playing this checkerboard game and no reward was necessary after they learned it.

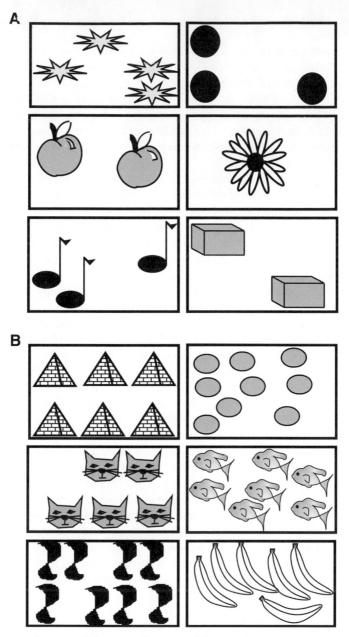

FIGURE 18.8 These sets of objects are illustrative of those used by Brannon and Terrace (1998) in their astonishing experiment with rhesus monkeys showing that the rhesus could order these sets just from the number of objects in the set. The sets of objects were shown to the monkeys on a touch-sensitive computer screen. (A) The monkeys were trained and tested on sets containing 1, 2, 3, or 4 objects. They could order these sets of objects regardless of size, shape, position, density, nature of objects, or color. (B) The monkeys were then tested without training on sets with 5, 6, 7, 8, and 9 objects. They again successfully ordered such sets just from the number of objects.

Mark and I immediately thought that some version of this checkerboard maze computer game would be useful for our work with primates and young children. We conferred with Matthew Peterson, and it will be included in MicroS.T.A.R., the version of S.T.A.R. to be used for young children and primates.

I strongly believe that animals can think, reason, and create at a much more sophisticated and higher level than generally supposed. They do not have the confounding language-analytic reasoning abilities that we humans have in addition to our spatial-temporal reasoning abilities. Furthermore, their response to music is not influenced by culture or peer pressure, as it is for humans. Thus I expect that applying our research program to primates should be especially fruitful.

PART V

The Future of Music as a Window into Higher Brain Function

BRIEF GUIDE

I have completed all the difficult technical material. Part V does contain some dramatic results from interesting and relevant experiments. Mainly, the remaining chapters summarize some important ideas, and I share some dreams and cautions with you.

CHAPTER 19

Child Brain Development and Adult Brain Reorganization

BRIEF GUIDE

Here I present some powerful experimental results that I think must be seriously considered as we look to the future of music as a window into higher brain function.

Clearly one of the most important concepts that I present in this book is that as the result of the Mountcastle columnar principle of mammalian cortex, *infants are born with far greater spatial-temporal abilities than previously understood,* ready for enhancing with the right environment. I contend that a newborn does not emerge with her or his cortex being a blank slate, ready to mold, but with a sophisticated brain that indeed is developing at a very rapid rate. If I had some say in government funding, I would give scientific studies in this area the highest priority. Now I want to describe several outstanding behavioral studies that support my hypothesis that infants are born with considerable spatial-temporal abilities. I will do this in a somewhat chronological order, beginning with the fetus.

ULTRASOUND STUDIES OF FETUS MOVEMENT

In 1981 Heinz Prechtl [1] began to study prenatal movements with **ultrasound** technology, which uses high-frequency sound waves to image the fetus in a safe manner. (Nowadays, almost all proud expectant parents show off ultrasound pictures of the fetus.) He would observe fetuses weekly for 1 hour, and analyze the data from videotape. Prechtl began his studies with the expectation that fetal movements might resemble the postnatal repertoire of behavioral spatial-temporal patterns to a small extent. After more than 10 years of continuous study, he came to the surprising conclusion that "fetal movements, without any exceptions . . . can all be observed again after birth (either immediately or some only many weeks after birth). This means that there are no movement patterns observed in the fetus which are specific for the prenatal period and non-existent after birth."

Furthermore, he emphasized that "the other unexpected observation in these studies was the fact that there exists no period of amorphic and random movements. In fact all fetal movements are right from the beginning at 7.5 to 8 weeks patterned and easily recognizable." His research studied the timetable of emergence of many of these recognizable and classifiable fetal movement patterns. Each fetus studied had a very similar time course of development for each of the patterns.

I find Prechtl's work really fascinating and extremely relevant to my hypothesis that infants are born with far greater abilities than previously understood. Again I would emphasize that we are just beginning to understand the role of outside influences on the fetus. In particular, as noted below in the brilliant work of DeCasper [2], auditory input to the fetus does influence auditory choice of the neonate.

I would urge great caution though to anyone trying to influence the fetus development through, for example, constant music input applied to the mother's stomach. It is far too early to know the effects of such a program. It is possible, for example, that the common sequential time development of movement patterns of the fetus observed by Prechtl [3] could be disrupted by premature overstimulation through the auditory system. *I strongly doubt that this is the case, but I would advise moderation.* I have always been quoted as saying that there are no known bad side effects of listening to Mozart, but caution is required with the human fetus. I do *not* recommend that your human fetus be exposed to 12 hours a day of Mozart, as Fran Rauscher did with the fetal rats [4] in her study.

NEONATE AUDITORY PREFERENCES

Anthony DeCasper and collaborators [5] have done a series of ingenious experiments that demonstrate that two-day-old neonates have definite auditory preferences that were dependent on their fetal experiences. How is this possible to scientifically determine? Tony devised the extremely clever design shown in Fig. 19.1, which allows these quantitative measurements to do done. He measures the average sucking rate of each newborn. Then he takes two auditory stimuli to be contrasted, for example, the newborn's mother's voice and another woman's voice. For some newborns, he presents the mother's voice when its sucking is faster than average and the other woman's voice when its sucking is slower than its average; for other newborns the reverse schedule is presented. In each situation, the newborn will adjust its sucking rate to hear its mother's voice. He was also able to show that after the newborn had adjusted to the appropriate sucking rate (for example, higher than its original rate) to hear the mother's voice, it would readjust if the presentation schedule was reversed.

I am impressed with DeCasper's experiments. He and I discussed the possibility of using his experimental design to test some sort of Mozart effect on the discrimination abilities of newborn infants. His proposed design was indeed extremely clever, and he plans to implement it when he can fit it into his schedule.

ADDITION AND SUBTRACTION BY INFANTS

Karen Wynn [6] showed that five-month-old infants can calculate the results of addition and subtraction operations on small numbers of items. The key idea used by Wynn is that *infants will look longer at a sequence of events that does not make sense or is incorrect than at a sequence that is correct or makes sense.* In other words, infants look longer at unexpected events than they do at expected events. Thus Wynn argued that if these infants can compute the results of simple arithmetic operations, they would look longer at a wrong result shown to them than at a correct result shown to them. Wynn's experimental design is shown in Fig. 19.2.

I believe that Wynn's results are very powerful. They demonstrate an ability to effectively add and subtract, which is a quite high level brain function. To further emphasize the significance, I mentioned in Chapter 18 that the

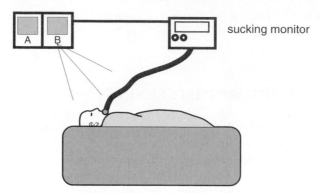

FIGURE 19.1   Schematic design of DeCasper's ingenious experiment showing that two-day-old infants prefer their mother's voice. Sucking on the (nonnutritive) nipple connected to a computer, the newborn infant can produce either the mother's voice or another woman's voice. The mother's voice would be played if the infant sucks faster (or slower) than its own average sucking rate and the other woman's voice was played if it sucks slower (or faster) than its average. Some infants get one choice of rates (faster, slower) and some the other to get their mothers' voices. It was found that infants adjust their sucking rates to get their mothers' voices. It was also shown that under a reversal of the sucking rate conditions, the infants would change their strategies to again get their mothers' voices.

analogous and successful experiment [7] following Wynn's design was done in the wild with rhesus monkeys! *Amazing!*

I suggest that these dramatic results are consistent with the trion model and its predictions that mammals are born with the abilities to quickly learn to do spatial-temporal reasoning. That this ability includes addition and subtraction must definitely be investigated in more detail. A study of Mozart effect priming in Wynn's experiment could be very insightful.

INFANTS' PREFERENCES FOR SPECIFIC STRUCTURE IN MUSIC

Carol Krumhansl [8] has demonstrated that four-month-old infants have a remarkable preference for hearing Mozart sonatas as they were written as compared to "unnatural" versions. As shown in Fig. 19.3, two versions of each of 16 Mozart minuets were prepared as stimuli. In the natural version, pauses lasting two beats (of duration 0.96 sec) were added at the end of a musical phrase as determined by the authors' "intuition" (and in coincidence with the perception of 14 adults). There were either four or six phrases (each phrase being 2, 4, or 6 measures long) in each stimulus. In the unnatural versions, the

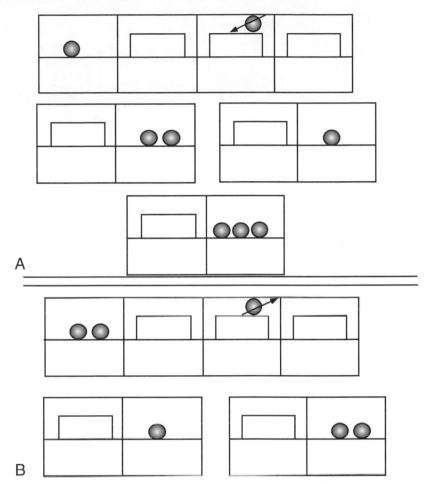

FIGURE 19.2   Highly schematic design of Wynn's clever experiment showing that five-month-old infants can do some form of addition and subtraction. (All objects are identical.) (A) Addition: As shown from left to right, first one object is placed in front of the infant. Then a screen comes up and, as observed by the infant, a hand with a second object goes behind the screen. The hand comes out without the second object. Then the screen is removed. There are either one, two, or three objects present. The infants spend longer looking when the number of objects is either one or three, rather than the "expected" number of two. (B) Subtraction: Two objects are placed in front of the infant. Then a screen comes up and an empty hand goes behind the screen. The hand comes out with one object in it. Then the screen is removed. There are either one, two, or three objects present. The infants spend longer looking when the number of objects is either two or three, rather than the "expected" number of one.

FIGURE 19.3   The top music score is of the natural version of a Mozart minuet with a pause (of 0.96 sec), each inserted at a "natural" phrase boundary. The bottom score is of the unnatural version of the same piece with a pause placed *not* at a phrase boundary. The four-month-old infants in Krumhansl's experiment preferred to listen to the natural versions rather than the unnatural versions. They had not heard this music before.

pauses were placed not at the end of musical phrases but rather at inappropriate places.

The infants listened significantly longer to the natural version of the Mozart minuets as compared to the unnatural versions. This was true for each of the Mozart minuets. Again, these amazing results are consistent with our hypothesis. In fact, I would have considered it a real blow to the model of higher brain function as proposed by Xiao Leng and me if Krumhansl had found that these infants had *no* preference for the natural versions. Our model predicts that the inherent Mountcastle columnar neural language common throughout mammalian cortex has specific natural sequences. Furthermore, we believe that

Mozart expresses his music precisely in terms of this inherent spatial-temporal neural language (with its families of firing patterns containing "words" related by symmetries). Of course, we do not know the mapping between music and the internal brain language. However, as I previously stated, "Perhaps the cortex's response to music is the 'Rosetta Stone' for the 'code' or internal language of higher brain function."

TESTING THE SPATIAL-TEMPORAL ABILITIES OF VERY YOUNG CHILDREN

I have presented just a few of the relevant experiments that show the remarkable abilities of very young children. For example, Elizabeth Spelke [9] has demonstrated that four-month-old infants can mentally compute trajectories of objects in a quite sophisticated manner. I suggest that the remarkable results from the experiments of Krumhansl, Wynn, Spelke, and DeCasper are the beginning of our understanding of higher brain function spatial-temporal abilities of very young children. The old (but pioneering) notions of Jean Piaget [10], which state that these higher brain functions can occur only in older children, are not correct.

It is of immense importance and interest, especially to parents and educators, that scientists more fully explore the amazing higher brain function capabilities of these very young infants. Greater understanding will allow us to better determine how to ensure that each child reaches his or her maximum reasoning capabilities. Two informative and readable books for parents and educators are "Inside the Brain" by Ronald Kotulak, a Pulitzer Prize-winning science reporter for the *Chicago Tribune*, and "Magic Trees of the Mind" by Marion Diamond and Janet Hopson [11]. Marion is a world-class neuroanatomist whose research has added much to the knowledge of how positive experience can influence cortical connections; Janet is an outstanding interviewer.

A high-profile research project by Marion Diamond, Arne Scheibel, and colleagues examined Albert Einstein's brain with the hope of finding some hint that might help to explain his genius. They were not able to locate any definitive neuronal feature [12] that might be associated with his prodigious mental powers. (There was a hint of more "housekeeping" glial cells in certain cortical areas.) Yet this result can be turned around. It is extremely unlikely that adults or children with enormous higher brain function capabilities can be identified through neuroanatomical studies. Of course, severe higher brain function deficits through neglect are identifiable (see later discussion).

My research studies have concentrated on children three years of age and older. It is absolutely clear to me that it is vital to extend our studies to younger children, as young as possible. For example, some politicians have taken our Mozart effect results with college students and used them to justify having very young children listen to classical music. This must be scientifically studied.

With this in mind, Matthew Peterson, Mark Bodner, and I are designing the proper spatial-temporal training software along with appropriate tests. I think the development of Matthew's S.T.A.R. software for young children, MicroS.T.A.R., which can also be used for primates, is our answer. As discussed in Chapter 18, the spatial-temporal checkerboard maze computer game used in Japan with macaques could be a valuable part of MicroS.T.A.R. We are interested in testing the effect of repeated listening to the Mozart Sonata (K.448) on spatial-temporal abilities. We are also interested in evaluating possible enhanced spatial-temporal reasoning abilities resulting from music and movement programs with very young children. I have discussed such a study with Michelle Greenwell, a delightful young woman from Calgary in Canada, who teaches such programs to children as young as 18 months. Michelle is ready to do this study as soon as MicroS.T.A.R. is available for pretraining and post-training tests.

BRAIN DEVELOPMENT AND REORGANIZATION

Here I will briefly discuss not only brain development in young children, but some new work with adults on brain reorganization that is quite relevant to us older folks (see Chapter 21). It may never be too late to improve your higher brain function.

Much of our knowledge of brain development comes from the numerous and important animal studies from rats to primates. There are two major take home messages, both of which go back to the pioneering and seminal work of Hubel and Wiesel. In addition to their research showing the columnar structure of visual cortex that I had mentioned earlier, they showed that (i) there must be appropriate *competitive* sensory input into *both* eyes of the animal for the proper development of the visual cortex, and (ii) there is an early age time "window of opportunity" during which it is crucial that these appropriate sensory inputs be present. These results [13] were of great value in designing the present treatment of vision problems of young children.

The knowledge concerning point (i) on the competitive nature of the sensory input in shaping the brain has been greatly extended and generalized beyond the visual system. It is generally understood that, in accordance with the Hebb synaptic learning rule (see Fig. 8.1), certain synapses will strengthen and others will weaken due to the behavioral experiences of the animal. This is especially true for the young animal, at which time the brain is anatomically reshaped in terms of which synaptic connections among the neurons survive and are strengthened, and which connections actually disappear (as well as neurons dying). The knowledge about point (ii) concerning the age "window of opportunity" has also been increased and generalized beyond the visual system. I would say that in general these windows in humans are not the "tight closing ones" that one might expect. My own personal example is our research [14] presented in Chapters 13 and 14 showing that the enhanced spatial-temporal reasoning resulting from piano keyboard training with three-year-old preschool children was also present in seven-year-old 2nd grade children.

The actual brain developmental studies with humans are not as numerous for obvious reasons. There is one *heroic* neuroanatomical study of human infant brain development by J. L. Conel [15], who devoted his career to this work, which was published in seven volumes from 1937 to 1967. He obtained human brains at autopsies (within 24 hours of death) of presumably neurologically normal children at the eight ages of 0, 1, 3, 6, 15, 24, 48, and 72 months (with four to nine brains for each age). Conel then analyzed these brains, counting the number of neurons in each layer in a cortical column (of dimension 0.1 by 0.1 cm) for up to 49 different cortical regions. Rod Shankle at U.C. Irvine has taken Conel's valuable data and put them all in a computer data base. Rod and colleagues then used this data base to ask a number of very interesting cortical developmental questions. They obtained some fascinating results [16]. The reported results are of such interest and significance that I think the Conel data should be replicated. Clearly, Conel spent a lifetime gathering these data. However, with sufficient funding and the use of modern neuroanatomical techniques, this is a quite doable project. These cortical development results could be correlated with behavioral and higher brain function capability results for children of these ages. This knowledge would be of enormous use in designing the appropriate teaching and training materials for optimizing the higher brain function abilities of very young children.

The new brain imaging technologies of EEG, fMRI, MEG, MRI, and PET (see Chapter 6) have vastly expanded the brain development issues that can be studied. For example, the PET studies by Harry Chugani [17] are of great interest. His studies, showing which brain regions had the greatest blood flow and thus neuronal activity as a function of age, could be correlated with the neuroanatomical data of Conel. Harry is also well known for his dramatic studies showing huge cortical deficits in the Romanian orphan children who experienced extremely deprived upbringing.

A recent relevant example [18] of brain development in children comes from an MEG imaging study showing an increased cortical representation of the fingers of the left hand in violin players (compared to those of their right hand). The amount of cortical reorganization is correlated with the age at which they started taking lessons before the age of 12. But is bigger better, and for what?

It is clear that large deficits in size of a particular cortical region are signs of neuropathological deficits in cortical function associated with that region. It is also clear that use or training involving a cortical region will enlarge it. What is not clear is the converse question of whether a bigger than average cortical region, whatever the cause, gives better than average performance. You would think so, but is that correct? The problem is that nonuse of one cortical region leads to enlargements of neighboring cortical regions (up to the large cortical distance of one centimeter), even in adults, and not necessarily improved function in the enlarged cortical regions. This is an interesting avenue to pursue.

The pioneering studies of Michael Merzenich and Jon Kaas and colleagues [19] over the past 20 years have demonstrated in detail how the cortex reorganizes in primates, *even in adults*. Without use and sensory input, the cortical representation of a given body part gets smaller. The corresponding *neighboring* cortical representations (see the touch or somatosensory cortical body map of the rat in Fig. 7.5) of the neglected body part get larger.

A dramatic example in humans of reorganization of the cortex comes from examining the cases of arm amputees. V.S. Ramachandran [20], in his very readable book "Phantoms in the Brain," tells a fascinating story that is relevant to our research (see Chapter 22) with the Mozart effect. It is well known that these arm amputees experience the sensation of feeling in the missing arm, which brings the designation of phantom arm. Rama and colleagues found that tactile stimulation of the lower face on the same (and not the opposite side) side of the body as the phantom limb causes sensation in the phantom arm. As was the case with the animal studies, the body map of the cortex had reorganized and the cortical regions (the lower face and upper arm) next to the representation of the missing arm had enlarged. The fascinating finding was that touching the lower face lightly caused sensation in the face as well as the phantom limb. Using MEG imaging, Rama and colleagues have shown this enlargement of the lower facial and upper arm representations (on the same side as the missing lower arm) in the cortex.

But here is the really interesting part of the story. Many amputees experience awful pain associated with their phantom arms and report that they believe the pain is due to the fact that the phantom arm is stuck in one position and cannot be moved. Somehow the motor command cortical area for the amputees has perceived the phantom limb as stuck. Rama, who is not only a renowned neuroscientist but also an M.D. with a practice in neurology, came up with the ingenious idea that perhaps the amputee's brain could be tricked into thinking that the phantom arm had become real and was moving by using a mirror.

Rama built a virtual reality "device" from a dime store mirror and a cardboard box. The mirror is placed vertically inside the box with the top removed. The front of the box has two holes, through which the patient with an amputated hand inserts her hands. Her normal hand (say, the right one) faces the front of the mirror and to the right of it and her phantom hand (the left one) is on the back side of the mirror to the left of it. Rama then asked her to view the reflection of her normal hand in the mirror, adjusting her normal hand position until the reflected hand position coincided with her perceived position of her phantom hand. As Rama tells his story:

> She has thus created the illusion of observing two hands, when in fact she is only seeing the mirror reflection of her intact hand. If she now sends motor commands to both arms to make mirror symmetric movements, as if she were conducting an orchestra or clapping, she "sees" her phantom moving as well. Her brain receives confirming visual feedback that the phantom hand is moving correctly in response to her command. Will this help restore voluntary control over her paralyzed phantom?

The answer is yes: temporary control of the phantom was restored while the patient was using this virtual reality device (and stopped when the eyes were closed). The amazing thing was that after repeated use of the device at home over a number of weeks, a major brain reorganization occurred for one patient with a phantom arm. As told by Rama:

> "Doctor," he exclaimed, "its gone!" "What's gone?" (I thought maybe he had lost the mirror box.) "My phantom is gone." "What are you talking about?" "You know, my phantom arm, which I had for ten years. It doesn't exist any more. All I have is my phantom fingers and palm dangling from my shoulder!" . . . "Phillip—does it bother you?" "No, no, . . . ," he said. "On the contrary. You know the excruciating pain I had in my elbow? The pain that tortured me several times a week? Well, now I don't have an elbow and I don't have that pain anymore. But I still have my fingers dangling from my shoulder and they still hurt. . . . Unfortunately, . . . your mirror box doesn't work anymore because my fingers are too high up."

I suggest that you take a mirror as in Fig. 19.4 and try this illusion for yourself. Place one hand behind the mirror and hold it still while you look at the mirror and move the hand facing the mirror to experience the illusion of the movement of the fixed hand.

Rama had thus demonstrated a remarkable ability of the adult cortex to reorganize 10 years after the amputation. There was an immediate short-term effect and a permanent effect after 3 weeks.

I would suggest that it may be very useful to precede each session where the patient uses the virtual reality device with listening to the first movement of the Mozart Sonata (K.448). I predict that just as the Mozart Sonata accomplishes some sort of cortical priming for enhanced spatial-temporal reasoning, it should

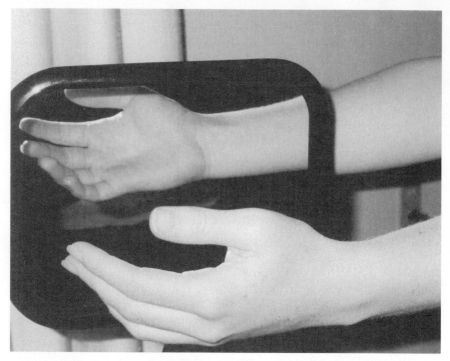

FIGURE 19.4   A left and right hand related by the symmetry operation of mirror reflection. Do this experiment for yourself following the instructions of Ramachandran. As in this photo, hold your right hand *fixed* behind a mirror and look at the reflected hand in the mirror. Move your left hand repeatedly back and forth in a pattern and experience the illusion of your fixed right hand moving together with the moving right one as you view the reflected hand.

facilitate the movement illusion and perhaps continue its effect when the eyes are closed. I will return to this illusion in Chapter 21, when I discuss our experiment in progress investigating the Mozart effect on recovery of finger movement following stroke.

PERFECT PITCH

Perfect pitch is the ability to identify any musical note without comparison to a reference note. Musicians must have what is called relative pitch, that is, the ability to identify any note in comparison to a reference note. Most people, including most musicians, do not have perfect pitch. A recent study by Gottfried Schlaug and colleagues [21] using MRI imaging may have located the

TABLE 19.1   MRI data on the size of the left and right planum temporale (PT) measured in area units of 0.1×0.1 cm, as well as the asymmetry δPT in terms of areas (right PT - left PT) divided by (right PT + left PT)/2 from Schlaug and colleagues. The data contrast musicians with and without perfect pitch and nonmusicians (also without perfect pitch). The numbers in brackets represent the standard deviations (see Chapter 13). The statistical significance of δPT for the perfect pitch group versus the nonmusician group is a probability less than 0.001. *Note that the perfect pitch group has smaller right PT than the average nonmusician (with no perfect pitch).*

Subjects	δPT	Left PT	Right PT
Musicians with perfect pitch (11 subjects)	−0.57 (0.21)	1097 (202)	611 (105)
Musicians without perfect pitch (19 subjects)	−0.23 (0.17)	1043 (183)	830 (178)
Nonmusicians without perfect pitch (30 subjects)	−0.23 (0.24)	896 (236)	736 (263)

physical basis of perfect pitch. They reported that the **planum temporale (PT)**, a region of the cortex that processes sound, is far bigger on the left side than on the right side in those professional musicians who have perfect pitch as compared to professional musicians without perfect pitch, and even more so as compared to nonmusicians (also without perfect pitch). The authors emphasize what they call the asymmetry δPT in terms of areas: (right PT − left PT) divided by (right PT + left PT)/2. I will examine their data, given in Table 19.1, since these data contain some features of importance that I have not seen discussed. Clearly these data show, as emphasized by Schlaug, that indeed δPT is more than twice as large for the perfect pitch musicians as for the nonmusicians. An important feature that was not discussed, however, is that while the size of the left PT for the perfect pitch musicians is larger than the left PT for the nonmusicians, *the right PT is smaller for the perfect pitch group than for the nonmusicians.* Furthermore, if we compare the musicians, perfect pitch versus no perfect pitch, this is more clearly evident: *Here the PT on the left are the same size, whereas the right PT size is considerably smaller on the average for the perfect pitch group than for the no perfect pitch group.*

In fact, perfect pitch seems to be the result of a smaller than average PT in the right cortex. I strongly suspect that, as discussed earlier in this chapter, having a smaller than average cortical area probably implies a lack of some higher brain function. In this case, I would expect that persons with a below-average PT in the right cortex would have a reduced ability in spatial-temporal reasoning. Note that I do not imply that people with perfect pitch might be deficient in spatial-temporal reasoning, only those with a very small right PT. There is a large standard deviation in these data in Table 19.1.

You might ask why I direct so much attention to this subject of perfect pitch (especially since it is not clear if having perfect pitch correlates with higher brain function). I have two reasons. First, two years ago I gave an invited talk at a conference on music education for young children that was attended by parents and educators. One speaker discussed Schlaug's results. Then he talked about his program to develop perfect pitch in young children as if this would be a big benefit in enhancing the reasoning capabilities of these young children. In the question period following this speaker's talk, I mentioned my previous concern that we should be cautious in using scientific data to support programs that go beyond their scope of validity, especially with very young children. My second reason will be evident when I discuss in Chapter 21 the fascinating rare neurological genetic disorder of Williams syndrome. Children with this disorder have seemingly above-average music ability and below-average spatial-temporal reasoning.

CHAPTER 20

Education: Music Training Plus Spatial-Temporal Training Improves Math

BRIEF GUIDE

I present arguments why I believe that music training will be greatly expanded in public schools, but also why it will become integrated into the standard curriculum. I suggest that this will happen because *music training can help raise math performance in a major way.* The material in this chapter is all readable.

WHY MATH?

The joke in real estate is that there are three factors that are crucial in buying a house: location, location, location. Likewise, there are three crucial factors in education: math, math, math. O.K., this is a joke, and reading and writing must

be of equal or more importance. But I am serious in stating the negative consequences of any child not being able to do math.

As we enter the third millennium, if one thing is clear, it is the tremendous
growth of technology. It is impossible to predict all the ways that (just to give a
few examples) biological engineering, computers, lasers, microelectronic circuits, and robotics will affect human society in the coming decades. However,
it is safe to say that the number of semiskilled jobs will continue to diminish.
Furthermore, businesses are no longer competing with those next door or even
those in the next state; they now compete around the world. In the future, there
will mainly be either high-tech jobs or low-tech jobs. I suggest that a child who
does not learn math will have little choice and fewer opportunities.

As I emphasized in Chapter 2, large-scale studies [1] have shown that 8th
grade children in the U.S. rank way below average in math performance among
developed countries. In particular, U.S. children are especially poor in doing
proportional math, that is, in comparing ratios of quantities. A simple example
shown in Fig. 20.1 asks (A) if you mix three cups of water and one tablespoon
of sugar, or (B) seven cups of water and three tablespoons of sugar, which is
sweeter?

Of course you may ask, what is the big deal about proportional math? The
big deal is fourfold:

1. As a professor of physics for 35 years, I can assure you that if your child
cannot do proportional math, the child will have difficulty with even the most
basic science, for example, with rate problems in biology, chemistry, and physics. Once a child falls behind at these beginning levels, the higher-level math,
science, and engineering courses may prove to be insurmountable. This will
rule out many high-tech jobs. I want to stress that I am not saying that every
child should aspire to a high-tech job, but that she should have the opportunity
and not be denied it by the time she is in elementary school.

2. O.K., you may now say, let's just devote more time teaching 6th graders
proportional math. Well, much research in math education by many eminent
scientists and educators has been devoted to the problem of teaching children
proportional math [2]. It is safe to say that until now there has been no breakthrough in improving the teaching of proportional math.

3. There are *many* higher levels of math, so proportional math is a very
crucial and obvious roadblock in a child's education.

4. Proportional math is a first academic hurdle that requires the children to
grasp the underlying concepts before they can master the material. Rote learning simply does not work.

Xiao Leng, Professor of Math at Pasadena City College, has nicely illustrated
point three with the students at her college (Fig. 20.2). Xiao has told me that
the students in her math courses are bright and serious, but they do not understand the concepts and so cannot do the problems. She attributes the falloff in

A

B

FIGURE 20.1 A simple example of proportional math that 8th grade children have difficulty with. (A) One tablespoon of sugar is mixed with three cups of water in the pitcher. (B) Three tablespoons of sugar are mixed with seven cups of water in the pitcher. Which is sweeter, case A or case B?

students taking more advanced math courses to this lack of understanding of the math concepts rather than a lack of interest. It is clear from Fig. 20.2 that most of these students will not readily be able to go into high-tech jobs. Xiao has devoted herself to developing and implementing computer software using spatial-temporal techniques to aid in teaching the concepts in her math courses. She has gotten striking success with her initial efforts.

I emphasized in Chapter 2 that a spatial-temporal approach must be used (in addition to the standard language-analytic approach) to teach math. For the *third* time in this book, let me offer you the following quotation from Richard Feynman, perhaps the most brilliant and influential physicist of the past 50 years. Here Feynman describes the interplay of spatial-temporal and language-analytic approaches [3]:

> It's like asking a centipede which leg comes after which—it happens quickly, and I'm not exactly sure what flashes and things go on in the head. I do know it's a crazy mixture of partially solved equations and some kind of visual picture of what the

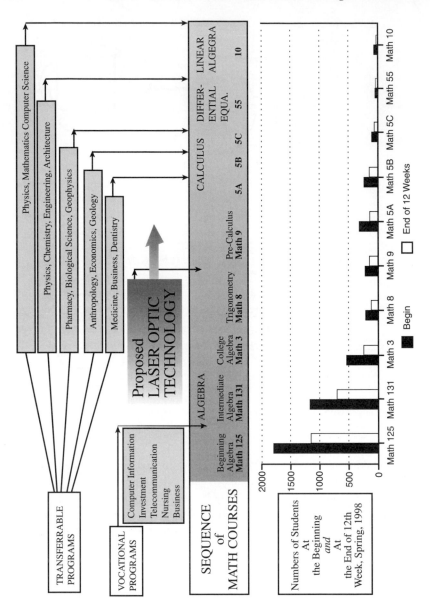

FIGURE 20.2   Math requirements for vocational and science programs at Pasadena City College as prepared by Xiao Leng. Shown below are the number of students in each math course at the beginning and end of the courses in Spring, 1998. (Note that the majority of the students at PCC take no math. Math 125 is essentially high school math and many students may have already taken it in high school.) It is strikingly clear that most of these college students are limited by their math and may have difficulty going on to high-tech professions.

equation is saying is happening, but not as well separated as the words I'm using. . . . Strange! I don't understand how it is that we can write mathematical expressions and calculate what the thing is going to do without being able to picture it.

In the following sections I will summarize our solution to improve the teaching of math. It has three parts:

(i)   Music training at an early age to enhance the cortical hardware to do spatial-temporal reasoning.
(ii)   Spatial-temporal training to teach math concepts.
(iii) Integrate (i) and (ii) into the standard language-analytic teaching of math.

MUSIC TRAINING ENHANCES SPATIAL-TEMPORAL REASONING

Xiao Leng [4] led the way to the prediction that early music training would enhance spatial-temporal reasoning. The preschool experiment by Fran Rauscher [5] showed that piano keyboard training for three-year-old children dramatically enhanced their ability to do spatial-temporal reasoning as compared to children in control groups.

As a result of these groundbreaking experiments, other groups around the country have replicated and expanded these findings [6]. Just recently I received a letter from D. Moody [7] in Florida, who has gotten great results. I expect that, just like Moody's experiment, other schools have brought music training back and documented improvements in the children's reasoning abilities.

These results that music training enhances spatial-temporal reasoning in young children were long term in the sense that the children were tested some days after their last piano keyboard lesson. *So we know that this enhancement lasts at least days.* In the scientific literature related to memory storage in the brain, this timescale is referred to as long term [8]. Thus long-term changes in neuronal connections in these children's brains have been made. I suspect that these changes must be reinforced through continued music training if they are to become truly long term. However, the timescale of days is certainly sufficient for this enhanced spatial-temporal ability to be of enormous use in an educational setting.

The ability to do spatial-temporal reasoning allows the child to make and maintain mental images, transform these images, and compare and evaluate them using symmetry relations. This ability is an innate one, which I have suggested is built into the Mountcastle columnar principle of mammalian cortex [9]. It is a marvelous ability that must be developed. As I have shown, piano keyboard training develops this spatial-temporal reasoning ability, which can then be used to think and reason and create, and in particular to learn difficult concepts in math and science.

There are many questions concerning the type of music training that will enhance spatial-temporal reasoning. Of crucial interest is how to optimize the role of music training and the corresponding enhancements of spatial-temporal reasoning in public schools with limited resources. We would want to know how different methods of music instruction appropriate for group settings (such as the methods used by Dalcroze, Orff, Kodaly, and others [10]) affect spatial-temporal reasoning. Some methods may work better than others for specifically enhancing spatial-temporal reasoning, and/or may work more efficiently in a public school setting. I will return to this shortly and present a program to evaluate these questions.

Our ongoing project with 2nd graders in the inner-city 95th St. Elementary School in Los Angeles has taken our program to the next level. The combination of group piano keyboard training and using S.T.A.R. to teach proportional math has been strikingly successful. I want to comment on several important points about our present music training:

(i) First, we see that the **window of opportunity** has not closed for these seven- and eight-year-old 2nd graders. The music training does give a large enhancement (27%) of their ability to do proportional math and fractions even after only 4 months of lessons.

(ii) I suspect that as the children get older, their music training must get more sophisticated to continue to enhance their spatial-temporal reasoning above that of children in control groups. Clearly 4 months is not enough for them to play, for example, Mozart on the piano, except for simple adaptations. I predict that as a child's piano playing abilities increase over a number of years of training and they are able to play the more complex Mozart, their spatial-temporal abilities will continue to improve.

I propose that it is the combination of the piano keyboard training and what they are playing that gives the best enhancements in spatial-temporal abilities.

(iii) Since listening to the Mozart Sonata (K.448) gives a short-term enhancement of spatial-temporal reasoning in college students, and repeated listening might even give longer-term enhancement, our 60-minute music training lesson now includes a brief listening time to this Mozart Sonata. By the way, most of these children had not heard classical music before they entered our program.

I want to share the following, perhaps even profound, story with you. The lessons (music training as well as S.T.A.R.) that we give to the children take place in the classroom of Linda Rodgers, where we keep our 20 piano keyboards and 20 computers. Other classes are given music training there in addition to Linda's class. When another teacher's class arrives for their music lessons, Linda takes her class into a smaller adjoining room that is not well sound isolated from the classroom. *Linda told me that her children spontaneously hum along when they hear the Mozart (K.448) being played to the children taking their music lesson from Stephen Cook. This is indeed a sophisticated thing to be able to do.* (I invite you to verify this sophistication: take the CD out of this book jacket and listen to the Mozart (K.448) and hum along.)

Because of this observation, Stephen will start to have the children play a very simple version that he arranged of the Mozart (K.448) while they listen to the original performance. Our goal now is to generate as large an enhancement of the spatial-temporal reasoning and math performance as we can from our program. It is hoped that subsequent studies can tease out the various components.

SPATIAL-TEMPORAL TRAINING USING S.T.A.R. TO IMPROVE MATH

As I discussed earlier in this book, it was clear to Wendy Boettcher and me [11] over five years ago that the appropriate computer software should be developed using spatial-temporal methods to teach math, in particular proportional math. Matthew Peterson quickly became (and remains) the chief architect and developer of the now proven and highly successful math video game S.T.A.R. and its evaluation program S.T.A.R. E.P. Again, for those of you who have a computer, slip the S.T.A.R. CD out of the book jacket and have fun with the great interactive demo that Matthew has prepared for you.

The chief goals of S.T.A.R. were to teach fractions, proportional math, and symmetry operations to 2nd grade children. These math concepts were all successfully included in S.T.A.R. in a manner that was readily understood and mastered by these children, as measured by S.T.A.R. E.P. The basic features of how Matthew incorporated these math concepts into S.T.A.R. are shown in Fig. 14.1.

The 2nd grade study using S.T.A.R., designed and carried out by Amy Graziano [12], involved 237 children from three schools. Three major results were found:

(i) The pilot study showed the teaching power of S.T.A.R. We had three groups: two groups of children from a school performing well below average in math, one getting S.T.A.R. training and one getting English language training on a computer, and a group from a school performing above average in math that received no extra training. After eight lessons, the S.T.A.R. group not only scored well above the English language group, but significantly above the group from the above-average school in our evaluation program. *Thus in one month, we were able to effectively level the playing field for these disadvantaged children in the math we were teaching them.*

(ii) In our main study at the 95th St. School, our S.T.A.R. E.P. results with different groups of children (see Fig. 14.4) showed how quickly they mastered the math concepts. We proposed that this gave strong support for our trion model of higher brain function, which predicted that S.T.A.R. is tapping into innate cortical processes of spatial-temporal reasoning that were used to teach the math concepts.

(iii) One group (Piano-ST) of children in the main study received both music training and S.T.A.R. training. A control group (English-ST) received English language training and S.T.A.R. training. After only 4 months, the Piano-ST group scored significantly higher than the English-ST group on the S.T.A.R. E.P. In particular, the *Piano-ST group scored 27% higher than the English-ST group on proportional math and fractions.*

The extension of S.T.A.R. to younger children using the software MicroS.T.A.R. is now under way. This is extremely important, since I suggest that it is possible to teach math concepts to two- and three-year-old children using spatial-temporal reasoning. Perhaps even more important is the use of MicroS.T.A.R. to evaluate possible enhancements of spatial-temporal reasoning through music programs for very young children. This has become a very high priority for me. Yet it is also clear that the S.T.A.R. software can and will be readily extended to teach difficult math and science concepts to older children, up to and including adults.

INTEGRATION OF MUSIC TRAINING AND S.T.A.R. TRAINING INTO STANDARD LANGUAGE-ANALYTIC MATH CURRICULUM

The next step is clear, and we are in the process of implementing it. We have shown that piano training plus S.T.A.R. training is successful in teaching the concepts of proportional math and fractions to 2nd graders. It is clear that this *should* allow these children to go on to master the more quantitative language-analytic word problem approach to proportional math and fraction problems. We are now in the process of trying to prove it.

Linda Rodgers is developing and implementing this integration of the piano keyboard training and S.T.A.R. training into math word problems. The children must also be taught some standard math that they are expected to know in the

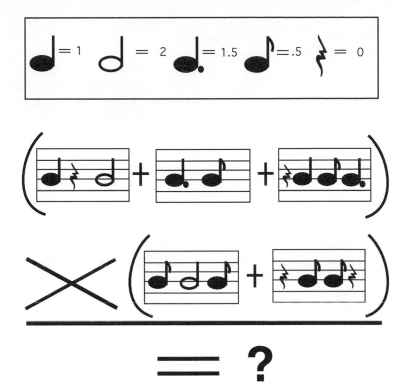

FIGURE 20.3 Illustration of example used by Linda Rodgers to combine the music training and S.T.A.R. training into 2nd grade math questions. The children must add the number of beats for each of the notes inside the left-hand bracket and then multiply this number by the number of beats inside the right-side bracket. The children have already learned their multiplication tables. They must do this in their minds, without using pencil and paper. Linda shows a selection of flash cards, and then after some tens of seconds asks the entire class to yell out the answer together, which is usually correct! This is a fine example of the children applying spatial-temporal reasoning abilities to solve a quantitative nontrivial math problem in their heads.

2nd grade. An example of how Linda is doing this is illustrated in Fig. 20.3 using flash cards from the music training lessons.

Even though the example shown in Fig. 20.3 involves addition and multiplication and not proportional math, I think that it beautifully illustrates the ability of these disadvantaged 2nd grade children to do nontrivial thinking and reasoning in their heads. This is a fine carryover use of the spatial-temporal training we have given them to their standard 2nd grade math. The children have learned to use spatial-temporal methods to solve problems taught to them, but can they transfer these methods to new and different problems? Clearly, the answer is yes: *These children in our program know how to think mathematically in their heads. This is a striking development.*

The second part of this integration program is to have a standardized written math test that will cover the proportional math and fractions material that these children know. The problem is that proportional math is not taught until the 6th grade. Michael Martinez, Professor of Math Education at U.C. Irvine, is helping to supply this crucial test ingredient in our program. Jill Hansen is about to try out the first version. If the children in our program can do better than average on standardized proportional math problems for older children, then no one can argue with our conclusions.

Well, this is almost correct. The one remaining hurdle is to demonstrate that any school, rural or urban, well funded or underfunded, can take our program and get our results. It must be shown that the successful teaching of proportional math, no matter how good the results look in one school, can be generated in any school. The M.I.N.D. Institute is planning a small study for the year 1999–2000 involving several schools. Although further studies will continue to improve our program, I believe that all parents and educators will want to see such a program in their schools.

EVALUATION OF MATH PERFORMANCE ENHANCEMENT THROUGH MUSIC TRAINING

It is very difficult to do long-term studies of the cumulative effect of years of music training on increased math performance. It is also very costly. Furthermore, many music training programs already exist. Which would be most effective for our purposes?

Based on our highly successful 2nd grade program [13], Amy Graziano, Matthew Peterson, and I proposed a new program [14] based on these results. We would quickly and cheaply evaluate the relationship between math performance enhancement and existing music programs as a function of the years of music training the children had. In particular, we would be interested in performance in proportional math and fractions which we showed S.T.A.R. could enhance in just 10 lessons.

Our program could be run in conjunction with any existing large-scale music program in any city. We could provide instructors to implement our S.T.A.R. training while existing music programs interested in collaboration would provide the students with a range of years of participation in their program. We would give 10 hours of S.T.A.R. training to these students. According to results from our published 2nd grade study, 10 one-hour lessons should cause S.T.A.R. E.P. scores to fall within the highest level of the learning curve. The program would take only one week to complete—we could administer one two-hour training session per day for five days.

We would also administer the E.P. both before and after S.T.A.R. training, in order to provide a baseline pretraining score as well as a post-training score. The S.T.A.R. software automatically keeps track of all scores on all levels every time the children use it. These data can be combined with pre- and post-E.P. scores, and then plotted against years and type of music training. This is a doable program that requires only modest financial support. The results would be of huge interest to educators, parents, and scientists.

What I have described in this chapter is just the beginning of the revolution to implement programs beginning in preschool that can fully develop the inherent cortical spatial-temporal reasoning abilities in every child through music training. This will be coordinated with school programs that utilize these enhanced spatial-temporal abilities to teach math and science through more developed versions of S.T.A.R. These programs will allow each child to reach her or his potential in math and science, and will also improve the ability to think, reason, and create.

CHAPTER 21

Clinical Implications

BRIEF GUIDE

My colleagues and I are studying a number of neuropathological disorders for which the Mozart effect and music training may be of large potential clinical relevance. The first published results for epilepsy and Alzheimer disease are discussed. Pilot studies are under way for stroke and Williams syndrome. The epilepsy results are extremely dramatic and hold great potential. All of this material is readable.

This chapter presents glimpses of hope for the treatment of several neurophysiological disorders. I will discuss the potential for new scientific insights into them, and will offer the possibility that the Mozart effect and music training can give some useful treatment.

There are many fascinating reports from music therapy that have clinical relevance. As we all are aware, music can have an enormous influence on our emotions. In music therapy, the therapist uses music to promote health and well-being, both mentally and physically [1]. My friend and colleague Kay Roskum, Professor of Music Therapy at Chapman University in Orange, California, and I have had numerous conversations about our mutual interests in how music can enhance brain function. Her studies [2] have centered on documenting the positive effects that music training can have on students, such as improving their self-esteem and behavior and motivation to attend school. I believe neuroscientists can learn an enormous amount from music therapy. The striking reports from music therapy can point the way to doing relevant controlled scientific experiments. As you have seen, my focus is to investigate how music can enhance spatial-temporal reasoning. *It is of vital importance for me to show that any behavioral results we obtain are not due to emotional factors or increased self-esteem.* The experiments I have presented in this book absolutely rule out such factors. For example, Fran Rauscher's rat study [3] and John Hughes' epilepsy study [4] (discussed in more detail below) present conclusive evidence.

I will present here the scientific studies (theoretical and experimental) that I have been associated with. These concern epilepsy, Alzheimer disease, Williams syndrome, stroke, Down syndrome, and disorders such as Parkinson disease that are related to neuromodulators. The first five are directly related to music as a treatment and experimental studies are under way in each one. The sixth, presented by Xiao Leng and me in 1991 [5], follows from the assumptions in Fig. 7.7 concerning the long (greater than seconds) inherent timescales involved in higher brain function. The ideas for this are purely theoretical and no experimental tests have been done. Yet I believe that the difficult experiments are warranted by the possibility of major clinical significance.

EPILEPSY

An amazing study was done by John Hughes [6] by monitoring the EEG of epileptic patients. In 23 of 29 subjects he found a dramatic and statistically significant reduction of abnormal firing in the cortex while listening to the first movement of the Mozart Sonata (K.448). *Some of these subjects, as in Fig. 21.1, were in a coma, ruling against any simple relaxation mechanism.*

The percentage of time that the patient in Fig. 21.1 had the readily identified, neuropathological, periodic ictal cortical firing events declined dramatically from 62% before the Mozart Sonata condition to 21% during the Mozart condition, and back to 50% following the Mozart condition. I have avoided the term "listening" here, since the patient in Fig. 21.1 was in a coma.

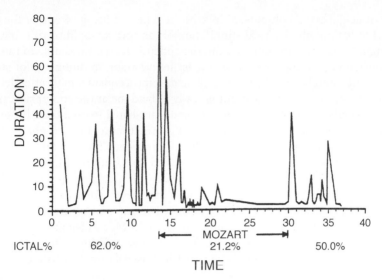

FIGURE 21.1   Dramatic example in John Hughes' EEG experiment of a decrease in duration of ictal episodes while an epileptic patient in a coma was played the Mozart Sonata (K.448). The duration of ictal episodes (in sec) is shown on the vertical axis and time (every 20 sec) on the horizontal axis. The pre-Mozart period is seen on the left, the Mozart period in the middle, and the post-Mozart period on the right. The percent is the time in that period with ictal rhythms. From Hughes *et al.* (1998).

Before discussing more details of John's published paper, I will present a little history starting with some ideas developed by Xiao Leng, John McGrann, and me [7] from the trion model. We predicted that an epileptic focus might be eliminated by patterned electrical stimulation:

Consider an epileptic discharge to be due to an abnormal firing of a large number of neurons in synchrony for periods of time.

There is a particular memory pattern present in most repertoires (see the upper left MP in Fig. 8.11) that has all trions firing together in synchrony, which we identify as the "Epileptic" MP, or EMP. In trion model simulations, the EMP can be enhanced via the Hebb learning rule after electrical stimulation so that an epileptic focus with after-discharge (about 3–6 Hz) is formed and spontaneous firing of the EMP occurs (as in animal models [8]). Following this, by using a small array of closely spaced stimulating electrodes out of phase, other MPs are enhanced via the Hebb rule, thus eliminating the dominance of the EMP. We urged that these predictions be tested in animal models. Any epileptic focus would involve many cortical columns. Here we envision that the repeated firing of the EMP in one cortical column as considered here would recruit the

EMP in neighboring columns. Similarly, the repeated firing of one of the patterned MPs through electrical stimulation of the cortex would recruit that MP in neighboring columns to eliminate the epileptic focus. I was able to interest the outstanding young neurophysiologist John Larson in doing a pilot study. We learned enough from the pilot study to develop a considerably better design. It remains on the back burner, but is ready to be done at the appropriate time.

In November of 1997, Mark Bodner and I presented invited talks [9] at the American EEG Association Annual Meeting in Baltimore. John Hughes, who is Professor of Neurology at the University of Illinois at Chicago and Director of the Epilepsy Clinic, gave a talk on documented case studies on how music had induced epileptic attacks. John and I were later discussing our respective talks, and I verified that none of the case studies had been induced by Mozart. So, with my previous ideas in mind, it occurred to me that what better way to reduce the epileptic ictal events than to listen to the Mozart Sonata (K.448) that we used in our Mozart effect studies [10]. I suggested this to John and gave him the Mozart Sonata (K.448) CD that I had used in my talk. About a week later, John called me with the classic "You are not going to believe this. . . ."— he had just analyzed the results shown in Fig. 21.1 with a patient in a coma.

Some of John's other results are just as interesting and dramatic as those in Fig. 21.1. Figure 21.2 shows the results from two patients who had focused ictal bitemporal (in the left and right temporal cortical areas) discharges. As shown, the Mozart Sonata reduced the number of discharges in the left temporal area but not in the right in patient CT, and in the right temporal area but not in the left in patient PR. The control music did not reduce the number of discharges in PR in either of the focused discharge sites. The control music was the same 1930s popular piano music [11] used as a control by Julene Johnson in her Alzheimer disease study [12].

One further interesting feature of John's data is that the slow second movement (Andante) of the Mozart Sonata (K.448) did not have the same powerful effect in decreasing the ictal spiking as the faster and more structured first movement (Allegro con spirito). This is only a qualitative observation, but if this were indeed true, it would tell us that there is something very special about the first movement. I am now taking this possibility very seriously!

John is continuing to collect data on the number of epileptic patients who have significant decreases in their ictal discharges during the Mozart condition. The number is now 29 of 36. Considering the wide variety of classifications and causes of epilepsy [13], this is truly dramatic.

He has also begun to look for longer-lasting effects by following a patient over 24 hours and repeating the Mozart condition once an hour [14]. These results should be very interesting. The prevalence of epilepsy in the U.S. may be as high as 2,000,000. Some very serious cases with young children cannot be controlled by drugs, and surgical removal of limited cortical areas is neces-

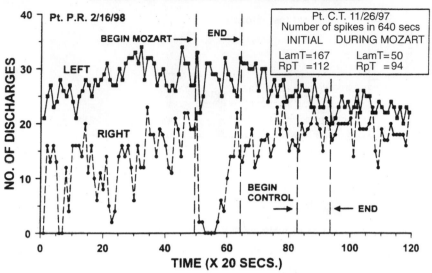

FIGURE 21.2   Effects of the Mozart Sonata (K.448) on bitemporal periodic epileptic discharges. The vertical axis shows the number of discharges (per 20 sec) and the horizontal axis is time (×20 sec). On the top right, in patient CT, a significant decrease is seen in the left but not in the right temporal area. The curves for patient PR show a clear decrease in the right but not in the left temporal area. Note that no change is seen during the control music (popular piano music from the 1930s). From Hughes *et al.* (1998).

sary. It is amazing that the young child's cortex can reorganize enough to properly function after such a procedure. However, imagine the consequences of a possible clinical treatment with the Mozart Sonata (K.448).

ALZHEIMER DISEASE

The case with Alzheimer disease [15] must be considered in more moderation than the epilepsy one since it represents a single case study. I first met Julene Johnson over five years ago while she was a graduate student collecting data on Alzheimer disease (AD) subjects who had been musicians. My mother-in-law Sylvia, who lived with my wife Lorna and me at the time, became one of Julene's subjects. Sylvia, an excellent pianist when young, has this dreadful disease and continued to play the piano until about two years ago. (Sylvia's decline in her memory and other cognitive functions seemed slower than that of the average AD patient, perhaps related to her piano playing.) Julene documented that AD

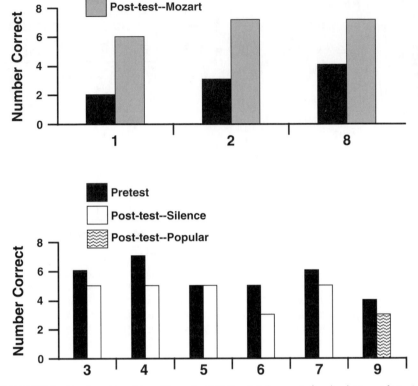

FIGURE 21.3   Results with subject AD on the PF&C task before and after (top) Mozart listening condition and (bottom) control conditions. Note the large improvement in post-test scores on all three testing sessions after the Mozart listening condition. For the control conditions, the post-test scores declined in five of the six sessions and remained the same in one. From Johnson *et al.* (1998).

subjects lost the language recognition of a familiar song before losing the music recognition. I next met Julene in Vienna, where she spent two summers working with Hellmuth Petsche. Julene was the subject JJ in my collaborative EEG coherence study [16] done at the University of Vienna.

I had talked with my colleague Carl Cotman, a world-renowned neuroscientist working on AD and Director of the U.C. Irvine Institute for Brain Aging and Dementia, about our Mozart effect experiments with college students. Carl is very open to novel ideas and immediately saw the value in trying such an experiment on AD patients. Julene was finishing her Ph.D. in Texas and I arranged for her to meet Carl. It was a match: Carl hired Julene to do clinical work with AD patients, and she would do our Mozart effect experiment.

Julene set about constructing a set of paper folding & cutting (PF&C) tasks analogous but much simpler than the ones used in the Mozart effect experiment with the college students [17]. Julene had nine separate testing sessions with one 72-year-old woman diagnosed with relatively moderate AD after neuropsychological and neuroimaging exams. It must be stressed that only upon autopsy after death can a diagnosis of AD be confirmed.

The experimental protocol for each of the nine sessions was:

(i)   two PF&C examples;
(ii) eight PF&C task items;
(iii) a 10-minute distracter to minimize potential practice and/or priming effects;
(iv) a 10-minute listening condition of either the Mozart Sonata (K.448), silence, or three popular piano tunes from the 1930s (performed by Peter Minton, PRCD 1054); and
(v)   eight PF&C tasks (different from those given in step (ii). The striking results are shown in Fig. 21.3.

The AD subject showed a huge increase (mean increase of 3.67 items) in the spatial-temporal PF&C task performance following all three Mozart listening conditions. She showed no increase (mean decrease of 1.17 items) following all six control conditions (silence or 1930s popular tunes).

Julene's results are extremely promising and she is continuing her studies with other AD subjects. Guided by the results in Fig. 21.3 and because there is such a wide range of degrees of AD, Julene is selecting subjects who do not show an increase in the silence control condition. Only these subjects are scheduled for further sessions, including the Mozart listening condition. I want to point out that a selection process like this (performing cuts in the data) is very common in **elementary particle physics** experiments as a technique to enhance the ratio of signal events to background events. The first results of this group study are very promising. It would be of great interest to see if repeated listening to the Mozart Sonata can give an increase in spatial-temporal reasoning over longer time periods.

WILLIAMS SYNDROME

Williams syndrome [18] is a rare (about 1 in 20,000 births) genetic brain disorder in which children are born with normal or even above-normal music and language abilities. They are exceptionally outgoing and friendly, however, they are extremely poor in spatial-temporal reasoning, contrary to what would be expected in normal children, in which above-average music ability correlates with above-average spatial-temporal reasoning [19]. Anecdotally, some people with Williams syndrome have above average musical talent. Although their attention span is usually very short, their attention for music is great. Most cannot read music, yet *some have perfect pitch or nearly perfect pitch* [20]. There is no known neurophysiological explanation for this extremely unusual set of higher brain function abilities. There are some interesting common physical characteristics (being pixielike) and physical limitations.

My friend and colleague Howard Lenhoff, Professor Emeritus of Biology at U.C. Irvine, first told me about Williams syndrome. Howard showed me how these general features were strikingly demonstrated in his extremely charming and exceptionally musically talented adult daughter, Gloria. These qualities are immediately evident in Gloria. She is a delight to talk to and to hear sing. She has performed in many concerts and appeared on a number of national TV shows, so perhaps you have heard or seen Gloria. In great contrast to her musical abilities, Gloria is extremely deficient in spatial-temporal reasoning.

Howard is a persuasive person and he quickly convinced me that the study of Williams syndrome held the potential of learning much about the brain. What interested me even more was the potential of improving the spatial-temporal reasoning of young children with this syndrome through music training. I thought that since our preschool study [21] showed a dramatic increase in spatial-temporal reasoning after only 6 months of piano keyboard training, it would be useful to do a pilot study with some Williams syndrome children by giving them piano keyboard training.

Amy Graziano, Jill Hansen, Howard, and I set out to do this study. Howard was able to locate enough young Williams children in southern California whose parents agreed to participate in our small study (four getting piano keyboard lessons and three getting no lessons as controls). Amy found music teachers who we would pay to give lessons in the childrens' homes twice a week for 12 months. Amy gave the teachers our music training protocol. Jill did the pre/post testing with the Wechsler WPPSI-R tasks used in our preschool study [22].

The pilot study was concluded in August, 1998, with negative results: the children did quite well in their music training, but we saw no significant improvement in their spatial reasoning. By the way, we compared their raw WPPSI-R scores and did not use the age-calibrated scores since these would not apply to the neurologically handicapped Williams children. I believe that perhaps one crucial reason for the failure to see an improvement in their reasoning was the fact that these children had very little attention for the WPPSI-R tasks. You might say that this could be expected for Williams children.

I propose that a simpler version of the S.T.A.R software is the answer to this testing problem. We had the opportunity of having two of the Williams children in our study, as well as Gloria Lenhoff, play with the introduction to one of the lower levels of S.T.A.R. It was immediately obvious to me that the children and Gloria had no attention problem and could do well with these introductory problems. In comparison, I remember that Gloria had great difficulty with similar problems we had presented to her several years ago in a more standard cardboard format that Laura Cheung had constructed as a precursor to S.T.A.R. What combination of attention, understanding what the task was, or actual reasoning ability was involved is not clear. However, I have no doubt that a simpler version of S.T.A.R. will solve this.

Further qualitative evidence that S.T.A.R. might solve the attention problem in the testing of spatial-temporal reasoning was our demonstration with **Attention Deficit Disorder (ADD)** children in the lab of James Swanson. ADD children in general have two sets of symptoms [23]: inattention (including being easily distracted, and difficulty following through on instructions) and hyperactivity-impulsivity (including difficulty awaiting their turn to do something). We had six 1st grade children with ADD who each played with an early version of S.T.A.R. for 10 minutes without one sign of inattention or hyperactivity (even while waiting for their turn).

When I have the resources to do the second experiment with Williams children, I intend to use the appropriate level of S.T.A.R. for all the spatial-temporal testing. However, I plan to combine the piano keyboard training with regular S.T.A.R. training. I strongly believe that this combined approach has the best chance to rewire their developing cortices to greatly enhance spatial-temporal reasoning.

I now return to the anecdotal evidence that many people with Williams syndrome have perfect pitch in addition to their extremely poor spatial-temporal reasoning. Let's consider again the discussion on perfect pitch in Chapter 19. As I emphasized in my discussion of the MRI results in Table 19.1, *the key feature of the musicians with perfect pitch was that the planum temporale (PT) cortical area in the right hemisphere was smaller than the right PT for the average person.* As further discussed in Chapter 19, it would seem that a cortical area that is way below average in size is probably not an advantage. Is this PT deficit in the right cortex hemisphere of musicians with perfect pitch associated with a poorer than average spatial-temporal reasoning ability, in particular those in this experiment [24] who had well below average right PTs? It would be interesting to correlate the size of the right PT with perfect pitch for the Williams people.

I want to close this discussion by telling you about the National Williams Syndrome Conference in July, 1998, where I gave an invited talk on our research. Most of the parents attended with their Williams children, and many had never seen another Williams child. As I mentioned earlier, their physical characteristics are clearly evident. As friendly and outgoing as the Williams people are with anyone, they were extremely attracted to their fellow Williams people. Further, it did not take a controlled study to observe their great enthusiasm and participation in all music events, scheduled and unscheduled.

STROKE

In the summer of 1997, I was talking with my longtime friend and colleague George Austin, an eminent neurologist and researcher on strokes, about our Mozart effect experiments. With his usual enthusiasm, George suggested that I try to see if listening to the Mozart Sonata (K.448) would enhance the fine spatial-temporal motor skills in cerebral stroke patients. In particular, he suggested the use of the finger alternating touching task, which I will call the FAT task. In this task, the patient would in sequence touch the thumb to the first finger, second finger, third finger, and fourth finger and then perform the return sequence for each hand, while the experimenter would time the task. If my belief that the Mozart Sonata (K.448) resonates with the common inherent cortical language is correct, it should enhance motor cortex function as well as spatial-temporal reasoning. Thus we should observe a decrease in the time for the FAT task for a hand impaired by stroke. George added that the stroke patients should be limited to those suffering from the nonhemorrhage or ischemic type [25].

I proceeded to put together an experimental protocol with the help of Lan Nguyen, an outstanding Clinical Professor on the faculty of the Medical School at U.C. Irvine. Lan gathered enough interesting demonstration data to warrant a pilot experiment. She then lined up four patients recovering from ischemic stroke for the experiment through Eric Feldman, Director of the Long Beach Rehabilitation Center. Our experimental protocol was quite similar to the one used with the AD subject presented earlier, only with the PF&C tasks replaced by three FAT tasks with each hand timed by the experimenter; in brief, the protocol was FAT tasks, distracter, listening condition, FAT tasks. The experiments were ably conducted by Miyoung Kim and Stephanie Schwartz. Up to eight experimental sessions were obtained for each subject. Each session had a listening condition of the Mozart Sonata, silence, or control music (alternating in successive sessions).

Although the data were suggestive of a positive Mozart effect enhancement, no conclusion could be drawn because of several factors:

(i)   The timing of the FAT tasks turned out to be not as quantitative as we had anticipated. Two of the patients were not able to sufficiently move the fingers in the impaired hand to have the thumb touch the fingers.

(ii) Sometimes the impaired hand would cramp during the session.

(iii) Large decreases in FAT timing occurred, but then for two subjects, there was a plateau in timing that was at a considerably longer time than for the good hand. Perhaps this was a muscle limitation effect rather than a cortical limitation effect.

After examining the data, Lan, Miyoung, Stephanie, and I decided, with the considerable help of Matthew Peterson and Jim Kelley, to modify the task in our protocol to one that would solve factor (i) and hopefully (ii). Matthew and Jim interfaced a small piano keyboard with a computer so that the patient would be able to depress several piano keys in sequence, while all the timings for each finger were being accurately recorded and analyzed in the computer. With this improvement, we will have not just a single overall time for the task, but highly accurate details of the time sequence. We are almost ready to implement this new protocol.

Finally, let's look at factor (iii) in light of Ramachandran's ingenious experiment [26] with the mirror and amputees with phantom hands (described in Chapter 19). Now imagine that your left hand has been impaired by an ischemic stroke in your right cerebral hemisphere. As seen in Fig. 19.4, there is a left and right hand related by the symmetry operation of mirror reflection. Do the following experiment for yourself: Hold your (impaired) left hand *fixed* behind a mirror and look at the reflected hand in the mirror. Repeatedly move the fingers of the right hand sequentially in a pattern and experience the illusion that the fingers of your fixed (impaired) left hand are moving together with moving the right one as you view the reflected hand.

We are now preparing to try out this mirror experiment with our stroke subjects to see if Rama's illusion will enable the impaired hand to go beyond the plateau associated with (iii). If so, we want to see if playing the Mozart Sonata (K.448) will further enhance the improvement brought about by the mirror illusion.

DOWN SYNDROME

Down syndrome is a chromosomal disorder that usually results in moderate to severe mental retardation and distinctive physical characteristics. Usually below normal development is noted in cognitive, language, social-emotional, and motor function. Even if Down syndrome is not detected before birth through amniocentesis, it is readily detected at the time of birth.

A few years ago I read about a recent scientific study that might allow me to design a simple research protocol to help very young Down children. I had a student, Nona Watson, write a term paper on this. Here, in brief, is my idea.

Michael Lynch [27] studied the babbling (production of prespeech syllables like "ba" and "da") of Down infants. He found that the onset of babbling is delayed some months in Down infants as compared to in normally developing infants. This then is a quantitative marker. My idea was simply to do a pilot experiment with two groups of Down newborn infants. One group would listen to the Mozart Sonata (K.448) for 10 minutes, twice a day for some 8 months or until babbling started, and a control group would listen to some popular soothing music for children for the same time periods. The idea would be to see if the Mozart group of Down infants would start babbling sooner than the control music group of Down infants. The results for these groups could then be compared to Lynch's results.

CONSEQUENCES OF INHERENT ULTRADIAN AND CIRCADIAN RHYTHMS IN NEUROMODULATORS

Another major clinical implication follows from our assumptions in Fig. 7.7 concerning long (greater than seconds) inherent timescales. In Chapter 7, we introduced the possibility of new timescales ranging from roughly seconds up to hours with these ultradian periods being related to or expressed by neuromodulators. In a very important experiment [28] from the lab of J. Justice, the presence of a circadian variation in the extracellular **dopamine** concentration in the rat brain was measured. (Note that the rat active period occurs during the dark part of the daily cycle, in contrast to humans.) *A highly statistically significant 58% increase of dopamine was found in the dark cycle as compared to the light cycle.*

Now imagine some neuropathology in one or more neuromodulators. For example, suppose that the natural dopamine levels in the cortex from the **substantia nigra** were impaired. The clinical application then would be in the treatment of **Parkinson disease.** Parkinson disease symptoms include tremor, rigidity of movement, and difficulty in starting and terminating movements. At present, the treatment of people with this disease is to try to keep the dopamine levels constant (for example, by giving the dopamine precursor L-DOPA). However, if our speculations were correct and, like the rat, the human dopamine levels in the brain have a circadian rhythm, one would want to simulate the rhythmic natural levels of dopamine rather than a constant rate in the clinical treatment. Furthermore, it is crucial to get the temporal phase of this cycle correct as illustrated in Fig. 12.1. So I would suppose that the L-DOPA dosage should be adjusted to keep the dopamine level higher during the day than at night.

Now imagine that there are natural ultradian rhythms as I have proposed for various neuromodulators, for example, a 45-minute rhythm. Then the clinical treatment of a neuropathology involving the neuromodulators with this ultradian rhythm must take this into account. I suggest that these ideas may be relevant for the treatment of such profound neuropathological disorders as schizophrenia and bipolar depression. It is with this in mind that I strongly urge that the ultradian rhythms in neuromodulators proposed in Chapter 7 be searched for.

This brings up another concept that I have followed in my scientific career. *An idea may be very speculative.* However, that does not mean that it should not be taken seriously. If the idea, even if unpopular, has a reasonable theoretical basis, is testable with modest resources, and the consequences of it being correct are major then the idea should be energetically pursued. Too often, however, the resources are not made available for this crucial type of science.

CHAPTER 22

The Spatial-Temporal Thinking Machine

BRIEF GUIDE

In this chapter I present some ideas and dreams about building a computer that can think and reason based on the spatial-temporal reasoning methods used in the brain. We are all aware of the enormous impact that electronic computers have had on our lives. Basically, the operations in present computers are addition and subtraction; the sophistication in what the computer does comes in the software we write. So, if one could combine the speed of the present computer with the ability of the brain to think using families of symmetry patterns developing in space and time, a whole new era would be here.

Throughout this book I have presented a model of higher brain function that predicts the built-in ability of the structured mammalian cortex to think, reason, and create using an innate internal neural language and grammar. Our model correctly predicted that music could enhance spatial-temporal reasoning, and the early neurophysiological results supporting these ideas have been published. I return to the insightful remarks of the late giant of brain theory, David Marr [1]:

> Let us look at the range of perspectives that must be satisfied before one can be said, from a human and scientific perspective, to have understood visual perception. First, and I think foremost, there is the perspective of the plain man. He knows what it is to see, and unless the bone's of one's arguments and theories roughly correspond to what this person knows to be true at first hand, one will probably be wrong. . . . Second, there is the perspective of the brain scientists, the physiologists and anatomists who know a great deal about how the nervous system is built and how parts of it behave. . . . And the same argument applies to the experimental psychologist. On the other hand, someone . . . with a small home computer . . . wants the explanation . . . telling him what to program. . . . He doesn't want to know about rhodopsin, or the lateral geniculate nucleus, or inhibitory interneurons. He wants to know how to program vision.

If I *really* understood how the brain thinks, I would be able to build a device based on these ideas. Well, I don't know how to build this thinking computer, but I think that it is useful to begin to try since I have had some success with the first two of Marr's points: namely, the model should make sense, and the behavior and neurophysiology should support the model. It is in this spirit that I proceed to discuss the building of a thinking machine.

As I mentioned in Chapter 1, it is evident that the present digital computer works on a totally different principle than the brain. It was only through linking hundreds of such computers together, each being millions of times faster than the computational time of the human brain, that IBM's "Deep Blue" was barely able to defeat the present world chess champion Garry Kasparov. The number of chess move possibilities looking ahead six to eight moves in many situations is just staggering! It becomes impossible for the computer to go through the possibilities that far ahead, whereas the chess Grand Master can. Imagine the technological impact of a computer that could do spatial-temporal reasoning like a chess Grand Master.

My colleagues and I have proposed that symmetry operations are a crucial feature of higher brain function and result from the spatial and temporal modularity of the cortex. It is interesting to stress the general role of pattern development in biological systems. Waddington [2], in referring to the growth of various animals, states "the dominant characteristic of biological proportions is that any given form usually exhibits the simultaneous operation of several rules of proportion, rather than of only one. And in discussing these proportions, it becomes extremely superficial to omit the time factor, since in the great majority of instances the proportions of a biological form change as it grows and develops".

This fits in nicely with our ideas of pattern development in the brain, as shown in the evolutions of the trion model spatial-temporal firing patterns and the symmetry relations among these patterns as they evolve dynamically. The symmetry operations arise naturally in the highly structured trion model of the cortex. A columnar network of a small number of trions has a large repertoire of spatial-temporal memory patterns, which can be excited. The MPs are related by specific symmetries: spatial rotation, mirror reflection, and time reversal, as well as other symmetry operations in this abstract internal language of the brain. These MPs can be readily enhanced by only a small change in connection strengths via a Hebb learning rule. Learning introduces small breaking of the symmetries in the connectivities, which enables a symmetry in the patterns to be recognized in the Monte Carlo evolution of the MPs. In Chapter 8, we presented detailed examples of the recognition of rotated patterns and time-reversed patterns via this procedure [3].

I propose that cortical columns are organized in a *very highly structured manner to form a cortical area*. It is this higher-level architecture that we have begun to examine in order to explore the further consequences of the concepts concerning computation by symmetry operations. I suggest that a hardware analog-digital implementation of this higher-level cortical area architecture of trion cortical columns should be "straightforward" owing to the localized and structured (in space and time) connectivity, and the discreteness of the firing levels [4]. A more "biological" version could also be considered in which these discrete quantities are allowed some spread to optimize the "behavior" of the model. I have had informative conversations concerning this feature with Carver Mead, a renowned expert at Cal Tech on building electronic circuits that simulate neurobiological systems. High-speed parallel computations would allow us to look for symmetry operations in a cortical area.

The following elements make up the structured connectivity that permits the notion of the minicolumn, column, and cortical area, to be called functional cooperative units in a dynamical processing sense:

(i)   The heavy interconnections vertically (excitatory and inhibitory) among the neurons through the cortical layers form the basis for the minicolumn.

(ii)   The (neurons in the) minicolumns are connected to neighboring minicolumns in the same column through horizontal connections in a weaker manner.

(iii)   The long-range connections between distant columns are still highly specific and yet still weaker in strength.

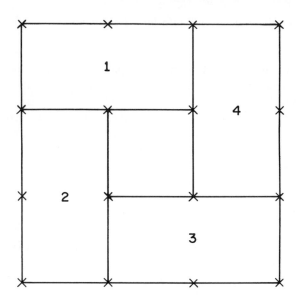

FIGURE 22.1   Four coupled six-trion columnar networks labeled 1–4 are mapped onto a 4 × 4 Go board (with the 16 vertices labeled by X's), illustrating the chunking of the board into groups of 6 vertices and the overlap of the columnar networks onto some of the vertices. We would map a few winning strategies of play in this Go game onto trion model evolutions and enhance these evolutions using the Hebb learning rule.

I think of at least three spatial scales of cooperativity when defining the functional units of minicolumn, column, and cortical area. The "global" MPs in the higher-level architecture of coupled columnar trion networks as in Chapter 8, which follow from the nature of weak intercolumnar connectivity between minicolumns, are products of the MPs from the individual columns. The specific temporal rotation and spatial rotation relations among the MPs were shown to be crucial in this cortical language and grammar [5].

Our crucial result and proposal is that the computations by symmetry operation discussed here are indeed involved in higher brain function. This book has been devoted to showing that this is true.

Consider now a small cortical area architecture of four coupled columns of trions as in Chapter 8. Then by some unspecified, very "clever" mapping of these firing patterns onto a logic problem, imagine that we can build a logic device. For example, insight into the solution of some simple "board" game would be a major advance toward building a thinking computer.

Some simple thoughts toward such a project of building a logic device to solve board games can be mentioned. Insights gained from analysis of chess show that when Master chess players recall a middle game position it takes place through the use of "local clusters of pieces." As I noted in Chapter 1, Chase and Simon [6] stated that the Chess Master's strategy in choosing a next move in a middle game is very interesting: "As we have shown, the board is organized into smaller units representing more local clusters of pieces. Since some of these patterns have plausible moves associated with them in long-term memory, the Master will start his search by taking one of these moves and analyzing its consequences." A second relevant well-known fact is that the organization of the visual information in the cortex is such that the receptive fields overlap in neighboring cortical columns.

We illustrated [7] these two features of (i) chunking or use of local clusters and of (ii) overlap in information in the simple example of a 4 × 4 **Go** game (Fig. 22.1): four coupled six-trion columnar networks labeled 1–4 are mapped onto a 4 × 4 Go board, illustrating the chunking of the board into groups of six vertices and the overlap of the columnar networks onto some of the vertices. We have in mind to map a few winning strategies of play in this 4 × 4 Go game onto trion model evolutions and to enhance these evolutions using the Hebb learning rule (Fig. 8.1) in a very rapid manner for the coupled networks. The goal would be to see if these winning strategies generalized to other moves.

Clearly, achieving this goal of having winning strategies generalized to other moves for any nontrivial board game is a challenge, but it is of enormous significance. Several excellent undergraduate students, including David Kirkman and David Sweet, have worked with me on these ideas. We examined **Reversi**, a much simpler game than Go. Although we found no large success, I am not discouraged and I plan to return to trying to build a thinking machine based on the trion model. It is a wonderful challenge, with a staggeringly important technological breakthrough as the goal.

CHAPTER 23

Final Thoughts

BRIEF GUIDE

In the previous chapters, I have presented details of the thirteen pieces shown in the brain puzzle figure that first appeared in the Prologue. I begin this final chapter by briefly summarizing them. Then I will make some general remarks that should not necessarily be ascribed to my good colleagues. Even though I think that the current knowledge presented in this book is just the "tip of the iceberg," or better yet a vein of gold leading to the gold mine, I cannot resist this opportunity to present my visions and dreams, as well as cautions about the future of the concept that "music enhances learning." Perhaps the most important comments concern the early development of all children's abilities to think, reason, and create.

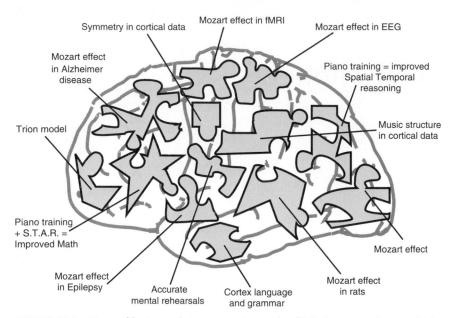

FIGURE 23.1   Pieces of brain puzzle in our ongoing study of "Music as a window into higher brain function." I have discussed all thirteen of them in this book and shown you how they all fit together.

THE THIRTEEN PIECES IN OUR BRAIN PUZZLE FIT

The goal of this book was to present my ideas on how we think, reason, and create, using music as a window into higher brain function. I have crossed many boundaries, including brain theory, neurophysiology, neuroanatomy, brain imaging, child development, music cognition, education, teaching of music, teaching of math and science, neuropathology, and psychology. In the Prologue, I presented our quest as an effort to explain and integrate a substantial number of puzzle pieces that, when assembled, would represent higher brain function. By carefully examining each piece (see Fig. 23.1) and the relationships among the pieces, I have tried to show you that it is *extremely* likely that we are on the right track.

In particular, the trion model provides the theoretical guide and the glue that ties together this entire story. As a mathematical realization of the Mountcastle columnar principle for mammalian cortex, it produced the crucial concepts on higher brain function. Among them are:

(i)   *Symmetry,* as I have stated and restated, is perhaps the most important concept.

(ii)   *Memory firing patterns in the cortex come in families related by symmetries.* This allows the recognition and use of these symmetries in how we think ahead in space and time.

(iii) *Natural time sequences* of the symmetry memory patterns occur. These would be of importance and common in all higher brain function.

(iv)   *An inherent cortical language and grammar,* discussed in Chapter 8, followed from the trion model. This neural language, basically one part of the brain talking to another part, should be common throughout the cortex and in all mammals. *Further, there are highly specific rules based on symmetry considerations for the grammar of this language.* The theoretical studies are just beginning to generate detailed results. (Remember that I consider the theory as a guide to experiment.) Experimental tests of this quite profound prediction of an inherent mammalian cortical language and grammar are quite doable.

(v)   *The striking trion music results of Xiao Leng focused all of our subsequent research on using music as a window into studying how we think, reason, and create, as well as provided a means of enhancing these higher brain functions.* Xiao and I predicted in 1991 that music could causally enhance spatial-temporal reasoning since both use the same cortical language and share common regions of cortical function.

This summarizes the two theoretical pieces (the trion model, and the cortex language and grammar) of the cortical puzzle shown in Fig. 23.1. The remaining eleven pieces involve the experiments that test and explore the predictions from the trion model. Again, these dramatic experimental results all support the theory, but by no means do they prove it. I am extremely pleased that it was the trion model theory that motivated these experiments. Although quite common in physics, it is quite rare in brain studies for theory to significantly influence experimental research. In the following, I briefly present the experimental results for these eleven areas.

(a) The first test of the trion model involved mental rehearsals. *The temporal durations of mental rehearsals of pieces of music lasting up to a few minutes were extraordinarily reproducible.* This was a crucial test for the Mountcastle spatial-temporal code (or cortical language) for higher brain function, and for our trion model, which is based on the Mountcastle code. My further studies in this area have been related to a less scientific goal, but with large general interest: Can this ability to do highly accurate mental rehearsals be related to top performance in sports, and be used to great advantage?

(b) The next test revealed the so-called Mozart effect, which provided the *first causal evidence that just listening to specific music enhances subsequent spatial-temporal reasoning in college students.* This experiment with Fran Rauscher, reported in *Nature* in November, 1993 (and expanded on in 1995), generated enormous interest. I believe that Franny's choice of the Mozart Sonata for Two Pianos in D Major (K.448) for our experiment will prove to be very fortunate. This is not to say that other pieces of music by Mozart or by other composers will not give the same results, but this remains to be shown. More on this later.

(c) The experiment with three-year-old preschool children showed that *piano keyboard training for 6 months led to dramatic improvement in spatial-temporal reasoning that lasted for at least some days after their last lesson* (rather than the short-term 10–15 minutes of the Mozart effect found with college students). Publication of these results in *Neurological Research* in 1997 led to even greater interest than for the Mozart effect since it had obvious educational implications. One of our experimental controls was a group of children who received word and number training on friendly commercial computer software. The piano keyboard group improved 35% more than this control group on spatial-temporal reasoning. (No group improved in spatial recognition, just as predicted.) We then predicted that these increased spatial-temporal abilities could be of benefit to the children in learning difficult math concepts. Matthew Peterson and I set out some 5 years ago to develop the necessary spatial-temporal math training software using our insight from the trion model on the neurobiological basis of higher brain function. The result of Matthew's long and ingenious efforts produced S.T.A.R.

(d) The next step showing that *piano keyboard training together with S.T.A.R. training leads to improved proportional math performance for 2nd grade children* has just been published with Amy Graziano and Matthew in the March 1999 issue of *Neurological Research*. I am writing the finishing touches on this book in April, 1999, so I can only speculate on the impact of this potential break-through in teaching difficult math and science concepts. I believe that this will have an even larger impact than either the Mozart effect or the Preschool study, even though more research must be done. I will comment further on this.

(e) The EEG coherence study of the Mozart effect provided the first experimental evidence for its neurophysiological basis. *There was a widespread increase in synchrony in cortical activity after listening to the Mozart Sonata (K.448) that carried over to the spatial-temporal task.* The striking findings have led to further EEG and new fMRI studies as described in Chapter 15. This experiment, done by Johannes Sarnthein in the EEG lab pioneered by Hellmuth Petsche at the University of Vienna, provides a model for our collaborative research with other such world-class labs.

(f) Demonstration of the presence of symmetry families of firing patterns in cortical data was done by Mark Bodner on the data acquired in the world-class neurophysiology lab of Joaquin Fuster at U.C.L.A. Mark's striking results were found using his new SYMMETRIC analysis on primate memory tasks. *These results showing families of memory patterns related by symmetries were just as predicted by the trion model.* This exciting breakthrough opens the door (a crack) to finding the code of higher brain function.

(g) *Experiments extending the Mozart effect to Alzheimer disease subjects* have been done by Julene Johnson in the Brain Aging lab of Carl Cotman at U.C. Irvine. Although we are in the early stages of the research, the potential for clinical benefits will be investigated.

(h) A startling demonstration of the Mozart effect in rats has been shown by Fran Rauscher in her lab at the University of Wisconsin, Oshkosh. As detailed in Chapter 18, her experiment has many profound implications. For example, *Franny's results showed that the increased spatial-temporal maze abilities of the Mozart group of rats lasted at least some 4 hours after the last listening condition.*

(i) The dramatic Mozart effect EEG study in epileptic patients was done by John Hughes in his Epileptic Clinic at the University of Illinois, Chicago. *John showed striking and statistically significant decreases in neuropathological cortical discharges in 29 of 36 epileptic patients while listening to the Mozart Sonata (K.448), even in patients in a coma.* The clinical implications of potential long-term effects are clearly of huge interest and thus worth careful investigation.

(j) The first fMRI studies of the Mozart effect were done by Tugan Muftuler in the lab of Orhan Nalcioglu at U.C. Irvine in collaboration with Mark Bodner and me. *In all four subjects examined so far, listening to the Mozart Sonata gave substantial and significant signals in the prefrontal cortex, whereas listening to control music did not excite this highest of thought areas.* As expected, all listening conditions excited the auditory cortex. These first fMRI results are extremely exciting, and the results from the next subjects will be of enormous interest. We will want to look at many other types of music. An exciting possibility is that fMRI brain imaging could be an indicator for which music besides the first movement of the Mozart Sonata (K.448) could give the behavioral enhancements in spatial-temporal reasoning as seen in the Mozart effect. This would be the beginning of the "Mozart effect meter" that Francis Crick had asked about.

(k) *Several important identifications of musical structure in cortical data were made with Mark Bodner and Amy Graziano.* These first results, presented in Chapter 17, are part of the enormously ambitious plan to determine the internal neural language of higher brain function. I will return to this below.

As I noted in the Prologue, these thirteen pieces in the scientific puzzle that I call "Music as a window into higher brain function" will each require much further research. *However, they all fit together.* For example, there are six separate Mozart effect puzzle pieces, all done in different labs. Together with the trion model predictions, these six experimental pieces on the Mozart effect, all from different perspectives and techniques, form an impressive cluster of results that support each other:

(b) college student behavioral studies from my lab at U.C. Irvine;

(c) EEG coherence studies from the University of Vienna;

(g) Alzheimer studies from the lab of Carl Cotman at U.C. Irvine;

(h) rat studies from the lab of Fran Rauscher at the University of Wisconsin, Oshkosh;

(i) epilepsy studies from the lab of John Hughes at the University of Illinois, Chicago; and

(j) fMRI studies from the lab of Orhan Nalcioglu at U.C. Irvine.

It is now no longer appropriate to consider these results as separate phenomena. I hope you now agree with me that they all fit into a coherent picture. In particular, the eleven distinct and exciting experimental results (a–k) are all supportive of the basic underlying trion model predictions that motivated them.

ACCEPTANCE OF NEW SCIENTIFIC IDEAS

Sometimes I am asked whether there are dissenting scientific views on our research. Several reports have focused on the Mozart effect behavioral studies, with some groups replicating our results and some groups failing to do so. Fran Rauscher and I [1] carefully discussed each of the failures and why their experimental designs were not relevant (mainly, they simply were not measuring spatial-temporal reasoning). As I just emphasized, there are now six separate and distinct Mozart effect experiments that form a body of knowledge that, together with the trion model theory, must be considered as a whole.

Edward O. Wilson, a pioneer for his seminal scientific studies of insect social life and a Pulitzer Prize-winning author, remarks in his book "The Diversity of Life" [2] on the universal problem of getting new ideas accepted by fellow scientists:

> First rule of the history of science: when a big, new, persuasive idea is proposed, an army of critics soon gathers and tries to tear it down. Such a reaction is unavoidable because, aggressive yet abiding by the rules of civil discourse, this is simply how scientists work. It is further true that, faced with adversity, proponents will harden their resolve and struggle to make the case more convincing. Being human, most scientists conform to the psychological Principle of Certainty, which says that when there is evidence for and against a belief, the result is not a lessening but a heightening of conviction on both sides. . . . Rule number two: the new idea will, like mother earth, take some serious hits. If good it will survive, probably in modified form.

In terms of Wilson's rules, I propose that we have more than survived. My noted neurophysiologist colleague Larry Stein first told me of a more succinct remark on new ideas: "First they say that it is not true, then they say it is not new, and then they say it is not you." I believe this book documents that it was indeed my many colleagues who developed the new ideas presented here.

I continue now with some stories and remarks that are relevant to the origin of the structured Mountcastle columnar principle for mammalian cortex, as well as the role of music in higher brain function. As an astute reader, I suspect that you may have asked yourself where those key components of our brains come from. These stories do not give answers, but they do give plausible insights.

EVOLUTION OF THE STRUCTURED CORTEX AND MUSIC

I was extremely pleased when I first heard that the renowned dolphin behaviorist Ken Norris was interested in the paper that Xiao Leng and I had written on higher brain function. Ken has spent his scientific career studying the group behavior of dolphins in the ocean [3]. At our first meeting, I immediately saw that he is just as dynamic and interesting as his fascinating books on dolphin behavior would indicate. It soon became clear to me how Ken's ideas meshed with Xiao's and mine. Our model of higher brain function is based on the trion model realization of Mountcastle's columnar principle of mammalian cortex. Ken was concerned with *rhythm or oscillation and its crucial importance in the organization of group behavior in animals. Although the columnar cortex is used by humans to think, reason, and create, its benefit to lower mammals in evolution was not evident to me until I talked with Ken. Clearly, doing higher math or listening to music is not relevant to lower mammals.*

I begin this discussion by quoting from Ken's fascinating presentation at the 1995 International Ethological Congress in Honolulu [4]:

> I believe . . . that there has been a single dominant theme in information transfer from the very beginning of life to the most complex manifestations of the evolutionary process we see today. . . . Oscillation, or if it is highly periodic, rhythm, has been the major means of organizing behavior. . . . The organization of animal groups by oscillatory behavior occurs because one animal must read the signals of another, . . . and it must extract relevant information from an overwhelmingly complex world. Hence rhythm or oscillation becomes the prime organizer of group behavior. The major function of such rhythm is to pinpoint where in a behavioral stream information of importance can be expected to occur. It pinpoints relevant information from a vast inundation of irrelevant or negative information.

For mammals, then, the assessment of this information allows each animal in the group to participate in the complex relevant behavior, since the bases of these rhythmic behaviors are built into the structured cortex, as I have shown earlier in this book. Back to Ken's paper:

> Rhythmically produced information seems basic, perhaps almost definitional of group processes where the coordination of many animals at once is required. . . . Let me describe . . . an accelerating spatiotemporal oscillation, [which] in its totality modulates the transition from one behavioral state to the next in the daily round of an entire school of dolphins. The . . . rhythms are the quintessential organizers of group process in these animals. Most, or perhaps all, of what these dolphins do as a school may have a rhythmic or oscillatory structure. A school of 40 spinner dolphins is at rest at midday, deep in flat, calm Kealake'akua Bay, Hawaii. The dolphins cruise slowly back and forth over the white sand 40 feet below in a tight school.

According to Ken, the school of dolphins then moves off the sand patch and out over the dark coral bottom. The dolphins, which were schooled tightly during rest, now spread out. They begin to vocalize and become moderately noisy, then slow down again. They become quiet, turn slowly around, and as they make it almost back to the original rest area, they begin to bunch together. Again to Ken's description:

> Later, . . . [the school] turns abruptly out toward the bay mouth again, spreads laterally, and speeds up again, . . . swimming a little faster than before. . . . [After another pause,] the school moves out toward the bay mouth moving faster than before. . . . [This] in-and-out oscillatory progression . . . goes on for two hours or more, and each time the dolphins turn for sea they speed more. All of a sudden the entire school bursts from the water in a beautiful series of clean, synchronized accurate leaps. . . . One can see for the first time their true synchrony. In totality, what we have been observing is a complex oscillation of an entire school in time and space. There is a rhythm of forth and back from the resting grounds toward the sea, there is a tightening and spreading of the school, there is a speeding and slowing, which is itself a progression toward faster and faster speed. . . . The entire behavior is, in other words, a complex spatiotemporal rhythmic pattern, oscillating from one behavior state, rest, into the next, feeding, and it points toward the feeding grounds offshore. . . . The dolphins race toward the setting sun, . . . diving synchronously into the deep scattering layer of squids, fishes and shrimps upon which they feed for much of the night. . . .
>
> Time-based behavior patterns have existed as long as there has been life. They are, in fact, an essential dimension of life. . . . Rhythms have come to have a coordinating function both in locomotion and in communication, internal and external. . . . It has reached an apex in the massive parallel processing systems of the mammalian cortex based on Mountcastle Columns."

I think that Ken's analysis is profound and will play a major role in future evolutionary investigations of the mammalian cortex. Furthermore, I suspect that this rhythmic dolphin behavior is somehow linked to the origin of music processing. Fran Rauscher's Mozart effect experiment with rats showed long-term enhancement of performance in a spatial-temporal maze. This implies that the rat's processing of music is similar to that of humans in some crucial aspects.

Rats, being nocturnal animals, are very auditory. Thus I suggest that they are constantly searching for patterns using the spatial-temporal analysis of their auditory input. I propose that such analysis is present in all sensory mammalian systems, though I cannot base this on firm data. However, there is a glimpse of such possible "searching for patterns" by cats as seen in some neurophysiological data from the cat visual cortex [5]. My suggestion is that the cortices of the rats in Franny's experiment were responding to the patterns in Mozart's music, which I believe resonate with the inherent structure of the mammalian cortex. If this is the case, the Mountcastle columnar principle for mammalian cortex is of crucial relevance to survival.

The foregoing evolutionary remarks now lead me to a philosophical discussion of the relationship between humans and animals. Darwin's theory of evolution led to contentious debates that continue to this day. Even for many people who intellectually acknowledge the truth of Darwin's theory, they support a belief that the human "mind" must be quite different, even though the underlying neural machinery may be similar in many aspects. In many ways, the human mind is decidedly different from that of animals, however, there are also many similarities. The main difference, of course, is the incredible usefulness of our human language, spoken and written. *As I have presented several times in this book, I propose that the structured Mountcastle columnar principle in mammalian cortex provides the basis for a common neural language and grammar, not only within an individual cortex, but throughout the entire species, and ultimately throughout all mammals. Furthermore, I suggest that this Mountcastle cortical language and grammar provides the basis for human language and the origin of music.*

This is a good place to relate one of my favorite accounts of the common human–animal bonds. This behavioral study has a very different twist, in that here *fishermen take the cues for their cooperative partnership from dolphins* in a highly successful fishing operation. As reported by marine mammal researcher Karen Pryor, in the coastal town of Laguna, Brazil, there is a recorded 150-year history of this [6]:

> [A] complex choreography has evolved in which the fishing is initiated and controlled by the dolphins. . . . The water at Laguna is extremely murky; visibility is less than a foot. The fishermen cannot see the fish and must depend on the dolphin's behavior to know when to cast their nets. The dolphin detect fish, round them up and deliver them to waiting fishermen near the shore. . . . This [is] strictly a business relationship, . . . mutual respect, but no obvious friendship.

The fishermen, each with a circular, weighted net, stand in a line, a net's diameter apart, in shallow water parallel to the shore. A few dolphins "station" themselves several yards on the seaward side of the men, floating or moving slowly in sight. A dolphin dives, and swims seaward, and the men get ready. According to Pryor:

> The dolphin reappears, usually in a few seconds, traveling toward the line of men. It . . . dives just out of net range, 15 or 20 feet from the line, making a surging roll at the surface that is quite different from normal respiratory surfacing. The men wait for the dolphin's signal and then cast their nets. Successful fishermen return to the beach and others replace them on the line. . . . Cues by the dolphins give the fishermen vital information. The timing of the roll indicates that fish are present; the direction of the dolphin's movement indicates the location of the fish.

So, we might ask, what do the dolphins get from this? Easy fishing. Pryor continues:

> When the nets fall, the fish schools lose their rhythm and cohesion and become easy prey. Individual dolphins, including females with calves, and at least one dolphin the fishermen said was more than 70 years old, can catch mullet with minimum effort. . . . The fishing appears to be initiated and controlled by the dolphins. Fishermen . . . wait along the shore in hope of a dolphin's arrival, and the process does not begin until the dolphin decides to start work. A working dolphin might move to another part of the beach, and immediately the men follow and set up their line there. . . . The fishermen do not call out, signal or attempt to affect the dolphin's behavior. . . . The Laguna fishermen do not think they train the dolphins. They never give them a fish.

Clearly, as noted by Pryor, her study describes a unique situation between the dolphins and the fishermen that cannot be easily duplicated or explained. However, I think her study has profound and broad philosophical implications for human interactions with animals. All can gain from having mutual interests and respect, and that respect depends entirely on the dominant human species being smart enough to realize this mutual benefit. These benefits must be considered in a long-term relationship, which perhaps can grow over years and centuries as in this dolphin–fishermen partnership.

A topic that has both evolutionary and philosophical implications is the origin of music and its role in human society. I certainly will not attempt to go deeply into this important subject, but briefly refer to the interesting study [7] by Anthony Seeger entitled "Why Suya Sing: A Musical Anthology of an Amazonian People" to illustrate a few concepts. Seeger's book documents his field studies on the role of music in a small Suya community in the South American rain forest. For example, Seeger describes in detail the very complex, fascinating, and sophisticated Mouse Ceremony, which one year began on January 24 and ended on February 7. The entire two weeks were dominated by extended periods of collective singing and dancing. My understanding of this study is that it demonstrates the cohesive role of music in the dynamics of the community's group behavior. Music is by its very nature patterned in space and time. In that sense, Seegar's account reminds me of Ken Norris' account regarding the importance and presence of patterned group behavior in spinner dolphins. The performance of song or music is obviously an important group behavior among birds, whales, and humans. It cannot be an evolutionary accident. Fran

Rauscher's Mozart effect rat experiment demonstrated this. Even though rats do not have a music like human music, the Mozart Sonata (K.448) appears to "resonate" with their columnar brain structure to enhance their ability to master a spatial maze.

That music plays so many strong and universal roles in human emotions is unquestioned. Further scientific results, when added to the present ones, should support our position that music, in particular the Mozart Sonata (K.448), enhances thinking in both humans *and* mammals. I suspect that this realization by the general public will generate philosophical debates that in turn will have substantial practical implications. I do not see these debates being limited to the academic philosophers, but being of concern to all humans with an ethical or moral interest in our world. I do not have the expertise or the vision to propose the details or results of these debates. However, I do believe that they will help reshape our interaction with the natural world.

In the beautiful and profound book about our close relatives the bonobos, Frans de Waal and Frans Lanting wrote the following [8]:

> When the lively, penetrating eyes lock with ours and challenge us to reveal who we are, we know right away that we are not looking at a "mere" animal, but a creature of considerable intellect with a secure sense of its place in the world. We are meeting a member of the tailless, flat-chested, long-armed primate family to which we ourselves and only a handful of other species belong. We feel the age-old connection before we can stop to think, as people are wont to do, how different we are. Many primatologists have experienced a profound change in their attitude towards anthropoid apes after making eye contact with one for the first time. The spark across the species barrier is never forgotten. Behind the ape's eyes, one can feel a powerful personality that resembles our own, both emotionally and mentally.

I now conclude with some dreams and cautions. Although I have formed these ideas from interactions with my many colleagues, I caution that they are not to be read as ascribed to them.

1. ROLE OF THE M.I.N.D. INSTITUTE

The M.I.N.D. Institute is not just an idea, but is now operating under the direction of me and my fellow Institute scientists: Mark Bodner (U.C.L.A.), Xiao Leng (Pasadena City College), Matthew Peterson (U.C. Berkeley), and Fran Rauscher (University of Wisconsin, Oshkosh). By now you will recognize the crucial scientific contributions of each of these young researchers to this story. My dream now is to endow the M.I.N.D. Institute so that Mark, Xiao, Matthew, and Franny might devote their full energies and scientific careers to exploring the profound implications of music on human intelligence.

It is absolutely essential that the neurobiological bases of these important behavioral and educational results be investigated at the highest scientific level. The M.I.N.D. Institute Scientific Board consists of five world-renowned researchers: Theodore Bullock (U.C. San Diego), Edward Jones (U.C. Davis), William Little (Stanford University), Jiri Patera (University of Montreal), and Martin Perl (Stanford University). They will help us to achieve and maintain these standards.

As I have presented all of this exciting research, you have read about the many fruitful collaborations with world-class laboratories. The structure of the M.I.N.D. Institute enables it to link directly to the community and to implement its research results in school systems, as well as in medicine. I fully expect that forthcoming scientific results will continue to have major educational and clinical relevance. You may keep up on ongoing developments by visiting our web site: www.MINDinst.org.

Caution: It is essential to the stability and productivity of this entire research program that funds become available soon to make the M.I.N.D. Institute permanent. I believe it is necessary to maintain a focused and concerted effort as we continue to explore the fascinating subject of the role of music in higher brain function.

2. MOZART AS THE ROSETTA STONE FOR THE CODE OF THE BRAIN

My ambitious goal and dream is to decode the internal cortical language for higher brain function, perhaps the most important frontier in science. Although, as outlined in Chapter 17, my colleagues and I have no clear-cut way to do this, we have developed a number of innovative and complementary approaches. I do *not* believe that the Mozart Sonata (K.448) is the only piece of music that can generate the many astonishing Mozart effect phenomena summarized earlier. However, since it does give these dramatic results, *I intend to focus on what can be learned from Mozart's music in general and from the first movement of the Mozart Sonata (K.448) in particular that will help decode the cortical language.* I quote Robert Harris, from his essential guide "What to Listen for in Mozart" [9]:

> What Mozart called melody and what we know as melody are two different things. Our notion of this musical element was bequeathed to us by the nineteenth century— a long, complete, musical sentence that has a form and structure all its own. Mozart never wrote a melody like that. His melodies were actually short phrases, generally four or eight bars in length, which were always heard in combination with other, similar phrases. The musical effect is something akin to a mosaic, with individual

pieces joining together to create a beautiful whole, as opposed to the expressive and
highly charged melodic lines of Romantic composers like Tchaikovsky and Chopin.

In his detailed examination of the score of one of the most familiar of Mozart's
works, "Eine Kleine Natchmusik," Harris states in connection with bars 9
and 10:

> There are seven harmonic changes in these two bars, and that's enough to balance
> off the four changes in the previous four bars. Two, four, eight (seven actually,
> because one beat is a rest), you can see why Mozart has been labeled a composer
> obsessed with symmetry, balance and form. Hidden in this innocent opening section
> of "Eine Kleine Natchmusik" is writing of the most fabulous complexity and purest
> symmetry.

Then Harris makes these incredibly profound remarks:

> Classical composers put themselves in a dangerous position, however, when they
> make the four-bar phrase the cornerstone of their musical language. For the dramatic
> success of their works, they had to make sure that listeners would hear those build-
> ing blocks as different, because if they did not, they would never understand the
> dramatic devices that would be applied to them. On the other hand, if each succeed-
> ing four-bar phrase were totally independent of the others, the music would degen-
> erate into chaos, a series of musical non-sequiturs. So, the challenge that Mozart and
> his colleagues faced was to create a series of phrases that sounded both different and
> related at the same time. Unity and variety—both had to be satisfied.
>
> It is here that Mozart the magician makes another appearance, the Mozart of
> subtlety and complexity. The means by which he creates unity in his works are so
> varied and well hidden that some musicologists have rebelled at the attempts of their
> colleagues to find relationships between musical ideas in his works, claiming that
> the experts are creating links of which the composer was unaware. This is almost
> assuredly untrue. There are so many connections in the music of Mozart that they
> cannot be accidental or spontaneous.

Here again I would like to relate the magical genius of Mozart in music with
the magical genius of Ramanujan in math. The last sentences from Harris make
it clear that it is in the sequential use of the music patterns that the real genius
of Mozart is most evident. Likewise, it may be so for Ramanujan in how he just
wrote down his math equations without proofs. These musical patterns and
their sequences in Mozart (as well as the thought processes in Ramanujan)
represent in some highest and purest form the internal neural language of the
brain and its patterns and sequences of patterns.

Thus I propose that the cortical response to the first movement of the Mozart
Sonata (K.448) can be used along with some representation of the corresponding
score as a Rosetta Stone for decoding the internal language for higher
brain function.

Caution: These remarks should be examined as serious scientific statements
that can be experimentally tested as I discussed in Chapter 17. They should *not*

be taken out of context and considered to be interesting yet fuzzy mysterious thoughts.

3. ROLE OF MUSIC TRAINING AND S.T.A.R. TRAINING IN OUR SCHOOLS

A recent front page story in the *Los Angeles Times* [10] told how a long-time $118 billion program has not been able to level the playing field in language and math between children in low and high demographic school systems. It is my dream that a new program that combines music training and S.T.A.R. training will level the playing field in math and science, not only for low demographic children, but also for girls.

I want to explain what I mean by leveling the playing field in math and science. It does not suggest that everyone has equally innate abilities or that every child can become an Einstein, or even an A student. It simply means that each child will be able to reach her or his full potential. At present, there are distinct but overlapping distributions of math and science achievement scores for children according to (a) low versus high demographics and (b) female versus male.

My dream is that our proposed program will level the playing field in math and science so that all of these distributions would shift up, and that there would remain only a single higher distribution, as shown in Fig. 23.2. That would be a worthy accomplishment!

The idea is that essentially everyone would increase their math and science performance, with the biggest shifts coming for the lowest-performing children, but substantial increases even for the brightest students. Regarding low versus high demographics, our 2nd grade study showed that the children in a below-average demographic school with S.T.A.R. training significantly outperformed a no lessons group from an above-average demographic school. Regarding girls versus boys, we found no significant gender difference in the 237 children in the entire study for their performance following the S.T.A.R. training, which is designed to avoid any language or cultural bias. So, this dream is at least off to a good start.

I am quite sensitive to the concept of equal encouragement for all children in math and science. My mother, born in New York around 1900, was strongly discouraged by her father from even going to college, while one brother became an engineer and the other a physician. My older daughter, Karen, was discouraged from taking wood shop and machine shop by her teachers in 8th grade

PERFORMANCE PREDICTION

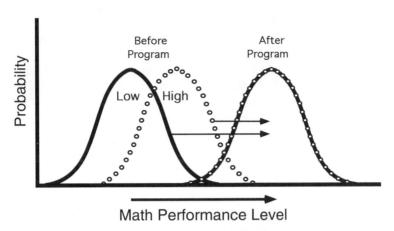

FIGURE 23.2 Highly schematic version of the probability of math scores for two groups (for example, low versus high demographics) of children. After our combined music training plus S.T.A.R. training, all children improved and the two distributions merged with a higher mean for each group. *This is an example of my dream of leveling the playing field.*

during the 1970s in Laguna Beach. Karen did take those classes, and she is now a mechanical engineer in charge of an engine maintenance team at United Airlines.

A fascinating anecdotal story of particular significance is the percentage of female physicists and mathematicians in Hungary compared to the U.S. In the U.S., less than 10% are women; in Hungary, roughly 50% are women. This comparison cannot be dismissed by saying that there are few physicists and mathematicians in Hungary, or that they are of low quality, or that the women in these fields are of low quality. There has always been a disproportionately large number of outstanding physicists and mathematicians from Hungary, including such stellar and familiar names as John von Neumann, Leo Szilard, Edward Teller, and Eugene Wigner. Only after World War II were women made welcome in these fields. My Hungarian sources tell me that already women are at the top of their graduating college classes in math and physics. This is very interesting. I would also note that the Kodaly method of teaching music (using group singing with hand movements in a sophisticated manner) starts for all children at a very young age in Hungary, and perhaps this plays a role [11].

Now back to our program. Piano keyboard training in conjunction with the spatial-temporal math software S.T.A.R. was dramatically successful in teaching proportional math and fractions in our study involving 2nd grade children [12].

Amy Graziano, Matthew Peterson, and I found that children at the inner-city 95th St. School in Los Angeles, when given 4 months of piano keyboard training along with the S.T.A.R. training, scored a striking 27% higher on proportional math and fractions than children given a control training along with the S.T.A.R. training.

Proportional math is usually introduced during the 6th grade and has proved to be enormously difficult to teach to most children using the usual language-analytic methods. Not only is proportional math crucial for all college-level science, but it is the first academic hurdle that requires children to grasp underlying concepts before they can master the material. Rote learning simply does not work. Children who do not master these areas of math are essentially ruled out of future competition for many high-tech jobs. Of course not all children should go into high-tech fields, but they should not be out of the running already in elementary school.

Our 2nd grade study presents a breakthrough in demonstrating that a combined program of piano keyboard training plus S.T.A.R. training allows disadvantaged 2nd grade children to master critical 6th-grade-level proportional reasoning concepts.

I have stated that the piano keyboard training in essence enhances the cortical connections or "hardware" for spatial-temporal reasoning, and that S.T.A.R. training capitalizes on spatial-temporal reasoning to teach difficult math concepts. I will now elaborate on these issues.

(a) Piano keyboard training: We have seen that after 6 months of piano keyboard training, three-year-old children show a dramatic improvement in spatial-temporal reasoning. We have also seen from the 2nd grade study that a 27% increase in S.T.A.R. performance was gained after only 4 months of keyboard training. So 2nd grade is not too late to begin piano lessons. However, my hope is that this enhancement effect will further increase with additional years of music training. Thus they should start in preschool. Further, I suggest that it strongly matters, as the children progress, what type of music they play: to play a Mozart Sonata may give the most benefit as far as increasing the cortical hardware for spatial-temporal reasoning. (This follows from my earlier remarks concerning Mozart's music.)

(b) S.T.A.R. was originally designed to reflect the ideas of symmetry and spatial-temporal reasoning gained from the trion model of higher brain function. We saw that S.T.A.R. training was rapidly mastered by the 2nd grade children. I suggest that this indicates that we are really tapping into inherent spatial-temporal reasoning abilities. Thus the more we learn about child brain development, the more we can improve and optimize future versions of S.T.A.R. I want to stress that S.T.A.R. is essentially nonverbal and without cultural bias. Furthermore, it is mainly self-teaching. Like video games, the children quickly learn what they must do to maximize their scores, which are always in front of them. The fact that they can immediately see how they are progressing is very important to them. All scores at each level for a child go onto her graph, which she can quickly learn to read.

(c) Computers are the key tool, but just a tool. They are now powerful enough, fast enough, and cheap enough for the S.T.A.R. training to work in any school. When I was working in 1957 on my Ph.D. thesis research in nuclear physics at Cornell University, I was using one of the first IBM 650 computers to do some computations. I would take my software (Fortran) program on a big deck of punch cards and sign up to run the campus computer by myself all night long. These same computations can now be done on a home personal computer in less than a minute.

(d) My dream is that the necessary further scientific studies, optimization studies for the music training, and large-scale expansion of S.T.A.R. into all grades from preschool to college be done in parallel as well as sequentially. There is no supportable reason why generations of children should be written off and deprived of the best education in math and science. I believe that many middle-class parents who read this book will make sure their children get the benefits from music training and S.T.A.R. training even if it is not provided in school. This will just widen the educational gap between children from low and high demographic homes. *The consequences of this entirely avoidable inequality in math and science performance are simply unacceptable in the U.S.*

(e) I have mentioned creativity a number of times, in particular in Chapter 9, but have not done any experiments on it. Let me return to my distinction between sequential thinking and creative thinking. Consider a specific problem to be solved, for example, in math, engineering, sculpture, or music composition. Contrast the two necessary yet distinct and complementary methods of solution as (A) the sequential method and (B) the creative method: (A) If the problem you have to solve is a slight variation of a quite familiar type (although even if it is very difficult), then perhaps the method of solution involves a fairly prescribed sequential series of mental computations that I call a sequential solution. For example, consider the paper folding and cutting tasks used in the Mozart effect experiments. (B) If a sequential solution to the problem at hand is not clear, then the mental processes in the creative solution involve rapidly picking out a potential solution from perhaps an enormous number, as in the middle or end of a chess game.

Unlike present computer chess programs, which sequentially examine all possibilities, a Master chess player in a short time comes up with one or a few potential solutions without even being aware or fully conscious of the mental process used in finding them. These solutions are complementary in that it is usually necessary to sequentially examine a creative solution for validity of the details. *Although I have not done the relevant research, my dream is that our program will enhance creativity with some appropriate version of S.T.A.R. It is my* strong belief that the appropriate means to evaluate creativity as I have it defined can be readily developed.

(f) I envision the use of S.T.A.R. to find young children with the potential of greatness in math (or science) even in underdeveloped areas in the world. Since S.T.A.R. is nonverbal and essentially without cultural bias, its use to detect a young child's innate spatial-temporal reasoning abilities might be quite appropriate. Perhaps you have heard of the movie *Searching for Bobbie Fisher* describing a search for the next great chess genius. In analogy with this, we might name this use of S.T.A.R. as "Searching for Ramanujan."

(g) I want to stress that although such factors as motivation, interest, self-esteem, and determination on the part of the child as well as the teacher are extremely helpful, they are not sufficient in learning difficult math concepts such as proportional math. Proportional math cannot be mastered through rote learning. Much research and resources have gone into teaching proportional math with no large success. I contend that it is our spatial-temporal approach that has broken this barrier for many children to learn proportional math. It is the child's understanding of proportional math that produces self-esteem not the other way around. I suggest that psychologists who suggest otherwise are doing a great disservice to parents, educators, and especially students of all ages. Fear of math comes from the inability to understand the concepts. As presented in a relevant, recent front page article [13], "For Students, Math Equals Fear," "many [students] at community colleges are blocked from careers or transfer to a university by an inability to pass [intermediate level] math courses." It is not sufficient to repeat the tired phrase "all that is needed is more self-esteem." Rather, the answer lies in new spatial-temporal methods to teach difficult math concepts.

The powerful combined approach of piano keyboard training and S.T.A.R. training should be easily generalized to teach other math and science concepts in a complementary manner to traditional language-analytic methods, and at a younger age. It must be shown that the results are large enough to be "cost-effective" in terms of the necessary school time and money. *Even one or two years of our combined approach will be extremely valuable to children.* I suggest that this is so since the children learn to think ahead mathematically several steps in their minds, and that they will never lose this major achievement. One of my favorite anecdotes is that related to me by Kimberly Kindy, a reporter for *The Orange County Register,* who was researching a story [14] on our newly published results with the 2nd graders [15]. Kimberly had gone to the school in Santa Ana and interviewed Eric Cerda, now eight years old, who had been in our pilot study with one month of S.T.A.R. training 15 months previous. She told in her article how Eric still retains and uses the math abilities he developed in the S.T.A.R. training. Kimberly told me that she also interviewed Carmen

Cerda, Eric's mother, and asked what is Eric's favorite subject. Carmen Cerda replied that it is math and that this developed after the S.T.A.R. training. (Kimberly had not included this in her article.) By chance, I met Carmen Cerda at the school just a week ago and had the pleasure of hearing the story first hand.

This brings up the necessity of developing a broad unified approach from pre-K to college-level education. Educators and scientists all over the world have shown considerable interest in our results. In particular, Chinese researchers have expressed an interest in this unified approach to Xiao Leng during her recent lectures in China.

Caution: Our proposed program may have profound implications. I fear that the U.S. educational system has far too much inertia to make the hard choices and changes and to put the resources into this program in the near future. It would be a shame to see the children in the U.S. fall even farther behind in math and science. A tremendous strength of the U.S. society is the independence of local school systems. However, more autocratic countries, such as China, may have an advantage because they can implement major educational changes throughout their entire school systems.

4. ROLE OF MUSIC IN CHILD BRAIN DEVELOPMENT

I conclude with how music might enhance child brain development, since it is perhaps the most important area in which science can make a positive impact. If I controlled science spending,

> *I would put 10 billion dollars into a 10-year program to improve our understanding of infant brain development and to learn how to optimize the child's neural hardware for thinking and reasoning. These children will determine the world's future. Let's give them the opportunity to reach their potential.*

This high level of funding would ensure that the best and brightest scientists would strongly consider devoting their energies to this enormously important field. I hope that this book has convinced you that it is not enough to simply know that the infant brain is complex and develops rapidly. The newborn infant brain is *not* a blank slate. We must learn what active inputs at each developmental stage will generate the most effective enhancement of brain function.

Clearly, the role of music in the spatial-temporal reasoning of infants and primates deserves much more study. My dream is that a simpler version of S.T.A.R. designed specifically for infants and primates—MicroS.T.A.R.—will play a pivotal role in both evaluating and enhancing the role of music. Matthew

Peterson, Mark Bodner, and I are now in the process of developing a spatial-temporal version of MicroS.T.A.R.

I have a special interest in this because of the many commercial and political distortions of the Mozart effect that are being aimed at eager parents. As mentioned earlier, one of the reasons that I wrote this book was to counteract the numerous misuses of our research. I discussed these cases in the Prologue. It is wrong to sell or even give away CDs and tapes of Mozart or Beethoven when stating that listening to the music will make your infant smarter or more creative. Our Mozart effect studies were with adults and focused on the Mozart Sonata (K.448). There is *no* information about other classical pieces of music, and there is *no* relevant research on the Mozart effect in young children. However, you can make your own informed decision. I suggest that reading this book has made you informed.

As a neuroscientist and grandparent, I encourage my daughter Karen to play Mozart to her two young sons even though the relevant research on young children has not been conducted. Our research has shown that piano keyboard training for three-year-olds enhances their spatial-temporal reasoning. One of my goals is to do research on whether the reasoning abilities of infants are enhanced by listening to different kinds of music. This research should begin soon. A possible pilot study of the effects of having children listen to Mozart starting at birth and continuing for several years is now being discussed with a parent group in Mobley, Missouri, who have just contacted me. I hope Mark and Matthew and I can work with them and get this valuable project started. It will of course involve the use of MicroS.T.A.R.

Caution: My main concerns are that the commercial exploitation of the Mozart effect will take advantage of the concerned parent's desire to improve their infant's reasoning abilities. There is no directly relevant research with infants. On the other hand, as a parent, you can observe your infant and check that there are no bad side effects from listening to classical music *in moderation*. In fact, you will probably see your child relax or become calm or go to sleep. However, I do not recommend the long-term playing of music to your fetus, as I discussed in Chapter 19. To summarize these cautions: I urge restraint in trying to influence the fetus's development through, for example, constant music input applied to the mother's stomach. No one knows the effects of such a program. It is possible that the common sequential time development of movement patterns of the fetus, as observed by Heinz Prechtl, could be disrupted by premature overstimulation through the auditory system. *I strongly doubt that this is the case, but I advise moderation.* I am fond of saying that there are no known bad side effects of listening to Mozart, but caution must be applied with the human fetus. My colleague Fran Rauscher advised me to add the same cautions for premature infants.

MY FINAL DREAM

I suspect that all of my dreams about music enhancing learning and the crucial role of symmetry in higher brain function will come true. Whether it will take 5–10 years or 20–30 years for these dreams to be fulfilled is unknown. I hope it is the shorter period, so that I can see the results. It would be wonderful if all children could begin to fully utilize their innate spatial-temporal abilities to think, reason, and create.

GLOSSARY

These definitions are quite brief and focused on the main use of the word or phrase in this book.

Action potential Electrical impulse sent out by a neuron down its axon when the neuron fires. It travels undiminished over the entire length of axon and all the branchings of the axon. See firing threshold.

Alzheimer disease Neurodegenerative disease that impairs memory, spatial orientation, and language and is eventually fatal. Slow period of deterioration is usually followed by rapid deterioration.

Amygdala Structure in the limbic system that is concerned primarily with emotion and forming emotional memories.

Anecdotal, causal, and correlational Anecdotal studies are not scientifically controlled, causal studies are controlled and show that the effect is caused by the treatment, and correlational studies are controlled and show that the effect is related to treatment but may not have been caused by it.

Angular momentum See spin.

Animal model Nonhuman experimental situation that is closely similar to a human experiment.

Anti-particle and annihilate See positron.

Apparent motion Display of discrete time sequence of sensory stimuli that appears continuous to the observer, as in television.

Attention deficit disorder (ADD) ADD children usually have symptoms of inattention and hyperactivity-impulsivity.

Autism, autistic Symptoms include extremely limited language function and very impaired social behavior.

Axis of rotation Line about which an object is rotated.

Axon Fiber through which a neuron fires and sends a signal (action potential) to junctions (synapses) of target neurons. The axon branches many times and the action potential goes down all the branches to reach roughly 10,000 synapses.

Axon hillock Location at the beginning of an axon near neuron cell body where the action potential starts.

Bell-shaped, gaussian, or normal distribution Distribution of results commonly found for test scores when there are a large number of subjects.

Blind to experiment When a subject or tester does not know the goals of the experiment.

Broken symmetry Precise symmetry that is broken such that the original symmetry form can still be recognized and plays a fundamental role.

Cartesian coordinate system System in which three coordinates or directions in space lie at 90 degrees to each other and can be used to specify the location of any point.

Ceiling and floor effects A ceiling effect occurs when a test is too easy for the subjects and a floor effect is when the test is too hard, in both cases limiting the range of the subjects' scores.

Cell body Main processing part of a neuron.

Circadian rhythm, ultradian rhythm, circadian pacemaker, or SCN A circadian rhythm is a cycle of behavior or neurophysiological function that occurs over roughly 24 hours. Ultradian rhythms are such cycles that repeat more than once in 24 hours. The suprachiasmatic nucleus (SCN) is a subcortical brain structure considered to be the circadian pacemaker that synchronizes circadian rhythms.

Clinical use Of practical use in treating some medical disorder.

Code or cortical language and grammar Internal language or code in which parts of the cortex communicate with other parts via spatial-temporal firing patterns of groups of neurons. A grammar indicates the presence of specific inherent rules of how these firing patterns can be fit together. I assume that this language and grammar are determined from the proposed Mountcastle columnar principle of mammalian cortex.

Cognition Processes in which the animal gains knowledge and becomes aware of its environment.

Coherence Correlation of EEG activity in two electrodes. This gives a measure of synchrony.

Column and organizational principle See Mountcastle columnar principle.

Competitive sensory inputs When two or more sensory inputs reach a cortical neuron, they determine the subsequent behavior of that neuron (perhaps via Hebb learning rules). For example, inputs from both eyes after human birth are necessary to realize proper binocular vision.

Control and experimental groups An experimenter divides her subjects into an experimental group to test a hypothesis and various control groups to rule out other confounding effects.

Cooperative phenomena or state See Cooperativity of functional unit.

Cooperativity of functional unit, linear and nonlinear effects Cooperativity of a functional unit of neurons follows from the nonlinear features, where the response of the functional unit is *not* simply the linear (arithmetic) sum of the individual neuronal responses. The Mountcastle minicolumn and column are cooperative functional units.

Corpus collosum Large bundle of axons linking the left and right hemispheres of the cortex.

Cortex, cerebral cortex, or neocortex Outermost part of the brain responsible for highest-level brain function. It has six identifiable layers and is about 0.2 cm thick. As put forward by Mountcastle in his columnar principle of mammalian cortex, it is made up of cortical columns.

Cortical areas, maps, receptive fields, and systems Cortex is divided into areas with distinct anatomical and physiological properties with a size on the order of cm. Many cortical areas make up a system such as the cortical visual system. The primary or first visual cortical area that visual stimuli excite is called V1 or area 17 or striate cortex. V1 has a complete map of the visual field seen by the eyes. Each neuron in V1 responds best to a visual stimulus in a given part of the visual field called its receptive field. The neurons in a cortical column in V1 have overlapping receptive fields. The neurons in a given minicolumn respond best to a visual bar with a specific orientation.

Cortical column and minicolumn Columnar structure about 0.08 cm in diameter going down through the cortical layers. The column is the fundamental neuronal network in the cortex according to the Mountcastle columnar principle. The column is comprised of substructures called minicolumns that are about 0.01 cm in diameter, which in the Mountcastle columnar principle are the irreducible processing units. See cooperativity.

Creative mode and sequential mode Temporal evolutions of memory firing patterns or MPs in the trion model cortical column have two quite distinct types. In the creative mode, MPs related by symmetries appear and reappear, whereas in the sequential mode, the MPs evolve in a more orderly manner. These modes are related to creative and sequential thinking. The values of the temperature or fluctuation parameter determine which mode the cortical column is in.

Critical period Early and appropriate stimuli are necessary during the critical period for proper functional development of cortical neurons in primates, for example, in vision. See window of opportunity.

Cycle, period, and temporal phase Time development of a system that repeats or cycles with a definite time period. Identifiable parts of this development have temporal phases with respect to each other (as in pushing a swing). See resonance.

Cyclically rotate Rotate in space or in time a periodic system with, for example, parts a, b, c, so that a goes to b, b to c, and c to a.

Cyclotron Device that maintains fast-moving protons in a circle (via a magnetic field) and accelerates them to higher energies with electric fields.

Demographics Statistical features of populations of people with regard to income, health, gender, and so on.

Dendrite and apical dendrite Dendrites are treelike branchings from the neuron cell body. The synapses or junctions with incoming axons are on the dendrites and the cell body. Apical dendrites go up through the cortical layers from pyramidal neurons.

Dendritic bundle Apical dendrites occur close together and form an anatomical bundle. Their function is not known, but it has been speculated that they form the anatomical basis for the minicolumn.

Discrete, bins, and continuous A continuous variable such as time (or length) can be made discrete by introducing time bins of specific duration so that a time interval is measured in terms of a discrete number of time bins.

Dopamine Neuromodulator that, among other functions, is important in movement. Loss of dopamine-producing neurons in substantia nigra can produce Parkinson disease.

Dorsal raphe nucleus Group of serotonin-releasing neurons that play a role in sleep and waking.

Downs syndrome Genetic neuropathology characterized by severe mental retardation and various physical abnormalities.

EEG (electroencephalogram), surface brain waves, and coherence analysis Recording of the electrical activity of the brain by placing electrodes on the surface of the skull. EEG coherence analysis correlates the electrical activity recorded from different electrodes and is important in determining how the electrical activity is "orchestrated."

Electric charge and electric field Electrons and the nuclear centers of atoms have electric charge. An electric field is produced by particles, electrons, and ions by the nature of their charge and their movement. These fields in turn cause forces on particles with electric charge.

Electrode and microelectrode Probe to measure electric field in the brain.

Microelectrodes can be used to monitor the firing of individual neurons.

Electron See proton.

Elementary particle physics Study of the basic forces in nature at the most fundamental level.

Epilepsy, ichtal events, and focused discharges Epilepsy involves abnormal, highly synchronized firing of groups of neurons that can spread to large parts of the brain and cause behavioral seizures. This neuropathology can be observed in nonseizure situations by observing ichtal or large spiking phenomena in EEG recordings, coming sometimes from specific brain regions.

Evolution of the brain The Darwinian evolution of mammalian cortex.

Families of memory firing patterns and symmetry families Concept that memory firing patterns come in families related by symmetries. This is a prediction of the trion model and has been observed in cortical data.

Feature detector Certain neurons undergo their maximum firing in response to a specific feature or property of the stimulus. For example, neurons in parts of the visual cortex respond best to bars of light. The minicolumns there are organized so that a given minicolumn responds best to a light bar of a given orientation.

Firing activity. See firing patterns and action potential.

Firing patterns and cortical firing patterns The trion model postulates that firing patterns are represented as a spatial-temporal code throughout the cortex at the minicolumn scale. This must be further tested using observed firing activity of cortical neurons.

Firing threshold and subthreshold
When the net electrical inputs to a neuron (within a small time window) exceed a threshold value, the neuron fires. Any electrical input below the threshold is subthreshold. See action potential and axon.

Fluctuation and temperature Fluctuations are random variations in a quantity, and temperature is a measure of the fluctuations. For example, variations in the release in neurotransmitter molecules in synaptic transmission upon arrival of an action potential can be (indirectly) related to the temperature parameter in the trion model.

Free throws in basketball Penalty shot that is practiced a great deal to improve accuracy, but remains a big difficulty for many players.

Frequency and frequency bands The frequency of a (periodic) wave is the number of times per second that the wave repeats. EEG data are usually divided into six frequency bands or bins.

Frontal, parietal, temporal, and occipital lobe of the cortex The four major subdivisions of each hemisphere of the cortex.

Functional MRI See MRI.

Glial cells Cells in the brain that act in supportive roles for the neurons and do housekeeping chores.

Go and Reversi games Go is a board game with two kinds of pieces and simple rules, however, the game has great sophistication. Reversi is another simple board game.

Gorilla user interface (GUI) Equipment interface to a computer designed by Jim Kelley for Koko and her gorilla friends so they can choose different music selections by pushing one of six buttons.

Hawthorn effect See statistical error.

Hebb learning coefficient ϵ Parameter setting the overall strength of the Hebb learning rule.

Hebb learning rule or Hebb synapse Change in strength of a synapse due to the combined firing activity from an incoming axon and the target neuron. It was first predicted by Donald Hebb 50 years ago and was identified neurophysiologically some 15 years ago.

Helmholtz Club A club of neuroscientists in southern California who meet once a month (for the past 16 years) at U.C. Irvine to discuss brain function.

Higher brain function Includes thinking, reasoning, creating, and processing information at some sophisticated level in the brain. For example, I usually talk of math, chess, and music as examples of higher brain function.

Hippocampus Subcortical brain structure crucial to short-term memory.

Ichtal See epilepsy.

Instructional learning See learning by selection.

Internal neural language See Mountcastle columnar principle.

Interpolate To estimate the value of a variable from neighboring values.

Ions, ion channels, and gates Ions are charged atoms and molecules. Neuron membranes on cell bodies, dendrites, and axons have channels that let specific ions pass in and out. These channels have gates that open and close to regulate these ion flows.

Language-analytic reasoning Thinking and reasoning using human language and equations. See spatial-temporal reasoning.

Learning by selection and by instruction Learning by selection occurs when a stimulus is rapidly associated with an inherent memory pattern. This happens in the trion model through a Hebb learning rule. Learning by instruction involves a slow process that finely adjusts many synaptic parameters to learn the information. Both involve synaptic change or plasticity.

Limbic system A subcortical group of brain structures, including the amygdala and hippocampus, that help regulate emotion and memory. (Some autonomous functions are regulated by limbic system structures, such as circadian rhythms by the SCN in the hypothalamus.) See circadian rhythm.

Magic genius An ordinary genius is one who produces marvelous results in, for example, math or music or science. If you are an expert in the field, after serious study you might understand how the result was produced. In contrast, a magic genius produces incredible results in a manner that is not understood.

Magnetic field Certain motions of charged particles and changing electric fields produce magnetic fields. The magnetic fields produced by brain activity are very small but can be measured in MEG imaging. Large external magnetic fields can be used to determine both the anatomical composition of the brain in MRI and the functional behavior of the brain in fMRI.

Map To take trion model time evolutions and translate them onto music or robotic motion. See cortical map.

Mean See probability.

MEG (magnetoencephalogram) Recording of the magnetic activity generated in the brain using SQUIDs.

Memory—very short term, short term, and long term Very short term memory last some seconds and is probably the active circulation of neuronal activity involving frontal cortex, the hippocampus, and other cortical areas in terms of patterns in space and time. Short-term memory refers to the holding of a limited amount of information for several minutes, presumably in briefly enhanced neuronal synaptic connections. Long-term memory has several stages that can last from hours to a lifetime.

Memory pattern (MP) The trion model postulates explicit and inherent spatial-temporal memory firing patterns. The MPs occur in families related by various symmetries and evolve in natural time sequences, forming the basis of higher brain function with a common cortical language and grammar.

Memory storage capacity Number of memory patterns that can be stored in a network of neurons.

Mental rehearsal (MR), mental imaging (MI), duration (D) of MR or MI, average duration ($\bar{D}$), and variations (V) Mental rehearsal is used by musicians, athletes, surgeons, and others to go over complex behavior in their brain without any sensory input as a supplement to actual rehearsal. Mental imaging is the use of such an internal brain process for any complex behavior. We have experimentally found that the temporal durations D of such MR or MI can be highly reproducible. The average of several D's is $\bar{D}$. The variation V is defined as the standard deviation σ divided by $\bar{D}$.

Microdialysis Means of separating and monitoring tiny amounts of neuromodulators in the brain.

Microelectrode See electrode.

MIDI (Music Instrument Digital Interface) and electronic music synthesizer System used to interface computer instructions with an electronic music synthesizer to play music.

M.I.N.D. (Music Intelligence Neural Development) Institute Community-based nonprofit scientific research institute that explores relationships among music, reasoning, and the brain to the benefit of society in education and medicine.

Minicolumn See cortical column.

Minimalist music Spare use of musical melody and rhythm, as in the music of Philip Glass.

Monte Carlo calculation Roulette game analogy used to show how to fully evolve the probabilistic trion model equations in time.

Mountcastle columnar principle and internal neural language or code for higher brain function As generalized and proposed by Vernon Mountcastle, all of the mammalian cortex is made of cortical columns that form the basic network. The column is composed of minicolumns, which form the irreducible processing unit of neurons. The basic internal neural language is activated in spatial-temporal firing patterns at the minicolumn scale in space and roughly 0.025 to 0.1 sec in time. Scientific support for the Mountcastle columnar principle continues to grow.

Mozart effect and Mozart effect meter The Mozart effect, as coined by the media, refers to our experiment in 1993 in which college students who listened to the Mozart Sonata for Two Pianos in D Major (K.448) experienced a subsequent short-term enhancement in spatial-temporal reasoning. A hypothetical Mozart effect meter is a device that would be able to predict whether a particular piece of music would give a similar enhancement. Perhaps this meter would involve some brain imaging such as fMRI.

MRI (magnetic resonance imaging) and fMRI (functional MRI) Large magnetic fields can align protons and atoms in the brain along the field direction. A small, rapidly varying magnetic field "tickles" these protons, causing them to emit light (not visible light). This allows brain anatomy to be visualized through MRI and, through fMRI, allows the measure of increased blood flow to determine function in response to some stimulus.

MSAC See SYMMETRIC analysis.

Multiplexing Having several copies of information being processed to back up the system in case of errors.

Musical motives and meter A motive is a short musical idea that can be used to generate a longer one. Time bins (see discrete) called beats are organized into meter with units called measures.

Natural sequences of MPs See memory patterns.

Neocortex See cortex.

Neural or cortical language and grammar Spatial-temporal code for higher brain function that is common throughout cortex with a specific inherent grammar as in the trion model.

Neurochemical or neurotransmitter and neuromodulator Neurotransmitter or neurochemical molecules released at synapses influence neuronal firing. The many neuromodulators are not as precisely specific in time and space in their effects.

Neuron   Basic cell in the brain that processes and communicates information.

Neurological   Clinically relevant neuropathology.

Neurophysiological   See physiological.

Nonlinear and linear   See cooperativity.

Normalized or scaled quantity   Raw data are converted to a normalized or scaled set of values through a statistical transformation. For example, individual probabilities are normalized so that the sum of all the various possibilities is equal to one. Data can be normalized for various subgroups, such as by age, to give scaled age scores.

Nucleus   Cluster or group of neurons in the brain, or the center of a cell, or the center of an atom.

Object-oriented platform   Computer animation software that allows you to generalize your programming easily to other examples.

Optical recording   Brain imaging technique for the cortex that uses the fact that reflection of light is dependent on the neural activity through, for example, modified blood flow.

P_L Probability of memory patterns remaining for one cycle in the system of coupled columns of trions.

Paper folding & cutting (PF&C)   Spatial-temporal reasoning task, used in our Mozart effect behavioral experiments.

Parkinson disease   Neuropathology in dopamine leading to motor problems.

Phantom limb   Sensation in a person with an amputated limb that the limb is still present.

PET (positron emission tomography)   Brain imaging in which a radioactive atom emits a positron which annihilates with an electron to give two photons that are then detected. These radioactive atoms travel more to regions that are being used in a cognitive task. Computer software tomographic analysis is used to reconstruct the brain use image.

Photon   When a charged particle changes its motion, it gives off electromagnetic radiation or light. Light comes in discrete particles or photons. See positron.

Physiological or neurophysiological   Relating to the function as opposed to the anatomy of the brain.

Planum temporale (PT)   Cortical region that processes sound.

Plasticity   See learning by selection.

Positron or electron anti-particle and annihilate   The positron as the electron anti-particle has the same mass and opposite electric charge (as well as some other quantities). Being the electron anti-particle means that a positron and an electron can annihilate each other to yield two photons.

Primary visual cortex or cortical area 17 or V1   See cortical area.

Probabilistic   Probability is explicitly used.

Probability (p), probability distribution, mean, standard deviation (σ), and standard error (s)   Probability p gives the odds that a certain event will take place. For example, the p for a coin toss to be heads is 0.5. The full results of a large number of coin tosses can be described by a probability distribution. The standard deviation σ is a measure of the spread of the distribution from its mean value. The standard error s is related to σ and the number of coin tosses. It can be decreased by increasing the number of coin tosses or subjects in an experiment, and is useful in comparing the results of different experimental treatments. See statistical errors.

Proportional math and rate problems Proportional math involves the comparison of ratios. It is very difficult for children to learn, and comes up in all natural sciences, for example, in rate of reaction problems.

Proton, neutron and electron The nucleus of an atom is made up of protons and neutrons. Protons have electric charge equal in size to that of the electron, but positive in sign. Neutrons have no electric charge. Neutrons and protons are about 2000 times heavier than an electron. Atoms have an equal number of electrons and protons.

Pyramidal neurons and inhibitory neurons Pyramidal neurons (they have this shape) are the primary excitatory neuron in the cortex. There are a few types of neurons that inhibit other cortical neurons.

Pythagoreans Followers of the ancient Greek philosopher and mathematician Pythagoras.

Quantitative MR (QMR) Our quantitative mental rehearsal program to be used in enhancing performance in sports.

Quark and fractional electric charge and confinement Quarks are the fundamental elementary particles inside the neutron and proton. Their electric charge is $\frac{1}{3}$ and $\frac{2}{3}$ in magnitude of that of the proton. It is conventionally thought that a free quark cannot be found in nature and so is called "confined."

Raw scores, scaled scores, and standardized age scores See normalized quantity.

Resonance Phenomenon in which an input optimally excites a system, for example, when you push a swing in the appropriate manner (or temporal phase) to build up the amplitude of motion. I suggest that certain music may resonate with the Mountcastle columnar organization of mammalian cortex.

Reversi game See Go.

Scanning electron microphotograph Image created by a beam of electrons traveling over a thin specimen slice.

Scientific notation System in which powers of 10 are written as a superscript, for example, 10^4 is 10,000.

Selectional learning See learning by selection.

Sequential mode See creative mode.

Serotonin An inhibitory neuromodulator.

Somatosensory Relating to the sensory system involved in touch.

Standard deviation See probability.

Standard error See probability.

Spatial recognition Tasks involved in recognizing, matching, copying, or classifying visual objects.

Spatial-temporal firing patterns Firing of groups of neurons expressed in patterns spatially and temporally, as in the trion model.

Spatial-temporal reasoning (ST) Thinking using pictures that evolve in space and time, especially important in math and science.

Spin, spin system, and angular momentum Angular momentum is associated with the rotation of particles. These atomic structures can also have intrinsic angular momentum, called spin. Spin systems describe just the spins of a group of particles.

SQUID (superconducting quantum interference device) Loop(s) of wire in a superconducting state used to measure tiny magnetic fields. See superconductors.

S.T.A.R. and S.T.A.R. E.P. S.T.A.R. is the Spatial Temporal Animation Reasoning software developed by Matthew Peterson to teach math concepts. S.T.A.R. E.P. is the corresponding evaluation program.

Statistical factor g or g(S) This g or g(S) factor accounts for the internal features of an idealized minicolumn and allows us to consider it as a single entity having three firing states S.

Statistical and systematic errors, and Westinghouse and Hawthorn effects An experiment can have two types of errors: a statistical error, which can be decreased by increasing the number of subjects and thus decreasing the standard error s (see probability), and a systematic error, which must be estimated or calculated to account for factors that are not directly controlled. For example, turning the lights on brighter might affect test scores, and I call such general effects not usually controlled for as Westinghouse effects. The Hawthorn effect is the increase in test scores by giving special attention to subjects, and is usually controlled by having an appropriate control group.

Statistical physics Branch of physics that deals with large numbers of objects in a probabilistic manner, employing sophisticated math.

Stimulus Sensory input that excites the cortex.

Stroke and ischemic type Brain damage resulting from vascular disorder. Ischemic stroke is non-hemorrhaging type.

Structured Relating to the inherent organization of the cortex, which is highly structured. See Mountcastle columnar principle.

Substantia nigra See dopamine.

Superconductors Materials that when cooled to an extremely low temperature (about −260 degrees centigrade) conduct electricity with no resistance. When made into a loop, they permit only certain "quantized" or discrete amounts of magnetic field though the loop as a way to measure these fields. Higher-temperature superconductors have been found.

Suprachiasmatic nucleus (SCN) See circadian rhythm.

SYMMETRIC analysis of cortical data firing patterns (SAC) SAC or SYMMETRIC analysis of cortical data is based on the trion model and specifically includes families of firing patterns related by symmetries. MSAC is the mapping onto music of SAC patterns.

Symmetry and symmetry operations α and Γ An object has symmetry when you can perform some transformations on it and the object still looks the same. Such transformations include rotation in space about a line and reflection in a mirror. Transformations α and Γ refer to symmetry operations on the memory patterns in the trion model.

Synapse and synaptic transmission Junction where the incoming axon reaches the dendrite or cell body of a neuron. The arrival of the action potential releases neurotransmitter molecules, which cross the synaptic gap to the target neuron.

Synaptic gap Small space separating the incoming axon from the target neuron at the synapse.

Synaptic learning rule See Hebb learning rule.

Synaptic vesicles Small containers for neurotransmitter molecules. The number of neurotransmitter molecules differs from vesicle to vesicle. The number of vesicles releasing transmitter when each action potential reaches the synapse is a statistical variable. These two statistical factors lead to the concept of a fluctuation parameter or temperature at the synapse, which is crucial to the trion model.

Systematic error See statistical error.

Temperature See fluctuation.

Thalamus Brain structure that acts as a relay station between sensory input and the cortex, as well as for cortical–cortical transfer of information.

Thinking machine A hypothetical future-generation computer that thinks, reasons, and solves problems using spatial-temporal reasoning.

Trial Each repeat of an experimental procedure can be a trial. For example, when you flip a coin 10 times, you have 10 trials of an individual coin toss.

Trion and trion model The trion model assumes the Mountcastle columnar principle. A trion is an idealized Mountcastle minicolumn with three levels of firing. The full mathematical model of cortical columns with Hebb learning is the trion model.

Ultradian rhythm See circadian rhythm.

Ultrasound Ultra-high-frequency sound that is used to noninvasively study body anatomy and function. In particular, it can be used to monitor the fetus.

Vesicle See synaptic vesicle.

Visual or receptive field See cortical areas.

Wechsler Preschool and Primary Scale of Intelligence Standardized test used in preschool study to assess spatial-temporal reasoning and spatial-recognition.

Westinghouse effect See statistical error.

White noise Sound having the composition of equal amounts of energy at each frequency and phases between them that are random, like the hiss you might hear from a radio not tuned to a station.

Williams syndrome Rare genetic brain disorder in which children are born with normal or even above normal music and language abilities. These children are exceptionally outgoing and friendly, but are extremely poor in spatial-temporal reasoning.

Window of opportunity Time period related to the existence of a neurophysiological critical period.

NOTES

CHAPTER 1

[1] Rauscher *et al.* (1993). This paper presented the first *causal* evidence that music enhances spatial-temporal reasoning, the ability to visually image patterns and transform them in space and time in your mind. This ability is of crucial importance in math and science. The results were immediately called the Mozart effect by the media.

[2] Sarton (1952), Allman (1976). The ancient Greeks made this connection between music and math, and it evens dates back to the Babylonians.

[3] Obler and Fein (1988).

[4] Empirical studies have suggested a relationship between music and spatial-temporal reasoning abilities. See Hassler *et al.* (1985), Barlett and Barker (1973), Hurwitz *et al.* (1975), Kalmar (1982), and Parente and O'Malley (1975).

[5] The most extensive of the studies [4] was done by Hassler *et al.*

[6] The famous Greek giants of math and philosophy had large groups of students and followers who carried on their work. The mathematician Pythagoras is perhaps best known by schoolchildren for his theorem in geometry that relates the three sides of a 90 degree triangle.

[7] See Cranberg and Albert (1988).

[8] Michelmore (1962); Clark (1971).

[9] Michelmore (1962); Clark (1971).

[10] Schattschneider (1990).

[11] The trion model of Shaw *et al.* (1985) was used; Leng and Shaw (1991) provided a causal relation between music and spatial-temporal reasoning.

[12] The short-term enhancements of spatial-temporal reasoning from the prior listening to the Mozart Sonata (K.448) were shown in Rauscher *et al.* (1993, 1995). The long-term enhancements from piano keyboard playing were shown in Rauscher *et al.* (1997) and Graziano *et al.* (1999a).

[13] Davenport (1932).

[14] Kanigel (1991) is a fascinating and readable story of this magic genius in math.

[15] S.T.A.R. E.P. is the evaluation program used with Matthew Peterson's S.T.A.R. software, the companion to this book, and is successfully used to teach math to young children using spatial-temporal methods. Both S.T.A.R. E.P. and S.T.A.R. have very little cultural or language bias and do not depend on prior math knowledge. Thus, I think that it could be used to find children with *huge* math potential.

[16] This article by Alikhan (1990), in a magazine put out by a company for its employees, was shown to me by a kind lady who had read about our Mozart effect studies and wanted me to be aware of the suspected large impact of South Indian Carnatic music on math and science.

[17] Chase and Simon (1973).

[18] de Groot A (1965).

[19] Chase and Simon (1973).

[20] The website is www.uschess.org.

[21] Deep Blue "cheated" when it defeated Kasparov. The chess experts and IBM computer experts who developed Deep Blue over many years had entered every move of every game played by Kasparov into its data base. Kasparov had no knowledge of any game played by Deep Blue, and IBM would not allow Kasparov to see even one prior game. This was hardly a fair match. For shame, IBM.

[22] Gardner (1983).

[23] Boettcher *et al.* (1994).

[24] Longhurst and Shaw (1999).

[25] Wendy Boettcher brought this crucial issue to my attention, and I immediately understood the relevance to our entire program. I owe a big debt to Wendy. We published this discussion in Boettcher *et al.* (1994).

[26] Graziano *et al.* (1999a).

CHAPTER 2

[1] These results were widely reported in the media. See, for example, "Students Weak in Global Tests," *Los Angeles Times,* November 21, 1996, p. A1.

[2] I would think that educators would want to do detailed studies of what the top countries of Singapore, South Korea, Japan, and Hong Kong were doing to get these

results. This would of course include their music programs, and the role of using spatial-temporal reasoning approaches to teach math and science in their schools.

[3] Grandin *et al.* (1998).

[4] Temple lectures and writes extensively on autism. See Grandin (1995b). Also, it is very interesting to read about people who have severe mental disabilities and yet are spectacularly gifted in some wonderful manner. See, for example, Treffert (1989). Temple has been able to enter mainstream society and has become extraordinarily successful.

[5] Graziano *et al.* (1999a).

[6] Hadamard (1945).

[7] Feynman (1949).

[8] Kemp (1998). Also see Gleick (1992).

[9] Sacks (1995).

[10] Grandin (1995a).

[11] Graziano *et al.* (1999a).

[12] See Leng and Shaw (1991) and McGrann *et al.* (1994).

[13] Piaget (1965), (1976)

[14] Papert (1980, 1993).

[15] Ferguson (1977).

CHAPTER 3

[1] Sarton (1952); Allman (1976); Obler and Fein (1988).

[2] Leng and Shaw (1991).

[3] Shaw *et al.* (1985).

[4] Mountcastle (1978, 1997, 1998).

[5] Hebb (1949).

[6] Bodner *et al.* (1997).

[7] Leng *et al.* (1990); Leng (1990).

[8] Petsche *et al.* (1993); Petsche and Etlinger (1998).

[9] Wynn (1992); Spelke (1990).

[10] DeCasper and Fifer (1980).

[11] Krumhansl and Jusczyk (1990).

[12] Peretz *et al.* (1994); Peretz and Morais (1993).

[13] Leng and Shaw (1991).

[14] Rauscher *et al.* (1993).

[15] Rauscher *et al.* (1995), Sarnthein *et al.* (1997); Hughes *et al.* (1998); Rauscher *et al.* (1998); Johnson *et al.* (1998); Muftuler *et al.* (1999).

[16] Rauscher *et al.* (1997).

[17] Graziano *et al.* (1999a)

CHAPTER 4

[1] Rauscher *et al.* (1997).

[2] Karplus *et al.* (1983).

[3] Graziano *et al.* (1999a).

[4] Rauscher *et al.* (1998).

[5] Bodner *et al.* (1997).

[6] Hughes *et al.* (1998).

[7] Johnson *et al.* (1998).

[8] Lenhoff *et al.* (1997).

[9] Mountcastle (1979, 1997, 1998).

[10] Norris (1995).

[11] Rauscher *et al.* (1998).

[12] See Patterson and Cohn (1978), Vassels and Cohn (1985). Koko is on the covers of these issues of *National Geographic*.

CHAPTER 5

[1] Weyl (1952); Kepes (1966); Eisenberg and Crothers (1979); Waddington (1966); Cole (1998); Schattschneider (1990).

[2] Please skim Fig. 5.3.

[3] Ramachandran and Blakeslee (1998).

[4] Pinker (1997).

[5] Rauscher *et al.* (1998).

CHAPTER 6

[1] For more detail on neuroanatomy and neurophysiology, see, for example, Zigmond *et al.* (1999).

[2] Hodgkin and Huxley (1952).

[3] Katz (1966, 1969).

[4] Little (1974).

[5] Little (1990); Shaw and Palm (1988).

[6] Shaw and Vasudevan (1974).

[7] Mountcastle (1978, 1997, 1998); Rakic (1988).

[8] See, for example, Damasio (1994); Zigmond *et al.* (1999).

[9] See Zigmond *et al.* (1999); Shaw *et al.* (1990).

[10] See Fuster (1995); Zigmond *et al.* (1999).

[11] See Zigmond *et al.* (1999); Katz (1966, 1969).

[12] See Leng and Shaw (1991) for my suggested role of them.

[13] Braitenberg and Schuz (1991).

[14] See, for example, Toga and Mazziotta (1996); Posner and Raichle (1994).

[15] Verzeano and Negishi (1960).

[16] Petsche and Etlinger (1998).

[17] Sarnthein *et al.* (1997).

[18] Cabrera *et al.* (1995). This volume is in commemoration of Bill Little's very rich scientific career over 40 years.

[19] Muftuler *et al.* (1999).

[20] Grinvald *et al.* (1981).

[21] For PET experiments relevant to music cognition see Sergent *et al.* (1992); Sergent (1993); Zatorre *et al.* (1994). Also see interesting PET experiment relevant to learning spatial-temporal game by Haier *et al.* (1992).

CHAPTER 7

[1] Mountcastle (1978, 1997, 1998).

[2] Mountcastle (1957); Hubel and Wiesel (1977); Goldman and Nauta (1977) Tootel *et al.* (1983); Goldman-Rakic (1984a, 1984b); Goldman-Rakic and Schwartz (1982); Rakic (1988).

[3] Seelen (1970); Braitenberg and Braitenberg (1979).

[4] Blasdel and Salama (1986); Bonhoeffer and Grinvald (1991).

[5] See Note 2.

[6] Blasdel and Salama (1986); Bonhoeffer and Grinvald (1991).

[7] Shaw *et al.* (1982).

[8] Roney *et al.* (1979).

[9] Masino *et al.* (1993).

[10] For further evidence of cortical structure see Jones *et al.* (1978); Gilbert and Wiesel (1983); Killackey (1983); Wiesendanger (1986); Leng *et al.* (1994); Asunuma (1975); DeFilipe *et al.* (1990).

[11] Hirsch and Gilbert (1991).

[12] Gilbert and Wiesel (1989).

[13] Rockland (1989); Rockland and Virga (1989).

[14] Churchland and Sejnowski (1988).

[15] Leng and Shaw (1991).

[16] See Gross and Meijer (1985); Hall and Rosbash (1987); Meier-Koll (1989); Konopka and Benzer (1971); Schulz and Lavie (1985).

[17] Brothers and Shaw (1989); Brothers *et al.* (1993).

[18] Poppel (1989).

[19] Bodner *et al.* (1997).

[20] Maxim *et al.* (1976); Bowden *et al.* (1978).

[21] Smith *et al.* (1992).

CHAPTER 8

[1] Shaw and Palm (1988).

[2] Hebb (1949).

[3] Cragg and Temperley (1954).

[4] Little (1974). For spin models in physics see Newell and Montroll (1953).

[5] Shaw and Vasudevan (1974).

[6] Little and Shaw (1975).

[7] Little and Shaw (1978).

[8] Shaw (1978).

[9] Shaw (1978).

[10] Mountcastle (1978).

[11] Roney and Shaw (1980).

[12] Roney *et al.* (1979).

[13] Fisher and Selke (1980).

[14] Wilson and Cowan (1972) showed that a population of neurons consisting of some with inhibitory interactions and some with excitatory interactions had three stable levels of firing.

[15] The dependence on two previous time steps rather than what was the usual one previous time step is very important. It allowed for an entirely new temporal complexity and sophistication in the trion firing patterns. See the arguments in Shaw *et al.* (1985).

[16] There are 3 possibilities of firing for each of the six trions in the column, giving 3^6, and the initial conditions depend on specifying two time steps, and thus there are 3^{12} possibilities, which is 531,441 initial states.

[17] Shaw *et al.* (1985).

[18] Leng and Shaw (1991).

[19] McGrann *et al.* (1991).

[20] McGrann *et al.* (1989, 1994); McGrann (1992).

[21] Shenoy *et al.* (1989, 1993).

[22] Edelman (1978, 1987); Changeux (1988). See Rumelhart and McClelland (1986) regarding instructional learning.

[23] McGrann *et al.* (1994). The choice of connections among the trion determines the repertoire of MPs. For other repertoires, see Shaw *et al.* (1985) and Silverman *et al.* (1986).

[24] McGrann *et al.* (1994).

[25] McGrann *et al.* (1994).

[26] Shaw *et al.* (1985).

[27] McGrann *et al.* (1994).

[28] Rauscher *et al.* (1995).

[29] Shaw *et al.* (1985).

[30] Shaw *et al.* (1998); Sardesai *et al.* (1999).

[31] Neumann (1956).

[32] Hirsch and Gilbert (1991).

[33] Little and Shaw (1975); Crick (1982). Crick's idea for short-term memory is very neat (but hard to test). Also see Marlsburg and Scheider (1986).

[34] Shaw *et al.* (1998).

[35] Shaw *et al.* (1982), Roney and Shaw (1980).

[36] Shaw *et al.* (1982), Roney and Shaw (1980).

[37] Chomsky (1975); Pinker (1994).

[38] Hutsler and Gazzaniga (1997).

CHAPTER 9

[1] Leng and Shaw (1991).

[2] If you had listened to the Mozart Sonata for Two Pianos in D Major (K.448) before trying to solve this PF&C item, you would have probably had an easier time with this difficult spatial-temporal task.

[3] See Chapter 1 for a discussion on the quantitative manner in which these chess titles are earned.

[4] Leng and Shaw (1991). Also see McGrann *et al.* (1991).

[5] Shaw and Vasudevan (1974) had shown the math relation between synaptic fluctuation and the fluctuation temperature parameter T in a model of Bill Little's (1974). Mintz and Korn (1991), Mintz *et al.* (1989), and Burnod and Korn (1989) have extensively studied the experimental details of synaptic fluctuations related to the effect of the neuromodulator seratonin.

[6] Leng (1990); Leng *et al.* (1990); Leng and Shaw (1991).

[7] Leng and Shaw (1991).

[8] These cortical structures for music are distinct from those associated with human language. See Peretz and Morais (1993); Peretz *et al.* (1994).

[9] Krumhansl and Jusczyk (1990).

[10] Treffert (1989) contains some extremely fascinating and amazing case studies.

[11] Brothers and Shaw (1989); Brothers *et al.* (1993).

[12] Shanbhag (1991).

[13] Ostling (1993).

[14] Sardesai (1993).

[15] Horn and Shaw (1990).

[16] Hubel and Wiesel (1977).

[17] Sardesai (1993).

[18] Leng (1990).

[19] Marr (1982).

CHAPTER 10

[1] Leng and Shaw (1991).

[2] Leng and Shaw (1991).

[3] Shaw *et al.* (1985).

[4] Shaw *et al.* (1988). See Fig. 9.

[5] We can expect deviations from exact symmetry in all of the quantities in the trion model and it will still maintain its dominant features as presented in this book.

[6] Petsche and Etlinger (1998); Petsche *et al.* (1993); Sarnthein *et al.* (1997).

CHAPTER 11

[1] Brothers and Shaw (1989).

[2] Richardson (1967); Coffman (1991).

[3] Brothers and Shaw (1989); Brothers *et al.* (1993).

[4] Brothers and Shaw (1989).

[5] Brothers *et al.* (1993).

[6] Brothers *et al.* (1993).

[7] Michon (1977).

[8] Burns (1968).

[9] Petsche and Etlinger (1998); Petsche *et al.* (1993).

[10] Zung and Wilson (1971); Zepelin (1986); Brush (1930).

[11] Lindauer (1961).

[12] Turek (1985); Menaker *et al.* (1978).

CHAPTER 12

[1] Einstein (1945).

[2] Rauscher *et al.* (1993, 1995); Sarnthein *et al.* (1997); Rauscher and Shaw (1998); Hughes *et al.* (1998); Johnson *et al.* (1998).

[3] Rauscher *et al.* (1998).

[4] Thorndike *et al.* (1986).

[5] Thorndike *et al.* (1986).

[6] Rama and I had met with Francis Crick some fifteen years ago and together founded the Helmholtz Club. Many neuroscientists in southern California meet monthly at U.C. Irvine to discuss how the brain works. Terry Sejnowski has been ably running the Helmholtz Club for many years.

[7] Rauscher *et al.* (1993).

[8] Leng and Shaw (1991).

[9] Rauscher *et al.* (1995).

[10] Sarnthein *et al.* (1997).

[11] These memory items were different from those used during Day 1.

[12] Rauscher and Shaw (1998).

[13] Sarnthein *et al.* (1997).

[14] Rauscher *et al.* (1998).

[15] Hughes *et al.* (1998, 1999).

[16] Johnson *et al.* (1998).

[17] Muftuler *et al.* (1999).

CHAPTER 13

[1] Leng and Shaw (1991).

[2] "Tuning Up Brains," *Los Angeles Times,* January 20, 1992, p. B1.

[3] Wechsler (1989).

[4] Wechsler (1989).

[5] Well, I promised you no equations so I hope you will not think this is too much to include. If you have not seen square roots, just estimate your result this way: Suppose you know that a quantity c squared or c times c equals d. You have a numerical value for d and you want to know what value c is. Simply choose some increasing values for c, calculate c times c, and compare with d. By having values on either side of d, you get your estimate. This way you get a good enough estimate for c. For example, let's say d equals 30. So, 5×5 is 25 and 6×6 is 36, so that we see that the square root of 30 is between 5 and 6. Much of science is knowing how to make simple estimates. You can always go back and do something more accurately if it is warranted. Perhaps the last giant in all of physics was Enrico Fermi (he died in 1954). Fermi could calculate anything! He held a weekly seminar and someone would show him the abstract of a new scientific paper. After reading the abstract, Fermi would proceed to the blackboard and reproduce the main results of the paper. Richard Feynman could probably have done this also.

[6] Rauscher *et al.* (1997). The exciting results of the first year were presented by Franny at an American Psychological Association convention (Rauscher *et al.,* 1994).

[7] McGaugh (1966); Shaw *et al.* (1990). Of course, we are interested in whether the music training enhancements of spatial-temporal reasoning can be made really long-term and last a lifetime. I expect that many years of training is necessary. We are all aware of skills or memories lasting a lifetime. Jim McGaugh offers this nice example which I suggest you try now:

> Get a pencil and paper, and *write* your name VERY SLOWLY. Now compare this writing to a sample that you have stored away from your first grade classes. You will probably note a remarkable similarity between the two.

Another powerful insight into the role of music in our brain is the fact that Julene Johnson, private communication, has documented in subjects with the dreaded Alzheimer disease that the memory of words in a familiar song is lost well before the melody.

[8] Rauscher *et al.* (1998). The effects here lasted at least 4 hours. *However, no one should even consider duplication of this experiment in children because of the enormous listening times involved.*

[9] Karplus *et al.* (1983).

[10] Boettcher *et al.* (1994).

CHAPTER 14

[1] "U.S. Students Weak in Math in Global Tests," *Los Angeles Times,* November 21, 1996, p. A1.

[2] Karplus *et al.* (1983).

[3] Graziano *et al.* (1999a).

[4] Wechsler (1989).

[5] Wechsler (1991).

[6] Karplus *et al.* (1983).

[7] Graziano *et al.* (1999a).

[8] Rauscher *et al.* (1997).

[9] Sarnthein *et al.* (1997).

[10] Such as the Dalcroze (1972), Kodaly (see Szonyi (1973)), and Orff (see Keetman (1970)) methods used extensively in Europe.

[11] Other programs include the Yamaha and Suzuki methods.

[12] Graziano *et al.* (1999b).

CHAPTER 15

[1] Petsche and Etlinger (1998).

[2] Petsche and Etlinger (1998); Andersen and Andersson (1968).

[3] Rauscher *et al.* (1995).

[4] Sarnthein *et al.* (1997).

[5] EEG recordings are always taken before and after each task such as the listening condition so as to compare the task recordings to these background recordings. Here the recording continued for a long time after the task.

[6] Cho *et al.* (1998).

[7] Muftuler *et al.* (1999).

[8] Sarnthein *et al.* (1998).

[9] Here active short-term memory or working memory refers to the situation where the relevant information is being maintained in measurable brain electrical activity. This might be contrasted to the case where the memory is temporarily stored in enhanced synaptic pathways for seconds up to minutes. See Shaw *et al.* (1990).

CHAPTER 16

[1] Shaw (1978).

[2] Mountcastle (1978).

[3] Patera and Shaw (1981).

[4] Shaw and Ramachandran (1982).

[5] Patera and Shaw (1981).

[6] Ramachandran and Blakeslee (1998) is a delightful and fascinating book.

[7] Hubel and Wiesel (1977).

[8] Blasdel and Salama (1986); Bonhoeffer and Grinvald (1991).

[9] Shaw et al. (1983).

[10] Pearson et al. (1983); Pearson (1985).

[11] Kruger and Aiple (1988).

[12] Ballard (1986).

[13] See, for example, references in MacGregor and Lewis (1977); Anderson and Rosenfeld (1988); Hinton and Anderson (1981); Palm and Aertsen (1986); Di Prisco (1984); Kohonen (1984); Hopfield (1982); Hopfield and Tank (1986); Seelen et al. (1988); Shaw and Palm (1988).

[14] Palm (1982).

[15] Hebb (1949).

[16] Shaw et al. (1993).

[17] See, for example, Verzeano and Negishi (1960); Perkel et al. (1967); Abeles (1982); Krone et al. (1986); Abeles and Gerstein (1988); Lestienne and Strehler (1987); Gray et al. (1989); Eckhorn et al. (1988); Gray and Singer (1989); Richmond et al. (1990); Singer (1990); Dinse et al. (1990).

[18] Shaw and Palm (1988); Patera et al. (1989).

[19] Bodner et al. (1999).

[20] Zhou and Fuster (1996).

[21] Fuster (1995, 1997).

[22] Bodner et al. (1997).

[23] Sarnthein et al. (1998).

CHAPTER 17

[1] Fuster (1995, 1997).

[2] This very stimulating atmosphere leads to a wonderful exchange of ideas and concepts.

[3] Hughes et al. (1998).

CHAPTER 18

[1] Readers, please send me any favorite published references that have some controls.

[2] Carter *et al.* (1999).

[3] Rauscher *et al.* (1998).

[4] Linden and Lanting (1992); Waal and Lanting (1997).

[5] Milner *et al.* (1968).

[6] Patterson and Cohn (1978); Vassels and Cohn (1985).

[7] Rauscher *et al.* (1998).

[8] Rauscher *et al.* (1993).

[9] Rauscher *et al.* (1997).

[10] Cheney and Seyfarth (1990).

[11] Brannon and Terrace (1998).

[12] Hauser *et al.* (1996).

[13] Wynn (1992).

[14] Hauser *et al.* (1996).

[15] Wynn (1992).

[16] Mushiake *et al.* (1998).

CHAPTER 19

[1] Prechtl (1994).

[2] DeCasper and Fifer (1980); DeCasper and Carstens (1981).

[3] Prechtl (1994).

[4] Rauscher *et al.* (1998).

[5] DeCasper and Fifer (1980); DeCasper and Carstens (1981).

[6] Wynn (1992).

[7] Hauser *et al.* (1996).

[8] Krumhansl and Jusczyk (1990).

[9] Spelke (1990).

[10] Piaget (1965, 1976).

[11] Kotulak (1997); Diamond and Hopson (1998).

[12] Diamond *et al.* (1985).

[13] Hubel and Wiesel (1977).

[14] Rauscher *et al.* (1997); Graziano *et al.* (1999a).

[15] Conel (1939–1967).

[16] Shankle *et al.* (1993).

[17] Chugani *et al.* (1987).

[18] Elbert *et al.* (1995).

[19] Merzenich *et al.* (1988); Kaas (1991); Recanzone and Merzenich (1993).

[20] Ramachandran and Blakeslee (1998).

[21] Schlaug *et al.* (1995).

CHAPTER 20

[1] "Students Weak in Global Tests," *Los Angeles Times,* November 21, 1996, p. A1.

[2] Karplus *et al.* (1983).

[3] Kemp (1998).

[4] Leng and Shaw (1991).

[5] Rauscher *et al.;* (1997); Rauscher *et al.* (1994).

[6] For example, the 42nd St. Fund project in New York City (Lisha Papert, private communication); project in Wisconsin under Frances Rauscher (private communication); Gardner *et al.* (1996).

[7] Drema Moody and I have discussed future projects.

[8] McGaugh (1966); Shaw *et al.* (1990); Fuster (1995).

[9] Mountcastle (1978, 1997).

[10] See [10] in Chap. 14.

[11] Boettcher *et al.* (1994).

[12] Graziano *et al.* (1999a).

[13] Graziano *et al.* (1999a).

[14] Graziano *et al.* (1999b).

CHAPTER 21

[1] See American Music Therapy Association Website www.musictherapy.org; Bruscia (1998).

[2] Roskum (1993).

[3] Rauscher *et al.* (1998).

[4] Hughes *et al.* (1998).

[5] Leng and Shaw (1991).

[6] Hughes *et al.* (1998).

[7] Leng *et al.* (1992).

[8] Wada (1986); Bolwig and Trimble (1989).

[9] Bodner *et al.* (1999); Shaw and Bodner (1999).

[10] Rauscher *et al.* (1993, 1995).

[11] Peter Mintun piano music.

[12] Johnson *et al.* (1998).

[13] Browne and Holmes (1997).

[14] Hughes *et al.* (1999). This first study looks encouraging.

[15] Johnson *et al.* (1998).

[16] Sarnthein *et al.* (1997).

[17] Rauscher *et al.* (1993, 1995); Sarnthein *et al.* (1997).

[18] Lenhoff *et al.* (1997).

[19] Hassler *et al.* (1985).

[20] Lenhoff *et al.* (1997).

[21] Rauscher *et al.* (1997).

[22] See Chapter 13 for details on the WPPSI-R spatial-temporal and spatial-recognition tasks that we used.

[23] Swanson (1992).

[24] Schlaug *et al.* (1995).

[25] Wiebers *et al.* (1997).

[26] Ramachandran and Blakeslee (1998).

[27] Lynch (1995).

[28] Smith *et al.* (1992). The extracellular dopamine level in the rat striatum was measured by microdialysis.

CHAPTER 22

[1] Marr (1982).

[2] Waddington (1966).

[3] McGrann *et al.* (1994).

[4] McGrann (1992).

[5] Shaw *et al.* (1998); Sardesai *et al.* (1999).

[6] Chase and Simon (1973).

[7] McGrann *et al.* (1994).

CHAPTER 23

[1] Rauscher and Shaw (1998).

[2] Wilson (1992).

[3] Norris *et al.* (1994).

[4] Norris (1995).

[5] Pearson (1985); Pearson *et al.* (1983); Leng *et al.* (1994).

[6] "Fishermen Take Cues From Dolphins in Rare Partnership" by Karen Pryor, *Los Angeles Times,* March 26, 1990.

[7] Seeger (1987).

[8] Waal and Lanting (1997). Also see Linden and Lanting (1992). For discussion on what we can learn on human behavior from observing animals see Lorenz (1965). For an elegant story of evolution happening as scientists observe, see Weiner (1995).

[9] Harris (1991).

[10] *Los Angeles Times,* January 17, 1999, p. A1.

[11] A careful study seems worthwhile.

[12] Graziano *et al.* (1999a).

[13] "For Students, Math Equals Fear," *Los Angeles Times,* March 15, 1999, p. A1.

[14] "Educators awed by students' improved skills," *The Orange County Register,* March 15, 1999, p. A10.

[[15]] Graziano *et al.* (1999).

REFERENCES

Abeles, M. (1982). Local Cortical Circuits. Springer-Verlag, Berlin.

Abeles, M., and Gerstein, G. L. (1988). Detecting spatio-temporal firing patterns among simultaneously recorded single neurons. *J. Neurophysiol.* **60**, 909–924.

Alikhan, A. (1990). The S.I. factor? *TAJ In House Magazine,* 53–59.

Allman, G. J. (1976). Greek Geometry from Thales to Euclid. Arno, New York.

Andersen, P., and Andersson, S. A. (1968). Physiological Basis of the Alpha Rhythm. Appleton–Century–Crofts, New York.

Anderson, J. A., and Rosenfeld, E. (eds.) (1988). Neurocomputing. MIT Press, Cambridge, Mass.

Asanuma, H. (1975). Recent developments in the study of the columnar arrangement of neurons within the motor cortex. *Physiol. Rev.* **55**, 143–156.

Ballard, D. H. (1986). Cortical connections and parallel processing: Structure and function. *Behav. Brain Sci.* **9**, 67–120.

Barlett, H. C., and Barker, H. R. (1973). Cognitive pattern perception and musical performance. *Percept. Motor Skills* **36**, 1187–1193.

Blasdel, G. C., and Salama, G. (1986). Voltage sensitive dyes reveal a modular organization in monkey striate cortex. *Nature* **321**, 579–585.

Bodner, M., Zhou, Y. D., Shaw, G. L., and Fuster, J. M. (1997). Symmetric temporal patterns in cortical spike trains during performance of a short-term memory task. *Neurol. Res.* **19**, 509–514.

Bodner, M., Shaw, G. L., Gabriel, R., Johnson, J. K., Murias, M., and Swanson, J. (1999). Detecting symmetric patterns in EEG data: A new method of analysis. *Clin. Electroencephalography,* in press.

Boettcher, W. S., Hahn, S. S., and Shaw, G. L. (1994). Mathematics and music: A search for insight into higher brain function. *Leonardo Music J.* **4**, 53–58.

Bolwig, T. G., and Trimble, M. R. (eds.) (1989). The Clinical Relevance of Kindling. John Wiley & Sons, New York.

Bonhoeffer, T., and Grinvald, A. (1991). Iso-orientation domains in cat visual cortex arranged in pinwheel-like patterns. *Nature* **353**, 429–431.

Born, J., Hansen, K., Marshall, L., Molle, M., and Fehm, H. L. (1999) Timing the end of nocturnal sleep. *Nature* 397, 29–30.

Bowden, D. M., Kripke, D. F., and Wyborney, V. G. (1978). Ultradian rhythms in waking behavior of rhesus monkeys. *Physiol. Behav.* 21, 929–933.

Braitenberg, V., and Braitenberg, C. (1979). Geometry of orientation columns in the visual cortex. *Biol. Cybernetics* 33, 179–186.

Braitenberg, V., and Schuz, A. (1991). Anatomy of the Cortex. Springer-Verlag, Berlin.

Brannon, E. M., and Terrace, H. S. (1998). Ordering of the numerosities 1 to 9 by monkeys. *Science* 282, 746–749.

Brothers, L., and Shaw, G. L. (1989). The role of accurate timing in human performance and the code for higher cortical function. *In* R. Cotterill (ed.), Models of Brain Function. Cambridge Univ. Press, Cambridge, England.

Brothers, L., Shaw, G. L., and Wright, E. L. (1993). Durations of extended mental rehearsals are remarkably reproducible in higher level human performance. *Neurol. Res.* 15, 413–416.

Browne, T. R., and Holmes, G. L. (1997). Handbook of Epilepsy. Lippincott–Raven, Philadelphia.

Bruscia, K. E. (1998). Defining Music Therapy. Barcelona Pub., Barcelona.

Brush, E. N. (1930). Observations on the temporal judgement during sleep. *Am. J. Psychol.* 42, 408–411.

Burnod, Y., and Korn, H. (1989). Consequences of stochastic release of neurotransmitters for network computation in the central nervous system. *Proc. Natl. Acad. Sci. USA* 86, 352–356.

Burns, D. B. (1968). The Uncertain Nervous System. Arnold, London.

Cabrera, B., Gutfreund, H., and Kresin, V. (eds.) (1995). From High-Temperature Superconductivity to Microminiature Refrigeration. Plenum, New York.

Carter, A., Oliver, L., Dolhinow, P., Bodner, M., Peterson, M., and Shaw, G. L. (1999). Study of music preference of langur monkeys. Manuscript in preparation.

Changeux, J. P. (1988). Learning and selection in the nervous system. *In* D. de Kerckhove and C. J. Lumsden (eds.), The Alphabet and the Brain, pp. 43–50. Springer-Verlag, Berlin.

Chase, W. G., and Simon, H. A. (1973). The mind's eye in chess. *In* W. G. Chase (ed.), Visual Information Processing. Academic Press, New York.

Cheney, D. L., and Seyfarth, R. M. (1990). How Monkeys See the World: Inside the Mind of Another Species. Univ. Chicago Press, Chicago.

Chomsky, N. (1975). Reflections on Language. Morrow, New York.

Cho, Z. H., Chung, S. C., Lim, D. W., and Wong, E. K. (1998). Effects of the acoustic noise of the gradient systems on fMRI: A study on auditory, motor and visual cortices. *Magnetic Resonance Med.* 39, 331–336.

Chugani, H. T., Phelps, M. E., and Mazziotta, J. C. (1987). Positron emission tomography of human brain functional development. *Ann. Neurol.* 22, 487–497.

Churchland, P. S., and Sejnowski, T. J. (1988). Perspectives on cognitive neuroscience. *Science* 242, 741–750.

Clark, R. W. (1971). Einstein: The Life and Times. World Pub., New York.

- Coffman, D. D. (1991). Effects of mental practice, physical practice and the knowledge of results on piano performance. *J. Res. Music. Ed.* 38, 187–196.

Cole, K. C. (1998). The Universe and the Teacup: The Mathematics of Truth and Beauty. Harcourt Brace, New York.

Conel, J. L. (1939–1967). The Postnatal Development of the Human Cerebral Cortex I–VII. Harvard Univ. Press, Cambridge, Mass.

Cragg, B. G., and Temperley, H. N. V. (1954). The organization of neurones: A co-operative analogy. *EEG Clin. Neurophysiol.* 6, 85–92.

Cranberg, L. D., and Albert, M. L. (1988). The chess mind. In L. K. Obler and D. Fein (eds.), The Exceptional Brain. Guilford, New York.

Crick, F. (1982). Do dendritic spines twitch? *Trends Neurosci.* 5, 44–46.

Dalcroze, E. J. (1972). Eurhythmics, Art and Education. Benjamin Blom, New York.

Damasio, A. R. (1994). Descartes' Error: Emotion, Reason and the Human Brain. Avon, New York.

Davenport, M. (1932). Mozart. Scribner's, New York.

DeCasper, A. J., and Fifer, W. P. (1980). Of human bonding: Newborns prefer their mothers' voices. *Science* 208, 1174–1176.

DeCasper, A. J., and Carstens, A. A. (1981). Contingencies of stimulation: Effects on learning and emotion in neonates. *Infant Behav. Dev.* 4, 19–35.

DeFilipe, J., Hendry, S. H. C., Hashikawa, T., Molinari, M., and Jones, E. G. (1990). A microcolumnar structure of monkey cerebral cortex revealed by immunocytochemical studies of double bouquet cell axon. *Neuroscience* 37(3), 655–673.

de Groot, A. (1965). Thought and Choice in Chess. Mouton, The Hague.

Diamond, M., and Hopson, J. (1998). Magic Trees of the Mind. Dutton, New York.

Diamond, M. C., Scheibel, A. B., Murphy, G. M., and Harvey, T. (1985). On the brain of a scientist: Albert Einstein. *Exp. Neurol.* 88, 198–204.

Dinse, H. R., Kruger, K., and Best, J. (1990). A temporal structure of cortical information processing. *Concepts Neurosci.* 1, 199–238.

Di Prisco, G. V. (1984). Hebb synaptic plasticity. *Prog. Neurobiol.* 22, 89–102.

Eckhorn, R., Bauer, R., Jordan, W., Brosch, M., Kruse, W., Munk, M., and Reitboeck, H. J. (1988). Coherent oscillations: A mechanism of feature linking in the visual cortex: Multiple electrode and correlation analysis in the cat. *Biol. Cybernetics* 60, 121–130.

Edelman, G. M. (1978). Group selection and phasic reentrant signaling: A theory of higher brain function. In G. M. Edelman and V. B. Mountcastle (eds.), The Mindful Brain, pp. 51–100. MIT Press, Cambridge, Mass.

Edelman, G. M. (1987). Neural Darwinism: The Theory of Neuronal Group Selection. Basic Books, New York.

Einstein, A. (1945). Mozart: His Character, His Work. Oxford Univ. Press, New York.

Eisenberg, D., and Crothers, D. (1979). Physical Chemistry with Applications to Life Sciences. Benjamin/Cummings, Menlo Park, Calif.

Elbert, T., Pantev, C., Wienbruch, C., Rockstroh, B., and Taub, R. (1995). Increased cortical representation of the fingers of the left hand in string players. *Science* 270, 305–307.

Ferguson, E. S. (1977). The mind's eye: Nonverbal thought in technology. *Science* 197, 827–835.

Feynman, R. (1949). Space–time approach to quantum electrodynamics. *Phys. Rev.* **76**, 769–789.

Fisher, M. E., and Selke, W. (1980). Infinitely many commensurate phases in a simple Ising model. *Phys. Rev. Lett.* **44**, 1502–1505.

Fuster, J. M. (1995). Memory in the Cerebral Cortex. Bradford, Cambridge.

Fuster, J. M. (1997). The Prefrontal Cortex: Anatomy, Physiology and Neurophysiology of the Frontal Lobe. Lippincott-Raven, Philadelphia.

Gardner, H. (1983). Frames of Mind: The Theory of Multiple Intelligences. Basic, New York.

Gardner, M. F., Fox, F., Knowles, F., and Jeffrey, D. (1996). Learning improved by arts training. *Nature* **381**, 284.

Gilbert, C. D., and Wiesel, T. N. (1983). Clustered intrinsic connections in cat visual cortex. *J. Neurosci.* **3**, 1116–1133.

Gilbert, C. D., and Wiesel, T. N. (1989). Columnar specificity of intrinsic horizontal and corticocortical connections in cat visual cortex. *J. Neurosci.* **9**, 2432–2442.

Gleick, J. (1992). Genius: The Life and Science of Richard Feynman. Pantheon, New York.

Goldman, P. S., and Nauta, W. H. J. (1977). Columnar distribution of corticocortical fibers in the frontal association, limbic, and motor cortex of the developing rhesus brain. *Brain Res.* **122**, 393–413.

Goldman-Rakic, P. S. (1984a). Modular organization of prefrontal cortex. *Trends Neurosci.* **7**, 419–424.

Goldman-Rakic, P. S. (1984b). The frontal lobes: Uncharted provinces of the brain. *Trends Neurosci.* **7**, 425–429.

Goldman-Rakic, P. S., and Schwartz, M. L. (1982). Interdigitation of contralateral and ipsilateral columnar projections to frontal association cortex in primates. *Science* **216**, 755–757.

Grandin, T. (1995a). Thinking in Pictures. Doubleday, New York.

Grandin, T. (1995b). How people with autism think. *In* E. Schopler and G. B. Mesibov (eds.), Learning and Cognition in Autism. Plenum, New York.

Grandin, T., Peterson, M., and Shaw, G. L. (1998). Spatial-temporal versus language-analytic reasoning: The role of music training. *Arts Ed. Policy Rev.* **99**, 11–14.

Gray, C. M., and Singer, W. (1989). Stimulus-specific neuronal oscillations in orientation columns of cat visual cortex. *Proc. Natl. Acad. Sci. USA* **86**, 1698–1702.

Gray, C. M., Konig, P., Engel, A. K., and Singer, W. (1989). Oscillatory responses in cat visual cortex exhibit intercolumnar synchronization which reflects global stimulus properties. *Nature* **338**, 334–337.

Graziano, A. B., Peterson, M., and Shaw, G. L. (1999a). Enhanced learning of proportional math through music training and spatial-temporal reasoning. *Neurol. Res.* **21**, 139–152.

Graziano, A. B., Peterson, M., and Shaw, G. L. (1999b). Evaluation of math performance through music training. To be published.

Grinvald, A., Cohen, L. B., Lesher, S., and Boyle, M. B. (1981). Simultaneous optical monitoring of activity of many neurons in invertebrate ganglia using a 124-element photodiode array. *J. Neurophys.* **45**, 829–840.

Gross, G. A., and Meijer, J. H. (1985). Effects of illumination on suprachiasmatic nucleus electrical discharge. *Ann. N.Y. Acad. Sci.* **453**, 134–146.

Hadamard, J. (1945). The Psychology of Invention in the Mathematical Field. Princeton Univ. Press, Princeton.

Haier, R. J., Seigel, B. V., MacLachlan, A., Soderling, E., Lottenberg, S., and Buchsbaum, M. S. (1992). Regional glucose metabolic changes after learning a complex visuospatial/motor task: A positron emission tomographic study. *Brain Res.* **570**, 134–143.

Hall, J. C., and Rosbash, M. (1987). Genes and biological rhythms. *Trends Genetics* **3**, 185–191.

Harris, R. (1991). What to Listen for in Mozart. Penguin, New York.

Hassler, M., Birbaumer, N., and Feil, A. (1985). Musical talent and visual-spatial abilities: A longitudinal study. *Psychol. Music* **13**, 99–113.

Hauser, M. D., MacNeilage, P., and Ware, M. (1996). Numerical representations in primates. *Proc. Natl. Acad. Sci. USA* **93**, 1514–1517.

Hebb, D. O. (1949). Organization of Behavior. John Wiley & Sons, New York.

Hinton, G. E., and Anderson, J. A. (eds.) (1981). Parallel Models of Associative Memory. Lawrence Erlbaum, Hillsdale, N.J.

Hirsch, J. A., and Gilbert, C. D. (1991). Synaptic physiology of horizontal connections in the cat's visual cortex. *J. Neurosci.* **11**, 1800–1809.

Hodgkin, A. L., and Huxley, A. F. (1952). A quantitative description of membrane current and its application to conduction and excitation in nerve. *J. Physiol.* **117**, 500–544.

Hopfield, J. J. (1982). Neural networks and physical systems with emergent collective computational abilities. *Proc. Natl. Acad. Sci. USA* **79**, 2554–2558.

Hopfield, J. J., and Tank, D. W. (1986). Computing with neural circuits: A model. *Science* **233**, 625–633.

Horn, D., and Shaw, G. L. (1990). Vertex neurons and rapid object classification. Unpublished report. University of California, Irvine.

Hubel, D. H., and Wiesel, T. N. (1977). Functional architecture of macaque monkey visual cortex. *Proc. Roy. Soc. London Ser. B* **198**, 1–59.

Hughes, J. R., Daaboul, Y., Fino, J. J., and Shaw, G. L. (1998). The "Mozart Effect" in epileptiform activity. *Clin. Electroencephalography* **29**, 109–119.

Hughes, J. R., Fino, J. J., Melyn, M. A. (1999). Is there a chronic change of the "Mozart Effect" on epileptiform activity? A case study. *Clin. Electroencephalography* **30**, 44–45.

• Hurwitz, I., Wolf, P. H., Bortnick, C. B., and Kokas, K. (1975). Nonmusical effects of the Kodaly curriculum in primary grade children. *J. Learning Disabilities* **8**, 167–174.

Hutsler, J. J., and Gazzaniga, M. S. (1997). The organization of human language cortex: Special adaptation or common language. *Neuroscientist* **3**, 61–72.

Johnson, J. K., Cotman, C. W., Tasaki, C. S., and Shaw, G. L. (1998). Enhancement in spatial-temporal reasoning after a Mozart listening condition in Alzheimer's disease: A case study. *Neurol. Res.* **20**, 666–672.

Jones, E. G., Coulter, J. D., and Hendry, S. H. C. (1978). Intracortical connectivity of architectonic fields in the somatic sensory, motor, and parietal cortex of monkeys. *J. Comp. Neurol.* **181**, 291–348.

Kaas, J. H. (1991). Plasticity of sensory and motor maps in adult animals. *Annu. Rev. Neurosci.* **14**, 137–167.

Kalmar, M. (1982). The effects of music education based on Kodaly's directives in nursery school children—From a psychologist's point of view. *Psychol. Music,* Special Issue: Proc. 9th Int. Seminar on Research in Music Education, pp. 63–68.

Kanigel, R. (1991). The Man Who Knew Infinity: A Life of the Genius Ramanujan. Scribner, New York.

Karplus, K. R., Pulos, S., and Stage, E. K. (1983). Early adolescent's proportional reasoning on "rate" problems. *Ed. Studies in Math.* **14**, 219–233.

Katz, B. (1966). Nerve, Muscle and Synapse. McGraw–Hill, New York.

Katz, B. (1969). The Release of Neural Transmitter Substances. Charles C. Thomas, Springfield, Ill.

Keetman, G. (1970). Elementaria: First Acquaintance with Orff-Schulwerk. Schott, New York.

Kemp, M. (1998). Feynman's figurations. *Nature* **394**, 231.

Kepes, G. (ed.) (1966). Module Proportion, Symmetry, Rhythm. George Braziller, New York.

Killackey, H. P. (1983). The somatosensory cortex of the rodent. *Trends Neurosci.* **6**, 425–429.

Kohonen, T. (1984). Self-Organization and Associative Memory. Springer-Verlag, Berlin.

Konopka, R. J., and Benzer, S. (1971). Clock mutants of *Drosophila melanogaster. Proc. Natl. Acad. Sci. USA* **68**, 2112–2116.

Kotulak, R. (1997). Inside the Brain: Revolutionary Discoveries of How the Mind Works. Andrews & McNeel, Kansas City, MO.

Krone, G., Mallot, H., Palm, G., and Schuz, A. (1986). Spatiotemporal receptive fields: A dynamical model derived from cortical architectonics. *Proc. Roy. Soc. London Ser. B* **226**, 421–444.

Kruger, J., and Aiple, F. (1988). Multimicroelectrode investigation of monkey striate cortex: Spike train correlations in the infragranular layers. *J. Neurophysiol.* **60**, 798–828.

Krumhansl, C. L., and Jusczyk, P. W. (1990). Infants' perception of phrase structure in music. *Psychol. Sci.* **1**, 70–73.

Kyriacou, C. P., and Hall, J. C. (1986). Interspecific genetic control of courtship, song production and reception in *Drosophila. Science* **232**, 494–497.

Leng, X. (1990). Investigation of higher brain functions in music composition using models of the cortex based on physical system analogies. Ph.D. thesis, University of California, Irvine.

Leng, X., and Shaw, G. L. (1991). Toward a neural theory of higher brain function using music as a window. *Concepts Neurosci.* **2**, 229–258.

Leng, X., Shaw, G. L., and Wright, E. L. (1990). Coding of musical structure and the trion model of cortex. *Music Perception* **8**, 49–62.

Leng, X., McGrann, J. V., and Shaw, G. L. (1992). Reversal of epileptic state by patterned electrical stimulation suggested by trion model calculations. *Neurol. Res.* **14**, 57–61.

Leng, X., McGrann, J. V., Quillfeldt, J. A., Shaw, G. L., and Shenoy, K. V. (1994). Learning and memory processes and the modularity of the brain. In J. Delacour (ed.), The Memory System of the Brain. World Scientific, Singapore.

Lenhoff, H. M., Wang, P. P., Greenberg, F., and Bellugi, U. (1997). Williams syndrome and the brain. Scientific American, December, 68–73.

Lestienne, R., and Strehler, B. L. (1987). Time structure and stimulus dependence of precisely replicating patterns present in monkey cortical neuronal spike trains. Brain Res. 437, 214–239.

Lindauer, M. (1961). Communication among Social Bees. Harvard Univ. Press, Cambridge.

Linden, E., and Lanting, F. (1992). Bonobos, chimpanzees with a difference. National Geographic, March, 46–53.

Little, W. A. (1974). The existence of persistent states in the brain. Math. Biosci. 19, 101–120.

Little, W. A. (1990). The evolution of non-newtonian views of brain function. Concepts Neurosci. 1, 149–164.

Little, W. A., and Shaw, G. L. (1975). A statistical theory of short and long term memory. Behav. Biol. 14, 115–133.

Little, W. A., and Shaw, G. L. (1978). Analytic study of the storage capacity of a neural network. Math. Biosci. 39, 281–290.

Longhurst, M., and Shaw, G. L. (1999). Mathematicians and music: Further insights into higher brain function. Submitted for publication.

Lorenz, K. (1965). Evolution and Modification of Behavior. Univ. Chicago Press, Chicago.

Lynch, M. P., Oller, D. K., Steffens, M. L., Levine, S. L., Bassinger, D. L., and Umbel, V., (1995). Onset of speech-like vocalizations in infants with Down syndrome. Am. J. Mental Retardation 100, 68–86.

MacGregor, R. J., and Lewis, E. R. (1977). Neural Modeling. Plenum, New York.

Malsburg, C. V. D., and Schneider, W. (1986). A cerebral cocktail-party processor. Biol. Cybernetics 54, 29–40.

Marr, D. (1982). Vision. Freeman, San Francisco.

Masino, S. A., Kwon, M. C., Dory, Y., and Frostig, R. D. (1993). Characteristics of functional organization within a rat barrel cortex using intrinsic optical imaging through a thinned skull. Proc. Natl. Acad. Sci. USA 90, 9998–10002.

Maxim, P. E., Bowden, D. M., and Sackett, G. P. (1976). Ultradian rhythms of solitary and social behavior in rhesus monkeys. Physiol. Behav. 17, 337–344.

McGaugh, J. L. (1966). Time-dependent processes in memory storage. Science 153, 1351–1358.

McGrann, J. V. (1992). Further theoretical investigations of the trion model of cortical organization. Ph.D. thesis, University of California, Irvine.

McGrann, J. V., Shaw, G. L., and Shenoy, K. V. (1989). Recognition of rotated objects in trion model of cortical organization. Abstract presented at the 22nd Annual Meeting of the Society of Mathematical Psychology, Irvine, J. Math. Psychol. 34, 367.

McGrann, J. V., Shaw, G. L., Silverman, D. J., and Pearson, J. C. (1991). Higher-temperature phases of a structured neural model of cortex. Phys. Rev. A 43, 5678–5682.

McGrann, J. V., Shaw, G. L., Shenoy, K. V., Leng, X., and Mathews, R. B. (1994). Computation by symmetry operations in a structured model of the brain. *Phys. Rev. E* **49**, 5830–5839.

Meier-Koll, A. (1989). Ultradian rhythms in cerebral laterality tested by a verbal dichotic listening paradigm. *Int. J. Neurosci.* **47**, 115–124.

Menaker, M., Takahashi, J. S., and Eskin, A. (1978). The physiology of circadian pacemakers. *Annu. Rev. Physiol.* **40**, 501–526.

Merzenich, M. M., Allard, T., Jenkins, W. M., and Recanzonne, G. (1988). Self organizing processes in adult neocortex. *In* W. V. Seelen, G. L. Shaw, and U. M. Leinhos (eds.), Organization of Neural Networks: Structures and Models. VCH, Weinheim, Germany.

Michelmore, P. (1962). Einstein, the Profile of the Man. Dodd & Mead, New York.

Michon, J. A. (1977). Holes in the fabric of subjective time. *Acta Psychol.* **41**, 191–203.

Mintz, I., and Korn, H. (1991). Serotonergic facilitation of quantal release at central inhibitory synapses. *J. Neurosci.* **11**, 3359–3370.

Mintz, I., Gotow, T., Triller, A., and Korn, H. (1989). Effect of serotonergic afferents on quantal release at central inhibitory synapses. *Science* **245**, 190–192.

Mountcastle, V. B. (1957). Modality and topographic properties of single neurons of cat's somatic sensory cortex. *J. Neurophysiol.* **20**, 408–434.

Mountcastle, V. B. (1978). An organizing principle for cerebral function: The unit module and the distributed system. *In* G. M. Edelman and V. B. Mountcastle (eds.), The Mindful Brain, pp. 1–50. MIT Press, Cambridge, Mass.

Mountcastle, V. B. (1997). The columnar organization of the neocortex. *Brain* **120**, 701–722.

Mountcastle, V. B. (1998). Perceptual Neuroscience: The Cerebral Cortex. Harvard, Cambridge.

Muftuler, L. T., Bodner, M., Shaw, G. L., and Nalcioglu, O. (1999). fMRI of Mozart effect using auditory stimuli. Abstract presented at 7th Meeting of International Society for Magnetic Resonance in Medicine, Philadelphia.

Mushiake, H., Sata, Y., Ishikawa, T., Saito, N., Sakamoto, K., and Tang, J. (1998). Behavioral analysis of a path-finding task performed by Japanese monkeys. 24th Annual Meeting of the Society of Neuroscience, Abstract 71.5, Los Angeles.

Neumann, J. V. (1956). Probabilistic logics and the synthesis of reliable organisms from unreliable components. *In* C. E. Shannon and J. McCarthy (eds.), Automata Studies. Princeton Univ. Press, Princeton, N.J.

Newell, G. F., and Montroll, E. W. (1953). On the theory of the Ising model of ferromagnetism. *Rev. Mod. Phys.* **25**, 353–389.

Norris, K. S. (1995). Rhythms as modulators of behavior in animals. Presented at the International Ethological Congress, Honolulu, Hawaii, August 1995.

Norris, K. S., Wursig, B., Wells, R. S., and Wursig, M. (1994). The Hawaiian Spinner Dophin. Univ. California Press, Berkeley.

Obler, L. K., and Fein, D. (eds.) (1988). The Exceptional Brain: Neuropsychology of Talent and Special Abilities. Guilford, New York.

Ostling, A. (1993). Application of the trion model to speech recognition and synthesis. REU Summer Program Internal UCI Report, University of California, Irvine.

Palm, G. (1982). Neural Assemblies. Springer-Verlag, Berlin.

Palm, G., and Aertsen, A. (eds.) (1986). Brain Theory. Springer-Verlag, Berlin.

Papert, S. (1980). Mindstorms: Children, Computers and Powerful Ideas. Basic, New York.

Papert, S. (1993). The Children's Machine: Rethinking School in the Age of the Computer. Basic, New York.

Parente, J. A., and O'Malley, J. J. (1975). Training in musical rhythm and field dependence of children. *Percept. Motor Skills* 40, 392–394.

Patera, J., and Shaw, G. L. (1981). Dynamics of firing patterns in the visual cortex. 11th Annual Meeting of the Society of Neuroscience, Abstract 59.5, Los Angeles.

Patera, J., Shaw, G. L., Slansky, R., and Leng, X. (1989). Model of adaptive temporal development of structured finite systems. *Phys. Rev. A* 40, 1073–1087.

Patterson, F., and Cohn, R. H. (1978). Conversations with a gorilla. *National Geographic,* October, 438–465.

Pearson, J. C. (1985). Information processing within cortical columns: The role of interacting assemblies. Ph.D. thesis, University of California, Irvine.

Pearson, J. C., Diamond, D. M., McKennan, T. M., Rinaldi, P. C., Shaw, G. L., and Weinberger, N. M. (1983). The neuronal coding of rotating bar stimuli in primary visual cortex of cat. 13th Annual Meeting of the Society of Neuroscience, Abstract 238.9.

Peretz, I., and Morais, J. (1993). Specificity for music. *In* F. Boller and J. Grafman (eds.), Handbook of Neuropsychology, Vol. 8. Elsevier, Amsterdam.

Peretz, I., Kolinsky, R., Tramo, M., Labrecque, R., Hublet, C., Demeurisse, G., and Belleville, S. (1994). Functional dissociations following bilateral lesions of auditory cortex. *Brain* 117, 1283–1301.

Perkel, D. H., Gerstein, G. L., and Moore, G. P. (1967). Neuronal spike trains and stochastic point processes. II. Simultaneous spike trains. *Biophys. J.* 7, 419–440.

Petsche, H., and Etlinger, S. C. (1998). EEG and Thinking: Power and Coherence Analysis of Cognitive Processes. Austrian Academy of Sciences, Vienna.

Petsche, H., Richter, P., von Stein, A., Etlinger, S., and Filz, O. (1993). EEG coherence and musical thinking. *Music Perception* 11, 117–151.

Piaget, J. (1965). The Child's Concept of Number. Norton, New York.

Piaget, J. (1976). The Grasp of Consciousness: Action and Concept in the Young Child. Harvard Univ. Press, Cambridge, Mass.

Pinker, S. (1994). The Language Instinct. Morrow, New York.

Pinker, S. (1997). How the Mind Works. Norton, New York.

Poppel, E. (1989). The measurement of music and the cerebral clock: A new theory. *Leonardo* 22, 83–89.

Posner, M. I., and Raichle, M. E. (1994). Images of Mind. Scientific American, New York.

Prechtl, H. F. (1994). Principles of early motor behavior. *In* C. Faienza (ed.), Music, Speech and the Developing Brain: The Case of the Modularity of Mind. Guerni, Milan.

Rakic, P. (1988). Specification of cerebral cortical areas. *Science* 241, 170–176.

Ramachandran, V. S., and Blakeslee, S. (1998). Phantoms in the Brain. Morrow, New York.

Ramanujan, S. (1957). Notebooks of Srinivasa Ramanujan, Vol. I & II. Tata Institute of Fundamantal Research, Bombay.

Rauscher, F. H., and Shaw, G. L. (1998). Key components of the Mozart Effect. *Percept. Motor Skills* **86**, 835–841.

Rauscher, F. H., Shaw, G. L., and Ky, K. N. (1993). Music and spatial task performance. *Nature* **365**, 611.

Rauscher, F. H., Shaw, G. L., Levine, L. J., Ky, K. N., and Wright, E. L. (1994). Music and spatial task performance: A causal relationship. Paper presented at the 102nd Annual Convention of the American Psychological Association, Los Angeles.

Rauscher, F. H., Shaw, G. L., and Ky, K. N. (1995). Listening to Mozart enhances spatial-temporal reasoning: towards a neurophysiological basis. *Neurosci. Lett.* **185**, 44–47.

Rauscher, F. H., Shaw, G. L., Levine, L. J., Wright, E. L., Dennis, W. R., and Newcomb, R. L. (1997). Music training causes long-term enhancement of preschool children's spatial-temporal reasoning. *Neurol. Res.* **19**, 2–8.

Rauscher, F. H., Robinson, K. D., and Jens, J. J. (1998). Improved maze learning through early music exposure in rats. *Neurol. Res.* **20**, 427–432.

Recanzone, G. H., and Merzenich, G. H. (1993). Functional plasticity in the cerebral cortex: Mechanisms of improved perceptual abilities and skill acquisition. *Concepts Neurosci.* **4**, 1–23.

Richardson, A. (1967). Mental practice: A review and discussion. *Res. Quart.* **38**, 263–273.

Richmond, B. J., Optican, L. M., and Spitzer, H. (1990). Temporal encoding of two-dimensional patterns by single units in primate primary visual cortex. I. Stimulus–response relations. *J. Neurophysiol.* **64**, 351–369.

Rockland, K. S. (1989). Bistratified distribution of terminal arbors of individual axons projecting from area V1 to middle temporal area (MT) in the macaque monkey. *Visual Neurosci.* **3**, 155–170.

Rockland, K. S., and Virga, A. (1989). Terminal arbors of individual "feedback" axons projecting from area V2 to V1 in the macaque monkey: A study using immunohisto-chemistry of anterogradely transported *Phaseolus vulgaris*-leucoagglutinin. *J. Comp. Neurol.* **285**, 54–72.

Roney, K. J., and Shaw, G. L. (1980). Analytic study of assemblies of neurons in memory storage. *Math. Biosci.* **51**, 15–41.

Roney, K. J., Scheibel, A. B., and Shaw, G. L. (1979). Dendritic bundles: Survey of anatomical experiments and physiological theories. *Brain Res. Rev.* **1**, 225–271.

Roskum, K. L. (1993). Feeling the Sound, the Influence of Music on Behavior. San Francisco Press, San Franciso.

Rumelhart, D. E., and McClelland, J. L., and PDP Research Group (eds.) (1986). Parallel Distributed Processing. MIT Press, Cambridge, Mass.

Sacks, O. (1995). An Anthropologist on Mars. Knopf, New York.

Sardesai, M. (1993). Application of the trion model in object classification and memory storage. Ph.D. thesis, University of California, Irvine.

Sardesai, M., Figge, M., Bodner, M., Hansen, J., Quillfeldt, J. A., Ostling, A., Vuong, S., and Shaw, G. L. (1999). Toward a cortical language and grammar inherent in the trion model. Submitted for publication.

→ Sarnthein, J., von Stein, A., Rappelsberger, P., Petsche, H., Rauscher, F. H., and Shaw, G. L. (1997). Persistent patterns of brain activity: An EEG coherence study of the positive effect of music on spatial-temporal reasoning. *Neurol. Res.* **19**, 107–111.

Sarnthein, J., Petsche, H., Rappelsberger, P., Shaw, G. L., and von Stein, A. (1998). Synchronization between prefrontal and posterior association cortex during human working memory. *Proc. Natl. Acad. Sci. USA* **95**, 7092–7096.

Sarton, G. (1952). Ancient Science Through the Golden Age of Greece. Dover, New York.

Schattschneider, D. (1990). M. C. Escher: Visions of Symmetry. Freeman, New York.

Schlaug, G., Jancke, L., Huang, Y., and Steinmetz, H. (1995). *In vivo* evidence of structural asymmetry in musicians. *Science* **267**, 699–701.

Schulz, H., and Lavie, P. (eds.) (1985). Ultradian Rhythms in Physiology and Behavior. Springer-Verlag, Berlin.

Seegar, A. (1987) Why Suya Sing: A Musical Anthropology of an Amazonian People. Cambridge Univ. Press, Cambridge, England.

Seelen, W. V. (1970). Zur informationsverarbeitung im visuellen system der wirbetiere. *Kybernetik* **7**, 89–106.

Seelen, W. V., Shaw, G. L., and Leinhos, U. M. (eds.) (1988). Organization of Neural Networks: Structures and Models. VCH, Weinheim, Germany.

Sergent, J. (1993). Mapping the musician brain. *Human Brain Mapping* **1**, 20–38.

Sergent, J., Zuck, T. S., and MacDonald, B. (1992). Distributed neural network underlying musical sight-reading and keyboard performance. *Science* **257**, 106–109.

Shanbhag, S. J. (1991). Motion and the trion model of the cortex. REU Summer Program Internal UCI Report, University of California, Irvine.

Shankle, R., Rafii, M. S., and Landing, B. H. (1993). Functional relationships associated with pattern development in human cerebral cortex. *Concepts Neurosci.* **4**, 77–87.

Shaw, G. L. (1978). Space–time correlations of neuronal firing related to memory storage capacity. *Brain Res. Bull.* **3**, 107–113.

Shaw, G. L., and Bodner, M. (1999). Music enhances spatial-temporal reasoning: Towards a neurophysiological basis using EEG. *Clin. EEG*, in press.

Shaw, G. L., and Palm, G. (eds.) (1988). Brain Theory, reprint volume. World Scientific, Singapore.

Shaw, G. L., and Ramachandran, V. S. (1982). Interpolation during apparent motion. *Perception* **11**, 491–494.

Shaw, G. L., and Vasudevan, R. (1974). Persistent states of neural networks and the random nature of synaptic transmission. *Math. Biosci.* **21**, 207–218.

Shaw, G. L., Rinaldi, P. C., and Pearson, J. C. (1983). Processing capability of the primary visual cortex and possible physiological basis for an apparent motion illusion. *Exp. Neurol.* **79**, 293–298.

Shaw, G. L., Silverman, D. J., and Pearson, J. C. (1985). Model of cortical organization embodying a basis for a theory of information processing and memory recall. *Proc. Natl. Acad. Sci. USA* **82**, 2364–2368.

Shaw, G. L., Silverman, D. J., and Pearson, J. C. (1988). Trion model of cortical organization and the search for the code of short-term memory and information processing. *In* J. Levy and J. C. S. Delacour (eds.), Systems with Learning and Memory Abilities, pp. 411–435. Elsevier, New York.

Shaw, G. L., McGaugh, J. L., and Rose, S. P. R. (eds.) (1990). Neurobiology of Learning and Memory, reprint volume. World Scientific, Singapore.

Shaw, G. L., Kruger, J., Silverman, D. J., Aertsen, A. M. H. J., Aiple, F., and Liu, H. C. (1993). Rhythmic and patterned firing in visual cortex. Neurol. Res. 15, 46–50.

Shaw, G. L., Sardesai, M., Figge, C., Bodner, M., Quillfeldt, J. A., Landau, S., and Ostling, A. (1998). Reliable short-term memory in the trion model: Toward a cortical language and grammar. 21st Annual Meeting of the Society of Neuroscience, Abstract 71.9, Los Angeles.

Shenoy, K. V., Kaufman, J., and Shaw, G. L. (1989). Learning by selection in the trion model of cortex. Abstract presented at the 22nd Annual Meeting of the Society of Mathematical Psychology. J. Math. Psychol. 34, 367.

Shenoy, K. V., Kaufman, J., McGrann, J. V., and Shaw, G. L. (1993). Learning by selection in the trion model of cortical organization. Cerebral Cortex 3, 239–248.

Silverman, D. J., Shaw, G. L., and Pearson, J. C. (1986). Associative recall properties of the trion model of cortical organization. Biol. Cybernetics 53, 259–271.

Singer, W. (1990). Search for coherence: A basic principle of cortical self-organization. Concepts Neurosci. 1, 1–26.

Smith, A. D., Olson, R. J., and Justice, J. B. (1992). Quantitative microdialysis of dopamine in the striatum: Effect of circadian variation. J. Neurosci. Methods 44, 33–41.

Spelke, E. S. (1990). Principles of object perception. Cognitive Sci. 14, 29–56.

Swanson, J. M. (1992). Schoolbased Assessments and Interventions for ADD Students. KC Pub., Irvine, Calif.

Szonyi, E. (1973). Kodaly's Principles in Practice. Boosy and Hawkes, London.

Thorndike, R. L., Hagen, E. P., and Jerome, M. S. (1986). The Stanford-Binet Intelligence Scale. Riverside Publishing, Chicago.

Toga, A. W., and Mazziotta, J. C. (1996). Brain Mapping: The Methods. Academic Press, San Diego.

Tootel, R. B. H., Silverman, M. S., DeValois, R. L., and Jacobs, G. H. (1983). Functional organization of the second cortical visual areas in primates. Science 220, 737–742.

Treffert, D. A. (1989). Extraordinary People: Understanding "Idiot Savants." Harper & Row, New York.

Turek, F. W. (1985). Circadian neural rhythms in mammals. Annu. Rev. Physiol. 47, 49–64.

Verzeano, M., and Negishi, K. (1960). Neuronal activity in cortical and thalamic networks. J. Gen. Physiol. (Suppl.) 43, 177–195.

Vessels, J., and Cohn, R. H. (1985). Koko's kitten. National Geographic, June, 110–113.

Waal, F. D., and Lanting, F. (1997). Bonobo: The Forgotten Ape. University of California Press, Berkeley.

Wada, J. A. (ed.) (1986). Kindling. Raven, New York.

Waddington, C. H. (1966). The modular principle and biological form. In G. Kepes (ed.), Module, Proportion, Symmetry, Rhythm. George Braziller, New York.

Wechsler, D. (1989). Wechsler Preschool and Primary Scale of Intelligence, revised edition. Psychological Corp., San Antonio, Texas.

Wechsler, D. (1991). Wechsler Intelligence Scale for Children, 3rd edition. Psychological Corp., San Antonio, Texas.

Weiner, J. (1995). The Beak of the Finch: A Story of Evolution in Our Time. Vintage, New York.

Wiebers, D. O., Feigin, V. L., and Brown, R. D. (1997). Handbook of Stroke. Lippincott–Raven, Philadelphia.

Wiesendanger, M. (1986). Redistributive function of the motor cortex. *Trends Neurosci.* **9**, 120–125.

Wilson, E. O. (1992). The Diversity of Life. Harvard Univ. Press, Cambridge, Mass.

Weyl, H. (1952). Symmetry. Princeton Univ. Press, Princeton, N.J.

Wilson, H. R., and Cowan, J. D. (1972). Excitatory and inhibitory interactions in localized populations of model neurons. *Biophys. J.* **12**, 1–24.

Wynn, K. (1992). Addition and subtraction by human infants. *Nature* **358**, 749–750.

Zatorre, R. J., Evans, A. C., and Meyer, E. (1994). Memory mechanisms underlying melodic perception and memory for pitch. *J. Neurosci.* **14**, 1908–1919.

Zepelin, H. (1986). REM sleep and the timing of self-awakenings. *Bull. Psychonomic Soc.* **24**, 254–256.

Zhou, Y. D., and Fuster, J. M. (1996). Mnemonic neuronal activity in somatosensory cortex. *Proc. Natl. Acad. Sci. USA* **93**, 10533–10537.

Zigmond, M. J., Bloom, F. E., Landis, S. C., Roberts, J. L., and Squire, L. R. (eds.) (1999). Fundamentals in Neuroscience. Academic Press, San Diego.

Zung, W. W. K., and Wilson, W. P. (1971). Time estimation during sleep. *Biol. Psychiatry* **3**, 159–164.

INDEX

A

Academic achievement, 6–8
Action potential, 54–55
Aertsen, Ad, 218
Alzheimer disease
    Mozart effect, 38, 285–287
    short term memory loss, 115–117
Amygdala function, 58, 60
"An Anthropologist on Mars," 21
Apostolos, Margo, 132, 138
Art, visual, 138–139
Aschenborn, Wiebke, 240
Atmur, Bob, 134
Austin, George, 290
Autism, 18–19
Axons, electrical properties, 55

B

Bach, Johann Sebastian, 167
Basketball, 155–158
Beethoven, Ludwig von, 179, 320
Belinfante, Frieda, 148–150
Bell-shaped distributions, 173
Biases, in research, 239–240
Bodner, Mark, 209, 221–237, 240–251
Boettcher, Wendy, 12, 15, 184
Bohr, Niels, 20
Bonhoeffer, T., 76
Bowden, D. M., 85
Brain
    activity, 54–58
    code, Mozart as, 312–314

complexity, 54
cortex
    basic network, 73–74
    cognition and, 31
    connectivity, elements, 297–298
    evolution, 307–311
    features, 58–63
    firing patterns
        analysis, 234–235
        monkeys, 36–37
        SAC, 234
    grammar
        inherent, 107–112
        significance, 118–120
    information processing models,
        218–222
    inherent patterns, 128–131
    language, 107–112
    memory patterns and, 114–115
    neural link, 61
    pattern recognition, 105–106
    pitch location, 267
    planum temporale, 267
    primary visual, 215–217
    priming, 265–266
    right hemisphere, 177
    spatial structure, 76–81
    structured, 31
    SYMMETRIC analysis, 223–224
development
    music role, 319–320
    studies, 262–266

Brain (*continued*)
  functions
    model, 30–31
    similarity, 30
    symmetry, 101–106
  imaging
    overview, 63–64
    types
      EEG, 65–66, 205–210
      MEG, 66–69, 264
      microelectrodes, 64–65, 215–227
      MRI and fMRI, 71, 209–210
      optical recording, 71–72, 77
      PET, 69–71, 263
  magnetic fields, 67–68
  neurons
    action potential, 54–55
    cortical link, 61
    description, 54
    firing threshold, 54
    types, 57–58
  reorganization, 262–266
  subcortical regions
    creative modes, 122–127
    sequential modes, 122–127
  theory, history, 88–93
Braitenberg, Valentino, 51
Brannon, E. M., 248–250
Broken symmetries, 49, 110
Brothers, Leslie, 83, 147–154
Bullock, Theodore, 312

C

Carnatic music, 9–10
Carter, Allisa, 241–242
Cartesian coordinate system, 132
Causation, distinction, 6
Cell body, 54
Chase, W. G., 10, 299
Chen, Jemmy, 221
Cheung, Laura, 188, 289
Chess
  computer, 296, 317–318
  music link, 7
  sequential solution, 124–125
  spatial-temporal reasoning, 10–12
  strategies, 299
Children, *see also* Infants
  brain development
    MEG studies, 263–264

  music's role, 39–40, 319–320
  Mozart effect study, 33–34, 751
  spatial-temporal reasoning, 261–262
  TV habits, 18
Chugani, Harry, 263
Churchland, Patricia, 81
Circadian rhythms, 81–83, 292–293
Clemmons, Helen, 19
Codes
  brain, 312–314
  Mountcastle, 152
  neural language, 37
Cognition, 31–32
Columnar organization principle
  description, 74
  mathematical realization, 91–93
  in new borns, 255
Computers
  chess, 317–318
  importance, 317
  thinking, 296–299
  training, 178–184
Conel, J. L., 263
Cook, Stephen, 275
Cooper, Leon, 89
Cooperative phenomena, 89–90
Cooperative state, 90
Cooperativity, 78–80
Corpus collosum, 60
Correlation, distinction, 6
Cortex
  cognition and, 31
  columns
    spatial structure
      analysis, 76–81
      composition, 73–74
  connectivity, elements, 297–298
  evolution, 307–311
  features, 58–63
  firing patterns
    analysis, 234–235
    inherent, 36–37
  grammar
    inherent, 107–112
    significance, 118–120
  information processing models, 218–222
  inherent patterns, 128–131
  language, 107–112
  memory patterns and, 114–115
  neural link, 61
  pattern recognition, 105–106

pitch location, 267
planum temporale, 267
primary visual, 215–217
priming, 265–266
right hemisphere, 177
spatial structure, 76–81
structured, 31
subcortical systems, 58, 60–61
SYMMETRIC analysis, 223–224
Cotman, Carl, 286
Counting skills, 168, 179
Cragg, B. G., 90
Creative modes, 122–127
Crick, Francis, 89, 167
Cyclotron, 70

D

Dance, trion model, 131–133
Darwin, Charles, 309
DeCasper, Anthony, 257
Deep Blue, 11–12, 296
Degenerative short-term memory, 115–117
Dendrites, description, 54
Dendritic bundles
    description, 76–77
    minicolumn link, 92
Development
    MEG study, 263–264
    music's effect, 39–40, 319–320
Diamond, Marion, 261
Differential equations, 20
Dolhinow, Phyllis, 240–242
Dolphin behavior, 307–311
Dopamine, 292
Down syndrome, 291–292

E

Earl, Tina, 25, 196
Edelman, Gerald, 89, 100
EEG, *see* Electroencephalogram
Einstein, Albert
    brain, examination, 261
    on music, 7
    spatial-temporal reasoning, 20
Einstein, Alfred, 162
Electroencephalogram
    coherence studies, 167–168, 206
    description, 65–66
    frequency bands, 207

mental rehearsal, 151–152
Mozart effect, 206–210
Electron function, 55–56
English language, S.T.A.R
    main study, 194–202
    pilot study, 191–193
    spatial-temporal training, 275–276
Epilepsy, 38, 282–285
Errors, testing, 173–176
Escher, M. C., 8
Evolution, brain
    human, 307–311
    primate, 40
Experimental design, 173–176

F

FAT tasks, 290–291
Feature detector, 135
Ferguson, Eugene, 28
Fetus movement, ultrasound, 256–257
Feynman, Richard, 20, 271, 273
Feynman diagram, 20
Figge, Chris, 115, 243–244
Filling-in, 216–217
Firing thresholds, 54, 215–217
Fisher, Bobby, 11
Fisher, Michael, 93
Frostig, Ron, 72, 77
Fuster, Joaquin, 65, 234, 237

G

Gabriel, Roger, 234
Gardner, Howard, 12
Gauss, Carl Friedrich, 7
Gaussian distributions, 173
Genius, magic, 3–4
Gilbert, C. D., 77
Glass, Philip, 165, 241, 243, 245
Glial cells, 261
Go game, 299
Gorilla
    Foundation, 40
    Koko and Michael, 40, 243–245
    User Interface, 243–245
Grammar, cortical
    description, 107–112
    significance, 118–120
Grandin, Temple, 18–19, 21–22
Graziano, Amy, 15, 187–202, 275–279

Grice, Bonnie, 176
Grinvald, A., 76

H

Hahn, Krista, 188
Hahn, Sabrina, 12
Hansen, Jill, 45, 115, 288
Hardy, G. H., 9
Harris, Del, 157–158
Harris, Robert, 312–313
Harth, Erich, 76
Hassler, Marianne, 6
Hawthorn effect, 175
Hebb, Donald, 31, 88
Hebb learning rule
  brain development, 262–263
  description, 88–89, 90
  memory, 111
  short term memory, 111, 118–119
  text recognition, 135–136
Hebb synapse, 88–89
Hebb training coefficient, 99–100
Heisenberg, Werner, 20
Hippocampus function, 58, 60
Hodgkin, Alan Lloyd, 56
Honeybee dance, 153–154
Hubel, David, 74, 76, 135, 215, 262
Hughes, John, 38, 168, 282–285
Huxley, Andrew Fielding, 56

I

Illusions, visual, 212–217
Infants, *see also* Children
  cognition, 31–32
  math skills, 257–258
  music structure, 236–237, 258
  neonate, auditory preferences, 257
Internal clocks, 152–154
Internal neural language
  decoding, 37, 229–237
  description, 30–31, 108–115

J

Johnson, Julene, 38, 285–287
Jones, Edward G., 58, 60, 312
Junctions, *see* Synapses
Justice, J., 85, 292

K

Kaas, Jon, 264
Kac, Mark, 9–10
Kasparov, Garry, 11, 296
Katz, Bernard, 58, 90
Kelley, Jim, 15, 290–291
Keyboard, *see* Piano keyboard
Killackey, Herbert, 80, 83
Kim, Miyoung, 195, 290–291
Kirkman, David, 299
Kotulak, Ronald, 261
Kruger, Jurgen, 218–219
Krumhansl, Carol, 31, 258–261
Ky, Katherine, 162–168

L

Language
  –analytic reasoning
    application, 10
    importance, 19
  cortical
    inherent, 107–112
    memory patterns, 114–115
  neural, internal
    decoding, 37
    description, 30–31
  pre, music as, 31–32
  –ST reasoning, interplay, 271, 273
Lanting, Frans, 311
L-DOPA, 292
Learning
  keyboard
    advantages, 195–196
    effect, duration, 34
    pre-school study, 178–184
    spatial-temporal reasoning, 36
  memory patterns, 96
  music
    academic achievement, 6–8
    math enhancement
      Einstein's view, 7
      enhancments, 200–201
      intergration, 276–278
      reasons, 278–279
      relationship, 22–28
    pilot study
      description, 170–171
      results, 176
    preschool study

keyboard, 33–34, 36
press accounts, 169–170
in schools, 314–319
spatial reasoning, 8
spatial-temporal reasoning, 273–275
science, 22–28
selectional, 99–101
structional, 100–101
symmetry breaks, 297
Left-handedness, 177–178, 263–264
Leng, Xiaodan, 30, 122–132, 229–237
Lenhoff, Howard and Gloria, 39, 288–289
Limbs, phantom, 46
Little, William, 79, 90, 95, 312
Longhurst, Maren, 12, 15
Los Angeles Lakers, 157
Lupu, Radu, 4, 161
Lynch, Michael, 291

M

Magic genius, concept, 3–4
"Magic Tress of the Mind," 261
Magnetic fields, 67–68
Magnetic resonance imaging, 71, 209–210
Magnetoencephalogram, 66–69, 264
Marr, David, 138–139, 296
Mathematicians, interviews, 12–15
Mathematics
  ability, 273
    importance, 269–271
    infants, 257–258
    primates, 248–251
  counting skills, 179
  curriculum, S.T.A.R integration, 276–278
  music enhancement, 22–28, 278–279
  number recognition, 179
  proportional
    enhancement, 200
    importance, 270
    introduction, 316
    learning, 7
  S.T.A.R.
    evaluation program, 186–188
    first version, 189–191
    main study, 194–202
    pilot study, 191–193
    results, feature, 188–189
    via spatial-temporal training, 275–276
  student ranking, 186

study, 18
theories, major, 20
mathematics, 22–28
Matrix theory, 20
McCulloch, Warren, 88
McGrann, John, 96, 103, 109–110
Mead, Carver, 297
MEG, see Magnetoencephalogram
Memory
  epileptic seizure effects, 243
  short-term
    degenerative, 115–117
    long-term vs., 183
    measuring, 118–119
    Mozart effect, 274
    synchrony, 210
  spatial-temporal sequences, 30
Memory patterns
  and cortical language, 114–115
  in coupled columns, 112–113
  epileptic, 283–284
  global, 298
  learning properties, 96
  natural sequences, 96–99
  recognition, 107
  repertoire, 101–105
  symmetries
    families, 222–223
    relation, 297
Mental imaging, 151–152
Mental rehearsal
  description, 148–149
  experiments, 149–152
  quantitative, 154–158
Merzenich, Michael, 264
Michon, J. A., 151
Microelectrodes, 64–65
Middleton, Fiona, 240–241
M.I.N.D. Institute, 311–312
"Mindstorms: Children, Computers and
  Powerful Ideas," 28
Minicolumns
  as processing unit, 79
  representations, 73–74
  in trion model, 93–96
Monte Carlo evolutions
  creative modes, 125–126
  in dance, mapping, 131–133
  in motion, mapping, 131–133
  in music, mapping, 127

Monte Carlo evolutions (*continued*)
  natural sequences, 96–99
  sequential modes, 125–126
  visual art, 138–139
Montroll, Elliot, 83
Moses, Edwin, 154
Motion, trion model, 131–133
Mountcastle, Vernon, 30–31, 58, 73–74, 74
Mountcastle code, 152
Mountcastle organization principle
  concepts, 302–303
  description, 30–31
  evolution, 40
Mozart, Wolfgang Amadeus
  composing, 10
  cortical language, 160
  genius, 313
  math abilities, 8
  minuets, 258, 260–261
  music, structure, 236–237
  simple melodies, 179
Mozart effect, 6, *see also* Sonata for Two Pianos
    in D Major (K.448)
  Alzheimer's disease studies, 285–287
  animal model, establishment, 247
  as brain code, 312–314
  child development, 39–40
  clinical, 37–39
  coining, 4
  cortical priming, 265–266
  Down syndrome, 291–292
  education, 36
  EEG analysis, 206–210
  epilepsy studies, 282–285
  experiments
    description, 162–163
    follow-up, 163–167
  exploitation, 320
  fMRI studies, 209–210
  further studies, 167–168
  language ability, 119–120
  meter, 167
  neuroscience, 36–37
  philosophical consequences, 40
  press accounts, 4
  primates, 240–245
  puzzle pieces, 305–306
  rats, 245–248
  reaction, 6
  sequential reasoning, 126–127

  short-term memory, 274
  spatial maze performance, 36, 36–37
  stroke, 290–291
  structural aspects, 236–237
  timescale, 245–246
  Williams syndrome studies, 288–290
MRI, *see* Magnetic resonance imaging
MSAC, 234
Muftuler, Tugan, 71, 209
Multiplexing, 118
Murias, Michael, 66
Music
  brain development, 319–320
  carnatic, 9–10
  chess link, 7
  cortical data, 231, 234–235
  evolution, 307–311
Music instruction methods, 274
  mental rehearsal
    description, 148–149
    experiments, 149–152
  meter, 234
  Monte Carlo evolutions, mapping, 127
  motives, 231, 234–235
  perfect pitch, 266–268
  as pre-language, 31–32
  structure
    cortical resonance, 236–237
    infants preferences, 258, 260–261
  tempo, 84
  training
    academic achievement, 6–8
    keyboard
      advantages, 195–196
      preschool study, 34, 36
    math enhancement
      Einstein's view, 7
      evaluation, 278–279
      integration, 276–278
      reasons, 200–201
      relationship, 22–28
    pilot study
      description, 170–171
      results, 176
    preschool study
      description, 33–34
      press accounts, 169–170
    in schools, 314–319
    on science, 22–28
    spatial-temporal reasoning, 8, 273–275

trion model
  general features, 128–131
  variations, 127–128
  Williams syndrome link, 268
"Music with Changing Parts," 165, 245

N

Nalcioglu, Orhan, 71, 168, 209
Natural sequences, 96–99
Neumann, John von, 110, 315
Neural language
  decoding, 37
  description, 30–31
Neuromodulators
  inherent rhythms, 292–293
  periodicities, 143
  release, 61
Neurons
  action potential, 54–55
  cooperativity, 80
  cortical link, 61
  description, 54
  filling-in, 216–217
  firing threshold, 54, 215–217
  types, 57–58
Neurophysiology, 212–217
Neurotransmitters, description, 56–57
Nguyen, Lan, 290–291
Norris, Kenneth, 40, 307–309
Number recognition, 179

O

Object assembly test
  description, 171
  preschool study scores, 181–182
Oliver, Lori, 240–243
Optical recording, 71–72
Ostling, Annette, 134–136

P

Palm, Guenther, 88
Paper folding and cutting tasks
  Alzheimer's patients, 287
  EEG analysis, 207–208
  Mozart effect experiment, 163–166
  solution methods, 124–125
Papert, Seymour, 28

Parkinson disease, 292
Paterson, Penny, 243
Patera, George, 93, 212, 312
Pavarotti, Luciano, 244
Pearson, John, 96, 215–217
Perahia, Murray, 4, 161
Perl, Martin, 312
Perfect pitch, 266–268, 284
Performance, sports, 154–158
PET, *see* Positron emission tomography
Peterson, Matthew, 15, 184–202, 275–279
Petsche, Hellmuth, 31, 144, 205–206
Pfund, Randy, 157
Phantom limbs, 46
Photons, definition, 69–70
Physical spin model, 93
Piaget, Jean, 27, 261
Piano keyboard
  advantages, 195–196
  training
    effect, duration, 34
    pre-school study, 178–184
    results, 316
    spatial-temporal reasoning, 36
Pinker, Stephen, 51
Plastino, Janice, 131–132, 149
Pitts, Walter, 88
Poppel, Ernst, 84
Positron, definition, 69
Positron emission tomography, 69–71
Prechtl, Heinz, 256
Preschool study, 33–34, 178–184
Primates
  cortical firing patterns, 36–37
  evolution, 40
  math abilities, 248–251
  Mozart effect, 210–215
Probability, 173–176
Proportional mathematics
  description, 7
  introduction, 316
  proportional, 270
  skills, enhancement, 200
Pryor, Karen, 309–310
Pyramidal neurons, 57
Pythagoreas music, 7

Q

Quantum theory, 20

R

Ramachandran, V.S., 212–213, 264–265, 291
Ramanujan, Srinivasa, 8–9, 313
Rappelsberger, Peter, 206
Rauscher, Frances, 32, 158–168, 176–184
Rats, Mozart effect, 245–248
Reasoning, see Spatial-temporal reasoning
Recognition
  number, 179
  patterns
    cortical, 105–106
    memory, 107
  spatial, 171
  speech, 134–135
  symmetries
    rotation, 107
    time, 107
  text, 135–137
Reflection, mirror, 44
Rehearsal, mental
  description, 148–149
  experiments, 149–152
Repetition, rhythmic, 165
Reversi, 299
Rhythm, repetitive, 165
Rinaldi, Pat, 215–217
Robertson, Richard, 59
Robotic motion, control, 132–133
Rockland, K. S., 77
Rodgers, Linda, 19, 274–277
Roney, Kathleen, 77, 92
Roskum, Kay, 282
Rossini, Antonio, 7
Rotation symmetry
  description, 45–46
  recognition, 107

S

Sacks, Oliver, 21
Sardesai, Milind, 135–138
Sarnthein, Johannes, 206–210
Scales, spatial and temporal, 81–83
Scheibel, Arne, 92, 261
Schlaug, Gottfried, 266–268
Schroedinger, Erwin, 20
Schuz, Almut, 61
Schwinger, Julian, 20
Science, music training and, 22–28
Scientific notation, description, 54

Seeger, Anthony, 310
Sejnowski, Terry, 81
Selectional learning, 100–101
Self-awakening, 152–153
Selke, Walter, 93
Sequential modes, 122–127
Serotonin, 126
Shakespeare, William, 84
Shanbhag, Sharad, 132–134
Shankle, Rod, 263
Shenoy, Krishna, 96, 101–102
Silverman, Dennis, 96, 218–220
Simon, 10, 299
Singing training, 178–184
Single subjects, 242–243
Sonata for Two Pianos in D Major (K.448),
    see also Mozart effect
  analysis, 235–237
  movements, effects, 284
  on PF&C tasks, 208–209
  preschool study, 33–34
  reasoning enhancement, 167
  selection, 160–162
  short-term memory, 274
  spatial maze performance, 36–37
Space, description, 46–49
Spatial maze performance, 36–37
Spatial recognition, 171
Spatial scales, 81–83
Spatial structure, 76–81
Spatial-temporal animation reasoning
  advantages, 25–26
  application, 318
  child development, 39–40
  design goals, 316–317
  evaluation program, 186–188
  features, 25
  first version, 189–191
  importance, 15
  key component, 31
  main study, 194–202
  math curriculum, 276–278
  pilot study, 191–193
  results, feature, 188–189
  in schools, 314–319
  symmetry program, 51
  Williams syndrome children, 288
Spatial-temporal reasoning
  chess, 10–12
  children, testing, 261–262

computer's ability, 296–299
features, 19
language analysis, interplay, 271, 273
left-handedness link, 177–178
music
    keyboard, 34, 36
    Mozart's, 160
    training, 8, 273–275
patterns, 221, see Memory patterns
primates, 248–251
S.T.A.R. training, 275–276
Speech
    recognition, 134–135
    synthesis, 134–135
Spelke, Elizabeth, 261
Spin model system, 90–95
Sports performance, 154–158
SQUIDS, 68
Standard errors, 173
Stanford Achievement Test, 192, 202
S.T.A.R., see Spatial-temporal animation
    reasoning
Statistics
    errors, 175
    factor g, 92
    in testing, 173–176
Stein, von Astrid, 206–209
Stroke, 38–39, 290–291
Structional learning, 100–101
Superconductivity, 68, 90
Swanson, James, 65–66
SYMMETRIC analysis, 119
    description, 223–224
    music, application, 231, 234–235
    relevant steps, 224–225
Symmetries
    analysis, 222–227
    application, 44
    brain functions, 101–106
    broken, 49
    family groups, 105
    memory patterns, 297
    operators, 223
    patterns, 225
    in physical systems, 93
    reflection, 44
    relationships, 48–49
    rotation
        description, 45–46
        recognition, 107

space, 46–49
time
    recognition, 107
    sequences, 46–49
"Symmetry," 49
Synapses
    description, 54
    types, 57
Synaptic learning rule, 31
Synchrony, 210
Systemic errors, 175
Szell, George, 130
Szilard, Leo, 315

T

Tachicki, Ken, 221
Tasks
    FAT, 290–291
    PF&C
        Alzheimer's patients, 287
        EEG analysis, 207–208
        Mozart effect, 163–166
        solution methods, 124–125
    WPPSI-R
        measures, 171
        scoring procedures, 173–176
Television viewing, children's, 18
Teller, Edward, 315
Temperature parameter, 97, 125–127
Temperly, H. N. V., 90
Tempo, 84
Temporal scales
    evidence, 83–85
    spatial scales vs., 81–83
Terrance, H. S., 248–250
Testing issues, 173–176
Text recognition, 135–137
Thalamus function, 58, 60
Thinking
    generation, 54
    machine, 118, 296–299
"Thinking in Pictures," 21
Trimble, Virginia, 152–153
Third International Math and Science Study, 18
Ticheli, Frank, 236
Time sequences
    description, 46–49
    recognition, 107
Training, see Learning

Trion model
  brain language, 127
  concepts, 302–303
  creative modes, 122–127
  dance, 131–133
  description, 93–96
  generalization, 142–144
  memory patterns
    and cortical language, 114–115
    in coupled columns, 112–113
  motion, 131–133
  music
    general features, 128–131
    variations, 127–128
  natural sequences, 96–99
  rotation recognition, 107
  sequential modes, 122–127
  speech, 134–135
  tests, 303–305
  text recognition, 135–137
  time reversal, 107
  visual art, 138–139
Turing, Alan, 88

U
Ultradian rhythms, 81–82, 292–293
Ultrasound, fetus movement, 256–257

V
Vasudevan, R., 58, 90
Verziano, Marcel, 64
Violin, 147–148
"Vision," 138–139
Visual art, 138–139
Visual illusions, 212–217
Vivaldi, Antonino, 243
Vuong, Sydni, 115

W
Waal, Frans de, 311
Waddington, C. H., 296
Walter, Bruno, 84
Watson, Nona, 291
Wechsler preschool and primary scale of
    intelligence-revised
  measurement, 171
  procedures, 173–176
  scoring, 187–188
  Williams syndrome children, 288
West, Jerry, 157
Westinghouse effect, 175–176
Weyl, Herman, 49
"What to Listen for in Mozart," 312–313
"Why Suya Sing: A Musical Anthology of the
    Amazonian People, 310
Wiesel, Tortsen, 74, 76, 135, 215, 262
Wigner, Eugene, 315
Williams syndrome
  description, 287–288
  Mozart effect studies, 288–290
  music link, 268
  spatial abilities, 39
Wilson, Edward O., 306–307
WPPSI-R, Wechsler preschool and primary
    scale of intelligence–revised
Wright, Eric, 122
Wynn, Karen, 249, 257–259

Y
Yedidia, Jonathan, 125
Young, Daniel, 154–158

Z
Zhou, Yong-Di, 223